FLYING COLT

by

ROBERT S. CAPPS

authorHOUSE

1663 LIBERTY DRIVE, SUITE 200
BLOOMINGTON, INDIANA 47403
(800) 839-8640
www.authorhouse.com

First published by AuthorHouse 09/28/04

ISBN: 1-4184-7383-9 (e)
ISBN: 1-4184-7382-0 (sc)

Printed in the United States of America
Bloomington, Indiana

This book is printed on acid-free paper.

*An historical, recreated diary of the author's World War II
experiences as a B-24 Liberator pilot in the 456th Bombardment Group
(Heavy), Fifteenth Air Force, Italy, from December 1943 to July 7,
1944. Includes experiences of other crew members, historical pictures,
records, and charts. Includes summaries of bomb group's history prior
to that time and afterward.*
    1. Liberators in World War II, Fifteenth Air Force, Italy 1944
    2. 456th Bombardment Group (Heavy), 304th Wing
    3. Air War, World War II, 1944

Alexandria, Virginia

DEDICATION

This book is dedicated to the estimated 1,050 combat crew personnel of the 456th Bombardment Group (Heavy) who served on the 105 Liberators that were lost, and particularly to the 910 of these who were either killed or originally listed as missing in action (MIA) throughout the Group's service in Italy during World War II. Many of those that were originally listed as missing in action were in reality killed and have not been heard from since. Some MIAs have since reappeared, as I have attempted to report in this book.

ACKNOWLEDGMENTS

In writing this history I did not rely solely on my own memory and my own personal records. I have attempted to assemble as much information from all available sources, as time would permit, to recreate the events as they actually happened, as closely as I could recreate them. Thus, the book, particularly the "daily diaries" of Chapters 3 and 4, include information compiled from many sources. It is composed of many official and private diaries.

The name, "Flying Colt," was taken from a comment, reportedly attributed to the movie actor Andy Devine, a good friend of our Group Commander, Col. Thomas W. Steed. The two were waiting for the Group's crews to come into the Officers' Club at Muroc Army Air Base for a cocktail hour after a day's flying activity. When he saw some of the crews arriving, Andy Devine told Col. Steed, "Here come your Colts." Someone in the Group's public relations activity picked up the name "Colonel Steed's Flying Colts," and the name stuck.

I relied heavily on information provided by survivors of the 456th Bombardment Group (Heavy); on information obtained from the U. S. Air Force Libraries at Bolling Air Force Base, Washington D.C. and at Maxwell Air Base, Alabama; on information obtained from the records of the National Air and Space Museum and the Smithsonian Institution in Washington D.C.; and on research into the National Archives in College Park, Maryland.

In particular, much of the information was obtained from the following sources, not in order of importance:

(1) A copy of the 456th Bombardment Group's final statistical report given to me by Dr. David Edward Tavel, formerly a Lieutenant Colonel, aircraft commander and pilot, and the Group Operations Officer. This statistical report covered the period from February 1, 1944 to May 8, 1945, and it was prepared by Capt. Paul A. Doorley, the Group Statistical Officer, with inputs from Col. Tavel, and Major Gilbert W. Smith, Group Intelligence Officer. It was signed by Colonel Thomas W. Steed, Commanding Officer.

(2) The valuable history, "456th Bomb Group History - 1943 Steed's Flying Colts 1945," published for the 456th Bomb Group Association by the Turner Publishing Company, Publishers of Military History, 412 Broadway, P.O. box 3101, Paducah, KY 42002-3101, Phone: (502) 443-0121. This important book was compiled and largely written by Frederick H. Riley Jr., a former bombardier of my 746th Squadron, with help from many of the Association's members. Leadership of the energetic Riley, chairman of the Association's book committee, historian, and current president, was assisted by the great leadership and abilities of James Watkins, secretary/treasurer of the Group's Association, and Edmund Moore, the Association's travel coordinator. Each of these hard working members were former members of the 456th Bomb Group and were

viii

very active in maintaining the 456th Group Association, an association of surviving members.

(3) Frederick Riley Jr. read the draft of this manuscript and made valuable comments and contributions from his records.

(4) The autobiography, unpublished, "World War II History," by Douglas C. Richards, formerly a Lieutenant Colonel and Squadron's Operations Officer of my 746th Squadron.

(5) The diary and records of Lt.Col. Werner C. "Judge" Foss Jr., then a Lieutenant bombardier in my 746th Squadron, who flew missions with my crew.

(6) The diary of S/Sgt Thomas S. Delaney, radio operator and gunner on my crew for half of his missions, in his "World War Two Diary, 12/5/42 to 9/21/45."

(7) The notes of Robert H. Vanderlaan, navigator of the 745th Squadron who finished his missions on the same day that I did and sailed home to the United States on the same ship with me to New York.

(8) Much information was obtained from surviving members of the group at annual meetings conducted by the 456th Bomb Group Association.

(9) Historical records obtained in the Headquarters USAF History Library at Bolling AFB, Washington D.C. and information provided by the USAF Historical Research Agency at Maxwell Air Force Base, Montgomery, Alabama.

(10) The official "War Diary" of the 456th Bomb Group kept by the then 1st Lt. Gilbert W. Smith, Captain John D. Gilder, and others of the 456th Headquarters Detachment. In many instances I have copied their diaries verbatim.

(11) The Headquarters 304th Bomb Wing (Heavy) historical records.

(12) The National Air and Space Museum's Photo Archives Division and its Customer Service Branch, particularly the assistance of Brian Nicklas.

(13) The World War II records of the Fifteenth Air Force.

(14) A statistical study provided by Joseph W. Shuster, a former pilot of the Group, in his "Preliminary Compilation of Data on the Combat Record of the 456th Bomb Group, 304th Bomb Wing, 15th Air Force, Italy, 1944 and 1945."

(15) Photographs provided by the San Diego Aerospace Museum, San Diego, California, and the Liberator Club, 15817 Bernardo Ctr. Dr. #102-124, San Diego, CA 92127-2353 (Phone: 619-679-1957).

(16) Many photographs were provided by Richard C. Hood who was formerly in the 746th Squadron Intelligence Section, and Joseph W. Shuster a pilot in the 746th Squadron.

(17) Some photgraphs were provided by Fred Riley the president and historian of the 456th Bomb Group Association.

Table of Contents

Chapter 4 COMPOSITE DIARIES OF THE GROUP'S NEXT 34 MISSIONS(From May 9, 1944 to July 7, 1944)... 300

PHOTOGRAPHS & CHARTS

FOREWORD

This book is a history of events as seen from the perspective of a Liberator bomber group, the 456th Bombardment Group (Heavy) in Italy, that took part in the great air war in Europe during World War II. It covers the history of the Group from its inception in 1943 to July 7, 1944, with a summary of events afterwards. Chapters 3 and 4 are a composite of many official and private diaries obtained from sources as outlined in the previous *Acknowledgments*.

The Luftwaffe dominated the skies over Europe when the 456th Bomb Group arrived in Italy in January 1944. Heavy bombers were being blasted from the skies by the Luftwaffe every time the Allies attempted to bomb in Central Europe.

On August 17, 1943 the Eighth Air Force lost an unsustainable 60 planes and 600 airmen when it raided targets at Regensburg and Schweinfurt in Germany. Sixty more planes and 600 more airmen were lost on a second attack against Schweinfurt on October 14, 1943. Raids deep into German controlled airspace had been halted after these two raids, and didn't resume until February 1944 because the Allies didn't have fighters that had enough range to escort our heavy bombers.

When Army Air Force raids deep into German controlled airspace resumed in February, 1944, many additional heavy bomber groups had arrived in Italy, including the 456th Bomb Group. Although we still didn't have escort fighters with long enough range to protect us, it was believed that many heavy bombers attacking targets in a coordinated attack at the same time would disperse Luftwaffe fighter defenses sufficiently. The Luftwaffe would have to spread its fighter defenses between three fronts, Italy, England, and Russia, now that we were flying bombing raids from Italy.

Control of the air over Europe was a necessary prelude to the invasion of Europe from England. Everyone agreed that without control of the skies, an invasion could not be attempted. Unknown to us in the heavy bomber groups at the time, the big three world leaders, Stalin, Churchill, and Roosevelt had set the invasion date for Europe in early June 1944, five months after we arrived in Italy.

Not enough has been written about that great, decisive air battle for domination of the skies over Europe which lasted from February 1944 to June 1944. Much has been written, justifiably, about the great air battle for control of the skies over Great Britain in the critical "Battle of Britain" during the summer of 1940, when the Royal Air Force achieved domination of the skies over England and prevented the German invasion of England from Europe. But the critical air battles for domination of the skies over Europe that enabled the Allied invasion of Europe from England, has not been given sufficient recognition.

The diaries of this book cover the period from the beginning of 1944 to July 7, 1944, a few weeks after the Allied air forces had gained air superiority over the German Luftwaffe in Europe. That day, July 7, 1944, was selected as the last day reported as a daily diary in this book because that happened to be the day that I completed flying fifty-one missions with the Group and I earned a ticket back to the United States. The Luftwaffe was defeated by that time. in time for the Invasion of Europe, project Overlord, in June 6, 1944. The last bomber of the 456th Bomb Group that was shot down by an enemy aircraft occurred in August, 1944.

I attempted to provide some perspective and background, throughout the book, to point up how our Bomb Group's effort fit into the overall picture of what was being accomplished in the master plan of that great war. The book will bring back poignant memories for many readers who participated in that great experience.

Many readers will think I included too much trivial information for each day's activities, whereas other readers will feel that I didn't include enough detail. At the risk of occasionally boring the casual reader, I have provided much minutiae in the daily diaries of some of the missions included in Chapters 3 and 4. More information has been preserved in the archives for some of each day's missions than for others, because the records of some missions were incomplete after being knocked around for more than fifty years. I only wish that I could include more detail than I did.

I found minor conflicts in the records while researching facts, and I had to make a judgment concerning which was the most accurate. In most cases, I used the official reports that the 456th Bomb Group made to its higher headquarters, the 304th Bombardment Wing (Heavy) as the best information.

I decided to write this history of my experience in the 456th Bombardment Group (Heavy) after I made a visit to the Italian farm in the Foggia Valley of Italy where we flew our Liberators off a dirt runway during World War II. The runway was located one third of the way between Stornara and the village of Stornarella in southeastern Italy. It was about thirty miles southeast of the city of Foggia.

Many poignant memories sped across my mind as I wandered through the olive trees of the tranquil farm, on the edge of a wheat field, where we had pitched our tents in 1944. The setting aroused vivid memories and strong emotions.

As I explored the landscape that day, I saw that an old farm house on a knoll at the end of the large wheat field was essentially the same now as it had been more than fifty years ago. The old farm building was confiscated during the war for use by our 456th Bombardment Group (Heavy) as bomber group headquarters. That farm house was the nerve center from which operations of the group's four heavy bombardment squadrons, the 744th, 745th, 746th (my squadron), and 747th were directed. A couple of smaller, stucco covered "tuffi" brick buildings with A-frame roofs, located near the farm house, were other structures that were still there, that had been there when the bomb group was active during the war.

Those two tuffi brick buildings were the site of much nervous agonizing and anticipation by aircrews immediately before takeoff on our life-threatening bombing missions. The two brick buildings were used as aircrew briefing rooms, navigators' and bombardiers' study rooms. This was the site of many anxious and frightening moments for crew members because it was here in the early mornings before each bombing mission that crew members were told for the first time what their enemy target would be for that day. We saw for the first time, as we entered the tuffi-brick building, how long the yarn was on the huge map at the end of the room that told us how far into enemy territory we had to fly that day. We were told how many German fighters would be expected to attack us, and how many huge 88mm and

105mm enemy antiaircraft guns would be firing from the ground trying to kill us.

Many familiar faces failed to appear at each of these pre-mission briefings. They were the crewmen who were shot down on the previous mission. New, unfamiliar faces constantly appeared from the States to take their places as replacements. Each crewman knew, in the back of his mind, that the next mission could be the one where fate would select him as one to be shot down, maimed, taken prisoner of war in one of the dismal Nazi Stalags, or killed. An unexpected catastrophe could come swiftly and violently to anyone of us during the combat missions briefed in that farm building, as new faces that continually appeared at the briefings kept reminding us.

Those olive trees, and the golden wheat fields that were at their edge, had been the scene of much heartache, comradeship, tension, anxiety, excitement, and at times, extreme pleasure during my youth. Some of the memories were not happy ones, but many are happy ones now, now that the life-threatening pressures of those days are many years behind.

I began to reminisce as I wandered around the farm. A light summer breeze rippled the stalks of wheat in the lush, golden fields on the edge of the olive groves. That wheat field once held a 4,800- foot, heavy-bomber runway, steele matted taxiways, and 62 four-engine, 33 ton, Consolidated B-24 "Liberator" heavy bombers parked on individual, dispersed ramps around it. In January 1944, an unbelievable cyclone of human activity suddenly descended on this quiet, peaceful farm. In only a few weeks, an incredible storm of activity had transformed this calm wheat field into a bustling industrial complex. That was made possible by hard working, dedicated ground support personnel, working long hours under adverse conditions in winter weather, and by the application of much Yankee ingenuity and improvisation.

Massive numbers of ground support vehicles and huge amounts of materiel began to arrive at this field. Arrival of the first B-24 heavy bombers started on February 1, 1944. Arrival of aircrews from the United States, in addition to the ground support personnel already here, now made a total of 2,000 people (380 officers and 1620 enlisted men). Huge Army olive-drab tent cities were created among the olive groves to house the personnel. People, the massive amount of ground support equipment, fuel, bombs, ammunition, and other supplies that continued to arrive, rapidly transformed this sleepy farm land into an enormous beehive of industrial activity.

As hard as I continued to search those placid wheat fields and olive groves in Italy, I found little evidence to suggest the incredible activities and heroic deeds that were performed there by enthusiastic, energetic, young ground crews and aircrews. Although we were apprehensive about being shot at, and homesick, our youthful hearts were touched by fire. We were making sacrifices that would have been unthinkable a couple of years earlier. If you were able to ask any of the intrepid heroes who had performed there, each would tell you that he was only doing his duty as he had been trained to do it. Any unbiased observer would characterize their behavior as heroic; that is, brave, noble, many times fearless, and marked by valiant courage.

I glanced out over the wheat field and recalled the many friends, most in their early twenties, who had left that runway never to return. Some of the lucky ones were able to bail out over enemy territory and be taken prisoner where they lived under harsh conditions in enemy prison camps. Some were able to return to this runway with horrible, painful, sometimes crippling battle scars, but they were able, at least, to continue living while many lost their lives.

Many faces and names of those who had lost their lives crossed my mind. They were all young boys in the prime of life. They had been hand-selected for service in the Army Air Corps because of their excellent health, intelligence, and enthusiasm, only to lose their lives in violent, sudden death. They lost their lives in aerial battles four miles above such World War II strategic bombing targets as aircraft factories, airfields, railroad yards, and oil fields. Many of their bodies were lost over such famous wartime targets as Ploesti, Regensburg, Klagenfurt, Friedrichshaffen, Moosbierbaum, Bucharest, Budapest, Vienna, Munich, Odertal, and Wiener Neustadt, but some were killed in crashes on that wheat field, while we watched in horror.

I was transferred into the 456th Bomb Group in December 1943 with three other young aircrew officers, 2nd Lts. Douglas S. Morgan, Gail J. Scritchfield, and Edward J. Heffner. Three of us, pilots, had been together for more than a year and a half, and Heffner, a bombardier, had been with us half a year. We arrived here at this wheat field in Italy in January, 1944. We shared a close camaraderie. We were all very young, eager, patriotic, and anxious to begin the great adventure of flying combat missions. We were billeted together, ate together, and shared leisure hours together for many months before we arrived in Italy.

Within four months of our arrival at this field, by May 23, 1944, all three of my comrades had been killed. Each met violent deaths in air crashes while flying B-24 Liberators. Later, another friend, a tent mate of mine, Lt. Nicholas Colletti, a bombardier was shot down in flames and killed.

When I completed my 51 missions on July 7, 1944, the rest of my crew had only half that many, because I flew nineteen missions before they joined me. For that reason, the rest of my crew was not eligible to return to the states with me when I finished my official combat tour. When I was given orders to return to the States, my copilot 2nd Lt. Sydney H. Brooks, was checked out as first pilot and given command of our ship "Porky." Two weeks after he took command of my crew, on a mission July 21, 1944, "Porky" had a wing knocked off by enemy fire and it collided with another plane in his formation. Porky spun violently to the ground out of control, and the other plane exploded. Only nine parachutes were seen to come from the two planes carrying twenty crew members. That happened three minutes after Porky had dropped its bombs on the Brux oil refinery in Czechoslovakia.

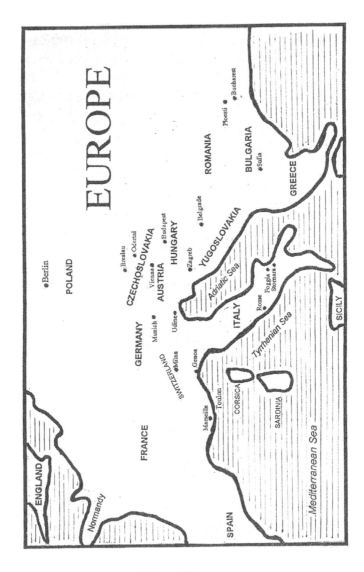

Map of Europe

Fear is a very important problem facing every soldier in combat, and it was a fact that pervaded the lives of all officers and airmen while flying from the runway that had been constructed in the wheat field. Everyone is fearful when being shot at, a normal reaction of participants of battles in war throughout the ages. Training, strong character, and dedication to duty are necessary to overcome fear, and the men that flew in the B-24 Liberator bombers from this field had the right stuff to do their job in the face of their fears. The 456th Bombardment Group (Heavy) earned two Presidential Unit Citations for its efforts during the time I flew with it.

Because of the present tranquillity of the farm, it would be difficult for anyone to imagine, today, what dynamic history had taken place there. The two tuffi brick buildings that had been a place of much torment and stress for aircrews during the war years were now being used as farm equipment storage rooms, and there was no evidence now to show how they had been used. I looked inside, and they were now filled with tractors, plows, reaping machines, and other farm equipment. The buildings now looked very peaceful.

When I arrived at the Italian farm for the first time, late in January, 1944, I had my twenty first birthday. By then, I had already been commissioned a 2nd Lieutenant in the Army Air Corps, trained as a combat pilot, checked out as a first pilot (commander of a ten man aircrew of the B-24 four engine bomber). I only had a total of 487 flying hours, and only 250 of them in the B-24 bomber that I was about to fly into combat with nine other men's lives dependent on my skills.

I was typical of pilots in my group. Very few pilots had more flying time, or were much older. Those with more flying time and older had been appointed to leadership positions, as flight commanders, squadron commanders, operations officers or they were given positions on the group commander's supervisory staff. My squadron commander, Major Paul T. Golden, commander of my 746th Bombardment Squadron (Heavy), was in his early twenties, and most aircrew members of his squadron were younger than he. Our handsome, redheaded squadron commander was a medical student with five and a half years of college when he entered the Army Air Corps, including four years of ROTC at the University of San Francisco. Our young operations officer, Captain Frederick Weston Hyde, Jr., also in his twenties, was a graduate of West Point.

As I gazed out over that sleepy wheat field, again reminiscing, I didn't know why it was my fate to survive when so many others died, but I have cherished every moment of life since that time, knowing how lucky I was to be selected to keep living. I know that most other aircrew members who survived the war with me feel as I do. The experience makes you appreciate your time on earth the way few other experiences can. Survivors of the experience share an emotional bond that is difficult to explain to others who have not had the experience. That mutual bonding and respect is tacitly felt whenever aircrew survivors get together. Survivors have organized the 456th Bomb Group Association and they meet annually.

My visit to that tranquil Italian farm inspired me to recreate this history of the 456th Bombardment Group (Heavy) as accurately as I could. I will apologize in advance for any misspelled names or other errors that may have slipped through our close proof- reading of the many details.

I have included copies of the original Battle Orders when I could find them in the archives. Some Battle Orders are missing after being kicked around for fifty-three years. Although some of the Battle Orders that I have included are difficult to read, and they are less than perfect, I have included them because they provide some valuable information. Most of the Battle Orders that I have included are legible.

Chapter 1
THE ROAD TO ITALY

The road to Italy started, for most of us, soon after the Japanese sneak attack on Pearl Harbor on December 7, 1941. An estimated eighty-five percent of the members of the 456th Bombardment Group (Heavy) that I flew with in Italy had no prior military experience, nor had they ever been in an airplane. We were civilians who had to be trained to become soldiers, airmen, pilots, navigators, bombardiers, engineers, aircraft maintenance technicians, intelligence specialists, and many other specialties that were needed to run a heavy bombardment group.

An estimated fifteen percent of all members of the original 456th Bomb Group had pre-Pearl Harbor military experience. They obtained that experience in either the very small Army, were graduates of West Point, had a small amount of military training in the Reserve Officer Training Corps (ROTC) while they attended various universities and colleges around the country, or they had served in their state's National Guard. Those that had some prior military experience were usually assigned to positions as leaders or they were made members of the commander's staff, to help organize, lead, and direct the rest of us.

The vast majority of our Group, and indeed the majority of all of the nation's military forces that fought in World War II, were civilians before the Japanese bombed Pearl Harbor. Most members of the 456th Bombardment Group were formerly doctors, lawyers, students, newspaper reporters, grocery clerks, truck drivers, engineers, salesmen, accountants, chemists, statisticians, teachers, and many other trades and professions. We had members who were from every state of the United States.

Although the 456th Bombardment Group (Heavy) was made up of citizens with many diverse professions and trades, we all had a common, overriding, uniting goal of defeating the three hated Axis countries, the Germans, Italians, and Japanese. Members of our 456th Bomb Group arrived in Italy reasonably well trained, motivated, and our morale was very high. We knew exactly what we were fighting for, and we had no doubts about the reasons we were there. We had no doubts about the support we had from the home front in the United States.

The spirit of national purpose, unity, and cooperation that was aroused in the United States by World War II has never been matched before or since that time. Although a total of 12 million men and women of the prewar labor force of the United States had gone into the armed services, more than 21 percent of our nation's total prewar work force, the production of our country's economy as measured by the Gross National Product was increased by 69 percent during the years 1941 to 1944. That increased production was made possible by the entry of almost 19 million women into the work force, by a well-motivated work force, and by much overtime work by those who were working.

The life of most citizens of the United States was disrupted by the war effort, and almost every family had a friend or relative in the military service. In an unprecedented move, the entire industry and manpower of the United States had been completely mobilized for the war effort by the Federal Government. There was a huge draft of all eligible manpower for the armed forces. The Federal Government established rationing of meat, sugar, gasoline, automobiles, tires and rubber products, and many other consumer and producer items. The price of everything was controlled by a newly formed Office of Price Administration. After the Japanese sneak attack on Pearl Harbor on December 7, 1941, during which Japanese diplomats were still in Washington D.C. negotiating peace treaties with our government, the war became a very popular and necessary one.

President Franklin D. Roosevelt had clearly identified our national objectives earlier in a speech before Congress. We were fighting for a world which guaranteed four essential freedoms for everyone: freedom of speech, freedom of worship, freedom from want, and freedom from fear. These four freedoms were widely publicized afterward by the news media, movie industry, and on posters and billboards. These were the freedoms that the three aggressive military dictatorships, Germany, Italy, and Japan, were forcibly taking from their citizens. It helped to develop a common, patriotic dedication to our country's goals and a strong desire to work hard to protect them for ourselves and to regain them for the citizens of Germany, Italy, and Japan and for the countries they raped, plundered, and enslaved.

Before the out break of World War II, the United States was a very different country to live in than it is now. It is difficult for those born after the war to realize what it was like, because the war caused such a great, revolutionary change in the social, political, and economic customs of Americans, as well as those of the rest of the world. The war stimulated a recovery from the Great Depression, it caused a sweeping revolution in technology, it developed our industries, and it brought about a social revolution that radically changed the way Americans viewed the world and themselves.

Our country was just beginning to emerge from a prolonged economic depression. More than twenty-five percent of the non-farm labor force was still out of work when war started in Europe in 1939, and there was little prospect that jobs would become available. The average employee who was fortunate enough to find a job in 1939 was only paid a little more than $100 a *month*, or only $1,266 a *year*. Those with jobs worked hard, with strong work ethics, for fear of losing their jobs and for fear of joining the vast unemployed work force.

In medicine, there were no antibiotics to use, and if you came down with an infection in your body, of any kind, it was life-threatening. The first antibiotics available to fight infections - penicillin and sulfa drugs - became generally available later during the war.

Before World War II, transportation by bus, auto, and railroad, which were the only practical means of travel for the average citizen, was very crude and slow by today's standards. The nationwide speed limit for automobiles during World war II was 35 miles per hour. There were no super highways, and practically all roads were dangerous two-lane ones, with many arterial stop signs along the way that further slowed traffic.

People did not travel much in those days, compared with today's standards. World War II quickly changed that! The war caused an explosive revolution in transportation and travel that has continued to expand up to the present time. One reason for the small amount of travel before World War II was that the severe economic depression of the 1930's did not allow it. Most people had a difficult time merely feeding, clothing, and housing themselves and their families, and there wasn't much money in people's budgets left for unnecessary travel.

Commercial air travel was almost nonexistent, except for a rare privileged few of our wealthier citizens. Air travel was very dangerous and unreliable during bad weather conditions, and aircraft were not as mechanically reliable as they are now. The new twin-engine Douglas DC-3 was the most advanced commercial transport aircraft at the war's outbreak. The plane only carried thirty to forty passengers, and it took about 24 hours, when weather permitted, to fly from New York City to Los Angeles. The plane made three or four refueling stops along the way. Weather delays were frequent and fares were expensive. It cruised at 155 MPH with a range of 900 miles. Because its passenger cabin was not pressurized and oxygen was not available for passengers, it didn't cruise much above 10,000 feet, with a maximum of 15,000. Thus the DC-3 had to fly in the clouds most of the time in bad weather because it could not fly above the clouds. Passengers had a rough, dangerous ride. There was no radar, as we now have, to provide direction and control of aircraft from the ground.

Electronic navigation aids for aircraft were very poor. They consisted primarily of low frequency radio beams that were poorest when they were needed most during bad weather. The radio signals were jammed by static from radio signals emitted by thunder storms. The country was covered by a network of light beacons on the ground that could be used as navigation aids during visual flight conditions, but they were useless in bad weather. Pilots could fly across the nation from one coded, flashing light beacon on the ground to the next beacon, when weather permitted them to be seen.

Recovery from the Great Depression of the 1930s did not start in the United States until most industrialized nations in Europe began, hastily, to build up their military forces starting in 1939, and orders for war materials began to flood into our factories long before Pearl Harbor brought us into the war. These orders helped put many of our unemployed workers to work, and it began to build up our country's aircraft and munitions industries. Thus they began to build an industrial base that helped us prepare for the war to come.

Except for the three Axis countries, Germany, Italy, and Japan, which had huge buildups of their military forces during depression years of the 1930s, all other countries including the United States, had grossly neglected their military preparedness. The reason for this was that most governments had isolationist foreign policies, and the long depression of the 1930s had severely reduced the amount of money that governments had available to spend on armaments. Most countries rationalized that World War I was the war to end all wars because it was so horrible. The international *League of Nations* was expected to establish cooperation among nations and peaceably solve all problems that arose between them by negotiation, rather than by war (Just as the present *United Nations* was later expected to do after World War II).

The three Axis Powers took advantage of this naiveté of other free, democratic nations, knowing that other nations didn't have the will or military capability to oppose them. The rest of the free world watched the hateful aggression and atrocities that were being committed by the Axis bullies, and the free nations stood by, helpless, while millions of people became victims and slaves of Germany, Italy, and Japan.

When war finally began in Europe in 1939 with the German invasion of Poland, the three Axis Powers had overwhelming military power compared with the weak and poorly equipped armies of all other countries. Military weakness of free world countries encouraged the three Axis bullies to expand their territory through military aggression, rape, and enslavement of innocent countries.

The United States was surrounded by two great oceans that seemed insurmountable by potential enemies, considering the crude state of military technology at the time. The policy of the United States since the turn of the twentieth century was to keep a strong U. S. Navy to protect it from foreign invasion by water. Naval force was expected to make a large U.S. Army unnecessary, and the U.S. Army was in a small, pitiful condition when war broke out. Before 1939 there were no weapons such as long range aircraft or missiles, such as we have today, with sufficient range to span the oceans to harm us, so most people felt secure.

The policy of our government was isolationistic since World War I, and the United States remained aloof of what was happening across the two oceans that protected us. Lip service, weak embargoes, and feckless diplomacy were all that our government relied upon to right the wrongs they saw. We didn't have sufficient military power to back our diplomatic will, when diplomacy failed. We were powerless to oppose military force on land and the Axis Powers knew it.

In September 1939 the U.S. Army consisted of only 200,000 men, and this included the 26,000 men that were in the Army Air Corps, a small corps within the Army. By June 1941 the Air Corps had only 1,257 combat ready planes, and they were generally inferior to the German Luftwaffe's high performance planes. The Luftwaffe had almost four times that number of planes and it was increasing its numbers rapidly.

Well publicized atrocities performed by armies of Hitler of Germany, Mussolini of Italy, and armies of Hirohito of Japan, for many years before the United States entered the war, had put public sentiment in America overwhelmingly against these Axis bullies. The news media publicized their outrageous and barbaric deeds: Atrocities committed by Japanese armies in Manchuria during the 1930s; ruthless mass bombings of innocent Polish, Belgian, Dutch, French, and English cities by German bombers; book burnings and other barbarisms perpetrated by the Nazi against Jews in Germany; German forced labor camps; the Italian Army invasion of weak and powerless Ethiopia; and the repression of free speech by all of these totalitarian Axis countries.

Each of these three barbaric Axis aggressors had used despicable "total war" tactics that devastated innocent civilian populations and cities with punishment more severe than it gave armies it opposed. This was the first war in modern history where more civilians were killed than military personnel. All of this appalled the entire free world. Unlawful aggression by the Axis powers threatened the security and liberty of everyone. Arrogant German submarines were ruthlessly sinking innocent merchant ships, including American ships, on the high seas and in the waters close to our shores.

The climax, which finally swayed public opinion of the United States in favor of taking the drastic step of actually going to war against the Axis powers, came when the Japanese made their infamous sneak attack on Pearl Harbor in the morning of Sunday, December 7, 1941.The United States declared war on Japan the next day. The United States didn't declare war on Germany and Italy, but on December 11, 1941, before we declared war on those two countries, they declared war on the United States. The action of Germany and Italy made us clearly at war with them too. This galvanized American public opinion in support of war, and it motivated an unprecedented, astounding all-out national effort to defeat the three Axis Powers.

The Road To Italy For Most Of Us In The 456th Bombardment Group (Heavy) Started Soon After The Japanese Attack On Pearl Harbor.

A great amount of training was necessary to convert us civilians to soldiers capable of performing the necessary technical chores required to operate a heavy bombardment group. The small nucleus of leaders we had, about fifteen percent of our Group who had some pre-Pearl Harbor military training and experience, had to have specialized training to prepare them to fly the new, state of the art B-24 Liberator, and to fight this unprecedented type of war. No one had experience with this new type of warfare and it required much training.

The new Liberator airplane had a crew of ten: two pilots, a navigator, bombardier, engineer, radio operator, nose turret gunner, ball turret gunner on its underbelly, upper turret gunner, tail turret gunner, and waist gunner (the radio operator and engineer usually manned one of the two guns in the waist). These positions, for each of the Group's 62 planes, had to be manned by training civilians who had never been in or near an aircraft. Large numbers of ground support troops, necessary to keep the planes flying, also had to be trained. All of these positions had to be filled by training civilians from all walks of life to perform the necessary highly technical duties needed.

Training usually started with the recruitment, examination, and selection process to get the most suitable people for each position. The Air Corps had a high priority that allowed it to take the most educated and qualified recruits and draftees that were available to the Army. The reason for this was that most of the Air Corps jobs were of a highly technical nature and they required a great amount of intelligence, skill, and education to learn them. Most jobs in the Army's infantry didn't require such qualified people.

After selection for the Air Corps, recruits were given an intense preflight training or officers' training school for officers, and basic training for enlisted men with the purpose of converting civilians to soldiers. This was followed by many months of technical training, such as pilot, bombardier, navigator, engineering, gunnery, or radio operator training for the aircrew positions. Ground support personnel were sent to aircraft mechanic, intelligence, meteorology, administration, dentistry, flight surgeon, chaplain and other such specialized training schools to fill the many maintenance and support positions needed in the 456th Bombardment Group to keep the planes flying.

As people completed their individual specialized training, and became qualified to perform their particular technical functions, they were assigned to the 456th Bomb Group where final operational training as a unit was supposed be accomplished at Muroc Army Airbase to prepare them and the Group for combat. As it actually turned out, much of this training had to be learned on the job, the hard way, in Europe, under fire. The reason for this was that there were not enough B-24 aircraft and associated equipment available at Muroc, or anywhere else in the United States, to properly prepare the 456th Bomb Group at Muroc for combat in Europe.

This training deficiency was also experienced by most other heavy bombardment groups that were in training in the United States, preparing to go overseas, because the shortage of aircraft and spare parts was nationwide. Most other groups had the same problem. Our Group, and most other heavy bombardment groups, were hastily sent overseas into combat without adequate training because of the war emergency. The Group arrived in Italy poorly prepared for combat duties.

Group Activated June 1, 1943, Then It Makes Four Moves In Four Months.

Another problem confronted by the 456th Bomb Group after it was activated, a problem that interfered with its ability to prepare for combat, was that it was required to make four changes of station in less than four months. The 456th Bombardment Group (Heavy) was activated June 1, 1943 at Wendover Army Air Base, Utah. It moved to Gowen Army Air Base, Boise, Idaho on July 14, 1943, and Colonel Thomas W. Steed, a handsome West Point graduate (Class of 1928), took command on that day. At that time the Group had only a small nucleus of personnel, a cadre of 66 officers and 237 enlisted men of the 2,000 people it needed. This nucleus of personnel was provided by the 18th Replacement Wing at Salt lake City, Utah and the 29th Bombardment Group at Gowen A.A.B.. Later, about one third of the Group's combat crew strength was provided by the 470th Bomb Group, Mountain Home, Idaho.

The Group was moved again, its second move in two weeks, from Gowen A.A.B. to Bruning A.A.B., Nebraska, on July 30, 1943. Key personnel were sent to receive specialized training at the Army Air Force School of Applied Tactics at Orlando, Florida during July and August of 1943. On September 5 the Group was moved a third time, this time to Kearns A.A.B., Utah. It only remained at Kearns until September 29, 1943 when it was ordered to move for the fourth time to its first "permanent" station, Muroc A.A.B., California to complete the Group's final operational training in preparation for combat before going overseas. (Muroc is now called Edwards Air Force Base.)

Shortage Of Liberators And Parts Needed For Training.

The Group was designated to be shipped overseas on December 1, 1943. Because of the exigencies of war, the Group was expected to complete three months training in a little more than one month, by the time it had settled in at Muroc. To make matters worse, it had a gross shortage of planes and equipment to do the job. The Group was constantly short of B-24s for training. During July the Group had no assigned aircraft, during August it had 4 planes, in September it had 15, and on November 1, 1943 it had 28 B-24s assigned but only 13 were flyable because 10 were grounded for maintenance and 5 were grounded for lack of parts. The old, worn B-24s that had been transferred into the 456th Bomb Group from the 2nd Air Force were in bad condition. A fact that aggravated the problem was that maintenance personnel, aircrews, and ground support people were all leaning their jobs and becoming familiar with the Liberator. Comparing notes with people who were in other heavy bomb groups during this time, it is evident that many others were experiencing the same problems while training in the United States.

An experience noted by Lt. Steven E. Hansen, copilot on Lt. Stanley A. Sagert's crew, illustrates the kind of problem facing combat crew training at Muroc. While on a routine training mission, his plane lost two engines and the two remaining ones were faltering. Lt. Sagert made a quick decision to put his heavy bomber down on the nearby Owens Dry Lake, California, not knowing if the soggy dry lake would hold the heavy bomber after recent heavy winter rains. F/O Werner C. "Judge" Foss (promoted to Lt. Col. in the USAFR after the war), the crew's bombardier, quickly located a small emergency airstrip nearby as an alternative, and Sagert, with help from his copilot to keep the plane airborne, struggled through an exploratory pass over the runway to investigate its suitability for landing. The small airstrip had no buildings around it. The plane's last two operating engines began to falter during this pass over the runway and Sagert had to make an emergency landing. The crew was able to land the crippled plane safely on the short deserted landing strip on two failing engines.

Lt. Hansen credits the quick action of "Judge" Foss' in finding the strip, and the flying of Lt. Sagert, for saving the lives of the crew. Foss gives much of the credit for flying the crippled Liberator, which required considerable strength when two engines were inoperative, to the able assistance of the strong Hansen. Hansen said that this wasn't the only time the crew experienced a loss of engines during their training. Other crews had mechanical difficulties with the worn liberators they had to fly.

The base at Muroc was not prepared to receive a Liberator Group, and many problems were encountered, most important of which were a lack of supplies and spare parts for B-24 airplanes. In addition, Muroc was isolated, out in the middle of the Mohave Desert, and its buildings and installations were poorly equipped.

The Group's personnel strength was finally nearing its authorized strength of 377 officers and 1627 enlisted men. A small detachment of Operational Training Unit personnel, Training Unit Number 2 of IV Bomber Command, was temporarily assigned to the Group to help it train and to assist in the Group's preparation for combat. Actual training during this time, in spite of the fact that most personnel worked around the clock, was very minimal. Training included a small amount of formation flying, high altitude bombing, gunnery, navigation, and calibration.

The most serious deficiencies in training before the Group had to depart for overseas was a lack of sufficient high altitude formation flying as a group, flying heavily loaded planes. In addition, there was not sufficient bombing and gunnery practice. These were all vital requirements to prepare the Group for combat, particularly in Europe. For example, until we arrived in Italy, none of our aircrews had flown aircraft loaded down so heavily as we flew them in Italy. The published maximum combat weight for takeoff in the B-24, published in our operating manuals was 56,000 pounds, and the maximum *emergency* gross weight for takeoff under *wartime conditions* was specified in the B-24 operating manual as 71,200 pounds. Many of our missions in Italy exceeded the maximum *emergency* gross weight, and all exceeded the weight that crews flew with at Muroc. It was on our first successful combat mission in Italy, at Grottaferrata, that our pilots flew such heavily loaded planes at 20,000 feet, in a Group formation of forty planes, and dropped bombs in formation. For some of our Liberator's gunners, firing at Luftwaffe Me-109s that were firing at them was the first time that they fired their guns at a target in the air. The Group had to learn on the job, for the most part, under pressure of combat.

When inspectors at Muroc, who were inspecting the Group's preparedness for overseas movement, asked Colonel Thomas Steed if his Group was prepared for combat, his honest answer was that it was not. He was pressured by successive calls from higher headquarters, all the way up the Air Corps chain of command to the Pentagon, to change his official assessment about his Group's readiness for combat. He did not change his view. His personal integrity and professional judgment would not allow him to change his honest assessment of the Group's readiness.

He knew that the 456th Bomb Group was not prepared for combat, but he also knew it would be ordered overseas anyway, because of exigencies of the war. He commented that his men wanted to get on with the show, and that the 456th would "fight one hell of a war." As we shall see in following chapters, it did!

Air Echelon Departs For Overseas December 3, 1943.

This was the day the road to Italy from Muroc began for the 456th Bomb Group's **Air Echelon** of flying personnel. (The **Ground Echelon** went to Italy separately by ground transportation, as explained below.) The Group received its orders to go overseas, regardless of its training deficiencies, and its B-24s began flying from Muroc Army Air Base to Hamilton Field, California where 62 new B-24H Liberators, painted olive-drab, were picked up. Some of the Air Echelon moved to Hamilton Field in their own planes, and others traveled by rail.

The Air Echelon moved to Hamilton Field by squadrons, with the 746th Squadron first to move, and the 745 Squadron last to move. Twelve officers and eight enlisted men of the Group headquarters staff made the trip with the Air Echelons of various squadrons. Colonel Steed and Lt. Col. Walter C. Phillips flew with Lt. Edward Meyer and his crew of the 745th Squadron. While at Hamilton Field the Group's Air Echelon was outfitted with other necessary equipment, in addition to their planes.

From Hamilton Field the crews flew their new Liberators along the south Atlantic route to Tunis in North Africa. This was much of the same route that Pan American Airways had pioneered a few years earlier. The route was supervised and serviced by the Air Transport Command of the Air Corps. Most of the Group's crews flew their new B-24H's to Tunis, Tunisia by taking a route from Hamilton Field with stops at Palm Springs, California; Memphis, Tennessee; Palm Beach, Florida; Puerto Rico; Trinidad; Belem and Natal in Brazil; Dakar, French West Africa; Marrakech and Casablanca, French Morocco; Oran, Algeria; Oudna and Tunis in Tunisia; before flying north to Italy. The Group was delayed in Tunis most of January 1944 because the new airbase in Italy was not ready to receive them.

The Group's First Casualty Occurred On January 5, 1944.

While in Tunis, the first casualty was suffered by our Group when Lt. George A. Rowley, a pilot, was killed instantly by a German butterfly bomb, and S/Sgt Charles Fagg a member of his crew lost an eye in the accident. S/Sgt Fagg was sent home. The treacherous Germans were notorious for leaving butterfly bombs as booby traps to entrap Allied personnel.

Steve Hansen, Lt. Stanley A. Sagert's copilot, reported that Sagert, who was a school friend of Rowley's, found a discarded B-24 propeller and made a grave marker by chiseling Rowley's name on the propeller.

The Group's combat crews and their Liberators remained in Tunis during most of January, 1944. They took advantage of that time to fly much needed practice missions and to become familiar with their new planes. Some had individual nose art painted on their Liberators while in Tunis.

Headquarters Staff Began Arriving At Stornara, January 23 to 26 January 1944.

Some of the Group Headquarters staff, of the **Air Echelon**, arrived at the new airfield at Stornara, Italy while the rest of the Group's Air Echelon remained in Tunis. Captains Robert Carlin and Arthur M. Fox were the first, coming to Stornara on January 23. Lt. Col. Walter C. Phillips arrived the next day, on the 24th. A light rain fell on January 24, but the weather during this period was generally sunny and frigidly cold. Colonel Steed, Major Dickerson, and Captain Kenneth W. Gruber reported for duty at the new airbase January 26, 1944.

The Group's First Liberator Crashes On January 30, 1944.

While enroute to Tunisia, a B-24 piloted by 1st. Lt. Christopher G. Agee exploded on takeoff from Dakar, French West Africa on January 30, 1944. Of the ten members of his crew, only one miraculously survived, Sgt. Bruce E. Ryan. Because there were some similar explosions in Italy that occurred later and were proven to be due to sabotage, I believe that it is highly probable that Agee's plane was also a victim of sabotage.

Group Headquarters Orders Pyramidal Tents Be Given To Aircrews.

Our Group headquarters issued an order on December 30, 1943 stating that combat aircrews were to be given the few large, more comfortable pyramidal five-man tents that were available. These larger tents had been occupied by hard working ground support personnel who had arrived at the new airbase before airplanes and aircrews had arrived. Personnel who were occupying the larger five-man tents were ordered to move into small one-man pup tents until more of the larger ones became available. In hindsight, it appears that the tent shortage was a direct result of the catastrophic Bari Harbor bombing mentioned in Chapter 3.

Needless to say, this was a severe blow to the morale of ground support troops, mostly hard working aircraft mechanics and staff who were required to give up their more comfortable large tents. Ground crews had spent much time and effort becoming settled in the larger tents, only to have to give them up and move into small, wet, cold one-man pup tents, in the muddy field. Within a few months, sufficient large tents arrived so all personnel could live in them, but in the meantime it was a severe blow to morale of the ground support troops.

Liberators Arrive At Stornara On February 1, 1944.

The Group's four-engine B-24Hs began arriving at their new airfield near Stornara in Italy. The airfield was now ready enough to receive the 62 Liberators. Our new airbase was located one third of the way between Stornara, population of about 5,000, and the very small village of Stornarella, population only a few hundred. Stornara was only a mile and a half from our airbase. Our airbase was on the estate of an Italian commendatore, called *Incarnata Farm*. The padrone of the estate was a suave Italian officer named Capt. Guido Frangipani who wailed continually about being dispossessed. Our airfield was on his farm. The farm was located about thirty miles southeast of the city of Foggia. The town of Cerignola, population of 18,000 people, was about six miles from our airfield and it was much larger than Stornara. Many maps don't show Stornara, but they usually show Cerignola. Cerignola was allegedly an Italian Fascist stronghold that contained many refugees from Foggia, a city that was heavily bombed, and many of our Group found the general populace rather diffident and aloof during the first few weeks. Almost all of the people seemed to wear black. Men's suits, women's dresses, men's hats, and women's shawls were all black.

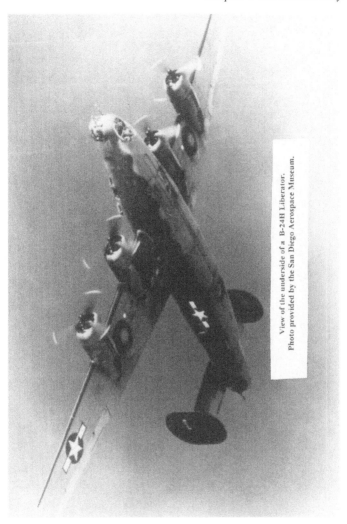

View of the underside of a B-24H Liberator.
Photo provided by the San Diego Aerospace Museum.

Underside View Of A Liberator

A B-24M in flight. Photo courtesy of the San Diego Aerospace Museum.

View Of A B-24 In Flight

I was interested in the fact that the ancient ruins of Cannae were only 15 miles southeast of our airbase. It was at Cannae that the great Carthaginian general, Hannibal, outnumbered almost two to one, lead his troops to destroy 70,000 Roman soldiers *in one afternoon* in 216 B.C. As a comparison, *in twelve years of war* in Vietnam, 58,000 American troops were killed. Hannibal aroused my interest so that I wrote a biography of Hannibal many years later (*Hannibal's Lieutenant: a Unique Biography of the Brilliant Hannibal* (1994), Manor House Publications of Alexandria, P.O. Box 19427, Alexandria, Virginia 22320-0427.)

Many other B-24 and B-17 heavy bombardment groups of the Fifteenth Air Force were being established around Foggia at the time of our Group's arrival. The 456th Bomb Group's 4,800 foot runway, taxiways, and 62 dispersed parking ramps had been hewn out of the farm's wheat field by bulldozers, then they were covered with steel matting to receive the Liberators. Ground crews had arrived at the airfield earlier and pitched their tents by January 25, preparing for the Group's airplanes. I and my three buddies, Lieutenants Heffner, Scritchfield, and Morgan arrived there with the ground crews, before the aircrews arrived with their planes.

The Ground Echelon Begins Its Road to Italy from Muroc.

Non-flying personnel of the 456th Bomb Group started their trip to Italy with a train ride from Muroc to Camp Patrick Henry, Virginia, near Hampton Roads, with some arriving there as early as December 4, 1943. The Ground Echelon was given final processing for overseas, then it waited for a huge convoy of Liberty ships to assemble. Finally, on December 13, 1943, the first part of the Ground Echelon was transported to Newport News and put on separate transport ships. Headquarters Detachment's officers, including myself and my three buddies, Second Lieutenants Gail J. Scritchfield, Douglas S. Morgan, and Edward J. Heffner, were put on the *S..S John Cropper.* Many of our Group were put on the *S.S. Timothy Dwight.* Some, including Sgt. Richard C. Hood of the 746th Squadron, sailed on the *S.S. Joaquin Miller.* Our huge convoy of ships finally departed Newport News and Hampton Roads on December 15, 1943. A fleet of Navy warships sailed with us and protected our huge convoy during the voyage. We still didn't know where we were going.

We experienced a very rough sea voyage on stormy winter Atlantic seas during which most of us became sea sick, and during which we heard rumors that a Liberty ship in our convoy had actually split in half. The Liberty ship that Sgt. Richard C. Hood sailed on, the *S.S. Joaquin Miller,* developed a crack during rough seas and had to return to port for repairs. After repairs, he and his party sailed to Italy at a later date. We traveled at about 9 knots per hour because our ship was sailing in formation with many other ships and it had to keep its position in the formation. Our convoy of ships had to take a circuitous "S" shaped route around the Atlantic Ocean to avoid German submarine wolf-packs that were taking a huge toll of merchant shipping in the Atlantic Ocean.

After spending Christmas and New Years on the Ships, the convoy finally sailed through the Straight of Gibraltar in the dark of night on January 5, 1944. We didn't know where we were going, but as soon as we passed the Straight of Gibraltar we knew it wasn't England. From there, two of the ships that had 456th Bomb Group personnel aboard took different routes. Those of us sailing with the Headquarters Detachment's officers on the *SS John Cropper* sailed from the Straight of Gibraltar to Syracuse, Sicily, near historic Mt. Etna. We stopped there to get further orders about where we were supposed to go next. The fluid ground war situation, or the desire to keep our destination secret, prevented our ship's captain from knowing our seaport destination in Italy until the last minute. From there we were ordered to go to Taranto, Italy, in Italy's heel, and the first of our troops touched land in Taranto at 1105 hours, January 11, 1944.

It has been documented that the Japanese Admiral Yamamoto got his idea for his sneak attack on Pearl Harbor after studying the success of this British raid on Taranto Harbor. Taranto was the site where the British made a surprise attack on the Port of Taranto on November 11, 1940 with obsolete Swordfish carrier aircraft that caught the Italian Navy by surprise. All of Mussolini's battleships were in port and they were severely crippled or sunk.

While waiting for the train in Taranto, Lt. Gilbert W. Smith of our Group Headquarters Intelligence noted in his diary that Italians in the station at Taranto all begged for food, and some had oranges to barter for it. He said that for two lumps of sugar the piccolini sang "Roll Out the Barrel." There were a few bomb craters at the station, our first evidence of war.

From Taranto we rode in a frigidly cold Italian train with open windows, no glass in them, that only had cold, hard, solid wood seats. We traveled on the train with members of the 454th Bomb Group. The train only had three coach cars and two box cars, a mixture of German, French and Italian types, no windows. Our rustic train pulled out of Taranto at 1625 hours. We traveled all night at a slow speed, traveling at a maximum of up to 25 miles per hour.

At each train stop along the way, Italian civilians and soldiers prayed for rides on our train. At one stop, a carabiniere eased his way into our compartment telling a love story and showing photos of his girlfriend. About midnight, at one stop, two policemen (polizie) and their two alleged prisoners talked themselves into a ride, and the prisoners appeared as enthused about their luck at getting the ride as their guards were. The next event occurred when the train engineer and his coal stoker refused to pull out of the next station until we gave them some supper. After someone in our party gave food to them we pulled out. We could see war damage from the train under the light of the full moon on a bitterly cold night. Everyone and his brother claimed to be working for the railroad, to get a ride, and we arrived in Cerignola with no less than thirteen conductors crowded on board of our three small coach cars. We arrived in Cerignola thoroughly chilled at 1100 hours on January 12, 1944. I became violently sick with the Grippe on this train ride, vomiting many times out a cold open window, and I had to be taken to an Italian Catholic hospital for a few days. I received very good care by Catholic nuns before rejoining the rest of the officers at a pink farm house.

Our Group headquarters detachment was first billeted with the 301st Bomb Group. Then Major Leonard A. Weissinger, Group Adjutant, negotiated for a farm house to be used as temporary quarters for the headquarters officers. It was a nearby pink masonry farm house that was fairly new, one of Mussolini's state-owned cattle farms. It was at this pink farmhouse that I rejoined the rest of the headquarters officers and my buddies, Lieutenants Scritchfield, Heffner, and Morgan. It was a comfortable but cold place to live, and we stayed there until it was time to be transported in Army trucks to our new airbase near Stornara. Many of us had our first showers in a long time in the cold cattle-washing shed of the farm. The weather was very cold and we only had ice cold water to use in the cattle showers.

We had a few meals as guests of the 301 Bomb Group mess hall, nearby, our best meals since leaving Muroc. The Headquarters of the 301st Bomb Group was located in a winery, the Pavoncelli Winery. It was still operating, and we could buy a bottle of white or red wine for eleven Lira (11 cents) with a nine Lira deposit on the bottle. We had a light rain in the afternoon of January 24, and in the evening Lt. Col. Walter Cal Phillips gave us a talk in the stable of our farm. He told us about our current situation, and he reminded us to maintain a proper military bearing. He said that the ground personnel were to begin moving to our new airbase the next day, on January 25.

On January 26, 1944 the Mayor of Stornara was called upon to recruit some laborers, laundresses, and barbers. Skilled Italian laborers were paid seventy-five Lira a day in Allied occupation money (75 cents), and unskilled laborers were paid fifty Lira a day (50 cents). A hair cut and shave was seven Lira (7 cents).

Although the pink farm house was very crowded, it was comfortable, and it was the first experience for many of us at living in Europe. The small bathroom had a bidet, as well as a toilet, a novelty for most of us Americans who weren't sure how it was supposed to be used. During the time we spent in that farmhouse, waiting for our airfield to be completed, my longtime traveling buddies and I found a very good friend and companion in the 746th Squadron's flight surgeon, the very likable, handsome Capt. Louis A. Tripi (a gynecologist in civilian life). We became acquainted with many other officers during those anxious two weeks of living in close quarters, not knowing what our future fate would be. We had come to know many of them on the *SS John Cropper* during our long sea voyage, cooped up on the small Liberty ship for almost four weeks. Among the officers occupying the farmhouse were the very congenial gentlemen, Thomas M. Perkins (Assistant Adjutant), Howard I. Neff (Intelligence), Burton L. Olmstead (engineering), Thomas L. Huff (Technical Inspector) and Major Leonard A. Weissinger (Group Adjutant). We all speculated about what would happen to us next.

Our first jolt with the reality of what was in store for us aircrew members came during the time we were eating at the B-17 bomber base nearby at Giulia, temporary home of the 301st Bomber Group (Heavy). The 301st was our host for some of our warm meals until we could get our own mess kitchens operating. The group was already established and regularly flying combat missions. We ate in a tent with combat aircrews of the 301st. I will never forget the serious, shocked, worn, and dejected looks on faces of B-17 crew members as they arrived in the mess tent where we were eating, after they had returned from flying a very rough bombing raid into Germany.

The 301st crew members all looked stunned, strained, emotionally drained, and very fatigued. They talked amongst themselves about how their buddies had been shot down on the mission, the number of parachutes they had seen coming from the falling planes, and planes that had blown up without any chance of men bailing out. They had animated discussions about the dense clouds of flak that came up from hundreds of 88mm antiaircraft guns firing at them from the ground. They talked about the large swarms of German Messerschmitt-109 and Folke Wolf-190 fighter aircraft that had relentlessly attacked their unescorted bombing formations. Missions over the Alps into Germany, Austria, Hungary, and raids to Rumania had to be conducted without fighter escort at that time because our fighters did not have the required cruising range.

It was there, in that mess tent, we began to realize that it was not going to be a fun and games experience. Nevertheless, in my youthful optimism I still didn't believe that I was going to be one that was shot down, and I couldn't wait to get into combat to see the great spectacle of air combat that they were talking about. It sounded very exciting. Furthermore, I couldn't wait to fly an airplane again, as it had been more than two months since my last flight.

We were finally transported by truck to our new airfield on January 27. The field had no airplanes on it. My three buddies and I were assigned to different squadrons. Heffner, Morgan, and Scritchfield were assigned to the 744th Squadron and I was assigned to the 746th Squadron, located on the other side of the runway. We were deposited on bare, damp ground in olive groves. We were instructed to pitch one man pup tents on the hard, moist ground like boy scouts. The olive groves became muddy quagmires at times from rain mixed with human activity. Sunny Italy did not live up to its press clippings, as rain and even a some snow fell that winter.

The *SS Timothy Dwight* took another route to Italy from the Straight of Gibraltar with its members of the Ground Echelon. It went to Bizerte, Tunisia before going to Naples, Italy, landing there on January 19, 1944. The 745th Squadron, after driving all night in open Army trucks in frigid weather from Naples, arrived at the 301st Bomb Group encampment in Giulia at 0230 hours on January 22. The 744th and the 747th Squadrons arrived there in the dawn of January 23, 1943. The airmen of my 746th Squadron, and parts of the 747th Squadron, arrived in Cerignola during the night of January 24, and they spent the night in the Teatro Mercandante in Cerignola before being transported by GI truck to their new airfield, nearby, the next day. The 746th and part of the 747th were the first units to arrive at our new airbase. The winter weather was cold, had rained the day before, and most of the Ground Echelon moved to the bare, wet ground of their new airfield on January 25, 1944. They pitched tents on the soggy ground for shelter.

Some of the 456th Bomb Group personnel docked at the port of Augusta, Italy, before being transported to Giulia, then to Stornara.

My Personal Training Experience Before Joining The 456th Bomb Group.

My specialized training experience before being assigned to the 456th Bombardment Group was probably typical of the other pilots in the Group. It was probably very similar to the training experience of others who had to be trained in other technical specialties that were required by the Group. The advent of long range heavy bombers, used by the new Air Corps, required specialized training of many navigators and bombardiers. Most gunners, engineers, radio operators, ground maintenance personnel, and other ground support specialties received technical training in a similar manner before they were assigned to the 456th Bomb Group.

My road to Italy started the day after the bombing of Pearl Harbor. I tried to enlist in the pilot training program of the Army Air Corps the next day, but I was told to go back to school until I had two years of college training. A few months later, I heard through the grapevine that the Air Corps was accepting anyone who could pass an examination that was supposed be the equivalent proficiency of two years of college, and I passed it. I was sworn into the Army Air Corps on April 27, 1942 after passing written and physical examinations in San Francisco. Only about twenty percent of the applicants were able to pass the rigid physical and written exams.

After being sworn into the Army Air Corps as a flying cadet in April, it wasn't until September that I received orders to enter the flying program. I learned later that the five month delay was due to a crash program the Army Air Corps had in progress, to construct many new training airbases and to procure thousands more training planes that were necessary to rapidly increase the number of cadets entering into the flying training program.

Classification.

In September 1942, I was ordered to the Classification Center at Nashville, Tennessee from San Francisco. The Classification Center gave us many more written, physical, and psychometric examinations over ten days. We were each interviewed by a psychoanalyst. Purpose of the exams was to classify us as either pilots, navigators, or bombardiers. I was rated as all three, so I was given my preference of becoming a pilot.

My faith in medical technology was given a severe, irreparable blow at the Classification Center. After we had passed the rigid exams, including days of rigorous, very detailed medical examinations and we were ready to be transported to our next base, a cadet sleeping on the cot near me died in the night of a heart attack. We didn't discover his death until we tried to wake him up to answer the bugle call for early morning reveille. I learned then and there about the limitations of medical science.

Preflight Training.

From Nashville, Tennessee I was sent to Maxwell Airbase, Montgomery Alabama to attend 10 weeks of intensive preflight training. The training included rigorous physical, military, and academic training. Its purpose was to develop sound bodies, stout hearts, and alert minds. A class system, upper and lower classes, was used with a fairly rough "hazing" process whereby the upper classmen put stress on lower classmen. I learned much later that the purpose of this hazing and tough physical training was to help identify those of us that did not have the mental and physical capability to withstand the stresses, strains, and fear that we would encounter in combat. Only a small percentage of our flying cadet class was eliminated ("washed out") of the program at this phase of the training, because we had been screened so thoroughly at the Classification Center.

Primary Flying Training.

Upon graduation from preflight school, I was sent to a civilian, contract-run Primary Flying School at Decatur, Alabama, the 65th Army Air Force Flying Training Detachment. The civilian school was called The Southern Aviation Training School. All the school's personnel, except for a few supervisory people, were civilians.

At Decatur, the hazing process was continued in a modified form, with the flying instructors providing the mental pressure on the cadet. The instructor had the power to wash out his student as a result of any day's performance, and many instructors did! This part of the training was the most stressful for us cadets, not only because it was the first time that most of us had flown and we didn't know what to expect, but because we had heard from our upper classmen that almost fifty percent of us would be "washed out" - i.e. eliminated from pilot training during primary training. None of us knew what it took to pass the course, so we all worked as hard as we could to avoid being one of the ones selected for washout.

The pressure was on us all during our stay at Decatur, because each day there were a few more cadets washed out. No one knew who would be next. There were four Air Corps officers on the base who flew a plane that the cadets came to call the "washing machine." It was given that name because whenever a civilian instructor scheduled one of his students for a check ride in the washing machine, before the student had finished most of the flying course, the cadet was almost always washed out of the program. We all had the ordeal of having to take a final check ride in the washing machine when we completed the course, but as long as you didn't screw up some way, by that time the check ride was usually successful. A major purpose of this stressful training was to identify those that didn't have the mental toughness needed for combat flying, as well as to identify those that didn't have the ability to fly. I believed that many who were washed out of the program could fly, but the instructors must have had a quota and selected those he felt were less qualified or less quick to learn..

The Stearman PT-17 could fly at a maximum speed of 125 MPH. We had 60 hours in the plane and 148 hours of academic and military ground training. My flying instructor was the civilian, T.V.Reeves, a very competent, no nonsense southerner with a drawl. I grew to like him and respect him very much. He was a very competent pilot and a good instructor. I soloed after seven hours. The time allotted for each cadet to solo was between eight and twelve hours, and if you didn't make it by then you had to ride the washing machine.

The PT-17 was a biplane, open cockpit, fabric covered, single engine plane with no radio. It had a 225 horsepower Continental radial engine and a fixed propeller blade. It was called the "Kaydet." All our planes were painted a neat, colorful blue and gold and they were lined up row upon row on the flight line. It was a beautiful sight. Our instructors were very competent civilian pilots, and the school's mess halls produced gourmet meals, the likes of which I have never seen in a military mess hall since. It made me think about the difference between government-run facilities and those run by private enterprise.

We learned to do loops, snap rolls, chandelles, lazy eights, put the plane in a spin, slow rolls, stalls, and many other maneuvers. We had many practice landings at different fields, all on grass. I learned that flying takes a combination of hard work and intense concentration. The fear of the "washing machine" was a great motivation for learning to do the job right. Flying in the open cockpit plane during January was very cold, even though we wore sheepskin-lined heavy flying suits, boots, helmets with goggles, and gloves. I was usually in a sweat because of my concentration and effort to avoid being washed out.

When final results were in at the end of our primary training, forty percent of our class, Class 43F, had been "washed out." I learned later that this was the same as the average washout rate for the entire Air Corps pilot training program from 1939 to 1945. Those that were washed out were usually sent to navigator or bombardier training, depending upon their qualifications, and they entered those programs.

Basic Flying Training.

From the civilian-run Primary Flying school at Decatur, the sixty percent of us who passed the primary course were sent back to Montgomery, Alabama where the military-run Gunter Field Basic Flying Training School was located. It was there that we had a 10 week course flying the Vultee BT-13 for 82 hours. It had a 450 horsepower engine and it was an all metal aircraft, except for the flyable surfaces which were fabric covered. It had a closed cockpit that protected us from the cold slipstream of air, a variable speed propeller, a fuel mixture control that controlled the fuel to oxygen ratio for the engine, a radio, and wing flaps. It did not have a retractable landing gear. It was affectionately called the "Vultee Vibrator" because of its vibrating characteristics.

We had night flying and instrument flying for the first time. We also flew some cross-country navigation trips. One pilot was killed while many of us watched, when he stalled his plane out on the base leg of his landing pattern and spun into the ground as he returned from one of our cross-country trips. We speculated that he forgot to extend his flaps. We had to get used to using flaps, mixture controls, and changing propeller pitch on the BT-13. We were introduced to more Link trainer instrument training. We had 141 hours of academic and military ground training at Gunter Field.

About thirteen percent of the cadets, of the sixty percent that had survived primary training, were washed out from this part of the program. Most of the flying instructors were Air Corps pilots, but my instructor was a veteran Royal Air Force pilot, Flight Officer Linton. He had experience flying in the Battle of Britain, and we all admired him. He wore the handsome blue R.A.F. uniform and decorations.

The Army mess hall at Gunter Field was a stark contrast with the civilian-run mess hall that we enjoyed at Primary Flying School! It was here in the Army mess that I first tasted horse-meat stew. It was clearly identified on the menu along with the other items on the menu, as horse meat. The menu was posted each day that it was served, on the wall of the mess hall. Dining in a slapdash Army "chow line" messing facility at Gunter Field was much different than dining at the civilian run messing facility of primary flying school at Decatur. At Decatur we had dignified table service, ate excellently prepared food with home-cooked pastries, and we had it served to us elegantly with table cloths and cloth napkins.

Advanced Flying Training.

From Gunter Airbase some pilots went to advance flying school for twin engine bomber training and others went to single engine fighter training. Since I wanted to be a fighter pilot, I went to the single engine Advanced Flying Training at Napier Field, Dothan, Alabama. This was the third and last phase of our training before we received our silver pilot wings and commissions as second lieutenants in the U.S. Army Air Corps.

In Advanced Flying School we flew the North American AT-6 for 88 hours. It was a very enjoyable, smooth flying all metal airplane. It had a retractable landing gear, closed cockpit, constant speed propeller, hydraulic flaps, a good radio, a smooth 600 horsepower Pratt & Whitney engine.

It had a single, low-slung wing, and a maximum speed of 210 MPH. It was a much more enjoyable plane to fly than the other planes we had flown. What made it even more enjoyable was the fact that we had heard that very few cadets washed out of this stage of the flying, so that pressure on us was lifted a little.

The pressure of washing out was reduced at Napier Field, but we had been trained to concentrate on the business of flying. The AT-6 was faster, heavier, and more complex. If you forgot to let your wheels down for landing you would wash out the plane and yourself. A few unfortunate cadets did make this unforgivable error! We learned to perform the "GUMP" check before each landing: check the Gas, Undercarriage, Mixture, and Propeller. We did more instrument flying and much formation flying. Our instrutors acted more like flight leaders and friends rather than the tough instructors we were used to having, and we were able to enjoy the flying without fear of being washed out of the program as long as we didn't make a gross error. Here we had 79 hours of academic and military ground training in addition to the flying training.

Cadet Robert S. Capps At Advanced Flying School

Cadet Robert S. Capps, June 1943

During Advanced Flying School, we had aerial gunnery training during a temporary duty trip to Eglin Army Airfield, Florida. There we fired our aircraft's guns at targets in the air that were being towed by other aircraft. We also fired at targets on the ground, in strafing excercises. I was not very good with my scores for air-to-ground firing, but I broke some records with my air-to-air gunnery scores. There was a severe shortage of the wire-mesh material that was being used as towed targets for us to shoot at for our aerial gunnery practice. The shortage of material caused the school to reduce the size of the targets that we fired at in the air to one-half of the normal size. Because the targets were reduced to half their normal size, the school decided to give us credit for two hits for every hit we placed in the target. Our bullets had colored wax on them, so that our bullets would leave a colored mark on the target as it passed through the wire mesh. Firing for score, I was able to get 96% of my bullets into the target; this gave me 192% as a score, an impossible score under normal circumstances, and it must have been the highest ever recorded. Anyway, it was the highest score in my cadet class.

Ten of us, out of the total of 200 cadets in my Napier Field class, were selected to go to Craig Field at Selma, Alabama to fly the hot combat fighter, the Curtis P-40 aircraft before graduation. (Selma later became famous for the 1965 voting rights march.) The P-40 had a 1,150 horsepower Allison engine and a maximum speed of 362 MPH. Since it had only one cockpit seat, none for an instructor, the first flight in the plane was a solo flight. We flew the P-40 after we were given extensive ground training, including a blindfold cockpit test of emergency procedures. It was a great thrill flying such a high performance plane for the first time, solo. The P-40 was the same aircraft that the "Flying Tigers" flew so successfully in China against the Japanese. Their planes had shark's teeth painted under their noses.

Lieutenants Douglas S. Morgan, Gail J. Scritchfield, and I were originally trained as fighter pilots in the Southeastern Training Command's flying school class of 43-F (graduating June 1943). Upon graduation from the pilot training course, the three of us had been assigned to the 439th Fighter Squadron at Dale Mabry Field, Tallahassee, Florida where it was rumored that we were to get North American A-36 fighter attack aircraft. We didn't know it at the time, but the A-36 was being modified to become the hot P-51 Mustang fighter by replacing the Allison engine with a supercharged British Rolls Royce engine, and by adding more fuel tanks. We didn't get these hot new P-51s as fighter escort in Italy until April 1944.

By the time that we were assigned to the 439th Fighter Squadron, the war in North Africa had been won and there was no longer fighting there. The demand for fighter attack aircraft had abruptly dropped off. However, many four engine bombers were coming off production lines, and the immediate need was for heavy bomber pilots, not fighter pilots. Our entire fighter squadron was transferred to the 382nd Bombardment Group at Pocatello, Idaho where we were given combat crew training in B-24 heavy bombers. All of us fighter pilots were disappointed by the transfer from fighters to bombers, and some of the pilots felt so bad about it that they refused to fly the huge four engine monsters. Those that refused to fly B-24's were removed from flying status, grounded, and made supply officers. I wanted to fly, so I willingly completed combat crew training as a bomber pilot with my friends Morgan and Scritchfield. While I started the training as a copilot to Lt. Larry Riesen, I was later checked out as a first pilot to fly the B-24 as an aircraft commander before being assigned to the 456th Bomb Group.

Combat Crew Training.

At Pocatello we learned all about the B-24 during our operational training program with the 382nd Bomb Group. I learned later that this was a replacement training unit, one that trained aircrews to fill in the ranks of other fighting groups going overseas. We flew night, day, on instruments, on long range navigation flights over water (one flight from Pocatello to Hawaii and back), on bombing and gunnery flights, and on formation flights with other huge B-24's. It was an intensive ground and air training course. I logged 250 hours flying time during this course.

After being accustomed to the tight and precise formation flying in fighter aircraft, my fighter-trained buddies and I had a difficult time abiding so many other pilots who could not fly formation very well. They were atrocious formation flyers. Many of them blamed their poor ability to fly good formation on the fact that the B-24 was less stable than other planes, but my buddies from the old fighter squadron knew better. We were able to keep our B-24s neatly tucked close to the other planes of the formation.

Flying close formation was very important later in aerial combat. Tight formations concentrated the ten machine guns of each Liberator in the formation into a close knit, lethal, aggregation of guns available to fire at attacking enemy fighter planes. For example, a seven-airplane box of B-24's would have 70 guns to fire at attacking enemy fighters. A tight knit bomber group having six closely knit boxes of seven airplanes each would menace attacking fighter with 420 guns. Our guns contained tracer bullets, so that approaching fighters were intimidated by a large number of tracer bullets, to let them know we had many guns firing at them.

Furthermore, when bombing in formation, the tightness of the pattern that bombs make when they hit the ground is dependent upon the tightness of the formation of planes in flight when bombs are dropped. If the formation of airplanes is tight when the bombs are dropped, the pattern of the bombs that hit the ground target will be tight and close to the target. The bombs on the ground will be spread out if the formation of bombers is spread out.

It was while we were preflighting for an evening training flight at Pocatello that we watched a B-24 in the traffic pattern getting ready to land. As I watched the Liberator turn from its base leg to its final approach for landing, all four of its engines suddenly stopped at the same time. The plane rapidly smashed head first into the ground, and it became a huge ball of fire. The entire crew was killed before our eyes. This was not an encouraging sight for my crew about ready to take off on a long night practice mission. I learned later, that engines of early B-24D models used Chandler-Evans (CECO) direct metering carburetors which had a bad history of "freezing up" when air temperature and humidity conditions were right. A freeze-up of the carburetor would stop fuel from reaching the engine and that would cause the engines to quit. I always wondered how many planes were lost this way before the problem was discovered. We lost a few other planes in training, but I never learned whether it was for that reason or not.

The B-24 was also having many other problems at that time with fuel leaks, fuel booster pump problems, hydraulic system malfunctions, and aircraft fires. Later models of the B-24, and even later B-24D's, were fitted with the more reliable Bendix-Stromberg injection type carburetor that solved the problem of freeze up. Liberator models B-24 G, H, and J's that I flew in overseas combat were relatively flawless, compared to our training B-24Ds. A large share of the reason for this reliability had to be credited to our hard working maintenance crews, because they had much more experience with the aircraft by the time we were in Italy. The B-24 was rushed into production, because of the wartime emergency without the normal research, development, and testing that we are used to accomplishing now on military aircraft. Liberators were constantly being modified throughout the war, and they were eventually made into a superb, reliable bomber.

After completing our combat crew training in B-24's at Pocatello, four B-24 crews including mine were all assigned to the 20th Tow Target Squadron at Wendover Field, Utah to get more flying time while waiting for an overseas assignments. Though we didn't know it at the time, top military planners were expecting an invasion of Italy to provide many more heavy bomber bases within a few months. England already had too many airfields, and the flying weather there was rotten.

While waiting for our orders to go overseas, we flew stripped down B-24 aircraft that had all heavy armor removed. These lighter B-24's could fly about 15 miles an hour faster than other B-24's and 25 miles an hour faster than B-17's. We used them to tow targets for gunners of other bombers to shoot at for gunnery practice. This enabled us to get more flying experience in the bomber while we waited for overseas orders to come through. I was able to get checked out as a first pilot of the Liberator during this assignment. In addition to a few stripped down B-24's, we also had a stripped down twin engine Martin B-26 aircraft (renamed the Advanced Trainer-23) for towing targets for heavy bombers' gunners to fire on. I was anxious to get as much flying as possible, so I volunteered to fly anything anytime. I was able to fly the "hot" B-26 that had two 2,000 horsepower engines. The B-26 was called the "flying prostitute" because it had no visible means of support. Its wings were so short they didn't look as though they could support such a large plane in flight.

The Boeing B-17 "Flying Fortress", which was used in the early bombing raids from England, was given much more notoriety than the Johnny-Come-Lately B-24 "Liberator". The B-24 was designed after the war in Europe had started, four years after the B-17 was first flown on July 28, 1935; the XB-24 first flew December 29, 1939. The B-24 was faster, carried a heavier bomb load, could fly further, and it had better engines than the Boeing B-17. Many more B-24's were produced and put into combat. Regardless of all this, the B-24 received much less publicity than the B-17.

The 20th Tow Target Squadron operated out of five different airbases during our short sojourn in it while waiting for overseas orders. We were on airbases at Wendover, Utah; Casper, Wyoming; Pierre, South Dakota; Sioux City, Iowa; and Boise, Idaho.

During this duty I had the great pleasure of meeting Captain James Stewart, the movie actor. He was operations officer of a heavy bombardment squadron and I was assigned to tow targets for his crews on a gunnery mission. I had no idea who he was when I was first ordered, along with another pilot, 2nd Lt. Larry Riesen, to meet a "Captain Stewart" at base operations to arrange a gunnery mission. I was pleasantly surprised when I recognized him as the famous movie idol. I was even more pleasantly surprised when he turned out to be such a nice guy. He behaved like "one of the regular guys" rather than the celebrity that he was. He was a real gentleman. I learned from some of his pilots that admiring women created such a commotion over him when he went in to the local town, even tearing his uniform for souvenirs, that he elected to stay on the airbase most of the time. Later, his squadron was sent overseas to the Eighth Air Force in England and he became group commander. He flew combat missions, risking his life, just like the rest of us.

Lt. Edward J. Heffner, a bombardier, was also assigned to the 20th Tow Target Squadron after completing his B-24 combat training. He was kept busy doing various duties while we all waited for our overseas orders. There were three other B-24 combat crews in the squadron marking time, expecting overseas orders.

When we first landed on the runway at Pierre A. A. B., South Dakota, there were numerous fat, ring-necked pheasants running across the runway, in the path of our aircraft. At our first opportunity, another officer and myself borrowed a skeet gun, shells, and a Jeep, and drove to a ravine at the edge of the runway in the direction where we saw the pheasants flee. In less than two hours the two of us shot 72 huge ring necks and the firemen of the base fire department volunteered to prepare a sumptuous pheasant feast for us. Since we had the only aircraft on the base at the time, as the local bomb groups had already left for overseas duty, the firemen had ample time to prepare the dinner for us.

Wartime gasoline rationing and the lack of available ammunition for guns for the civilian populace had severely reduced the number of pheasant hunters in South Dakota. The lack of hunters to thin the crops of pheasant caused pheasant to multiply to such an extent that they were a severe hazard to local farms. There was no legal limit to the quantity of pheasant that could be shot, and the state legislature was considering a law that would offer a bounty for all pheasant killed to reduce their sudden phenomenal population growth.

Capps, Morgan, Heffner, And Scritchfield Ordered To Join The 456th Bomb Group At Muroc.

On November 26, 1943 we were on a couple of weeks of temporary flying duty at Pierre Army Air Base, from our home base at Casper Army Air Base, Wyoming, when we finally received our orders to go to Muroc Lake Army Air Base, California for assignment to the 456th Bombardment Group (Heavy) as replacement crew members. Our entire

20th Tow Target Squadron was dissolved and every one of its members were ordered to become replacement aircrew members for different bomber groups that had already been ordered overseas. We didn't know it at the time, but we had been in a "holding status" waiting for more territory to be liberated in Italy so that more heavy bomber airfields could be built there. The Allies had begun the invasion of Italy in September 1943, and initially they advanced northward up the Italian peninsula very rapidly. Many new airfields were being planned for Italy, as planners expected the land to be liberated by Allied forces. Heavy bombers were flying from airfields in Italy, close to enemy lines, within three months by December 1943.

Muroc was a mystery name. All of us who were headed for Muroc couldn't find anyone who knew where the airfield was located. Pierre A.A.B. only had a skeleton "housekeeping" unit because the resident bomb group had already departed for overseas a few months before and the base didn't have the normal administrative personnel available to help us. No one had ever heard of Muroc A.A.B.. We went to the local railroad depot to see if railroad clerks on duty there knew where the airbase was located and how we could get there. After much searching and discussion with one another, and many telephone calls for about forty-five minutes, the railroad clerks finally found a small train stop called "Muroc" on the map. After some more telephone calls, we determined that was the place.

We took a train, and after two days' travel, the train dropped us off in the middle of the hot Mohave Dessert at a spot where there wasn't a living sole around except for one railroad clerk in a one room wood shack that was being used as a train station. The railroad employee told us to use his telephone to call the airbase for transportation. An army truck eventually arrived to drive us many miles through the Mohave Desert to the airbase The base is now called

Edwards Air Force Base, where the space-shuttle now lands occasionally on the Muroc Dry Lake.

Soon after we arrived at Muroc, we learned that the 456th had already departed for overseas. We were told that we would be supplied with overseas equipment, then we would be sent to catch up with the ground echelon of the 456th that was traveling by ground transportation to its port of embarkation. The flight crews had departed earlier by air. We had no idea where we were going overseas. As far as we knew, our destination could be England, Italy, Alaska, or the Pacific. Our destination was secret information kept from us. Written military orders were always purposely vague, for security reasons.

We had a strong indication that we were not going to the Pacific combat theater of operations, to fight the Japanese, when we were finally issued some heavy fur-lined winter flying clothing. Then, we were ordered to travel by car, plane, and train to catch up with the Group's ground personnel at Camp Patrick Henry, Virginia. The Pacific combat area was thus ruled out, so we believed that we were headed for either England, Italy, or Africa.

There was a rich and famous movie actor, George Montgomery, on the American Airlines DC-3 airliner that carried the four of us buddies from Los Angeles to Washington D.C. He was wearing an enlisted man's uniform with the rank of corporal. The plane made at least five stops on the way to Washington, and passengers were asked to get off at each stop while the plane was refueled. It was at three of those stops that this rich and famous movie actor, a corporal and older than me, saluted me while we were off the plane. I was only a twenty-year old second lieutenant, I admired him, and I felt like saluting him rather than the other way around. We were all taught that the military code of conduct is that you salute the uniform, not the individual. But I was very young, inexperienced, and embarrassed.

To this day, I remember how Ed Heffner would wake up singing a song from the new stage musical, "Oklahoma": "Oh what a beautiful morning, oh what a wonderful day, I've got a wonderful feeling, everything's going my way." He had seen the new musical in Los Angeles during our last leave before going overseas. That song succinctly expressed the youthful optimism of the four of us. I was 20 years old, and none of the others were older than 21 years. We couldn't wait to get into aerial combat with the hated Nazi enemy, although we all had a lingering homesickness and we did not relish leaving our families and loved ones behind. It was the first time we had been away from home. We were all facing the adventurous unknown together.

The four of us replacements aircrew members finally caught up with the rest of the group's Ground Echelon at Camp Patrick Henry, just in time to board the Liberty ship, *S.S. John Cropper,* and we journeyed to Italy as previously described above.

We still did not know where we were going because it was kept a secret from us. I'm convinced now, long after the war, that top military planners weren't sure we would be able to go to the part of Italy where they had planned to put us because the Allied ground forces were still battling over the ground where our airbases were supposed to be built. Most of us weren't sure whether we were going to England, Africa, or Italy. Italy had only recently been invaded by the Allies on September 9, 1943, only three months before we sailed from Virginia, so Italy was not high on our expectation list. However, when we passed through the Straight of Gibraltar we assumed it was either Africa or Italy.

Allied ground forces had been stalled by the Germans below the German Gustav Line, which ran east and west on a line south of Cassino Abbey, south of Rome. When we finally arrived at our new airbase near Stornara we could occasionally hear heavy guns firing at the front lines when conditions were favorable. To guard against air raids, shelter trenches had to be dug near our tents, and we were ordered to keep our metal helmets and gas masks handy. Mustard gas had been used by the Germans in World War I, and we had to be prepared for that to happen again. Major Leonard A. Weissinger, our Group Adjutant, used to bother us considerably (to say the least) when we failed to get into our shelter trenches during enemy air raids.

When I was transported to our new airfield, personnel of each squadron, the 744th, 745th, 746th (mine), and 747th set up one-man pup tents in improvised, separate campgrounds in olive groves that surrounded the wheat fields. The 744th and 745th Squadrons were on one side of the runway, and the other two squadrons established their camp grounds on the other side. There were a few larger army pyramidal tents in the tent cities, but they were occupied by the first troops to arrive at the airfield a few days before. The olive groves provided some protection and camouflage from possible German air raids. Front lines of battle and the ever-threatening German ground forces were about eighty-five miles to the north.

Most of us in the 456th Bomb Group weren't aware of it at the time, but a great catastrophe, discussed in the next chapter, had occurred in Bari Harbor shortly before the 456th arrived in Italy. It was one that had a profound impact on our creature comforts around camp, base supplies, and other items for our operations. Stove pipes, light bulbs, and valves to regulate the flow of 100 octane gasoline for our improvised heaters were difficult to come by, and we had to make foraging trips into nearby villages and towns to buy them from the destitute Italian people who needed the money for food. When we offered to buy a light bulb from an Italian, for example, a family member would run into his house and unscrew one to bring out to us. They needed the money for food for their families. Germans had a scorched earth policy as they left the area, taking all livestock and everything edible that they could find as they retreated from the area. Italians in that part of Italy were very poor peasants before the German army did this, but the German action made local Italians even more impoverished.

Lt. Fred Riley of my 746th Squadron heard that some people stole the light bulbs when they visited hotels in Bari on temporary duty there.

Our main food rations at our airbase at Stornara were army K-rations in cardboard boxes and C-rations in cans and boxes. These were augmented by whatever our imaginative army cooks could find to improve them. Crusty Italian white bread was one of the better additions they found to add to the meals. The army C-rations included Spam, soup, beans, beef stew, dehydrated potatoes, dehydrated eggs, dehydrated milk, instant coffee, pickles, jam, peanut butter, pancakes, and margarine, among other items. We had steak on rare occasions. One of those occasions was the day our Liberators arrived from Tunis, on February 1, 1944. Each of us had our own aluminum mess kits that we would bring through a long "chow line." After eating, we would get into another line to wash our mess kits in a series of three steel drums filled with hot water, disinfectant soap, and rinse water.

We were all looking forward to arrival of our Liberator fleet. I was anxious to start flying again.

Chapter 2
THE BIG PICTURE: WHY WE WERE IN ITALY

Priority Mission: Air Superiority Before June 1944.

The first, most urgent priority mission of the 456h Bombardment Group in Italy, and of all U.S. Army Air Force bombardment groups in Europe, was the destruction of the German Air Force (Luftwaffe) in the air and on the ground *before June 1944.* That priority had a profound influence on the 456th, although we at group level didn't know about that magic date at the time because it was "Top Secret" information known only to a few top military leaders and planners.

Roosevelt, Churchill, and Stalin, the top leaders of the allied war effort against the Axis powers, had held a conference at Tehran on the Black Sea which ended on December 1, 1943. They agreed to a plan for an allied invasion of Europe, code named "Overlord" to begin in June 1994. They also agreed that it was absolutely necessary to destroy the German Air Force, and to have complete control of the air over Europe before Overlord could be attempted. Victory in the battle for air supremacy was regarded as a necessary prelude to any invasion of Europe. The destruction of the Luftwaffe and attainment of allied air superiority had a higher priority than the decisive strategic bombing of other German war making capability. After allied air superiority was attained, the overall objective was to destroy by bombing, finally, the rest of Germany's war making capability. That was the "big picture" as envisioned by our planners.

The Strategic Bombing Concept.

The strategic bombing concept used by heavy bombers in Europe during World War II, the concept of destroying Germany's ability to wage war by bombing strategic targets that would accomplish that purpose, was originally developed during World War I by the great Brigadier General William (Billy) Mitchell. During that war, Mitchell developed the concept of having two distinct types of air forces, with two distinct missions: one air force mission was to give direct support to ground forces, controlled by ground commanders, later termed "Tactical Air Forces;" and another distinct air force, with an independent mission of strategic bombing behind enemy lines, to destroy enemy airpower and enemy's industrial war making capability, later termed "Strategic Air Forces." Mitchell's concept was to wage a total war that not only meant fighting enemy armies on the ground, face to face, but to carry the war to the enemy's homeland to destroy its industrial ability to wage war through bombing specific strategic targets.

Mitchell forcefully carried on a crusade for this concept after World War I. His efforts were met by the vigorous opposition of superior officers who were infantry officers controlling Army policy. The Army Air Service was a small, subordinate branch of the Army. Mitchell also met overwhelming opposition of the United States Navy in War Department debates, and by Navy's strong political lobbying in the United States Congress against his plan. The Navy not only feared that scarce money would be diverted from Navy appropriations to the purpose of building long range bombers, but the Navy also feared that the Army Air Service would take over part of the mission of the Navy, that of finding and intercepting enemy battleships at sea.

Mitchell was eventually court-marshaled and drummed out of the service, but Army Air Service visionaries that followed him continued his crusade. During January 1933, after much effort by visionary pioneers in the Air Service who believed in Mitchell's concepts, the War Department officially stated that the role of Army aviation would include long range reconnaissance operations. This required long range aircraft in addition to the short range aircraft that were designed and dedicated specifically to support the Army ground forces.

During the 1930's, leaders of the Air Service succeeded in having a few long range bombers built. The first "modern" long range bomber, ordered in the 1933-36 time period, was the Martin B-10. It was an all metal two engine monoplane with retractable landing gear and a top speed of more than 200 miles per hour. Its range was 1,370 miles, it could carry a bomb load of 2,200 pounds, and it had a service ceiling of 24,000 feet. It had two Wright R-1820 engines with 775 horsepower each. It could fly as fast as most fighter planes of its time.

The Flying Fortress And Liberator.

The Boeing B-17 long range "Flying Fortress" was designed in 1934 and it made its maiden flight July 28,

1935. By December 7, 1941, only a handful were in service. It had four engines, at a time when practically every other bombing plane of the world was powered by not more than two engines. The B-17 could fly faster, higher, further and carry a greater bomb load than any other plane at the time. It could cruise at 165 MPH, carry a bomb load of 5,000 pounds, had a range of 1,850 miles, and it had a service ceiling of 35,000 feet. It was heavily armed, giving rise to the name "Flying Fortress." By May 1945, 12,726 of them had been built. The average cost of the B-17 was $187,742.

In January, 1939, five years after the B-17 was designed and after much technological progress had been made, the U. S. Army Air Corps asked the Consolidated Aircraft Corporation to produce B-17's as a second source of the B-17 bomber. The company told the Air Corps that it could build a better bomber than the B-17 in as short a time as it would take to become a second source for producing the B-17. The first XB-24 flew on the afternoon of December 29, 1939. The first B-24s went to the British in December 1940. The British named the plane the "Liberator" and the name stuck. It had a tricycle landing gear. The B-24 could carry a larger bomb load than the B-17, it was faster, it had much longer range. It could carry a bomb load of 8,000 pounds, had a range of 3,200 miles, a maximum speed of 303 MPH, a wartime cruising speed more than 200 MPH, and a service ceiling of 28,000 feet. During world War II, our bombing true airspeed at 20,000 feet of altitude was usually between 200 and 220 MPH. The only advantage that the B-17 had over the B-24 was that it had a higher service ceiling. By 1945, 18,481 Liberators were produced and delivered. The average cost of the B-24 was $215,516.

Although the B-17 Flying Fortress received more publicity than the B-24 in the news media and in Hollywood movies, almost 6,000 more of the better performing B-24s were produced. Greater publicity for the Flying Fortress was due in large part to the fact that the B-17 had been in existence for many years before the war, receiving much publicity from its advocates to encourage Congress to buy them, and it was first to fly in combat for the Army Air Corps in Europe. Furthermore, a famous Hollywood movie star, Clark Gable, flew as a crew member in the B-17, providing much more publicity for it. The B-24 which was a better plane, and many more of them were produced, received little publicity compared to that of the B-17.

During the war, the United States and Britain were the only countries that were mass producing long range, four engine heavy bombers. The German Air Force (Luftwaffe) and the Soviet Air Force regarded close air support of ground troops as their primary duty because these air forces were a part of, and subservient to, their armies. Thus, they were under the command and control of army commanders who were ground officers and they had to abide by decisions made by ground commanders who were primarily interested in having air power that provided direct support in the front lines for their ground forces. German and Russian combat bombers were only one and two engine types designed primarily to support ground troops with tactical bombing. They could not carry the heavy bomb loads as far as the American and British four engine bombers, as required for strategic bombing.

The Royal Air Force in Britain was a separate service, equal in status with Britain's Army and Navy. Thus the autonomous RAF had more influence on the type of aircraft that it procured, and it devoted a portion of its austere budget during the depression years to four engine long range strategic bombers.

Reorganization Of The Army Air Corps.

The autonomy and status enjoyed by the RAF in Britain had a great influence on the United States Army Air Corps.

There was a growing demand to reorganize the Army Air Corps. The need to give the Air Corps more autonomy and to reduce the influence of Army ground-warfare commanders on air doctrine, particularly long range bombing doctrine, was becoming generally recognized. This became more obvious after the Battle of Britain in 1940 when it became apparent that air power was to play a much more important role in modern warfare. With Germany controlling mainland Europe, long range bombing of the Axis powers by the Allies was going to become very important.

On June 20, 1941, the Army's air arm was formally elevated to a higher level within the War Department of the United States, from its lowly status as a corps within the Army organization. The Army's new air arm was named the Army Air Force (AAF), headed by a Chief who became an Army Chief of Staff for Air. General Henry H. Arnold who became the new Chief of the AAF headed two new subordinate branches, the Army Air Corps and the Army Air Force Combat Command.

Outbreak of war caused congress to increase the amount of money spent on the military budgets of all services, so that more money became available for long range bombers. Thanks to the vision, persistence, and planning of early Air Corps leaders, some of whom had their careers ruined by their superiors, long range strategic bombers were available when we needed them when war broke out.

British And Americans Agree On A Master Plan, But Disagree On Methods.

British and Americans, who were charged with accomplishing the task of destroying the Luftwaffe on the western front had agreed to a master plan for a bomber offensive at a meeting in Casablanca, Morocco in January, 1943.Russians were not doing long range strategic bombing, although they were destroying many Luftwaffe aircraft during their tactical fighting in support of their army on the eastern front. It was up to the British and Americans to be charged with the strategic mission of destroying the remaining Luftwaffe capability as a first priority.

Britain's Royal Air Force and the United States Army Air Force disagreed on the best bombing procedure to use in achieving the goal of destroying German war-making capability. The RAF wanted to mass bomb general areas at night and the USAAF thought the most efficient procedure was to bomb pin point military targets during daylight, when specific military targets could be seen..

The RAF bombing doctrine was to fly at night and "mass" or "area" bomb cities to destroy industrial areas and workers' homes. The R.A.F. expected its mass bombing of industrial areas to cause a shortage of manpower in German factories and to disrupt communications in industrial areas. It was hoped this would destroy the Nazi war making ability, and eventually destroy German will to fight the war.

The British, from their experience during the Battle of Britain in 1940, believed that daylight bombing could not be accomplished without prohibitive losses of their bombers. British fighter planes (Spitfires and Hurricanes) were able to shoot down so many German bombers during the Battle of Britain when Luftwaffe bombers attempted to attack England during daylight hours, that Germans had to discontinue daylight raids because their losses of aircraft were too great. The Luftwaffe learned that it could only bomb safely at night when defending British fighter pilots and ground based antiaircraft gunners could not see them to shoot them down.

The problem that switching from daylight to nighttime bombing created for German bomber crews during the Battle of Britain in 1940, was that bombardiers could not see specific military targets from the air during darkness of nighttime. All lights on the ground were blacked out by the British. This fact prevented Luftwaffe aircraft from finding military targets visually, then bombing them.This was a much more efficient use of the scarce bomber resources to destroy enemy war making capability. The only alternative for the Luftwaffe was to "mass" bomb general areas at night because only general areas could usually be located with reasonable accuracy at night. Airborne radar had not been perfected at the time for use as navigation and bombing devices, and to enable bombers to "see" through cloud cover and darkness. Air to ground radar bombsights were developed later.

The British also believed that there was another problem with American plans to bomb during the day. In addition to the problem of prohibitive losses expected from enemy fighter attacks during daylight hours, the British asserted that the prevailing weather conditions in Europe would prevent bombardiers from seeing the ground much of the time. Weather commonly formed protective cloud cover over European targets, especially during winter months, so they couldn't be seen much of the time. The RAF believed that this would prevent the USAAF from bombing German targets a large share of the time, making attempts to bomb in daylight inefficient. Another British skepticism was belief that Americans could not bomb precisely in daylight while they were being harassed by heavy enemy fighter attacks and by massive numbers of German antiaircraft guns firing at them from the ground. The British view was that the American plan would not work.

The USAAF Master Bombing Plan.

The American plan (Air War Plans Division, Air Staff, 1942, originally developed in September, 1941, before the Japanese bombed Pearl Harbor, but still valid in 1943) was to use the secret Norden or Sperry bomb sights for precision bombing of specific, pin point targets from high altitude during daylight hours when targets on the ground could be seen. The USAAF believed that this would be a more efficient use of bombs dropped and that it would achieve the objective of more quickly and efficiently destroying Germany's ability to make war. The original USAAF plan identified 177 specific targets that would destroy the war making ability of Germany if these targets were destroyed by bombing. The selected targets were listed in seven categories:

1. German aircraft plants
2. Submarine yards (not reachable from Italy)
3. Transportation
4. Electric power
5. Oil
6. Aluminum
7. Rubber

Americans did not believe the British plan for mass bombing of industrial cities was a very efficient way of getting the job done because area bombing of London by the Germans during the 1940 Battle of Britain and afterward did not succeed in destroying the will of the British to fight, nor did it cause a shortage of British manpower. British production had actually increased after many German mass bombings of British cities.

American leaders (USAAF) put their faith in firepower and armor that was carried aboard the heavy bombers, and in the quality of their air crews. The long range, four engine Boeing B-17 "Flying Fortress," and later the faster and longer ranged B-24 "Liberator," had each been designed with ten 50 caliber Browning machine guns to defend the bombers against fighter attack. USAAF bombers also had protective armor and self sealing fuel tanks. For planning purposes, each bomber group was originally projected to fly a tight formation of 36 bombers on each of its missions. With 360 guns in each group firing on attacking fighters, it was originally believed that this would be adequate to defend the bombing formations over Germany from fighter attack.

Bomber formations were expected to be self sufficient for their own defense, and it would allow precision daylight bombing, using the new, secret, accurate Norden or Sperry bombsights. Large numbers of bomber groups attacking Germany at the same time in different areas were expected to disperse Luftwaffe defensive fighter capability so that enemy fighters would be thinly distributed over the bomber formations. This was the general USAAF plan.

USAAF planners believed it was not realistic to compare Luftwaffe bomber losses over England during the Battle of Britain with those expected for the more heavily armed B-17's and B-24's over Germany. During the Battle of Britain, Germany only had light, short range two-engine bombers that did not have the heavy armament, range, and defensive fire power that American four-engine Flying Fortresses and Liberators had specifically designed into them. German bombers were originally designed for direct tactical support of German ground forces, because German ground warfare commanders, and Hitler, were making the important decisions. Luftwaffe's front line bombers were not designed as long range, heavily armed strategic bombers. Luftwaffe bombers did not have the range nor could they carry the large bomb load that USAAF flying fortresses could carry, nor did they have the defensive armament.

Originally, USAAF planners knew that our bombers had to fly unescorted into Germany because there were no long range fighters in existence at that time. Although weather would prevent visual bombing many days, as the RAF had insisted, the USAAF expected that the efficiency of precision bombing, when possible in good weather, would still make it the best and most efficient method of bombing. USAAF bombing was planned to be from high altitude, much higher than the German bombing altitude, to make ground based antiaircraft guns less accurate. The high altitude was expected to reduce the amount of flying time that enemy fighter planes would have left to spend attacking the bombers, after the fighters burned the fuel necessary to climb to the bombers' high altitude and intercept our bombers. German fighters could only carry enough fuel for less than two hours of flying time.

Regardless of their disagreement about bombing methods, the RAF and USAAF did agree at the Casablanca meeting of January 1943 that RAF planes would bomb at night and USAAF planes would bomb during the day, each using its own bombing doctrine. This was planned to provide around the clock bombing of German targets, and it would continually harass the German population and defenses, and interrupt work at industrial centers.

By the time the 456th arrived in Italy, one year later in January 1944, neither the British nor the American doctrine had been proven successful because neither had been fully tested.There hadn't been enough planes to fully test either bombing doctrine. The Luftwaffe was stronger than ever before, and it was rapidly growing larger every day. Each of the doctrines were vulnerable to legitimate questions.

(As it turned out, by 1945 the two bombing doctrines had become almost the same. Technological advances made during the war years, later, enabled both doctrines, the RAF and the USAAF, to become very much the same. Development of precision radar bomb sights enabled more precise bombing at night by the RAF. It also enabled the USAAF to bomb through clouds during daylight hours. In addition, Americans developed long range fighter escort for its bombers, which by the spring of 1944 gave the USAAF unqualified air superiority over enemy targets. Another development that drew the two doctrines closer together near the end of the war, Americans finally agreed to mass bomb Berlin and a few other targets in eastern Germany, under pressure from its allies, to confuse German transportation and communications on the eastern front in support of invading Russian armies.)

Fifteenth Air Force Formed.

The Fifteenth Air Force was formed in Italy on December 1, 1943 to divide the Luftwaffe fighter defense capability between three fronts: Western Europe, Italy, and Russia. This division of heavy bomber forces spread Luftwaffe forces thinner on each front, compared with what it would have been with only two fronts. Another reason that the Fifteenth was formed was to enable heavy bombers to reach many strategic targets that could not be reached from bases in Britain, but were reachable from Italy. In addition, many new airfields were needed just to accommodate the massive numbers of heavy bombers and crews that were ready to come to Europe from the United States. England was becoming saturated with heavy bombers and fighters, and some said that England was like a large airbase. Then too, flying weather in Italy was expected to be much better than in Britain and it would allow more missions to be flown.

The 456th Arrives In Italy During A Desperate Strategic Situation.

When the 456th Bombardment Group arrived in Italy, the strategic situation was becoming desperate, particularly in the minds of top planners who knew the time table, because the German Luftwaffe had more planes then than it ever had up to that time. We had no fighters with long enough range to escort our long range bombers into many of our most heavily defended priority targets in Europe. It was highly questionable, in the minds of our top leaders, whether or not the Luftwaffe could be destroyed by June 1944 in time for project Overlord to proceed. The Eighth Air Force had been flying missions from Britain against Germany, and it had experienced severe losses whenever it penetrated the German homeland. On August 17, 1943 the Eighth Air Force lost an unsustainable 60 planes and 600 airmen when it raided targets at Regensburg and Schweinfurt. Sixty more planes and 600 more airmen were lost on a second attack against Schweinfurt on October 14, 1943. This was a shock to the USAAF doctrine that heavy bombers could protect themselves and bomb visually and precisely in daylight.

Top planners realized that we would have severe losses of bombers if long range fighter escort was not available over heavily defended German, Austrian, Hungarian, Rumanian, and Czechoslovakian targets that were heavily defended by hundreds of Luftwaffe fighters and hundreds of 88 mm and 105 mm antiaircraft guns at each target. Despite bombings by British at night and heavy losses suffered by the USAAF in daylight raids up to the time of arrival of the 456th in Italy, German fighter production and Luftwaffe fighter strength was rapidly increasing.

It was learned after the war that this increased production of fighters was made possible by the fact that the German Third Reich had not fully mobilized its industry and manpower, and thus, it had much excess capacity in its production facilities to more than compensate for heavy losses suffered from RAF and USAAF bombing of aircraft industries. For example, even the production genius of the Third Reich, Albert Speer, Hitler's Minister for Armaments, who was credited with stepping up war production of factories during 1943 and 1944, rarely put factories on a double shift basis. Women were never fully mobilized as a manpower resource, as they were in Britain and the United States. Critical factories in the United States were operating on a three shift basis, around the clock, using men and women. These options were available to Germans but they were not utilized.

Thus, when the allies began bombing the existing German aircraft factories, the Nazis had enough unused capacity to disperse fighter production to other factories to protect it from bombing. Germany was actually able to increase its production of fighters after the Allies began bombing its aircraft factories. Much German production was accomplished in a "cottage industry" style, where numerous aircraft components were produced at dispersed locations and brought together and assembled at many locations.

Arrival of our Fifteenth Air Force bombers in Italy was planned to stop the rapid increase in production of German aircraft. Top of the list of our targets were aircraft, engine, and ball bearing production facilities. Fighter production actually increased.

It was learned after the war from Albert Speer's reports that our bombing of other targets, in particular the synthetic oil production and other oil producing facilities, and railway transportation necessary to transport needed war materials to fighting forces, did the most damage to German Luftwaffe's war making capability. In addition, the large numbers of irreplaceable Luftwaffe fighter pilots lost in the fierce air battles of early 1944 over enemy targets, in addition to planes and pilots lost on the Russian front, resulted in our most severe damage to German war capability. The introduction of large numbers of USAAF long range escort fighter planes by spring of 1944 helped to give us air superiority over many targets, and it helped to shoot down many more scarce Luftwaffe pilots.

Germany Produces Many Fighters, But It Has No Pilots, Fuel, Or Parts To Fly Them.

Although the number of German fighter planes being produced by the dispersed German aircraft industry continually increased during the war, as postwar studies have shown, our bombing of oil and rail targets, and Germany's loss of so many irreplaceable Luftwaffe pilots in the fierce air battles, was responsible for the Allies gaining air superiority over Europe in time for "Overlord." Our bombing resulted in severe shortages of fuel to fly the increased number of fighters that Germany was able to produce. Our bombing also created a shortage of ammunition and spare parts with which to service the fighters, and the fierce air battles over Nazi targets caused a critical shortage of trained fighter pilots to fly the fighters. In addition, there were many other strategic shortages that our bombings created.

Arrival of long range fighter escort for our bombers was a very welcome development to us bomber pilots. Until that time, our long range strategic missions flown deep into the heart of Europe allowed the Luftwaffe fighters to take a heavy toll on our bombers and crews. We learned that bombers needed escort fighters to protect them from swarms of Luftwaffe fighters that were aggressively defending their homeland. In the 456th Bomb Group, aircrews did not know about it, but a huge, secret, priority program was underway in the United States to extend the range of our fighter escort aircraft. Because our aircrews didn't know about the fact that escort fighter protection was coming, we had a dismal outlook for completing fifty missions. We gritted our teeth, expected the worst, and continued to do our jobs the best we could.

The 456th Bomb Group Arrives In Italy While The Luftwaffe Dominates The Skies Over Central Europe.

Also unknown to most of us in the 456th Bomb Group when we arrived in Italy and began flying missions in February 1944, was the June 1944 date for the invasion of France from England. It must have appeared to our supreme headquarters, which was planning for the invasion, that it was a low probability bet we would gain air superiority in Europe in time to allow the Overlord invasion. The Luftwaffe still dominated the skies!

Unknown to most of us, the USAAF began a crash program to add longer range to our fighters after the Eight Air Force's punishing Schweinfurt and Regensburg raids. Bombing missions into Gemany's heartland was stopped until our 456th Bomb Group and many other bomb groups had arrived in the Fifteenth and Eighth Air Forces by February 1944. It was realized that long range escort fighters were needed to escort our bombers, but until sufficient long range fighter escort became available, it was also believed that the massive numbers of heavy bombers attacking targets in coordinated bombings at the same time would disperse the defending Luftwaffe fighters so much that it would make our bomber losses sustainable. Bombings of strategic targets in Germany, Austria, and Hungary resumed in February 1944, before we had the necessary long range fighter escort.

The program to develop long range fighter escort began to pay off in early spring of 1944. First came the addition of drop tanks to P-38 and P-47 fighters, which added fuel they could carry, then in mid-April arrival commenced of large numbers of longer range P-51 aircraft, the best mass produced fighters of the European war. The new P-51 had an endurance of more than seven hours, whereas the Luftwaffe's defending Me-109 had less than two hours endurance. The P-51 could fly faster, higher, and longer than Luftwaffe fighters. This gave the P-51 a tremendous advantage. The P-38G was another modification to the P-38 that increased its internal fuel capacity by one-third, in addition to the fuel added by using drop tanks. Thus, starting in mid-April we began to get P-51s and P-38s with sufficient range to escort us to most of our strategic targets. In April 1944 the USAAF gradually began to gain air superiority over enemy targets in Europe.

Allied air forces were able to gain air superiority over Europe by the Spring of 1944, in time for Overlord, in spite of the increased German fighter production. German fighter production continued to increase during this entire period, but the Luftwaffe couldn't get the gasoline or pilots to fly them because of our strategic bombing and our fierce air battles over enemy targets. After air superiority over Europe was gained, the invasion of France from England was made possible and USAAF's heavy bombers then began to concentrate on destruction of the remaining German war-making capability. On June 6, 1944, during the enormous invasion of France, the Luftwaffe was so weak that it could only launch two fighter aircraft to oppose the thousands of our Allied aircraft and the thousands of naval vessels involved in the invasion.

The Disaster At Bari Harbor Where 456th Group's Supplies Lost.

There was one disaster that happened in December 1943, shortly before the 456th arrived in Italy, that had an enormous impact on the creature comforts of all the 456th Bomb Group's personnel and on the Group's air operations during the early days operations. Most of our base support supplies and equipment were sunk to the bottom of Bari harbor, located 70 miles southeast of our airbase on December 2, 1943. Unknown to most of us at the time, except as vague rumors because it was kept as top secret information by our government until recent years, the United States' second greatest shipping disaster of World War II - second only to the Japanese bombing of Pearl Harbor on December 7, 1941 was the German bombing of thirty ships crowding Bari Harbor on that night. This calamity occurred shortly after the new Fifteenth Air Force Headquarters staff had moved into Bari, Italy from Africa. It was one of the best kept secrets of World War II, and the "Top Secret" classification was only removed long after the war.

Vital supplies were lost in the Bari Harbor bombing. In addition to our creature comfort base supplies, were 100 octane gasoline, bombs, ammunition, food, clothing, trucks, tractor-trailor units lost. Many of the losses were vital supplies and equipment destined for support of allied ground forces of the U.S. Fifth Army and the British Eighth Army that were operating in Italy. In addition to the vast amount of supplies and equipment that were lost to the bottom of the Bari Harbor, the sunken ships and the bomb damage to the harbor facilities closed the harbor so that other incoming ships could not unload precious supplies for a long time afterward.

The disaster occurred one day after General J. H. "Jimmy" Doolittle arrived in Bari, Italy on December 1, 1943. The famous hero of the Tokyo Raid and then commander of the Fifteenth Air Force, had moved his headquarters from Tunis, Africa into a building recently occupied by the Italian Air Force in Bari (over objections of the Italians). The location of Bari was 70 miles southeast of where the Fifteenth Air Force heavy bomber airfields, including the 456th's airfield at Stornara, were being constructed around Foggia. General Doolittle was working late in his new office when the bombing of Bari harbor took place, and the bombing shattered windows of his office.

The Bari Harbor bombing results were devastating to the Allied war operations for the next few weeks. It had a profound impact not only on the standard of living and air operations of the 456th Bomb Group, but it undoubtedly slowed operations of ground forces in Italy. It severely hindered the air operations of the Fifteenth Air Force, delaying the top priority strategic bombing program of Europe targets. The Eighth Air Force, bombing from England, had to operate without assistance from the Fifteenth

Air Force for a longer period than had been planned before the disastrous bombing.

The Fifteenth, bombing from Italy was planned to require the Luftwaffe to divide the number of its available defensive fighters between raids from England and from Italy. Until the Fifteenth began its operations, the Luftwaffe could focus all of its available aircraft against the Eighth Air Force, and it was having a devastating effect. Top planners feared that the time schedule for project Overlord, planned for June 1944, may have to be postponed because of the huge losses being experienced by the Eighth and because of the delay at getting Fifteenth Air Force bombers and fighters operating in Italy.

Bari Harbor was under the control of a British port director because it was in the eastern part of Italy where the British Eight Army was operating. The British port director thought that Bari Harbor was so safe from any German air raid that he allowed lights to be turned on around the harbor to facilitate the difficult task of quickly unloading the thirty heavily loaded merchant ships that were crowded in the harbor.

Because twin engine C-47 aircraft were regularly flying around the port, in and out of a nearby airfield, and they looked much like some types of Luftwaffe bombers, he gave orders that none of the antiaircraft gunners on the merchant ships, or guns on shore, were to fire at aircraft unless he specifically gave the order to do so. He was afraid of having gunners shoot down one of the allied planes, and he expected no raid from the weakened Luftwaffe in Italy. But the Germans were more resourceful than he expected.

The day before the disaster, and again on the day of the attack, a fast German reconnaissance plane flew over Bari Harbor. The Luftwaffe pilot, Oberleutnant Werner Hahn, flying his lone Messerschmitt 210 reconnaissance plane at 370 MPH (very fast for that period) saw the harbor jammed with 30 merchant vessels. He reported back to his base in northern Italy that Bari Harbor was so jammed with fully loaded merchant ships, there was hardly room for another ship in the harbor.

That evening, the Luftwaffe commanders in northern Italy assembled 105 Junkers 88 bomber aircraft from bases in northern Italy, Greece, and Yugoslavia. A formation of these bombers, led by Oberleutnant Gustaf Teuber, entered Bari Harbor at an altitude of 45 meters and an airspeed of 200 MPH at 7:30 PM, flying low enough to remain under the allied radar screen, undetected.

They also dropped chaff, that many called "window," which were strips of tinfoil invented by the British in 1942 to muddle radar returns. Chaff was much like the tinsel that many put on Christmas trees as decoration. Our USAAF bombers in Europe successfully used it later. The German planes also dropped parachute flares to light up the harbor brilliantly, so they could clearly see their targets. Antiaircraft gunners on the ships and around the harbor had strict orders not to fire their guns, so the Luftwaffe bombers were unopposed. Luftwaffe pilots later reported that the bomb runs were very easy. They reported leaving the harbor with a colorful sight of burning ships, exploding and sinking ones.

The catastrophic result of the bombing was that 17 of the 30 ships in the harbor were sunk. The sunk and disabled ships closed the harbor for a long time, preventing urgently needed supplies from reaching allied ground forces and the newly developing Fifteenth Air Force bomber bases.

What made the bombing even more devastating, and very enigmatic, was that one of the ships, the SS John Harvey, was loaded with 100,000 tons of mustard gas in 100 pound bombs. The Harvey was not hit in the bombing, but explosions of nearby ships blew it up. The explosion released mustard gas, causing deaths of many seamen who were still on ships as well as many people on shore who were unlucky enough to be in the path of winds carrying the deadly gas. Because it was Top Secret information, that the ship was carrying a cargo of mustard gas, few officials had the need to know about it. Thus, when it was discovered that mustard gas had been released during the bombing, everyone except a very few who were in on the top secret information, believed that the Luftwaffe had used the gas during its bombing. Many Italians, as well as many high ranking allied officials, believed that Germans had used the gas. When we later arrived in Italy, we were instructed to keep our burdensome gas masks nearby at all times for many months afterward because we expected Germans to use gas, because many still believed that Germans had used the gas in Bari Harbor.

Allies were stockpiling the mustard gas to use in the event that Germans started using it again. Germans had first used the gas during World War I when they were desperate and losing the war. Although it was against the Geneva Convention to use mustard gas in World War II, the bombs were being stockpiled for possible use in retaliation, in the event that Germans began to use the deadly gas again. It is understandable why the information would be kept secret long after the war ended.

One thousand men were killed or missing in the bombing, and more than 800 casualties were hospitalized. Of the hospitalized, 628 suffered mustard gas injury.

An excellent book has been written about the Bari Harbor bombing: *Disaster At Bari*, by Glenn B. Infield, the Macmillan Company, New York, NY (1971). It provides many more details and heroic deeds that were performed by military personnel as a result of the bombing. The USAF Historical Research Agency at Maxwell Air Force Base, Montgomery, Alabama also has considerable information on the disaster.

The bombing had a serious effect on Allied operations in both, the Mediterranean and the European theaters. The loss of supplies practically stopped the rapid advance of allied ground forces up the Italian peninsula during the winter of 1943-44. From the initial invasion of the peninsula at Salerno on September 9, 1943 to November of that year, the British Eighth Army had rapidly progressed to the Sangro River, about 85 miles north of Stornara where the 456th airfield was being constructed. The U.S. Fifth Army had crossed the Volturno River and had reached the Liri Valley which led to Rome. But this rapid progress of the ground forces came to a halt, due in no small extent to the Bari disaster which caused a shortage of supplies. This slow down gave the German ground forces time to regroup and form their defenses along what became known as the Kesselring Gustav Line. The line ran east from the southern part of the Liri Valley, near Cassino the hinge, to the area where the British Eighth Army had progressed near the Sangro River.

The Desperate Situation In The Ground War As The 456th Starts Flying Missions.

Parts of the front lines, and German ground forces, were less than 85 miles to the northwest of our airbase when the 456th began to move on to its new airfield in January, 1944. When conditions were right, we could hear distant sounds of shelling coming from fighting at the front lines.

Just as the 456th was getting ready to fly its first mission in February 1994 a desperate situation developed in the ground war in Italy. The U.S. Fifth Army landed two divisions on a beachhead behind German lines at Anzio in Italy on January 22, 1944, just as the 456th was coming to Stornara, Italy. Anzio came close to being a huge disaster when German counterattacks almost succeeded in wiping out the beachhead. The Anzio beachhead was behind the German Gustav line that ran through Monte Cassino. The

456th and other Fifteenth Air Force bomber groups had to be temporarily diverted from their priority strategic targets in the European hinterland to drop bombs on German ground forces at Anzio and at Cassino.

Later, another important distraction of Fifteenth bombers from bombing its priority strategic targets came when the Russian ground forces advanced into Hungary and Rumania. High level decisions again required the Fifteenth Air Force's heavy bombers to bomb in direct support of ground troops in these areas. It gave tactical ground support targets temporary priority over its strategic targets.

This was the background and the general situation confronting the 456th Bombardment Group (Heavy) as it began operations in Italy and it explains the reason why it was there.

Chapter 3
COMPOSITE DIARIES
OF THE GROUP'S FIRST
COMBAT OPERATIONS
(From February 1, 1944 to May 9, 1944)

Although nervous, we were all anxious to start earning our pay and eager to find out what combat flying was going to be like. We wanted to learn how well we could do the job we were trained to do. In hindsight, with twenty five more years of experience in the Air Force, I realize now how poorly prepared we were for combat. The USAF today wouldn't send such poorly prepared crews into battle, but at that time nobody, not even our top military planners, had sufficient training or experience for such new type of warfare. It was a critical wartime emergency and there wasn't enough time to do anything else.

Tent City Life, Part Of Lt. J.J. Walker's Crew

No one knew exactly what to expect. There were many unplanned surprises, and everyone had to remain flexible, improvise and adjust to constantly changing, unexpected conditions while we gained experience the hard way. How well we were able to get the job done in view of all of the obstacles is a tribute to the character, competence, ingenuity, and hard work of the people involved.

February 1, 1944   Liberators Arrive At Stornara, Italy.

The group's new B-24H planes with their olive green paint began arriving at our airfield, and ground crews eagerly swarmed over soon as possible. In celebration of their arrival, steak for dinner!

Our base at Stornara was precariously close to the front lines of the ground war in Italy, only seventy miles at one point, and it was highly possible that we would have to evacuate the airplanes on short notice if German ground forces were to break through the Allied defenses. First orientation and training flights from our new field began the next day.

With the new tent policy of our headquarters, which ordered that aircrews were to occupy the larger pyramidal tents, I was told to move out of my temporary, small, damp, one-man pup tent into one of the larger tents. I was assigned an army cot, no mattress, in a tent that had a dirt floor, no lights, and no heat. It was already occupied by the very young, congenial, competent officers of 1st Lt. Dave E. Tavel's crew. (Dave, an optometrist in civilian life before the war, later moved up to the Group Headquarters Operations staff, and was eventually promoted to the grade of Lieutenant Colonel). Our tent included, in addition to Tavel, his bombardier, Lt. Nicholas J. Colletti; his copilot, Raymond J. Lorenz; and navigator, 1st. Lt. Anthony P. Thalmann. (Colletti was later confirmed killed while flying with another pilot on a mission to bomb the synthetic oil refinery at Blechhammer, Germany. Thalmann had to bail out over Yugoslavia because engines of his plane stopped running. He was able to evade capture by the Germans with assistance of Chetnicks in Yugoslavia and he returned to duty. Lorenz was unable to complete his missions for medical reasons, and Tavel completed all of his missions.)

It was too cold to take our clothes off in the tent until later when we were able to rig an improvised heating stove that burned dangerous, aromatic 100 octane gasoline. The same gas we had for flying our planes. I heard that our people learned how to construct the gasoline-burning stoves while they were being quartered with the 301st Bomb Group. The stove was made out of scrounged, makeshift parts that we obtained wherever we could ind them. The stove included an elevated 55 gallon tank outside the tent to store the gasoline, surplus quarer-inch tubing to bring controlled amounts of the gas into a sawed-off steel drum located on the center of our tent floor that acted as the stove where the gas was burned. The system included petcock valves to control the flow of gas from the tank outside to the sawed-off drum in the tent where the gasoline was burned, and black stovepipe to drain off fumes that were the products of combustion through a flap in the top of the tent. All parts of the stove were foraged from material found around our airfield, except the black three-inch stovepipe which we had to buy on the market in town. Stovepipe was difficult to find because everyone wanted the same thing, and the local market supply was quickly exhausted by all USAAF personnel looking for the same thing. There was no such pipe in the Army supply.

Until we gained experience with the heating system, we had some exciting experiences. The stove and pipe would become cherry red from excessive heat, and this threatened to burn our tent at its top where the stovepipe went out through a flap in the top of the tent. Some tents on our airfield actually burned down. We were always worried about explosions caused by vapors or leaks of 100 octane gasoline. Initially, explosions commonly occurred throughout our tent cities until we finally modified the stove by putting extra shutoff control valves in the line and it worked very well. Later we were able to burn 83 octane gasoline when it became available to reduce the hazard that 100 octane gas posed.

February 2 - 8, 1944   High Altitude Training Flights

Predominant conditions were rain, high winds, and mud. These conditions continued intermittently for the rest of February. Weather had to be good enough in the local area for us to takeoff and form our bomber formations, navigate to the target in visual conditions above or between clouds, and then be able to bomb the target visually. Airborne radar bombing equipment, that enabled bombing targets that were hidden by clouds, called "Pathfinder," did not become available to us until April. Orientation and training flights around our airfield, between rain clouds, were all that could be flown much of the time.

Weather was very cold and gasoline stoves that people had improvised continued to blow up nightly, burning some tents and occasionally causing minor burns to people.

I hadn't flown since November 15, 1943 in the States, when I received orders assigning me, and my three comrades, to the 456th Bomb Group. A Second Lieutenant's pay at that time was $150 per month plus $75 a month flying pay, for hazardous duty. However, if you didn't fly for a period of more than three months, you lost flying pay. I was about to lose some flying pay. Thank goodness, I was allowed to get some orientation flying on February 4, 6, and again on the 16th of February during Group practice flying sessions. Colonel Steed was well aware of the fact that none of us had ever taken a B-24 off the ground as heavily loaded as we would have to takeoff for our combat missions, and he knew that our Group had very little high altitude formation flying practice at the altitudes we would have to be flying.

The one practice high altitude formation flight in which I was able to fly revealed how unready and disorganized the group was. The group was awful at high altitude formation flying. Colonel Steed had acknowledged that problem to USAF inspectors back in the States when he was ordered to take his group overseas. The exigencies of war would not allow him more time to train his group, so the Colonel had to leave the States hoping to get many more high altitude formation training flights before his group was ordered on its first combat mission. Whenever the weather was good enough in the local area around Stornara, more training flights were conducted.

February 6, 1944   First Liberator Lost In Italy.

The first of my comrades, who had been with me for a year and a half, was killed on one of the orientation training flights discussed above. Second Lieutenant Douglas S. Morgan was flying as copilot on 2nd Lt. Willis D. Johnston's crew when their airplane crashed into a mountain in southern Italy while flying in clouds. All ten personnel aboard were killed. Some of us speculated that the crew read mountain altitudes from their map thinking they were shown in terms of "feet," as our maps in the States had always shown them, instead of "meters" as the maps we were using in Italy had them marked. If that were the situation, they would be flying too low to clear the mountains while flying blind in clouds.

February 10, 1944   First Mission Attempt: Grottaferrata, Italy.

The group's first combat mission was finally attempted. Rain and bad weather prevented our Group from flying its first combat mission until then. I didn't fly on this first mission because I still hadn't been assigned to a combat crew.

The night before the Group's first mission, the Group's Commander, Colonel Steed, visited each of his four squadrons one at a time to announce to an assembly of personnel that the first combat mission was to be flown the next day. He gave the men a spirited pep talk of encouragement. It was our first contact with our new group's commanding officer and I was very impressed. If Hollywood were casting the part for a movie, it could not have chosen a more handsome, charismatic leader to play the part. He was a personable, capable southerner, a West Point graduate, class of 1927. Somewhere along the line, one of his gung ho staff members called his crews "Colonel Steed's Flying Colts" and the name stuck. As sophomoric as it may sound to many in today's environment, most of us whose average age was in the early twentys and caught up in the patriotic fervor of wartime circumstances, were proud of the name.

The Group's first target on February 10 was to be German Army Headquarters at Grottaferrata, Italy. However the target could not be seen by bombardiers due to bad weather, as the formation flew over the target, and bombs could not be dropped on this mission. The Group encountered no enemy opposition during its flight. No flak nor enemy fighters were seen.

That target, rather than one of our high priority strategic targets in the underbelly of southern Europe, was selected because of the desperate situation that had developed in the ground war in Italy. Germans were massing for an attack against U.S. Army ground forces that had established a precarious amphibious beachhead landing at Anzio, just south of Rome, behind enemy lines. We had to help them out by bombing the German troops they faced.

February 12, 13, and 14, 1944   Training Flights.

The dismal attempt at formation flying that was demonstrated on the Group's first mission, on February 10, convinced almost everyone that more high altitude practice flights were needed. As discussed earlier, up to the time the Group arrived in Italy, pilots had never flown such heavy planes, nor had they flown them in group formation at such high altitude. These days were spent trying to improve the Group's high altitude formation flying ability. Three practice missions were flown, concentrating on high altitude formation flying above 19,000 feet. (Another one was flown again on the fourth day, February 15, as noted below.)

February 14, 1944   Number One Mission: Destroy The Luftwaffe.

Word came down from Maj. Gen. Nathan F. Twinning (who took over command of the 15th Air Force from Maj. Gen. James H. Doolittle on January 3, 1944) that the number one mission of the Fifteenth Air Force was destruction of the German Air Force (Luftwaffe) in the air, on the ground, and in aircraft factories before the planes could fly. He said that the war was now a personal battle between the USAF and the Luftwaffe. We had heard rumors of Luftwaffe pilots shooting at our men as they floated down in parachutes after bailing out of their airplanes.

Of course, Gen. Twinning did not mention the top secret invasion of Europe from England, Project Overlord, that was scheduled for May or early June 1944. None of us knew of the tight time schedule, which was less than four months away, for defeating the Luftwaffe so that the invasion could take place.

To top level USAAF planners, the situation must have been getting very serious. American planners had decided years ago to go with daylight bombing in the face of advice against it from the British. Daylight bombing had not yet been proven viable. Some members of congressional oversight committees were becoming highly critical of the USAAF and they were putting pressure on American top planners to reevaluate their strategy, and to keep its losses of bombers to a minimum. The basic decision by top military planners, which was to give highest priority for scarce national resources to winning the war in Europe before giving priority to winning the war against Japan in the Pacific Ocean, was also being put under strong pressure and constantly questioned by advocates of the Pacific war. The U.S. Navy, which had command of the war against Japan in the Central Pacific Ocean, had strong political allies in Congress. President Franklin D. Roosevelt was a former Assistant Secretary of the Navy and he naturally had a strong disposition to listen to Navy advocates.

Thus far, bombing raids into Germany from England were being hindered by bad winter weather over Europe that prevented visual bombing, just as the British had warned the Americans months before. As the British had warned, the Eight Air Force was suffering prohibitive loses from enemy fighters whenever weather cleared enough to allow visual bombing of German targets. The only two times that the USAAF had attempted to bomb deep into the heart of Germany, in August and November of 1943, when it bombed Regensburg and Scweinfurt, resulted in disasters for the USAAF because 60 heavy bombers and 600 airmen were lost on each raid. This was additional ammunition for critics of the USAAF doctrine, against the present plan for conducting daylight bombing in Europe. The daylight bombing concept was still on trial!

In the Fifteenth Air Force, so far, winter weather permitted only occasional raids from Italy into Germany and Austria. Only a meager nine bombing missions above the Alps to primary strategic targets were accomplished by 15th's bombers during the three months of its organization, from December 1, 1943 to the end of February 1944. Only one strategic bombing mission to Germany, seven to Austria, and one to Hungary, were all that could be accomplished in three months of operations. Thus, top planners must have been agonizing over the fact that there were less than four months remaining before the scheduled date for Overlord. It was generally recognized by Russian, British, and American top level planners that destroying the Luftwaffe and gaining complete control of the air over Europe was a necessary prelude to the invasion of Europe from England. Without control of the air, no invasion could be attempted. The Luftwaffe was stronger than it had ever been before, and it was growing stronger every day.

We learned after the war, from the United States Strategic Bombing Survey, that German fighter production increased from 2445 fighters per month in January 1944 to about 4,000 per month by September 1944. Destruction of the Luftwaffe within the next four months appeared to be a very long-shot bet, if not an impossible one, to those who knew about the Top Secret Overlord schedule. German fighters still ruled the skies over Germany, Austria, Czechoslovakia, Hungary, and Rumania. Our heavy bombers still had no fighters with enough range to escort them on long missions. This was necessary to protect us from massive enemy fighter attack, as had happened at Regensberg and Schweinfurt.

Missions to our primary strategic targets required us to fly from 700 to 850 miles distance from our bases in Italy. Our fighters at that time could only fly with us for 300 miles, flying back and forth over our slower bomber formations. This was far short of what we needed. Later, a procedure was worked out to keep fighters on the ground until long after the bombers took off, then our fighters would takeoff and fly directly to the target to give us "target cover." Many times this timing didn't work out very well. Germans knew the limitations of our fighter escort, tracked them on radar, and they took maximum advantage of our fighter shortcomings. Later, two 750 gallon drop tanks were added to our fighters flying escort, extending their flying range, but this modification was many weeks away.

Thus, we in the 456th Bomb Group as well as other bomber groups in Europe, suffered heavy Luftwaffe opposition until we began to get reliable long range fighter escort to help protect us. It wasn't until April 21st that a few long range P-51B and C Mustang fighters began to become operational enough to help us out, giving us some relief. The range of the P-38 was also increased by one-third due to modifications made by then.

Thus, when General Twinning said on February 14th that the war was now a personal battle between the USAF and the Luftwaffe, that meant, for the time being, it was primarily a war between USAAF heavy bombers and the Luftwaffe fighters in the air and German antiaircraft gunners on the ground.

Luftwaffe fighters took a heavy toll of bombers on many unescorted missions. However, our bombers' gunners took a heavy toll of enemy planes and their pilots, killing or maiming many of their most experienced pilots. Still, it was highly questionable whether or not the USAF or the Luftwaffe would emerge as winners of their war against one another, let alone reach a decision in four months.

It was a dismal outlook for bomber crews because we didn't know about the Top Secret crash programs that were in progress to bring us aid. There were many modifications to fighters in progress that would extend the range of our fighter escort by spring, and many more heavy bombers were in the pipeline coming to increase the number of bombers that would face the Luftwaffe, to help us out.

February 15, 1944   High Altitude Formation Training.

Another Group high altitude formation practice mission was flown at 20,000 feet. Considerable improvement has been made.

February 16, 1944   Assigned To Lt. Kenneth L. Boughner's Crew.

I was finally assigned to a crew so that I could start flying combat missions. I was to fly as copilot on Lt. Kenneth L. Boughner's crew because his regular copilot, Lt. John P. Eliopoulis, was transferred out of the group to fly fighters. We later heard a rumor that John had been killed while flying a fighter during a practice flight.

Boughner had a very competent crew consisting of the following members, in addition to myself: 2nd Lt. Clifford E. Bowdish, Jr., bombardier; 2nd. Lt. James C. Wellons, navigator; Sgt. Bernard P. Ketelhut, engineer; William G. Attencio, Jr., radio operator; Sgt. Everett S. Hayes, tail turet gunner; and Sgts Saul R. Holtzan, Duward M. Gardner, Leonard A. Dodge, gunners. Gardner is currently a member of the 456th Bomb Group association. The crew picture on the back cover shows 2nd Lt. Robert M. Abrams standing next to me, second from the left, instead of Bowdish.

Lt. Boughner's crew. Lt. Boughner standing far right, Lt. Capps next to him. Photo courtesy of Sgt. Richard C. Hood of the 746th Squadron Intelligence.

Lt. Ken Boughner's Crew, Copilot Lt. Capps

I was only 20 years old at the time and Hayes our tail gunner was 39 years old. To go overseas at 39 years of age during World War II required a special waiver. He had to sign special papers that indicated he was a volunteer. I made the mistake of writing home to my family about the "old man" on our crew; and every time I visited home after I had reached that age myself, everyone would ask me if I still thought 39 was an "old" age. As I write this book, I am 74 and in perspective, 39 now looks very young.

I was able to fly with Boughner for 1:30 hours on a practice flight in the local area today to get acquainted with him.

February 17, 1944   German Army Headquarters, Grottaferrata, Italy.

I flew my first combat mission, on this, the group's first mission where bombs were dropped. Bad weather had delayed an attempt to fly a combat mission from February 10 until this date. (The asterisk * before each date will indicate missions on which I was able to fly, in pages that follow. If no asterisk appears before the date, it means it was a mission on which I didn't fly.)

Ken Boughner was one of the established members of the 456th Bomb Group, so I had a foot in the door to begin flying combat missions with his crew. I was anxious to prove my worth and start earning my pay. There was always a question about how effective we would be, because none of us had previous combat experience.

A messenger came around to our tents in the olive grove at about 0430 hours on the cold winter morning of February 17, to wake us up for the mission. Still sleepy, we had a breakfast of dehydrated eggs, Spam, powdered milk, cereal, greasy bacon, bread, and instant coffee, eaten camp-out style from our aluminum mess kits, we then rode in the back of Army six-by-six trucks from our squadron tent area up to group headquarters on the hill to attend the mission briefing.

The briefing started at 0615 hours in one of the two stucco-covered limestone tuffi-brick buildings near the Group's farmhouse headquarters. We all wore our heavy sheepskin, fur-lined flight gear because the weather was still very cold. In a few weeks we were issued electrically heated suits that replaced the fur-lined suits. The attached crew picture, taken later, shows us wearing our new electric suits. Given the crude living conditions, and the early hour, we were a motley looking group because many were unshaven.

When we walked into the briefing building there were numerous metal crates on the floor to be used as chairs. These crates had been used to protect tail fins of bombs during their shipment from the states. Tail fins were shipped separate from the bombs themselves. On the wall at the end of the briefing room was a large map of Europe with red yarn leading from our air base at Stornara to the target, Grottaferrata near the Anzio beachhead in Italy, south of Rome. The Initial Point (IP) was identified. The IP was a point on the ground that began the selected 15 to 20 mile bombing run that bombardiers required to identify the target, and synchronize their secret Norden bombsights before release of the bombs.

The run from the IP to the target was a dangerous period for aircrews because it was during that time the plane had to remain at a constant speed, direction, and altitude for bombing to be accurate. It was a crucial period during which bombardiers had only a few minutes to identify their targets, and synchronize their bomb sights on it. Thus, for a period of 5 to 7 minutes our planes were sitting ducks for antiaircraft gunners on the ground. This was the best time for them to synchronize their guns, getting our speed, altitude, and direction for accurately shooting at us because we could not take evasive action.

The Norden bombsight was connected electronically to the aircraft's autopilot, and the autopilot responded to corrections in the aircraft's course that the bombardier made through his bombsight's direction gyro. On reaching the IP, pilot of the lead plane of the formation transferred control of his plane to the bombardier who then controlled the flight of the aircraft through movements and settings in his bombsight from the IP until bombs were released. After bombs were away, the pilot took back control of the aircraft, turning off the auto pilot, and we usually made a violent descending turn in formation to confuse enemy gunners on the ground.

In the early days, before the autopilots became reliable, some pilots preferred not to trust the autopilot and they flew their planes manually by following a needle on their instrument panel, the Pilot's Direction Indicator (PDI) that was moved by the bombardier's movements of the bombsight.

I didn't know many of the faces in the briefing room, because we didn't visit the tent cities of the other three squadrons except on rare occasions. We were always too busy with activities of our own, making our living areas livable and attending squadron meetings. We had meetings in our squadron tent cities on various subjects, such as discussions about various aircraft emergencies that we could encounter and survival procedures we intended to use in case of bail out over enemy territory. Personnel of each squadron stuck to themselves for the most part, between missions, and we only saw them at briefings and training sessions that were conducted at Group Headquarters.

Our briefing officers briefed us about the route to the target, expected weather (weather was usually checked in advance by a fast reconnaissance plane), enemy flak and fighter defenses that were expected (they said no enemy resistance was expected because the previous flight to this target on February 10 encountered no fighters or flak). We were given start engine time of 0745 hours, taxi time of

0750, and the lead aircraft took off at 0800 hours. The rest of us, thirty-nine more heavily loaded B-24s, making a total of forty Liberators, staggered off the dirt runway at one minute intervals.

Pilots were given a mimeographed piece of paper that had the position of each aircraft in the formation, the bombing altitude (20,000 feet), interplane frequencies (ours was the very high frequency, or "VHF," channel "B" with call sign "Bellboy Three.") Two other Bomb Groups of our 304th Bomb Wing, the 454th and the 455th, were scheduled to be ahead of us to at same target area, and they had call signs "Bellboy One and Two." Radio was only to be used in emergencies because radio silence was supposed to be maintained.

We were part of a massive bombing of German troop concentrations in the Anzio area to help ground forces of the 5th Army that were in a desperate situation. It was close to being a major disaster. The U.S. VI Corps of General Mark Clark's Fifth Army had made an amphibious landing behind enemy lines at Anzio, thirty-three miles south of Rome on January 22, 1944. These forces were about to be wiped out by the German army that had assembled its forces for a massive counter attack.

All Liberators of our 304th Bomb Wing loaded their planes for this mission with ten 500 pound general purpose bombs with nose fuses set at .1 seconds and .025 seconds on the tail fuses. Thus, our Group alone would be dropping 200,000 pounds of bombs on the German Headquarters at 0920 hours, and there were two other groups ahead of us dropping their bombs on the same target, the 454th Group at 0910 hours and the 455th Group at 0930 hours.

We were not briefed to have fighter escort. Unknown to us, our fighters, P-38's and P-47's, had been directed to make low level ground attacks in support of ground operations in the Rome area. Thus we had no fighter escort.

87

Navigators and bombardiers were given special information at our morning briefing, such as expected winds aloft, areas of heavy flak that were to be avoided, and courses to fly. Bombardiers also received special information pertaining to target recognition, aiming points, bombing altitude, bomb ballistics, bomb interval settings, and other information that had to be preset in the bombsight. Navigators and bombardiers worked together closely at the briefing, and they flew together in the nose section of our Liberators.

Gunners on our crews were given a special briefing about procedures for testing and firing their guns, enemy fighters expected, expected tactics that enemy fighter pilots would use, and a briefing about escape and evasion procedures to be used if we bailed out over enemy territory.

Most of us took notes that we put on our mimeographed handout sheets and kept with us as a "program" for reference during the mission. (I couldn't find a copy of the typed battle order for this mission, but copies that were used for other later missions, have been included in following text that describes those missions.)

Colonel Steed gave us a few words and the briefing officer gave us a "time hack" so that we all had the same time on our watches. Then we were dismissed to be taken to our planes riding in the back of Army six-by-six trucks.

Start engine, taxi sequence, and takeoff order were all controlled in radio silence by colored flares. Each pilot had a mimeographed "program" showing where he fit into the sequence. It showed the start engines time for his position in the formation. He had to watch for the plane that was to takeoff in front of him and leave his parking stand to fall in behind it in the proper sequence. It was all carefully choreographed to be done under radio silence for security purposes.

We took off on this day at one-minute intervals. On later missions, we used forty-five second takeoff intervals to save fuel and time required to assemble our formation. Hazards to aircrews included the possibility of crashing on takeoff, a time when the heavily loaded plane was strained to its maximum military rated emergency performance power from its four Pratt and Whitney engines, to get into the air. Until we arrived in Italy, none of our aircrews had flown such heavy aircraft. The combat weight published in our operating manuals was rated at 56,000 pounds, and the maximum emergency gross weight for takeoff under wartime conditions was specified in the B-24 operating manual as 71,200 pounds. I'm sure that after many crews added extra flack suits and extra ammunition for extra protection, more than the Group had specified, the takeoff gross weights of many planes exceeded this amount much of the time.

Pilots in our Group had never taken off in B-24s weighing more than 56,000 pounds until they came to Italy and had flown a combat mission for the first time. It was an exciting experience, taking off for the first time on the 4800 foot long dirt runway. The takeoff roll under these conditions was around 4,200 feet before the wheels left the ground. In addition to 5,000 pound bomb load for this day's mission, we had 2,783 gallons of hazardous, aromatic 100 octane gasoline on board, 500 rounds of ammunition for most guns and more for the two guns in the plane's waist, flak suits and helmets (which came on later missions), and our heavy flying clothing. Engines used during World War II were not as reliable as our modern ones. During takeoff, one engine failure would mean crashing in a flaming mass at the end of the runway or shortly after. An error in the crew's pre-takeoff check list, such as flaps not down twenty degrees, engine cowl flaps not closed, or control locks not unlocked, meant that we would crash like a bomb, in a huge ball of fire. We were fully loaded, and if we didn't have a headwind to help us, it took almost the entire runway just to get off the ground. It took a 4,200 foot takeoff roll on our 4,800 foot runway to accelerate to the necessary takeoff speed of 110 to 120 MPH. During my time in the 456th Group, none of our aircraft crashed on takeoff, but the 459th Group had ten aircraft crash on takeoff during that same period.

After struggling into the air, our lead ship would circle at a reduced speed over a predetermined point, and each bomber would climb after takeoff at an indicated airspeed of about 170 MPH to take its place in the Group formation. We then circled in formation until the rest of the bombers caught up.

Our forty B-24's flew in our standard formation of six Boxes, each Box consisting of six planes, with four of the Boxes having an extra plane called a "Tail end Charlie." This amounted to two waves of twenty bombers, and was the standard formation used by our Group until June 22, 1944, when the standard formation was changed from six Boxes to four Boxes. (Shown on the accompanying illustrations.)

The number of planes in each Box depended on how many of our B-24s were flyable for the mission For this day's mission, the first three Boxes,called the 1st Unit, flew in a V fomation of boxes, and it contained 20 bombers. The 2nd Unit also consisted of 20 bombers flying in a similar formation. The 2nd Unit flew behind and about 200 to 500 feet lower than the 1st Unit. The lead aircraft bombed at an altitude of 20,000 feet for this mission.

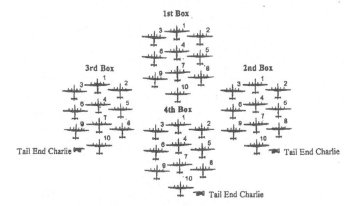

HEAVY BOMBER FORMATION
(Forty B-24s)
1st UNIT
1st Box

3rd Box

2nd Box

2nd UNIT
1st Box

3rd Box

2nd Box

Tail End Charlie   Tail End Charlie

This is the 456th Bomber Group (Heavy) formation used until June 22, 1944.

Six Box Formation - Before June 22, 1944

HEAVY BOMBER FORMATION
(Forty B-24s)

1st Box

3rd Box   2nd Box

4th Box

Tail End Charlie   Tail End Charlie

Tail End Charlie

This is the 456th Bomber Group (Heavy) combat formation from June 22, 1944.

Four Box Formation - After June 22, 1944

A Combat Box formation of 15th Air Force B-24s in flight over Austria.
Photo Courtesy of the National Air and Space Museum, Smithsonian Institution

Picture Of A Liberator Box Formation

Each Box was composed of six ships flying in two three-ship V formations, stepped down, making a total of six ships per Box, with a seventh ship flying as "Tail-End Charlie" below these when we had enough ships available for the mission. The Tail-End Charlie position of the last Box was considered by some to be the "Purple Heart Position" because, being last in the Box, it was viewed as the primary target of enemy fighters that attacked our formations from the rear.

After our Group formation was assembled, we rendezvoused with the other three groups of our 304th Bombardment Wing (Heavy), the 454th, 455th, and 459th over Stornara at 7,000 feet. After all bombers had been assembled, we climbed on course in a trail formation with the other groups of our Wing, at an indicated speed of 160 MPH, which was a true airspeed of about 200 MPH. We climbed at a relatively slow rate of climb, 200 feet per minute, to bombing altitude which was 20,000 feet. Climbing at an indicated airspeed of 160 MPH and keeping a low rate of climb, well below our planes' maximum performance capability, gave the rest of the ships in the formation a margin that allowed them to easily stay in formation and it was also an airspeed that gave us good fuel consumption for what we were doing.

In addition to enemy fire, other hazards to aircrews included fires or explosions from leaking fuel lines, always a hazard. There was the ever-present hazard of aircraft malfunction or fire, bad weather, getting lost and running out of gas, and the very real hazard of colliding with other aircraft while flying close formation. Dodging clouds, and the hectic period of assembling the entire forty plane group formation was a hazardous period, particularly while we were new at it. Two of my close buddies were killed when two aircraft collided directly over our airfield as they were preparing to land after a mission. Many of us watched that tragedy from the ground.

Our bombing altitude was 20,000 feet, where winter temperatures were around minus 30 degrees centigrade and no effective heating system on the B-24. Early Liberators had a hazardous, ineffective heating system that burned gasoline mixed with air, and at that altitude there was not sufficient air to make the system efficient. The system was eventually replaced by a system that required all aircrew to wear heated suits, and that did not work well either. The lack of an effective heating system required us to wear much heavy clothing during winter months to keep warm, and many aircrew members became victims of frostbite, particularly the gunners at the open-air windows in the waist of the bomber, and the turret gunners who were exposed on all sides by frigid air with only a thin layer of Plexiglas separating them from the frigid air outside.

Wearing so much gear was difficult to get used to at first. During winter months, we wore leather helmets with earphones and their wires that were plugged into aircraft radio systems. On later missions we wore regular army steel helmets over all of this on our heads. The helmets had to be stretched to cover all of this, throat mikes were strapped around our throats and plugged into the aircraft radios, we wore goggles, rubber oxygen masks pressed hard against our faces with their oxygen hoses plugged into the aircraft outlets (our planes' cabins weren't pressurized), heavy wool underwear next to our skin, wool gabardine outer flying suits over this, our Army .45 caliber pistols in leather holsters strapped to our shoulders, heavy sheepskin-fur leather pants and jackets worn over all this, Mae Wests (yellow life vests for water survival) on top of this, heavy flak vests on top of it all, heavy fur-lined gloves on our hands, and heavy fur-lined boots over our shoes on our feet. I wondered how much we weighed with all this. Later, many of us began to wear leather G.I. high-top boots rather than our low-cut Oxford style shoes because they were more serviceable for walking long distances, for escape and evasion, in case of bail out over enemy territory.

Wearing all of this and strapped to our seats by a seat belt was no place for someone who had claustrophobia. Somehow, it eventually became routine, and that problem didn't concern us when more important problems eventually dominated our thoughts. With the concentration that was required to safely fly the heavily loaded four-engine planes in close formation, and the excitement of entering enemy territory, we hardly noticed the discomfort of wearing so much restrictive equipment.

However, being strapped down with so much bulky clothing and equipment did become an obstacle to bailing out of the plane in an emergency, or evacuating the bomber on the ground rapidly, particularly if the aircraft was on fire and/or spinning out of control in the air. Most pilots believed that fires, particularly those near our aromatic 100 octane gasoline, were very difficult if not impossible to put out. We practiced procedures for evacuating the airplane as quickly and orderly as possible many times, because every second could mean life or death in an emergency. Pilots had control of an emergency alarm bell that could be heard throughout the airplane. When the bell rang three times it signaled the pilot's order for the crew to bail out. There wasn't much hesitation on any crew member's part when he heard the bell!

On nearing enemy territory where enemy fighters could be around, all ships pulled in to a much tighter formation for protection against an attack. Our standard combat formation was designed so that the maximum number of guns would come to bear on an enemy fighter plane attacking from any direction. For example, in the formation of forty aircraft for this day, there would be 400 fifty-calibre Browning machine guns available to fire at attacking enemy aircraft. If the formation was flown too loosely, many of the guns would be unnecessarily out of range to fire at some of the attacking enemy fighters. General Curtis E. LeMay, a famous future leader of the Air Force, is credited with designing this combat box formation while he was in an Eighth Air Force group during early bombing missions in Europe, and it was adopted as a standard by all groups in Europe.

At first, it was a difficult, unwieldy formation to assemble and fly properly at high altitude when our planes were heavily loaded. That is why it required so much practice. The B-24 had to have its center of gravity maintained at its ideal point, or its longitudinal stability would be poor. If the Liberator's loading by inexperienced or careless crews put the center of gravity too far aft of its proper position under heavily loaded conditions, the plane would not fly formation efficiently and easily in the thin air of high altitude. It would mush along through the air in a nose high attitude, causing it to burn much more fuel than normal.

It wasn't until we had the experience of many missions after this one that the 456th became expert at high altitude formation flying. Later, having many new inexperienced crews constantly coming into our group to replace those experienced crews that were shot down, made training them a constant challenge.

Our mission on February 17 was expected to be an easy, routine mission because it was a short bombing mission and it was the same target that the group flew over on February 10 without enemy opposition. The group had experienced no flak or enemy fighter attacks on that mission, the same target. Nearness of the target also led most of us to believe that our own fighter aircraft would have enough range to be able to defend us against Luftwaffe fighters in the area. That wasn't what happened!

Our freshman mission, expected to be what was known in the trade as a "Milk Run" turned out to be a tough indoctrination into combat. Enemy fighters seemed to be waiting for us at the target area. Two other heavy bomber groups were at the target ahead of us and they seemed to have stirred up a hornets' nest of enemy fighters. None of our own friendly fighters were anywhere in sight.

We saw fifteen Messerschmitt fighters (Me-210's) below us while we were enroute to the target. They were at an altitude of about 3,000 feet, but they didn't attack us.

As we approached our target, twenty-seven enemy fighters, fifteen Messerschmitt fighters (ME-109's) and twelve Focke-Wulfs (FW-190's), attacked our forty bombers. Each enemy fighter made numerous well organized gunnery passes, in pairs, on the rear of our formation, but some attacked from the 9 o'clock and 3 o'clock positions.

Most attacks came at us from the high rear. Enemy fighters had a top speed of about 390 MPH, much more than our formation's cruising speed. We were flying at a true airspeed of 226 MPH. In the air battle that followed, two of our B-24's were shot down and four other Liberators in our formation were damaged. Our gunners claimed two enemy fighters destroyed, one probably destroyed, and three enemy fighters damaged. A gunner in my 746th Squadron's formation, S/Sgt Louis E. Fuerstein, was credited with downing our first enemy aircraft, an Me-109.

The two crews lost were those of 1st Lt. John A. Eidson of the 745th Squadron, and 2nd Lt. Harry W. Bessler from the 747th. Only one parachute was seen to come out of Eidson's plane, and three out of Bessler's plane.

On my plane, Lt. Boughner flew the aircraft during our approach to the bombing run, so I was free to look out and observe most of the action. I only flew the aircraft after bombs were released, to give Boughner some needed rest, and by then the enemy fighters had gone away.

Because I wasn't flying, I watched the air battle. I was captivated by the sight of the famous, graceful, fast Me-109 and FW-190 fighters as their pilots established a well coordinated traffic pattern on us. I had seen the Luftwaffe fighters on newsreels in movie theaters and studied them in flying school. This was my first sight of them live, and I was fascinated by them. They twisted and turned their planes aggressively, unmolested by our own fighter planes because they were not around. Enemy pilots seemed to be having a good time punching holes in our bombers with deadly efficiency. They closed to within forty yards of our formation, so close that I could see the enemy pilots in their cockpits as they passed by. Our gunners' tracer bullets saturated the air around incoming enemy fighters to such an extent that I couldn't see how all those fifty caliber bullets could possibly miss. It must have been an intimidating sight for enemy pilots, and it must have taken tremendous courage for them to fly towards our formation, into that cloud of tracer bullets. I did see pieces coming off some of the enemy planes as our gunners struck their targets, however the enemy fighters continued to come at us.

It was the first time I had experienced most of our ship's machine guns firing at the same time. The firing caused our B-24 to vibrate violently, increasing the atmosphere of excitement. The hectic, animated discussions going over the ship's interphone added to the excitement as gunners nervously called out positions of the attacking enemy fighters, described planes going down, and counted the number of parachutes they saw blooming in the sky.

Again, it was the first time that I saw the ugly grey-black puffs of exploding 20 millimeter cannon shells coming from enemy fighters. The cannon shells burst around our plane like popping popcorn, some sprinkling shrapnel onto our plane. The 20mm shells had fuses on them that caused them to explode after a certain time if they did not strike a target, and I could see their ugly puffs bursting throughout our bomber formation, many of them near our plane.

The most unexpected sight was that of a huge, 33 ton, four-engine B-24 bomber exploding when hit by 20mm cannon. I could clearly see the Messerschmitts attacking 1st. Lt. John A. Eidson's plane off to my right, not far from my plane. The right wing tip of Eidson's bomber, from the engine out, was shot off. It came off in a great, colorful explosion that created a huge bright red-orange ball of fire, and the 33 ton B-24 spun in an unreal, tight, rapid spin, like a toy top. Until then, I would never have believed that such a large plane could be made to spin so fast. The centrifugal force of the tight, rapid spin of the plane must have prevented most of the crew from being able to bail out of the airplane. Only one chute was seen to get out.

The second of our planes shot down, 2nd. Lt. Harry W. Bessler's plane, was behind our aircraft, out of my sight, but I heard the gunners talking excitedly over our interphone describing it and reporting what they saw. Fighter planes did some damage to Bessler's bomber before we reached the Initial Point to start our bomb run on the target. The target was covered with ugly black bursts of antiaircraft shells, and German fighter planes refused to follow us into their own barrage of heavy flak. Bessler's plane was severely damaged by several direct hits of flak bursts during the bomb run. Coming off the target, heavily damaged and unable to keep up with the rest of the formation, Luftwaffe fighters resumed their relentless attack on his crippled plane to finish it off. German fighters always went after bombers that could not stay in the bomber formation because there were fewer guns firing at them, guns of one plane compared to many guns of bombers that were in the formation.

B-24 Over Italy With Wing Shot Off

A Liberator with its left wing shot off by enemy fire.
Photo provided by the San Diego Aerospace Museum.

B-24 With Wing Shot Off By Enemy Fire

Only one parachute was seen coming from Bessler's unfortunate plane. Later, it was learned that three parachutes were able to get out. Staff Sergeant Jesse Bradburn, a flight engineer on Bessler's plane, was one of those that bailed out. He had been wounded by enemy bullets. Wounded, Bradburn was captured by the Germans, hospitalized, then he escaped. After an interesting adventure, he was able to evade recapture with help from the underground workers behind enemy lines, and he returned to our base May 29, 1944.

Staff Sergeant Joseph Millman, also a flight engineer on Bessler's plane, had another interesting experience, which he later reported in summary in our 456th Bomb Group Association's Group History Book, published by the Turner Publishing Company in 1994. After the war, years later, many survivors joined the 456th Bomb Group Association and we learned many more details about what happened. Bailing out of the plane while injured, Millman was captured by Germans, hospitalized in a body cast, shipped to Germany, beat up, shot at, was traveling on a bombed train that was wrecked, put in solitary confinement, and starved. These were among his many interesting adventures. He reported that he was going to publish a book, "The Eleventh Passenger" to describe details of his unusual experiences. Millman is a member of the 456th Bomb Group Association.

The other man on Bessler's crew who was able to bail out was Sgt. Harold C. Lewis, Bessler's Tail Turret gunner. Sgt. Lewis was able to evade capture with aide from friendly Italian civilians and he returned safely to allied territory in June 1944, when the 8th Army moved north.

In the excitement, and because it all happened so fast with so much to see, I had little time to feel compassion for the twenty men of the crews that were shot down. When I saw Eidson's plane spinning in such a tight spin, I realized that it would be next to impossible for anyone to bail out of it, unless they happened to be near the open waist window in the rear of the plane. I felt very sorry for them at the time and I automatically visualized what it must have been like to be trapped in such a plane.

It was like a surrealistic adventure. I observed the entire scene as if it were an exciting, detached technicolor movie. We had a clear blue sky and at high altitude, the 100 octane gasoline burned with a beautiful red-orange color that made a colorful contrast against the blue sky. Seeing the aggressive, high performance ME-109 and FW-190 fighters, that I had only seen in movie newsreels previously, was an awesome, intriguing sight. I knew that we were in a desperate battle for our lives and my adrenaline was flowing, but I was so intrigued by the scene, and it absorbed so much of my attention, that I gave little thought to my own security or anyone else's. It was like an unreal adventure.

The flak at this target was graded as being moderate intensity, heavy guns, and accurate. It was the first time that I saw the ugly huge black bursts of flak coming from German 88mm antiaircraft guns whose gunners were trying to kill us. It was like fireworks, but on a much larger scale. Each menacing black burst had an orange core, and when it was close enough the loud explosions sprayed shrapnel across our plane and caused our B-24 to bounce a little from its flight path. Eight of our bombers, including mine, were damaged on this mission. For example, 1st Lt. Dave Tavel's plane, flying in the lead ship of the 2nd Unit had his astrodome hit by flak among other holes, and another plane, "Lassie Come Home" flown by Lt Richard Witkin of my 746th Squadron, had ten holes in its wings from flak and fighters.

The only clouds we encountered were a few altocumulus clouds below us at 12,000 to 14,000 feet enroute to the target. However, weather at the target was clear and visibility was unlimited.

We dropped 96.5 tons of general purpose 500 pound bombs (386 bombs) on the target area from 20,000 feet for the 1st Unit and 22,000 feet for the 2nd Unit at 1056 hours, on an axis of attack of 82 degrees magnetic. The bombardiers' bomb release interval setting was 100 feet. The temperature at 22,000 feet was minus 30 degrees centigrade. We flew at an indicated airspeed (IAS) of 160 MPH, which was a true airspeed of about 228 MPH at that altitude and temperature.

True airspeed (TAS) at altitude was more than IAS because the pilots' airspeed indicator relied on the impact of outside air on a measuring device (pitot tube). Since air becomes thinner as we climb to altitude we actually cruised faster than the pilots' airspeed indicator registered. For this mission, TAS for the bomb run was about 228 MPH.

Two bombers returned to our base with bombs, unable to release them on the target because of release mechanism malfunctions. One aircraft jettisoned its bombs in the target area because of malfunctions. Fifteen photographs taken at the target by cameras aboard our planes indicated there was a good concentration of bombs on the target. Results were later graded as fair by analysis of the photos.

Later, bombing of the Anzio area by heavy bombers on this and following raids, was credited with saving the beachhead. Many German troops and a whole Panzer division that were getting ready to attack our soldiers on the beachhead were destroyed by bombing.

On return to our base, we circled over the airfield as planes peeled off the group formation in an orderly sequence, one box landing its planes, one plane at a time until all were down.

The flight took five hours. After we had landed on our dirt runway, taxied to our parking hardstands, cut engines, we rode in army six-by-six trucks up to Group headquarters to be interrogated by intelligence personnel about the mission. We were met by our flight surgeon who rationed two ounces of medicinal whiskey per man, which most of us gratefully downed. After being on oxygen for five hours, with the rubber mask pressing hard against my face, it was a great relief to be safe on terra firma again breathing fresh air. We were all hyped up, excited from the experience, even before we drank the whiskey. Another very welcome sight was that of Red Cross workers who had set up a coffee and doughnut bar for us. We gratefully sampled their wares as we entered the intelligence interrogation room where we had to report everything that we had seen. It was my first combat mission, and the first mission where the 456th Group was able to drop its bombs on a target. I was glad that we finally experienced a combat mission and sampled enemy opposition, but we were sad about losing two crews and planes.

This procedure, from early morning wake-up call in our tents, breakfast, briefing on the hill at group headquarters, start engine, taxi, takeoff, bomber formation, cruise to the target, bomb drop, return, land, whiskey, coffee and doughnuts from the Red Cross, and debriefing by intelligence personnel became routine procedure for all missions afterward.

We heard that Winston Churchill, Prime Minister of England, congratulated the 456th Bomb Group on its excellent bombing results achieved on this mission.

February 18, 1944   No Mission.

I flew the Link Trainer to get some instrument flying practice. The trainer was installed at group headquarters so pilots could get some blind flying practice on the ground.

February 19, 1944   No Mission.

On the February 19, and again on the 20th, we had Red Alerts at our air base at Stornara, warning us that enemy aircraft were approaching to bomb or strafe our field. This caused everyone to grab shovels and begin digging fox holes for protection in the hard ground outside our tents. I always suspected that many of these air raid alerts were false ones, manufactured by the staff at group headquarters or at some higher organizational level, because it stimulated us into the unpleasant task of digging fox holes outside our tents. Something that they were constantly trying to get us to do, and something that none of us had a passion for doing. The weather was bitterly cold, making the task even less enjoyable. Cheap Italian labor was later hired to help us out.

We actually did have some enemy aircraft fly over our airfield at a later date, but by then our slit trenches were full of water and we were reluctant to dive into them.

Chaplain Theodore B. Mitzner conducted the first church service at group headquarters in a cold building on February 19.

February 19 - 25, 1944   Big Week.

A coordinated attack, often called the **"Big Week,"** was launched against the Luftwaffe in the air and German aircraft industry on the ground during this period. It was an all-out effort conducted by all heavy bombers of the RAF at night and the USAAF in England and Italy during the day. It was a direct challenge to the Luftwaffe's superiority in the air over Europe. Since the Fifteenth Air Force was formed in November 1943, the overall top USAAF command in Europe, known as the U.S. Strategic Air Forces Command (USSTAF) located in England, had planned a "Big Week" against the German aircraft manufacturing industry to give it a smashing blow. It was also aimed at giving the Luftwaffe a smashing blow in the air and on the ground. The project was called "Operation ARGUMENT," and it was to be a coordinated precision bombing of key parts of the German aircraft industry by the RAF Bomber Command at night, and the Eighth and Fifteenth Air Forces' heavy bombers in daylight. It was a round-the-clock effort.

After many weather delays, and possibly some delay caused by the catastrophic German bombing of Bari Harbor that deprived the Fifteenth Air Force of many of its supplies, the operation officially began on February 19 with an RAF night attack. Next, the Eighth Air Force in England which carried the main load of Big Week, started with an attack on February 20 that went deep into Germany, bombing the industrial complex at Leipzig and an eastern German complex called the Tutow complex. This first Eighth Air Force mission consisted of 1,028 heavy bombers accompanied by 832 USAF escort fighter planes and sixteen fighter squadrons of RAF Spitfires and RAF Mustangs. It was the largest number of bombers and fighters to be assembled up to that time. It was a direct challenge to air superiority of the Luftwaffe over Germany. The Eighth also flew follow-on missions into Germany, although with fewer planes, on 21, 22, 24, and 25 February.

The Fifteenth Air Force's more established bomber groups in Italy made raids into Germany and Austria on February 22, 23, 24, and 25, all that weather would allow, but the Fifteenth didn't have nearly as many bombers as the Eighth Air Force to send on its raids. Some of the Fifteenth's heavy bombers were diverted from strategic targets to bomb in support of our ground troops at the Anzio beachhead because of the emergency situation that had developed there in the ground war.

During Big Week, from February 20 through 25, the Eighth Air Force sent approximately 3,300 bomber sorties, the Fifteenth Air Force sent about 500, and the RAF sent 2,300 over Germany at night in support of Operation Argument. These bombers dropped about 10,000 tons of bombs, about as much as the Eighth Air Force had dropped during its entire previous first year of operations from England. The USAAF lost about 230 of its heavy bombers, an average of around 7 percent of its striking force, during Big Week and twenty-eight fighters were lost to enemy action. The Luftwaffe lost 450 planes during Big Week, an unsustainable loss rate for its pilots. From that time, the Luftwaffe went into a slow but steady decline in power. During February 1944 the Luftwaffe lost 33.8 percent of their total operational fighter force in all theaters of operations, including the Russian front, and it lost 17.9 percent of its fighter pilots. The Allies could replace its bombers, fighters, and crews from the United States, but the Luftwaffe could not replace its experienced fighter pilots.

Big Week was terminated due to forecast bad weather on February 25.

The 456th Bomb Group was ordered to bomb strategic targets in support of Big Week, but it was prevented by bad weather. Our Group had to wait until after Big week to commence bombing strategic targets in the Nazi homeland in the underbelly of Europe. Our Group was ordered to bomb the Graz Thalerhof Airdrome in Austria on February 21, but it was delayed one day because of weather. The next day, with the same bad weather conditions at Graz, the Group was ordered to bomb Brod, Yugoslavia, but again weather foiled the attempt, discussed below.

As mentioned earlier, for reasons described in Chapter 2, the great air battles over enemy targets during which so many Luftwaffe pilots were lost, turned out to be more important than the bombing of aircraft factories. A report made in the summer of 1944 by Adolph Galland, leader of Luftwaffe fighters, stated that "Between January and April, 1944, our (Luftwaffe) daytime fighters lost over 1,000 pilots," and he continued to say that these included the loss of his best fighter squadron. Galland reported that the time has come when his fighter defense capability is "in sight of collapse."

Although German fighter production continued at a healthy pace, and planes were replaceable, trained pilots were not. The German pilot training program had as a big problem, in addition to the poor winter weather, a severe shortage of fuel by the spring of 1944. The fuel shortage was the result of the Fifteenth Air Force, Eighth Air Force, and Royal Air Force combined bombing of oil and transportation facilities. The USAAF lost many planes and crews, but it had a steady stream of replacements coming from the states, something the Luftwaffe could not match.

February 22, 1944   Railroad Installations, Sibenik Harbor, Yugoslavia (An Alternate Target)

Our Group's third accredited mission, with Colonel Steed in the lead plane, tried to bomb Brod, Yugoslavia, in support of Big Week. Weather caused our planes to bomb the alternate target, German railroad installations at Sibenik Harbor, Yugoslavia where the weather was clear.

Thirty-nine planes took off at 0830 hours and two planes returned early because of engine problems. Brod had an undercast of clouds that covered seventy-five percent of the target, but it was clear at the secondary target, Sibenik. Only twenty eight bombers were able to drop bombs on the secondary target because of bomb release malfunctions on the other planes in the formation, but the target was completely destroyed. Fourteen pictures of the target were taken by K-22 cameras aboard our bombers.

The Group dropped 69.75 tons of 500 pound general purpose bombs (279 bombs) at 1344 hours from 20,000 feet. Four Liberators returned their bombs to our base and the others jettisoned their bombs before returning home. No enemy fighters were seen, and flak was classified as ineffective. The bomber formation returned to base at 1441 hours, and logged a total flying time of 7:10 hours after they had landed. The crew I was assigned to fly with did not fly on that mission.

On the same day, February 22, the Fifteenth Air Force sent other groups above the Alps into Germany in support of Big Week. Target cover was provided by 122 P-38's, and withdrawal cover for the bombers was provided by 63 P-47's. One formation of 118 B-24's bombed an assembly plant at Obertraubling with good results, but it ran into 120 enemy fighters and 14 of their Liberators were shot down. At the same time, a formation of 65 B-17's from the Fifteenth Air Force dropped 153 tons of bombs on a Messerschmitt component factory at Regensburg, losing five of its bombers. The Fifteenth Air Force lost one P-38 fighter and one P-47 for the day.

February 23, 1944   Weather Abort Enroute to Orvieto, Italy

This was the day that our Group was scheduled to fly its fourth mission, to Orvieto, Italy. I was assigned to fly on it as copilot with Boughner's crew. Our planes were loaded with fragmentation bombs, and we were scheduled to have British Spitfires as escort on the mission for the first time. This would have been my second mission, but the group was recalled because of bad weather reported at the target while we were over the Adriatic enroute to Orvieto. I logged 1 hour and 10 minutes. Naturally, no credit was allowed for this mission, but it was good practice for the Group.

On this day, Italian troops arrived at our airfield, assigned to the 456th for duty (Italy had surrendered to the Allies in September, 1943). There were fifty enlisted men, one sergeant, and one second lieutenant. They were wearing quite a mixture of uniforms, and they were put in pup tents at the east end of our field.

February 24, 1944   No Mission.

Foul weather everywhere, so no missions could be flown.

February 25, 1944   Weather Abort Enroute To Graz, Austria.

Today was the fifth attempt by the group to fly a mission, this time to bomb the Graz airfield in Austria in support of Big Week, but weather prevented bombs from being dropped and our planes returned to our air base with their bombs.

We lost one plane on the mission. A Liberator flown by Lt. George H. Gutting Jr. of my 746th Squadron had to make an emergency crash landing on a neighboring bomb group's airfield with his bombs aboard. On landing, the bombs broke loose from their racks and rolled around in the aircraft's bomb bay. No one was injured, but the plane was so damaged that it had to be scrapped.

Up to this point, for all of February, the group attempted to fly five missions, but succeeded in getting credit for only three because of bad weather.

February 26 - 28, 1944   No Mission.

Bad weather persisted, either in our local area or in potential target areas for five days after the attempt to bomb Graz. Weather had to be good enough in all areas at the same time: weather in the local area had to be good enough to enable the assembly of the formations of bombers and climb to high altitude; enroute weather had to be good enough to fly formation visually to the target; and target weather had to be good enough to see the target and visually bomb it.

The mare in the farm's stable, located behind the Group Headquarters, had a colt on February 28. It attracted a considerable number of interested people, and it temporarily provided some much needed diversion.

Some troops went into town on February 28, to the Teatro Mercandante in Cerignola, to see Louise Albritton the movie star and her troupe of USO performers. Some reported that it was a pretty good show.

February 29, 1944 Weather Abort Enroute, Budapest, Hungary.

An early morning wake-up at 0500 hours. We were briefed at 0630 hours for a mission to bomb Budapest, Hungary, but the mission was canceled after we were airborne because of weather. I logged 2:10 hours of flying time, but no mission credit.

Weather continued to be bad for the most part of March, and only thirteen targets could be bombed during the month by the 456th Bomb Group. Only three of the thirteen targets were to our primary strategic targets in Austria and Bulgaria. As a result, many times during March, our bombers had to return to Italy and drop bombs on secondary targets as a last resort. One secondary target, one that was a great help to British and American ground forces in the Italian ground war, was the railroad marshalling yards at Rimini, Italy. The weather there and at other targets in northern Italy were always more reliable for bombing when the primary target above the Alps could not be bombed. The railroad yards at Rimini and at other Italian railroad "choke points" were demolished, disrupting the flow of essential resources from northern Europe to German ground forces that were tenaciously fighting our 5th and 8th Armies in Italy.

A Note About Mission Credit.

A word must be said about the method that our headquarters had established for counting accredited "missions." The Eighth Air Force in England was the first USAAF organization to start bombing in Europe on a consistent basis. The Eighth Air Force in England established a policy of limiting the number of missions that aircrews had to fly before they earned a ticket to return to the states for a rest. On a statistical basis, at the expected aircraft loss rate of seven percent per mission that the Eighth Air Force was experiencing in the early days, the average bomber crew should be shot down almost two times by the time it completed 25 bombing missions into the heartland of Germany. However, some of the missions were "milk runs," missions to lightly defended targets in France and other areas outside of Germany and Austria. For morale purposes of its crews that were facing such a situation, the Eighth Air Force established 25 missions as the standard number of missions required to be flown in order to earn a ticket home and rest in the States. Later, lower than expected loss rates caused the official number of missions to be increased to 35.

In the Fifteenth Air Force, which was organized after the Eighth was formed, a different standard was established. We were bombing many of the same targets in Germany and Austria, but many targets we bombed were "milk runs" in Italy, Yugoslavia, and Bulgaria. Fifty missions was the standard requirement for a ticket home in the Fifteenth Air Force, but a system of giving credit for two missions, or double credit, for each long mission flown to highly defended strategic targets in Germany, Austria, Hungary, Czechslovakia, and Rumania was established. Longer missions gave enemy aircraft much more opportunity to shoot us down, and those missions were usually to more heavily defended targets that had many more enemy fighters and flak guns shooting at us. Only one mission was accredited for short missions. Thus, our missions to targets in Germany, Austria, Hungary, Rumania, and Czechoslovakia were given double credit for each single mission (sortie) flown, whereas bombing missions to targets in Italy, Bulgaria and Yugoslavia were only awarded one mission credit for each mission (sortie) flown.

As it turned out, a few of the two-credit missions were not as tough as some of the one-credit types. I flew on 38 bombing sorties, but was given official credit for 51 missions in the accounting toward a ticket home. I received extra credit for 13 of the tougher, longer missions that I flew. This was close to the 35 missions required in the Eighth Air force, and it was about average for aircrews of the Fifteenth Air Force at the time that I was flying combat missions..

March 1, 1944   No Mission.

No mission this day because of bad weather.

By March we were beginning to gain much more confidence in our flying ability, and our formation flying began to improve significantly. Our ground crews were also becoming more experienced and suited to the routiine. The past few months were training experiences for all of us.

Aircrews were issued heavy bullet-proof flak vests and regular Army infantry steel helmets. The helmets had to be stretched to be able to fit over our leather helmets and earphones. We learned to use our steel helmets as wash basins, by improvising tri-pods made with three sticks tied together, and used them as resting places for the helmets when we washed. We soon learned to take complete baths out of the helmets.

Some pilots decided to sit on their flak vests, to protect their "family jewels" from enemy shell bursts coming from below the plane, rather than wear them to protect their torsos from flying flak. I wore mine as a vest. Some crew members scrounged or borrowed more than one flak vest for extra protection. I always wondered how much additional weight this added to our planes that were already overloaded.

We were getting more settled into our tents and we were improving our crude living conditions. A steady supply of water, better and more sanitary messing facilities, and plans for some recreational clubs were developing. The Group began construction in February of semi-permanent installations such as kitchens, mess halls, latrine boxes. This program was gradually completed by native and troop labor. More of the large five-man pyramidal tents had become available for the ground personnel. Supplies were gradually being received so that by March of 1944 adequate shelter was provided for all personnel. Improvised stoves and local building materials had been used to winterize tents and offices.

One of our pilots, Lt. Harry Ragland, used his engineering expertise to build our only shower in the 746th Squadron. When it became available, we had to stand in line to use his ingenious shower structure, and each one who used it had to hand pump the water he would use from fifty gallon drums on the ground up to another fifty gallon drum above the shower so the water would gravity-feed through the shower head. The energetic and handy Harry was a moving force in designing and building an officer's club out of tuffi limestone bricks, a major project. Harry is currently a member of our 456th Bomb Group Association.

I was on a special committee to buy some liquor for our club. A couple of us was provided a jeep to visit some Italian distilleries in the area and it was an eye-opener. The health and cleanliness standards of these distilleries were the lowest possible, but we figured that the alcohol would kill many of the germs. We watched workers brush away swarms of ever-present flies to reach the bottles they were filling with spirits. Wine, champagne, and cherry brandy were our first purchases. Spumonte champagne was only seventy cents a bottle, so I could afford to sample my first taste of it. I became drunk for the first time of my life.

As another additional duty between missions, I was assigned along with another officer, the task of dismantling and inspecting emergency life rafts and survival gear that were stored on top of our Liberator's fuselages. The rafts were available for emergency use in the event that we had to ditch our B-24s in water. The B-24 had poor ditching characteristics because weak bomb bay doors would collapse on impact with water during an emergency landing attempt, allowing water to rapidly fill the plane and the plane would sink very fast. Thus, the life rafts were of questionable value, but still they had to be inspected regularly.

The other officer who was with me inspecting the life rafts was a competent, eager, personable young West Point graduate, Lt. Richard E. Beck. He also had an additional duty as an assistant operations officer, assistant to another competent West Pointer, Captain Frederick Weston Hyde, our squadron's operations officer. I came to like and admire them both very much. We had a tricky job of doing the inspections of the life rafts between rain showers that made the top of the airplanes very slippery. The frequent rain also exposed the rafts and survival gear to water if we had their access doors open. We could only inspect them when weather was good and when the planes weren't flying.

Lt. Beck was later killed on a mission to Ploesti on May 5th. Captain Hyde (promoted to the rank of colonel after the war) was shot down on August 22, 1944, on a raid to Blechhammer, Germany. All of our operations officers that I knew were shot down before they completed fifty missions. One of our operations officers, Major Douglas C. Richards (later promoted to Lt. Colonel), was able to make a forced landing on a small, 1500 foot, landing strip at Vis, Yugoslavia. He was rescued, returned to Stornara, and he continued duty with the 746th Squadron for the rest of the war. Richards and Hyde are currently members of our 456th Bomb Group Association.

The young colt in the stable behind group headquarters was attracting many admirers and growing rapidly.

March 2, 1944   German Troop Concentrations Near Anzio, Italy.

The Group flew its fourth accredited mission in six attempts. My crew was not selected to fly on that one. The Group lost one plane in a tragic crash as a result of this mission.

The German Tenth Army was threatening our 5th Army's beach head position at Anzio again with a new drive. This day's mission bombed German troop concentrations that were massed on the road between Cisterna and Velletri, Italy, ready to attack our ground forces that were stranded in the beachhead area.

After a 0530 wake-up call in their tents, a C-ration breakfast, and a ride up to attend a 0630 briefing at Group headquarters, aircrews were driven to their Liberators for a 0730 stations time. Start engines time was 0740 for all aircraft flying in the 1st and 2nd Boxes, 0750 for the 3rd and 4th Boxes, and 0800 hours for the 5th and 6th boxes. Colonel Steed in the lead bomber started to taxi to the end of the runway at 0750 hours, then he coaxed his heavily loaded Liberator off the bumpy dirt runway at 0800 hours. Thirty-eight more of the group's B-24s followed his plane off the runway at one minute intervals. There were seven aircraft that aborted the mission, and returned early. One returned early because gasoline was siphoning from the right side of the aircraft, four bombers had inoperative superchargers, one had an engine detonating, and one had a runaway propeller.

DETAILED OPERATIONS BRIEFING

1. a) Battle Order:

2 MAR.
Date: ~~20 Feb~~ 1944

1st Unit, 1st Box

Formation Leader: WARD, Col STEED, GRUBER AP 637 AP

No.3: NEWHOUSE   AP 283   Dep Leader: ANDREWS & CLARK, RR 284
                   No.4: NILSSON   AP 297
No.6: LASSITER   AP 345   No.5: PALIS   AP 635

2nd Box

Leader: PHILLIPS   AP 470
No.3: HAVILAND   AP 661   Dep Leader: DEMELIK   AP 595
                   No.4: BISHOP   AP 658
No.6: MAPA   AP 311   No.5: GREENSTONE   AP 634
                   No.7: RIDDLE - RAWLINSON 287

3rd Box

Leader: MILLER   AP 268
No.3: RUDD   AP 295   *dikkson* Dep Leader: GRIFFIN   AP 276
     DESPEROCK   No.4: ~~JONES~~ WM.   AP 291
No.6: ~~JACKSON, W.L.~~ AP ~~256~~ 212   No.5: BARRASSO   AP 290
                   ~~No.7: JACKSON, G.Y. AP 279~~

2nd Unit, 1st Box

Leader: LAMPLEY & TAVELL AP 222
No.3: BOWERING   AP 189   Dep Leader: SAGERT, GOLDEN AP 480
                   No.4: CUTTING   AP 486
No.6: BOUGHNER   AP 199   No.5: THOMAS   AP 492
                   ~~No.7: RICHARDS, D.G. AP 485~~

2nd Box

Leader: TOWNSEND   AP 231
No.3: KRISPINSKY   AP 643   Dep Leader: WITKIN   AP 477
                   No.4: LEE   AP 214
No.6: PHIFER   AP 501   No.5: SMITH   AP ~~222~~ 233
                   No.7: HILLMAN AP 285

3rd Box

Leader: DOUGLASS & CLARK, W.D. AP 304
No.3: LISZEWSKI   AP 292   Dep Leader: RICHARDS, N.O. AP 217
                   No.4: CALLAN   AP ~~445~~ 330
No.6: MEYER   AP 309   No.5: KEY   AP 177
                   No.7: MONAHAN   AP 334

Colonel Steed flew his plane in a race track pattern in left turns at 8,000 feet until the rest of the Group's planes caught up with his, and completed forming the six-Box formation. Colonel Harmon Lampley Jr. and Lt. Dave E. Tavel were in the lead plane of the 2nd Unit. When the 39 plane formation was complete, Colonel Steed led it over Stornara to rendezvous with the other three groups of our 304th Wing, to form a trail formation of groups. The Wing's cruising formation was 454th Group in the lead, followed by the 455th, then the 456th stacked up to the right and the 459th on the left of the 456th and 1,000 feet below it. The Wing formation departed Stornara at 1000 hours climbing at an indicated airspeed of 160 MPH (200 MPH true airspeed), and a 250 feet per minute rate of climb to the bombing altitude of 23,500 feet for our Group. Cruising speed of the formation was 165 MPH (233 MPH true airspeed due to air temperature and altitude), to the target.

Weather enroute to the target was undercast with clouds as far as the coast, and with broken cumulonimbus clouds having tops reaching 30,000 feet until the bombers reached the Initial Point. From the I.P. to the target, there was forty-percent cloud coverage over the target area, with broken altocumulus clouds that had tops up to 14,000 feet. The outside air temperature was minus 42 degrees centigrade at 23,200 feet.

There were P-38s and P-47s over the target area for fighter cover, and they did a good job because our Group saw no enemy aircraft. Flak over the target area was composed of heavy guns, moderate intensity, and accurate. They were so accurate that nineteen of the Group's Liberators received flak damage in the target area.

Twenty-seven bombers successfully dropped 31.98 tons of cluster fragmentation bombs (533 bombs) on the German troops at 1111 hours from 23,500 feet for the 1st Unit. The bombardiers' bomb release setting was 300 feet. Though there was a forty percent cloud coverage at the target, bombardiers could identify the target sufficiently so that the bombs were well scattered over the target area. Eighteen photographs were taken of the target by our planes. After bombs were released, Colonel Steed led the formation in a prearranged descending right turn at 170 MPH indicated airspeed (240 MPH true airspeed), and a 500 feet per minute rate of descent, to confuse antiaircraft gunners.

Five planes did not drop their bombs on the target, but dropped their bombs prematurely, prior to reaching the target. When the five planes saw the lead plane of their Box, "St. Chris," flown by 2nd Lt. James A. Krispinsky of the 746th Squadron, drop its bombs prematurely, they dropped their bombs. They didn't know that Krispinsky's lead plane was forced to drop its bombs early because it took a severely damaging flak hit, and it had to return to our base from that point. The other planes of the box, with the deputy leader of the box Lt. Arthur F. Bowering of my 746th Squadron taking over the lead, remained with the Group formation. They flew home with the Group formation.

The Group formation returned to Stornara at 1227 hours. Two planes had to leave the Group formation and make emergency landings at San Giovani because of severe flak damage. Flying time was 5:25 hours. Personnel casualties on this mission were four killed, and two wounded, as discussed below.

I, along with many others, witnessed a tragic crash landing on our airfield when one of the severely damaged planes, Lt. Krispinski's "St. Chris," returned to our air base and was destroyed before our eyes, killing four men.

Since I wasn't scheduled to fly on that mission, and was idle, I was asked to squire officers of a replacement crew that had just arrived, around the squadron area. This was to give them an orientation of the area, acquaint them with our routine procedures, and give them an indication of what to expect. After escorting them around the squadron area, I noticed that one of our group's planes had already arrived over the field, getting ready to land, an indication that the group was starting to return from the Anzio mission. I took the new officers out to a position near the runway so we could closely watch our planes as they landed one at a time, to show the new airmen the landing procedure we used when we arrived over the field after a mission.

One of my 746th Squadron's planes, "St. Chris" number 42-52187 flown by 2nd Lt. James A. Krispinsky, evidently had much flak damage. I didn't know it at the time, but the plane had received three heavy direct flak hits that severely wounded the navigator, tail turret gunner, and they damaged the flight controls. The pilot, knowing he was going to have trouble on the landing, ordered his crew members to bail out. Five crew members, S/Sgts Carmon Allen, Leon Bashaw, Arthur Becker, Arthur Dejean, and Robert Donahue, bailed out near our field. Because of the severely wounded navigator, Lt. Raymond A. Pullman, who was very weak from loss of much blood and thus could not bail out, Krispinsky and his copilot, 2nd Lt. Craig Andrus, and the flight engineer, S/Sgt Wade E. Saunders, decided to stay with the aircraft and attempt to land it rather than bail out themselves. Our squadron bombardier, 1st Lt. Benjamin Smalley, also elected to stay with the plane because he was attending the severely wounded Pullman.

As the plane touched down near us on the runway, it was obvious that its right tire was flat, among other problems that became apparent as his plane moved erratically on the runway. It was about forty yards from where we were standing. Because of the flat right tire, and other possible problems such as loss of brakes and hydraulic fluid that may have troubled the landing, the plane suddenly veered off the runway to its right, coming directly at the me and my small party that was watching the event. Krispinsky's plane would have overrun us, except that the soft-plowed field that the plane ran into when it left the firm dirt runway, slowed the plane considerably. The nose wheel of the plane collapsed in the soft earth off the runway. When the nose wheel collapsed in the soft turf, the nose of the aircraft was rapidly destroyed by being ground down under the rest of the plane by its fast-moving forward momentum. The two pilots and the engineer who was standing between them were ground under the rest of the plane and killed instantly. The collapse of the nose wheel and destruction of the aircraft's nose section slowed the airplane to a halt, causing the giant craft's tail to rise vertically into the air, then it slammed back down to the ground in a horizontal position. It's nose section, along with the two pilots and engineer were completely gone, ground under the rest of the plane by its forward momentum..

As the tail of the plane came down and hit the ground, it began to explode into flames. We watched as Lt. Smalley, incredibly, came running out of the ball of fire, running as fast as he could from the open space created by the eliminated nose section. Luckily for Smalley, he was standing in the back of the plane adminstering morphine to Pullman while all this was happening, and while the front of the aircraft was being ground under. Firemen who had been alerted about the troubled aircraft immediately assisted Smalley. Krispinsky, Andrus, Pullman, and Saunders were killed instantly. They and Lt. Smalley were recommended for the Silver Star for their heroic action of attempting to save the life of Pullman at the risk of their own lives. The crew's tail turret gunner, S/Sgt Arthur L. Dejean, was awarded my squadron's first Purple Heart for the flak wounds he received on the mission. The five other crew members who bailed out of the plane as ordered by the pilot, landed safely and survived. Bashaw and Becker are currently members of the 456th Bomb Group Association.

This was an incredible indoctrination for the new crew that I was showing around, for their first day in our squadron.

Later, Sir Harold Alexander, Supreme Allied Commander in the Mediterranean, cited the Fifteenth Air Force for it effective support of the ground troops at Anzio.

March 3, 1944   Viterbo Landing Area #2 North of Rome (Alternate Target).

The group's fifth accredited mission in seven attempts was flown. I flew with Boughner on this mission. The Fifteenth Air Force wanted a maximum effort to bomb in the Budapest area this day, but weather required a change in orders to bomb in Italy.With Colonel Steed in the lead aircraft, thiry-four of our B-24s took off at 0826 hours. There were no early aircraft returns. The new orders for the 456th Group were to bomb the Viterbo Landing Area #2 north of Rome, but even that had to be aborted after our bombers flew up to the target area and couldn't see the target because it had eighty percent cloud coverage. No bombs were dropped today, and 32 Liberators brought their bombs back to our air base and landed with them. The other crews jettisoned their bombs rather than land with them.

Flak was heavy over the target, and fairly accurate. Six of our planes received flak damage. Ten enemy fighters were seen, but there was no damage from them. Two enemy fighters fired rockets at the formation at 1145 hours as the Group passed northwest of Rome. Dogfights of fighters were seen in the target area. Our P-47 escort fighters were successful at keeping the Luftwaffe from attacking our Group.

The thirty-four planes arrived safely over our base at 1229 hours and we logged 5:45 hours.

ORDER No 34

DETAILED OPERATIONS BRIEFING

1. (a) Battle Order: Date: 3 March 1944

1st Unit, 1st Box

Formation Leader: Lampley, Thomas AP 768
No. 3: Williamson AP 345   Dep Leader: Bowering, Reid 189
                    No. 4: Miller AP 501
No. 6: Rudd   AP 295   No. 5: Hillman   AP 285

2nd Box

Leader: Clark, W.D. AP 470
No. 3: Webster   AP 638   Dep Leader: Ward   AP 637
                    No. 4: Chandler AP 633
No. 6: Strombom   AP 634   No. 5: Ball   AP 595

3rd Box

Leader: Mulligan AP 290
No. 3: Scurzi   AP 214   Dep Leader: Nix   AP 233
                    No. 4: Jones AP 291
No. 6: Jackson, W.L. AP 276   No. 5: Ames   AP 212

2nd Unit, 1st Box

Leader: Sinclair, Jackson, C.Y. AP 475
No. 3: Monahan   AP 334   Dep Leader: Abernathy, Walker 275
                    No. 4: Greenstone AP 287
No. 6: Lane   AP 661   No. 5: Wallace   AP 311

2nd Box

Leader: Manlove, Hyde AP 492
No. 3: Snee   AP 477   Dep Leader: Randall   AP 486
                    No. 4: Lehner AP 199
No. 6: Boughner   AP 222   No. 5: Johnson   AP 231
                    No. 7: Little AP 304

3rd Box

Leader: Gardner   AP 292
No. 3: Key   AP 297   Dep Leader: Lassiter AP 312
                    No. 4: Richards AP 217
No. 6: Fleming   AP 309   No. 5: Passmore   AP 330

March 4, 1944   Abort at Briefing - Breslau, Germany.

I was scheduled to fly with Boughner's crew to Breslau, Germany. We never knew in advance where we were going on our missions because it was secret information, known only to a few people at group headquarters who had to do the planning. We were told about our target for the first time at the early morning Group briefings. On March 4 we walked into the briefing room very early in the morning, as usual, and all of us were shocked by the length of the yarn that we saw on the map of Europe on the wall at the end of the room. It designated the day's route for our mission. It went farther into Germany than we had ever gone before. In fact, it was so far that it was stretching the limits of endurance of the B-24, considering the extra gas we were then burning to stay in formation. The target was Breslau, Germany, seat of the German army headquarters. That target meant we had to pass through two enemy fighter belts on the way up to the target, each with hundreds of enemy fighters ready to attack us. By the time we had bombed our target and headed home, the fighters that attacked us on the way up would have refueled and they'd be ready to attack us again on the way back. It was definitely out of range for our escort fighters at that time, so we would have to do the whole thing on our own. It would be us bombers against their fighters and flak, deep into the airspace they controlled, and we would have to fight off four different fighter attacks.

Thank God, much to the delight of aircrews, after we took off and assembled our group formation, the mission was canceled due to bad weather. We logged 2 hours and 45 minutes in the air, but naturally received no mission credit. This was the group's eighth attempt to fly a mission, but only five were accredited.

We were told that as soon as the weather was good all the way to Breslau we would go there. In the meantime, we were advised to practice careful control of our aircraft's fuel consumption on our other missions in training for the Breslau mission. From that time on, every time we went into the briefing room for our early morning mission briefing, we were always afraid it would be Breslau. (As it turned out, a target near Breslau was to be my last mission, my fifty-first accredited mission, giving me my ticket home.)

March 5, 1944 No Mission.

The mission was canceled before briefing due to bad weather.

The group was officially designated Colonel Steed's "Flying Colts" on this day, so I was now a Flying Colt.

Pretty baby-blue electrically heated underwear and handsome British outerwear flying suits with fur collars were issued to us. The B-24 had woefully inadequate heating, and the temperature inside the aircraft wasn't much warmer than the minus 35 degrees centigrade that existed outside the aircraft at altitude in winter months north of the Alps. The direct-current electric suits, which we plugged into electric outlets located by our work stations in the plane, worked marginally well at first, but most crew members had chores that required considerable movement, and soon the electric wires in the suits became broken from the energetic movements required to do our jobs. Broken wires could not be repaired, and they would short out giving us mild shocks whenever we touched a metal object. I eventually disconnected my baby blue suit and used it as an extra layer of underwear for added warmth under the other heavy winter flying gear that we were using before.

Frost bite continued to be a problem, particularly among the waist gunners who had to stand by their guns in open windows near the subfreezing air and turret gunners with a continuous cold blast of air streaming over their thin Plexiglas turrets.

Those in our group with radios listened to Axis Sally and Lord Haw Haw who made regular propaganda broadcasts at 6:30 PM from Germany. They provided the best available American Broadway music, news of German victories, names of prisoners of war, and heavy propaganda that was so ridiculous that it was listened to with great amusement as a big joke. However, Sally had access to some of our secret information that led us to believe that German agents had infiltrated our units. Some German radio operators reported, on a few of our missions, the secret names of the pilots leading our formation and the secret names of our specific targets that we were on our way to bomb. These were broadcast to us while we were in the air on our way to the targets. Sally would tell us that a warm reception was waiting for us in the target area. This type of information was disconcerting to say the least.

We heard rumors that a T/Sgt in a nearby group was caught in the act of sabotaging B-24s. We heard that he was of German descent, a former member of the German-American Bund, and he was placing bombs in the nose-wheel wells of B-24's of his group so that his bombs would explode when the landing gear was retracted on takeoff. The story was that he was paid $1,000 (much money at that time) by German agents for every B-24 he destroyed. The sabotage took place in either the 454th Bomb Group located about eight miles to the west of our base, or the 459th that was about eight miles to our east. He was supposed to have been caught in the act and shot within forty-five minutes of his conviction. I do remember at least three times when we took off to assemble our 456th's formation, we saw a huge fire ball and a plume of smoke at the end of their runway. The story goes that he destroyed a quite a number of B-24s before a trap caught him. These groups lost ten planes on takeoff, during a period that the 456th Bomb Group lost none.

We all wondered what it must have felt like being a crew member in a plane at the end of the runway in that group, ready to take off, not knowing who would be next to blow up on takeoff. .

Records in the National Archives indicate that both groups, the 454th and 459th, lost planes on takeoff during a period that our Group lost none in the summer of 1944, so I suspect that one of those groups could have been the group concerned, but I couldn't find any information in the court martial records or other reports, to confirm this rumor. I did find record of a civilian who was caught and convicted of sabotaging one B-24 in a bomb group located in southern Italy.

Someone told me that military commanders, in wartime, had authority to execute spies without formal courts martial proceedings, so there may be none on record. I couldn't find anyone who had first hand information about the incident, but quite a few people had heard of the story. In the summer of 1944, security of our B-24s was suddenly tightened and twenty-four hour guard duty was ordered to be put on every one of our B-24s.

March 7, 1944   Viterbo Aircraft Landing Area #2, North of Rome.

Weather cleared enough so that our aircraft were finally able to bomb Viterbo Aircraft Landing Area #2, north of Rome, Italy. After a wake-up call at 0600 hours in their tents, breakfast, and a 0700 briefing at Group headquarters, aircrews arrived at their planes for an 0810 stations time.

Colonel Steed was in the lead plane, and he started his engines at 0820, then began to taxi to the end of the runway at 0830. He took off the runway at 0840 hours and 34 Liberators followed him at one minute intervals. After the Group formation consisting of six Boxes was completed, Colonel Steed led the Group over Stornara for a rendezous at 3,000 feet with the 454th Group. With the 456th Goup in the lead and the 454h Group echeloned up and to the right, Colonel Steed set course for Bari climbing at 250 feet per minute and 160 MPH indicated airspeed. This was necessary to gain bombing altitude before reaching the Initial Point that was so close. He turned around at Bari and headed back to Stornara so that the two groups would depart that town at 1020 hours and 10,000 feet, continuing to climb on course for the Initial Point.

DETAILED OPERATION BRIEFING

(a) Battle Order:

Date: 7 March 1944

1st Unit, 1st Box

Formation Leader: Col. STEED, Donolik   AP 768
No. 3: Bishop   AP 635   Dep Leader: Clark, R.R. Reid 595
No. 4: Zoe   AP 224
No. 6: Jackson   AP 293   No. 5: Darcasso   AP 290

2nd Box

Leader: Phillips   AP 470
No. 3: Newhouse   AP 220   Dep Leader: Haviland   AP 661
No. 4: Stromben AP 634
No. 6: Riddle   AP 633   No. 5: Wallace   AP 637

3rd Box

Leader: Miller, Ladd   AP 295
No. 3: Griffin   AP 276   Dep Leader: Desperock   AP 212
No. 4: Phifer   AP 501
No. 6: Nix   AP 233   No. 5: Hillman   AP 285

2nd Unit, 1st Box

Leader: Lampley, Tavel AP 477
No. 3: Palis   AP 217   Dep Leader: Golden, Lohnor 189
No. 4: Laszewski AP 292
No. 6: Smith   AP 275   No. 5: Feld   AP 312

2nd Box

Leader: Townsend AP 231
No. 3: Witkin   AP 486   Dep Leader: Richards   AP 489
No. 4: Gutting AP 452
No. 6: Sagert   AP 199   No. 5: Mapa   AP 311

3rd Box

Leader: Clark, W.B., Golden AP 330
No. 3: Key   AP 177   Dep Leader: Nilsson   AP 345
No. 4: Douglas AP 304
No. 6: Moyer   AP 306   No. 5: Herniban   AP 334

Three of our planes returned early without dropping bombs on the target. Two of the early returns were planes from my 746th Squadron. One 746th plane, number 489 flown by Lt. Douglas C. Richards, had superchargers on engines one and three malfunction, and one plane, number 189 flown by Lt. Albert M. Lehner, had a bad oil leak on number three engine. The other early return was from the 747th Squadron, plane number 177 flown by Lt. William Key, and it had number four engine detonating.

Fourteen P-47s gave the Group target cover. Nineteen enemy fighters were seen, but our escort fighters succeeded in keeping them from attacking our Group.

Weather enroute to the target was not ideal. In addition to fog near the mountains that covered twenty percent of the ground, there was a layer of clouds that covered sixty percent of the ground below the formation, and a layer of cirrostratus clouds at 21,000 feet above the formation. Over the target area, there was a sixty percent cumulus cloud coverage that obscured the target, with bases at 4,000 feet and tops at 8,000 feet. Visibility was 10 miles. Bombardiers were able to identify the target through breaks between clouds. The outside air temperature at 19,500 feet was minus 32 degrees centigrade.

Flak was negligible and none of our planes were damaged. Thirty-two of our 456th Group's bombers released 80 tons of fragmentation bombs at 1143 hours, with the lead ship flying at 20,000 feet and 160 MPH indicated airspeed, which was a true airspeed of 220 MPH. The bombardiers' bomb release interval setting was 300 feet. The target was completely covered with bombs and large explosions were seen in the target area after the bomb run. The explosions could have been oil tanks on the field. Seven photographs were taken of the target area by photographers on our planes.

The thirty-two planes in the formation returned safely to our base at 1341 hours. This was the groups eighth mission, and its sixth accredited mission. Combat time logged was 5:35 hours. It was another milk run that I missed.

There were many factors that determined which crews would be assigned to each mission as orders directing the mission came down to our headquarters from our 304th Bomb Wing headquarters. It was like rolling dice. When it was our turn to fly, we never knew whether our mission would be a milk run or a rough, dangerous mission. Our operations officers tried to rotate missions among crews so that there would be an equitable distribution. One factor was the in-commission status of our aircraft that determined how many crews would be needed. We didn't have pressurized cabins and ruptured eardrums were a common hazard when crews flew with bad head colds, so this condition was enough for the flight surgeon to ground a crew member until it cleared up. Our Group's medical records indicate that there were only seven groundings in a five week period caused by respiratory problems, so that wasn't a major problem.

I never had a health problem that prevented me from flying on any mission. However I did fly a few times with colds when I should have stayed on the ground, and I ruptured my right eardrum. Since I was anxious to get my missions finished, and return to the states, I never mentioned this to anyone except my friend Captain Louis A. Tripi, our squadron flight surgeon. He was an obstetrician before he entered the USAAF. He became a good friend when we were living together in the pink farm house before our airfield was completed. He was an outstanding gentleman with a wonderful attitude. I told him that I was eager to fly each mission that came up. He put some sulfa powder in my ear to kill an infection that developed in it, and he didn't ground me. He rationalized that these were emergency wartime conditions. Doctor Tripi distinguished himself with the local Italian populace by volunteering to deliver babies for the local town. Tripi was later awarded the Soldiers Medal for his performance of military duties.

I wanted to get my missions flown and return to the states as soon as possible. Axis Sally sometimes broadcast propaganda asserting that Germans were developing a secret weapon that would blast American bombers from the sky, and indeed, we kept seeing new weapons coming at us as time went on. First were pink, phosphorus antiaircraft shell bursts that we saw sprinkled through the normal ugly black flak bursts. The phosphorus was supposed to stick to our planes and set them on fire, but I never saw any that were successful. Next, proximity fuses were put on German antiaircraft shells so they would explode when they came within range of a plane, and these made them more effective. Then came rockets as new ammunition for the Luftwaffe fighters. Rockets came whistling through our formations at times, but they were not particularly effective. Next came attacks by new, sensational jet aircraft (Me-262s) but the Germans were never able to manufacture many of them, partially due to our constant bombing of their factories and fighter sweeps of their airfields. Later, rocket powered aircraft were added. We knew that the Nazi were shooting buzz bombs and V-1 rockets at England. This constant parade of new weapons gave at least some credence to Axis Sally's claims, and kept us guessing about what new weapon the treacherous and ingenious Germans would invent next to blast us out of the sky.

My own private philosophy was to fly my fifty missions as fast as I could, then return home to loved ones before such a secret super weapon, if any, was developed by the Germans. I didn't intend to make the USAAF a career after the war. I intended to leave the USAAF and finish my college training in mechanical engineering. We all had to fly fifty missions before we could return home, and it was like a roll of the dice that determined whether your name would come up on a milk run or a tough aerial battle. I knew that whether I flew my missions fast or slow, my chances for survival would be the same, except for the possibility of the new, revolutionary, secret weapon that Axis Sally talked about. My main motives for flying my missions as fast as I could were homesickness and a desire to get home to loved ones as soon as possible, poor living conditions in Italy, and a common sense of self preservation. I did succeed in beings the first pilot in our Group to finish fifty missions.

March 8, 1944 Weather Abort Enroute To Genoa Railroad Marshaling Yard, Italy.

Weather was good enough to allow thirty-four of our bombers to takeoff at 0729 hours and try to bomb the Genoa railroad marshalling yard, but bad weather did not allow the mission to be executed. Weather in the local area was too bad to allow our formation to assemble. The Group returned to our base at 0844. I flew on this mission and logged 1:30 hours. Three airplanes had returned early, before the rest of the Group's Liberators, two with gas leaks and one with its number four supercharger malfunctioning. All aircraft returned to base safely and landed with their bombs. This was the Group's tenth attempted mission, but no mission credit was given for this one. Although it wasn't a successful bombing mission it was another great learning experience for everyone involved. We were all honing our skills to greater perfection with each mission.

March 9 and 10, 1944 No Missions.

Spring rains prevented flying missions. Ground crews remained busy. The rains and lack of flying had a depressing effect on the aircrews because it gave us time to think about loved ones left back in the states. It also gave us time to think about our chances of getting fifty missions. We wrote letters home. Officers had to take their turns censoring letters written home by Group personnel. Although some of the letters were very interesting, I never liked the chore when it was my turn. Captain Chester R. Ladd has been appointed Group Operations Officer, S-3.

I took advantage of the stand-down to go see the dentist about a tooth that had been annoying me for sometime. That was an unforgettable experience! I believe the dentist was Captain Virgil C. Wanezak. His drill had to be operated mechanically by pumping his foot on a pedal for power as the equipment was not yet electrically powered. There wasn't suitable electric power on the base at that time, and the only dental tools he had available were borrowed. I believed that his original dental tool kit was laying at the bottom of Bari Harbor, a victim of the catastrophic December 1944 Luftwaffe bombing of our supplies on ships waiting to be unloaded.

As Captain Wanezak laboriously pumped a pedal that was similar to the old Singer Sewing Machine pedals that were manually operated before electricity, his slow-speed dental drill laboriously ground my tooth down to the extent that he was able to put in a temporary filling, and he told me to have the tooth refilled as soon as I returned to the states. It was a painful experience. On March 22, 1944 he received a complete Chest 60 MD with all the necessary dental tools. A tooth had to be very painful before I would think of trying that again!

To help us escape and evade capture for each mission we were issued a small survival kit to be used in case of being forced down in enemy territory. The kits contained a silk map of Europe, a fifty dollar United States Gold Certificate (well recognized by knowledgeable Europeans as exchange for gold), a small compass, small files, magnetized pencil clips that could be used as compasses, small pills that could be used to purify water, and other small items encased in a waterproof plastic pouch that we had to return after each mission. In addition, ambulances made the rounds of the aircraft scheduled on each mission before takeoff and distributed two morphine syrettes to the copilot, two to the bombardier, and one to the waist gunner. These were used to ease pain of wounded crew members when necessary, and they had to be signed for and returned to the dispensary by the bombardier after each the mission. We also had emergency first aid kits aboard the aircraft.

We were briefed by intelligence personnel about some areas that were known to be fluid, rural, safe areas where the Nazi did not have tight control, areas that we were advised to try to get to after bail out. Five specific highly classified underground resistance areas that we could make use of after bail out over enemy territory were shown to us.

In case of capture by the enemy, or internment in a neutral country, we were told that we must never indicate, inadvertently, that we were briefed to bomb a city as such. We were always briefed to bomb specific military objectives as targets in and around cities, such as manufacturing plants, oil production plants, or marshalling yards. Many of our airmen were beat up and/or killed, after they were captured in Axis countries, by citizens who believed we were bombing innocent civilians. Nazi propaganda and lies to German citizens led them to believe we were all gangsters from Chicago (as they had seen in American movies of the thirties) and that we were purposely killing innocent civilians.

On March 9, 1944 an aircraft mechanic of the 744th Squadron, Private Carmine Sirco, was killed on an Italian road off the base while he was returning to our airfield from a pass in town. He was struck by a British lorry.

March 11, 1944   Pontassieve Marshaling Yards Near Florence, And Airdrome At Iesi, Italy (Target of Opportunity).

Today was the first that weather cleared sufficiently to allow the next mission to be flown. I was selected, with Boughner's crew, to fly on this mission, and we received wake-up calls in our tents at 0615 hours. After breakfast and then a briefing at Group Headquarters starting at 0715, we arrived at our planes at 0815 hours.

Thirty-five bombers took off, starting with the lead plane at 0831 hours, to bomb the Pontassieve marshalling yards and railroad bridge near Florence, Italy, escorted by sixteen P-38s. Colonel Harmon Lampley, Jr. was in the lead aircraft, but when he aborted over the field because of a fuel leak, the deputy lead, Major Robert L. Reid, flying with 1st Lt. Arthur F. Bowering's crew from my 746th Squadron took over the lead. We were specifically briefed to be careful not to drop bombs on the valuable antique buildings and artifacts of Florence that had no military value.

Five of our Group's planes returned early without dropping their bombs on the target. One plane, Lampley's, had a gas leak, one had number three propeller governor malfunction, and three planes lost the Group formation in clouds during the initial assembly, never found it, and returned to our air base.

The mission was not very successful because atmospheric conditions caused the bomb sight of the lead aircraft of the 1st Unit of bombers to have frost develop on it. This prevented the lead bombardier from dropping his bombs on the primary target so none of the bombers of the 1st Box of the 1st Unit, a total of four aircraft that were waiting for the lead to drop its bombs, failed to drop their bombs.

ORDER No. 39

DETAILED OPERATIONS BRIEFING:

1. (a) Battle Order:　　　　　　　　　　　　Date: 11 March 1944

1st Unit, 1st Box

Formation Leader: Lumpley, Thomas AP 769
No. 3: Williamson AP 475　　　　　Dep Leader: Bowring, Reid 139
　　　　　　No. 4: Fhifer AP 275
No. 6: Budd AP 295　　　　No. 5: Millman AP 295

2nd Box

Leader: Clark, W.D. AP 470
No. 3: Lane A 481　　　Dep Leader: Ward AP 637
　　　No. 4: Wheeler A 533
No. 6: Strombom P 634　　　No. 5: Bell AP 595

3rd Box

Leader: Mulligan AP 290
No. 3: Scurzi AP 214　　　Dep Leader: Jackson AP 276
　　　No. 4: Jones AP 201
No. 6: Hix AP 203　　　No. 5: Shumacher AP 212

2nd Unit, 1st Box

Leader: Sinclair, Jackson, C.W. AP 279
No. 3: Donahon AP 334　　Dep Leaders: Abernathy, Walker
　　　No. 4: Greenstone AP 127
No. 6: J　　　No. 5: Wallace AP 211

2nd Box

Leader: Henlove, Gato AP 473
No. 3: Snee AP 477　　　Dep Leader: Kewall AP 436
　　　No. 4: Longmer AP 722
No. 6: Liddle AP 304　　　No. 5: Johnson AP 231

3rd Box

Leader: Gardner AP 292
No. 3: Key AP 297　　　Dep Leader: Lassiter AP 312
　　　No. 4: Richards AP 217
No. 6: Fleming AP 579　　　No. 5: Dinsmore AP 330

The lead aircraft of the 2nd Box had the same problem, a frosting up of its bombsight. However, the bombardier of the deputy lead plane of that 2nd Box didn't have the problem and his pilot took over the lead in time to bomb the target at the last moment.

Twenty-six bombers dropped 64.75 tons of general purpose bombs (259 bombs) at 1127 hours from 19,000 feet for the 1st Unit, and 20,000 feet for the 2nd Unit, on a magnetic heading of 339 degrees. The marshalling yards at Pontassieve and its immediate vicinity were hit by scattered bombs, but four bombardiers goofed and dropped their bombs in the environs of Florence. Some reported that they suspected a smoke screen over the marshalling yards at the primary target.

The four bombardiers of the Group's 1st Unit that couldn't drop bombs on Pontassieve dropped their bombs, 7.75 tons, on a target of opportunity on the way home, the airdrome at Iesi, Italy. They were flying at 20,000 feet. The airfield and buildings at Iesi received scattered hits.

Thus, a total of 72.5 tons of general purpose 500 pound bombs were dropped on the mission with only fair results. Seventeen photos of the targets were taken by photographers in our bombers. We encountered some inaccurate flak at four different sites enroute (Arezzo, Pescara, Sanseferrate, and near Empoli), but none of our Liberators received significant damage and no enemy fighters were encountered.

The formation of thirty Liberators arrived back over our airfield at 1306 hours and I logged 5:00 hours on the mission. I also logged my second accredited mission! It was a milk run. This was the group's eleventh mission to bomb a target, but it was only the group's seventh accredited mission because weather made four of them ineligible for credit.

Though we didn't see enemy aircraft on this mission, P-47's from the 325th Fighter Group that were escorting another bomb group mixed it up with a swarm of Luftwaffe aircraft that were beginning to contest the skies of northern Italy again. The P-47 Thunderbolts shot down nine Me-109's and one other enemy fighter while losing three of their own.

That evening was our first real spring evening with a mist on the meadows, a sallow moon and a wistful fragrance in the air. It made me homesick for home, but I knew that a return home was a long way off. I only had two missions, and forty-eight to go!

March 12, 1944   No mission.

No mission flown today because of rain.

A new power plant was installed, providing steady lights for our tents, and incidentally, power for our dentist. I should have waited a few weeks to have my tooth filled. Light bulbs were in short supply and we had to go into town to try to buy them on the market.

While walking around a neighborhood in Cerignola, looking for a store of some kind, a grubby looking, barefoot boy about ten years old tried to sell his sister as a prostitute. She was so unappealing that the thought never entered our minds, but when we asked the boy where we could buy a light bulb, he ran into his house and brought us one. He probably took it from one of the rooms in his house. We felt very sorry for his poor standard of living. The stench of sewage and garlic, and general poor health conditions that was evident in his neighborhood, and the boy in barefeet in cold winter conditions. We heard that the going price for light bulbs on the market was 200 to 300 of occupation Lira, so we paid him accordingly, with a generous tip. I felt so sorry for him that I would have given him all the cash I had, but I didn't have any spare cash.

March 13, 1944   No Mission.

It rained again.

We heard that the entire 747th Squadron came down with a severe case of the "GI's", as diarrhea was known in the Army. Needless to say, every squadron had a major review of its food handling procedures and equipment. We smelled extra strong disinfectant in the water we used to wash our aluminum mess kits from the large fifty-five gallon drums filled with soapy or germicidal water for the purpose, and there was an absence of flies around the mess tent for a while afterward.

The headquarters detachment now had about seventy Italians working for it. They were given many odd jobs ranging from police to plumbers, and they were relieving us of much manual labor. Their ages ranged from young children to men in their forties. I suspect, now, that when Axis Sally began broadcasting secret information about our missions that enemy agents were among these workers and were somehow providing her some of the information.

March 14, 1944   Snow, No Mission.

Large snowflakes covered our field today. Our Group was scheduled to bomb Sofia, Bulgaria, but weather was so poor that no missions were able to be flown from the 11th until the 15th of March.

The Group briefing room was being planned to be used as a movie theater that screened some of the latest Hollywood movies.

*March 15, 1944 Cassino, Italy

I flew on our group's shortest mission this day, to bomb the town of Cassino, Italy, a 3:15 hour round trip flight. It was so short that we tried to fly another mission in the afternoon, but the second mission was canceled. It was another milk run, but it was marred by a tragic error.

140

This mission was most notable because a few heavy bombers bombed our own troops. It was believed that a few planes from my Group may have been among them, and there was an investigation. Thank goodness, the bombardier on Boughner's crew, 2nd Lt. Clifford E. Bowdish, hit the correct target because we were flying in the 1st Unit, led by Colonel Steed, that bombed the correct target. We were flying number two position of the 2nd Box of the 1st Unit.

ORDER No 41   DETAILED OPERATIONS BRIEFING

Date: 15 March 1944

1. (a) Battle Orders

1st Unit, 1st Box

Formation Leader: Steed, Thomas   AF 187
No. 3: Lane (c)   AF 634   Dep Leader: Abernathy, Walker 635
        No. 4: Rudd (c)   AF 295
No. 6: Key   AF 172   No. 5: Leukuma   AF 595

2nd Box

Leader: Richards   AF 489
No. 3: Sagert (c)   AF 486   Dep Leader: Loughner AF 199
        No. 4: Cutting (c)   AF 222
No. 6: Yitkin   AF 477   No. 5: Meaahun   AF 334
No. 7: Beck   AF 492

3rd Box

Leader: Callan   AF 475
No. 3: Nilsson (C) AF 330   Dep Leader: Meyer   AF 309
        No. 4: Loughlse (c) AF 304
No. 6: Fayis   AF 512   No. 5: Weld   AF 217

2nd Unit, 1st Box

Leader: Longley, Jackson   AF 279
No. 3: Logowski (c)   AF 292   Capt Leader: Golden, Lehner AF 179
        No. 4: Miller (c) AF 368
No. 6: Nunimaker   AF 501   No. 5: Terral   AF 291

2nd Box

Leader: Lee (Gruber)   AF 214
No. 3: Ames (c)   AF 485   Dep Leader: Griffin AF 233
        No. 4: Demmerock (c) AF 212
No. 6: Smith   AF 279   No. 5: Tarrazzo   AF 290

3rd Box

Leader: Hairme   AF 635
No. 3: Pishon (c)   AF 287   Dep Leader: Webster AF 037
        No. 4: Phillips (c) AF 470
No. 6: Hard   AF 282   No. 5: Copeland   AF 641

Copy of the Original
458th Bomb Group Battle Order
Source: National Archives, Wash. D.C.

All bombers of the Twelfth Air Force (medium bombers) and Fifteenth Air Force (heavy bombers) were sent to bomb the small town of Cassino in an effort to help allied troops break through German lines at that point, where our Fifth Army had been stalled for months by German ground forces. Our Allied ground forces were massed to the south of Cassino ready for an attack, and the scenario was for them to follow our mass bombing of German troops positioned in the Cassino area, to their north, with a great push north to break through the lines.

All of us on Boughner's crew received a wake-up call at 0545 hours for this mission, and as usual we had a C-ration breakfast, then attended a briefing at 0645 at Group Headquarters. Colonel Steed was the leader of the Group formation, and his Liberator left our runway at 0800 hours. Thirty-five B-24s followed his plane off the runway at one minute intervals, then joined his in the air to form our standard group formation of six Boxes. Colonel Harmon Lampley Jr. was in the lead plane of the 2nd Unit.

Weather wasn't very bad enroute to the target, with only a few altocumulus clouds below us with bases at 12,000 feet and tops at 14,000, and above the formation was a high solid overcast of cirrus clouds with bases at 22,000 feet. Visibility was unlimited, and the temperature at 15,000 feet was minus 20 degrees centigrade.

Some flak was encountered on the mission at four different points of our route, at Pontecorvo, Esperia, Castel Forte, and at the target, Cassino, but it varied from moderate intensity to scattered, and inaccurate. None of our planes received reportable flak damage. We had P-38 fighter cover over the target, but no enemy fighters were seen on the mission.

Fifteenth Air Force heavy bombers pummeled the target, the small town of Casino. They reduced the town to rubble, with eleven hundred tons of bombs. Of this total,

143

53 tons of giant 1,000 pound GP bombs (106 bombs) were dropped by 18 of our 456th Bomb Group Liberators flying in the 1st Unit of our formation. They dropped from 14,000 feet at 1020 hours at 160 MPH indicated airspeed, about 220 MPH true airspeed, on an axis of attack of 290 degrees magnetic. These bombs, as revealed by three photographs taken aboard our planes, were well placed on the assigned target, the town of Cassino.

Unfortunately, seventeen planes of the 2nd Unit dropped 50.5 tons of the giant 1,000 pounders (101 bombs) on some other target from 14,000 feet on the same axis of attack and airspeed. Three photographs taken aboard these bombers revealed two strings of bombs hitting in the town of Venefro proper and the balance of the 2nd Unit's bombs were revealed to have fallen in surrounding hills around Venefro. Three of the Group's Liberators did not drop bombs due to bomb release malfunctions; and two of these brought their bombs back to our air base and the other jettisoned it bombs before returning.

The Germans were not dislodged, in spite of the heavy bombing, and they continued to hold their positions for many days after the bombing. The planned allied push north was a failure.

One possible contributing factor, accounting for this lack of progress by our ground forces after our massive bombing, could have been the fact that some bombers accidentally bombed our own troops that were waiting to the south of Cassino ready for a massed assault north as soon as the bombing was completed. A bomber group, flying ahead of our group, dropped forty of its thousand-pound bombs short of the target into Allied held areas, hitting our troops, killing 24 of them, and causing a total of 142 military and civilian casualties.

Next, ten miles away from the target, 17 heavy bombers (probably the 2nd Unit of our 456th Bomb Group formation) were suspected of dropping 101 of their thousand pound bombs by mistake on Venafro, where there was a concentration of troops and vehicles waiting for the push north. This mistake killed seventeen soldiers and it wounded seventy-nine more of our ground troops. In addition, forty civilians were killed by this erroneous bombing and one-hundred more civilians were wounded.

Nearby, at Cervaro to observe the action and watching this embarrassing event from a hill, and almost bombed themselves, were: Commander of the Fifth Army, General Mark Clark; Commander of the Allied Mediterranean Air Force, General Ira Eaker; Commander of Allied Armed Forces in Italy, Field Marshal Sir Harold Alexander; and many other important generals.

Later, General Clark attributed the error to "poor training and inadequate briefing of crews." He was entirely correct! Investigators later reported that the reason for bombing our own troops near Cassino was "poor air discipline on the part of two groups, malfunctioning bomb racks, lack of specific aiming points, and a heavy pall of smoke and dust after the first two raids."

The axis of attack that our bombers were briefed to take for our bombing of Cassino was east to west on a heading of 255 degrees magnetic from the Initial Point. This heading would have avoided flying over our troops that were massed on the ground around Venafro. However, because of a navigation error, the actual axis of attack was 290 degrees which brought our planes further south of the intended course, and over the town of Venafro where our ground forces were massed. Talking to some of our navigators afterward, they said that they were briefed to use a fork in the river south of Cassino as a check point to identify the small town to the north of the fork as Cassino, because Cassino was so small and difficult to identify from high altitude. There was a fork in a river a few miles south of Venafro that was similar to the fork in a river south of Cassino. It was not envisioned that the bombers would be coming so far south of course, over Venafro, at our early morning crew briefing and target study in Group Headquarters.

One ship from some prior bomb group had a bomb release error and it dropped its bombs accidentally on Venafro, starting a conflagration on the ground where our troops were located. Navigators of our 1st Unit of 18 bombers, led by Colonel Steed, were astute enough to note the error and that unit dropped its bombs on the correct target, Cassino.

Unfortunately, a nervous lead bombardier of our other unit of 18 planes, the 2nd Unit, saw this erroneous river fork, saw smoke coming from the previous bombing of Venafro, misread his map, dropped his bombs early on our own troops around Venafro, thinking it was Cassino. The other bombardiers of the 2nd Unit, seeing their leader drop his bombs, dropped theirs on the same erroneous target. This second unit dropped 101 of its huge thousand-pound bombs on Venafro and its surrounding hills, hitting some of our massed troops and vehicles that were waiting there for a big push. Their bombs narrowly missing our top commanders who were watching the bombing.

Of course, in hindsight, bombardiers and navigators should have thoroughly studied the maps along our flight path before taking off, but a few bombardiers evidently did not. All of us were still learning. The bombing of our ground troops and vehicles must have crippled, or at least slowed the ground forces' intended attack north. At any rate, the German Gustav Line held, and the Gustav line didn't budge as a result of the massive bombing.

Needless to say, we were no longer popular with the ground forces around Cassino after that day. That event wiped out the good reputation that we had, up to that time, with our ground troops. Heavy bombers, using similar close support bombing tactics to aid our ground troops at Anzio, who were in desperate need, were highly successful. Troops at Anzio looked upon the heavy bombers as heroes, and those at Cassino must have looked on us as bumbling bums.

The Cassino event was kept very quiet by our commanders, and I have never read much about it except in the National Archives. Either the news media never learned about it, or it was kept a secret.

The 36 planes of our Group formation returned over our airfield at 1111 hours and I logged 3 hours and 15 minutes. I also logged another, my third, accredited mission, but it was one that I wasn't proud of, even though the bombardier on my plane dropped his bombs on the proper target, Cassino.

Because this mission was so short, another mission was attempted in the afternoon of the March 15, to bomb the airfield at Aquino, Italy. Our Group bombers took off, but weather caused the mission to be aborted before reaching the target, and no bombs were dropped. I logged 2:25 hours on that second, aborted mission.

These were genuine "milk runs," but they gave us some more much needed practice at the procedures necessary to brief, get our planes ready and loaded with bombs, takeoff in proper sequence, form our group formation, navigate to the target, bomb it, return, and land all aircraft of the formation safely. As the Cassino error illustrated, we were still far from the efficient force that we were to become in a short while. The Cassino mission was the Group's eighth accredited mission, and of course the Aquino mission did not count.

March 16, 1944   Snow, No Mission.

A heavy wet snow began at dawn and continue to the afternoon. A stand-down order was given. We had more time to take care of chores around our camp, write our "V" mail letters, and to think about our loved ones left behind.

March 17, 1944   Bad Voslau Aircraft Plant And Airdrome, Vienna, Austria.

St. Patrick's day, the first that weather cleared enough to permit another mission. I didn't fly on this one.

All heavy bomber groups of the Fifteenth Air Force were scheduled to bomb aircraft component manufacturing factories, assembly installations, airdromes, and parked aircraft in the Vienna area on this day. Targets for Fifteenth Air Force heavy bombers included our target, which was the aircraft plant and parked aircraft on the Bad Voslau Airdrome (target time of 1300 hours), the Schwechat Airdrome aircraft assembly and factory installations (target time of 1305 hours), and the Fischmend Market Aircraft Components Factory (target time of 1315 hours).

Fighter escort included P-38 protection that started at Bosanski Novi, Yugoslavia to "the P-38s' prudent limit of endurance." Thunderbolt P-47s joined the bombers with air cover that started at the Initial Point, Lake Neusiedler, Austria, and continued protection to and from the target "to their prudent limit of their endurance." They did a good job because no enemy fighter attacked our Group.

Chapter 3 Composite Diaries of the Group's First Combat Operations

S-2.

ORDER NO 44

DETAILED OPERATIONS BRIEFING

Date: 17 March 1944

1. (a) Battle Order:

1st Unit, 1st Box

Formation Leader: Golden (Demelik) AP 768
No. 3: Feld (C) AP 292   Dep Leader: Abernathy (Lassiter) 31
No. 4: Fleming (C) AP 177
No. 6: Palis AP 297   No. 5: Paramore AP 330

2nd Box

Leader: Chandler AP 633
No. 3: Leukuma (C) AP 284   Dep Leader: Webster AP 634
No. 4: Rawlinson (C) AP 470
No. 6: Andrews AP 595   No. 5: Ward AP 637

3rd Box

Leader: Mulligan AP 290
No. 3: Desperock (C) AP 212   Dep Leader: Jones AP 233
No. 4: Miller (C) AP 268
No. 6: Ames AP 275   No. 5: Terrell AP 295
No. 7: Phifer AP 501

2nd Unit, 1st Box

Leader: Sinclair (Tavel) AP 279
No. 3: Snee (C) AP 477   Dep Leader: Clark (Scursi) AP 214
No. 4: Haviland (C) AP 641
No. 6: Wallace AP 283   No. 5: Napa AP 287
No. 7: Hillman AP 285

2nd Box

Leader: Gardner AP 475
No. 3: Richards (C) AP 217   Dep Leader: Moyer AP 309
No. 4: Little (C) AP 304
No. 6: Williamson AP 334   No. 5: Walker AP 635)

3rd Box

Leader: Townsend AP 231
No. 3: Bowering (C) AP 189   Dep Leader: Johnson AP 489
No. 4: Manlove (C) AP 492
No. 6: Randall AP 222   No. 5: Ensign AP 199

Copy of the Original
458th Bomb Group Battle Order
Source:NationalArchives, Wash, D.C.

149

Aircrews were awakened in their tents at 0630 hours, they had their C-ration breakfasts in a cold tent, rode in the back of six-by-six trucks up to Group Headquarters for briefing at 0740 hours, then were driven to their Liberators for a stations time of 0845. My squadron commander, Major Paul T. Golden, was in the lead aircraft for this mission. Major John R. Sinclair and my tent mate, Lt. Dave E. Tavel, flew in the lead aircraft of the 2nd Unit of the formation. Major Golden started his engines at 0855 and began taxiing to the end of the runway for a takeoff at 0905 hours. Thirty-six B-24s followed his plane off the dirt runway at one minute intervals to form our Group's six-Box formation around his plane. After our Group formation was complete, Major Golden led the Group over Stornara at 5,000 feet to rendezvous with the 454th Bomb Group.

Five of our Liberators returned to our airfield early, aborting the mission, because of mechanical malfunction. One early return, flown by Lt. Robert Ensign of my 746th Squadron, had a bad oil leak on number two engine. One B-24, flown by Lt. Charles E. Johnson of my Squadron, had number three engine run away uncontrollably. Another bomber, flown by 2nd Lt. J. J. Walker of the 745th Squadron, had two turbo superchargers become inoperative. One plane flown by Lt. Webster of the 747th squadron, had two generators and a propeller become inoperative; and a fifth bomber flown by Lt. John S. Mapa of the 747th Squadron returned because he had two superchargers become inoperative.

The 304th Wing was divided into two "Mini-Wings" for this mission: our 456th Group followed the 454th Group from Stornara at 1005 hours and 5,000 feet, climbing on course in a Mini-Wing formation; and the 459th Group led the 455th Group from Giulia at 1005 hours and 6,000 feet, climbing on course forming another Mini-Wing. The 454th Group was followed by the 456th Group flying slightly higher and to the right, and the 459th Group was followed by the 455th Group flying slightly lower and right of the 459th Group. The groups climbed enroute at 250 feet per minute rate of climb and 165 MPH indicated airspeed. The route of flight took the groups over Bosanski Novi, Yugoslavia, to the west end of Lake Balaton, Hungary, to the center of Lake Neusiedler, Austria (the Initial Point) and then to the target at Vienna.

No enemy fighters attacked the Group, probably because the weather on the ground was too poor to allow them to take off. There was a solid overcast of clouds at Vienna and its vicinity. The temperature at 19,000 feet was a very cold minus 42 degrees centigrade.

Flak was encountered at five different locations during the mission. The most intense flak was in the Vienna area where there were 300 heavy antiaircraft guns firing at our formations, and it was graded as intense, inaccurate (due to the effectiveness of our Window), with heavy guns. Moderate flak intensity was encountered at Mitski, and sparse bursts of flak were sprinkled throughout our Group formation at Wiener Neustadt, Makarsko, and Maljkovo. Thanks to the effectiveness of the "Window" that our planes dropped, only four of our Group's Liberators were damaged by flak.

Weather enroute out was clear over the Adriatic Sea with visibility 20 miles. On reaching the Yugoslavian coast it was clear with unlimited visibility. From Lake Balaton north an undercast of cumulus began to develop, and by the time the Group was within 50 miles of the Initial Point a solid undercast of clouds had developed. On reaching the target it could not be seen because the ground was completely covered by clouds.

There was a very heavy barrage of flak around Vienna, and thirty-one of our planes flew through it to drop a total of 59.55 tons of general purpose 100 pound bombs (1191 bombs) on the airdrome through the clouds on the basis of estimated time of arrival as determined by dead-reckoning navigation. Bombsights could not be used, and the results of the bombing couldn't be seen through the clouds. Bombs were dropped from 19,000 feet and an indicated airspeed of 160 MPH, a true airspeed of 222 MPH. The axis of attack was 294 degrees magnetic. The bombardiers' bomb interval release setting was 100 feet. One plane in the Group had a bomb release malfunction and did not release its bombs on the target.

Flak fire at 15th AF Liberators over Vienna, Austria.
Photo courtesy of the National Air and Space Museum, Smithsonian Institute.

15th A.F. Liberators In Flak Over Vienna, Austria

Our "Window," small strips of aluminum or lead that we dropped, confused their radar that was used to aim their guns. Enemy gunners on the ground resorted to barrage type firing with the intent of saturating the sky over the target with an intense, ugly black thick cloud of bursting shells. The massive barrage of hundreds of exploding shells over the target, that almost completely blackened the sky, looked as though a plane could not fly through it without being blasted to bits. It was very intimidating as our planes approached the target, but surprisingly, only four aircraft had slight damage from the flak.

After bombs were released, Major Golden rallied the group in a descending left turn to pass west of the town of Wiener Neustadt. From there the Group flew to Froszpetersdorf, then to a point east of Split, and directly to the base from there. The weather began to break up over western Yugoslavia on the route back, and snow could be observed covering the ground.

Thirty-two planes returned safely, reaching our airfield at 1538 hours. Flying time logged was 6 hours and 33 minutes. This was the Group's ninth accredited of the fourteen missions flown.

A bombardier from the 747th Squadron, Lt. William T. Carrington on Lt. Joeseph F. Leukuma's crew, in the plane that had his bomb rack malfunction, had to manually release his bombs at high altitude while standing on the catwalk of the bomb bay, without oxygen or a parachute, while the bomb bay doors were open and subfreezing air was swarming in on him. He did this as his plane was losing altitude because turbo superchargers on three engines of his plane were out of commission. The crew was able to return to base safely.

S/Sgt Thomas S. Delaney, radio operator on the plane of "Deuces Wild," reported that both the ball turret and the nose turret of the plane malfunctioned on the mission. Thus his plane lost the services of four guns. It was lucky that fighters didn't attack because his plane was flying the tail end position of the Group formation, one of the most vulnerable positions. He also reported that Sgt. William E. Halper, his nose turret gunner had to release a few bombs of his plane manually. Both Delaney and Halper were later assigned to my crew when I was given a crew of my own in May. Delaney is currently a member of the 456th Bomb Group Association.

March 18   Maniago Airdrome, Italy.

Today my crew was selected to fly again to bomb Maniago airdrome in Italy. When Fifteenth Air Force bombers last bombed airfields in the Udine area in the northern tip of the Adriatic, on January 30, that bombing effectively stifled the Luftwaffe in northern Italy until now. Since that time Allied Air Forces enjoyed substantial air superiority in northern Italy. The Luftwaffe gradually began to build up its strength in the area again. Luftwaffe fighter strength had reached a total combined strength of 235 planes at Aiello, Lavariano, Maniago, Osoppo, Gorsia, and the Udine airfields. The Luftwaffe was seriously challenging our control of the sky over northern Italy. In response to this challenge, to maintain air superiority there, the Fifteenth Air Force dispatched its largest task force to date with a total of 592 planes in a well coordinated attack to neutralize these airfields and to destroy the maximum number of enemy fighters in the air and on the ground.

First, three groups of P-38s, ninety-five planes, were sent on a low level strafing mission over these airfields, avoiding enemy radar, and it effectively held enemy aircraft on the ground. The P-38s also strafed railroad trains in the area. At the same time, a group of 113 B-17's made a feint toward Germany, as though they were headed to targets in the fatherland, that flushed up fighters in the Klagenfurt and Graz areas. After their feint, the B-17's turned west toward the Udine and Villaorba airfields where they dropped fragmentation bombs. Fighter escort for the B-17's downed seven ME-109's and two other types of Luftwaffe aircraft that had been scrambled to intercept them from the Klagenfurt and Graz areas.

When the B-17's finished their bombing runs on the Italian airfields, German fighters from Klagenfurt and Graz areas, that had been chasing them, began to run out of fuel, as had been planned in advance by our Fifteenth Air Force planners. These Luftwaffe fighters had to make emergency landings at the bombed airfields, or alternative fields nearby. Just as fighters from the Klagenfurt and Graz area were concentrated on the ground at Gorzia, Lavariano and Maniago fields, in addition to the normal complement of fighters that were already assigned to these fields, and on the ground, three task forces of Liberators consisting of waves of 72, 67, and 121 planes dropped a total of 32,370 fragmentation bombs on them. Only two enemy planes were able to get off the ground to intercept the B-24's. Our 456th Bomb Group Liberators were a part of this effort.

The 456th's portion of this mission, to bomb the Maniago landing field and aircraft dispersal area, amounted to a flight of thirty-four Liberators taking off at 0915 hours. Major Louis Abernathy of the 745th Squadron and Colonel James Leo Thomas Jr. of Group were leading the formation. Lt. Colonel Keneth W. Gruber and 1st Lt. Dave E. Tavel were leading the 2nd Unit of the formation. The 304th Wing's bomber groups were again divided into two separate Combat Wings, the first composed of the 459th Group leading the 454th Group which followed it flying up and to the right. These groups rendezvoused at 5,000 feet over Giulia Airfield, home of the 459th, then departed at 0900 hours climbing on course. The second Combat Wing was composed of the 455th Group followed by our 456th Group flying slightly lower and to the right, and we departed San

Giovianni Airfield, home of the 455th Group, at 0900 hours and 6,000 feet climbing on course. The climb on course was made at an indicated airspeed of 160 MPH (about 210 MPH true airspeed) and a 200 feet per minute rate of climb to our bombing altitude of 20,000. All four groups of the 304th Wing attacked the Maniago Airdrome and dispersal area with fragmentation bombs. Our programmed target time was 1100 hours, and we actually released our bombs at 1111 hours. The route of flight took our formations over Tremiti Island then to the Initial Point, San Vito Al Tagliamento to bomb Maniago Airdrome on an axis of attack of 342 degrees magnetic. We were supposed to have P-47 escort aircraft, but we never saw them. They were possibly engaged in dogfights out of our sight.

ORDER No 46

/ 18 March 1944

1. (a) Battle Order:

1st Unit, 1st Box

Formation Leader: Abernathy, Thomas AP 279
No. 3: Key (C)   AP 277.   Dep Leader: Nilsson, Clark,W.B. AP 297
                   No. 4: Andrews (C) AP 595
No. 5: Nix   AP 233   No.6: Amos   AP 768

2nd Box

Leader: Clark, W. D.   AP 470
No. 3: Lane (C)   AP 287   Dep Leader: Webster   AP 634
                   No. 4: Chandler (C) AP 633
No. 5: Mapa   AP 637   No. 6: Greenstone   AP 661

3rd Box

Leader: Miller   AP 212
No. 3: Jackson, W.L. (C) AP 285 Dep Leader: Smith   AP 275
                   No. 4: Lee (C)   AP 214
No. 5: Nunimaker   AP 501   No. 6: Barrasso   AP 290

2nd Unit, 1st Box

Leader: Gruber, Tavel   AP 475
No. 3: Walker (C)   AP 635   Dep Leader: Hyde & Bowering   AP 199
                   No. 4: Rudd (C)   AP 295
No. 5: _____ AP ____   No. 6: Passmore   AP 487

2nd Box

Leader: Richards   AP 489
No. 3: Boughner (C) AP 231   Dep Leader: Johnson   AP 189
                   No. 4: Cutting (C) AP 477
No. 5: Sagert   AP 492   No. 6: Ensign   AP 222

3rd Box

Leader: Callan   AP 217
No. 3: Monahan (C) AP 334   Dep Leader: Lassewski   AP 292
                   No. 4: Little (C)   AP 304
No. 5: Lassiter   AP 312   No. 6: Fleming   AP 309

Four of our planes returned early, one with an engine inoperative, one had a flight control problem, one had a gas leak, and another had a carburetor that became inoperative on reaching high altitude. Waist gunners, looking out of the B-24s from their open windows in the rear, and other gunners were valuable visual aids to the crew because they could see oil and gasoline leaks, loose cowling, and many other such discrepancies that other members of the crew could not see. They were able to detect many dangerous conditions for the crew.

The bombing formation used today was an unusual formation with all Boxes of each group spread out abreast with 18 bombers across (six Boxes across). At the I.P. the Boxes of the 2nd Unit positioned themselves abreast of the Boxes of the 1st Unit, with elements of the 2nd Unit echeloned right and left, unbalanced to the right.

Weather to the target was clear, visibility 10 miles, moderately hazy. Over the target a one-tenth coverage with cumulus clouds developed below the bomber formation. The outside air temperature at 19,500 feet was minus 26 degrees centigrade.

Flak was encountered near the target area, and it varied from intense, barrage type at Aviano to moderate at Udine and Venice, and scattered at Pola Auk and Latisano. No reportable damage to our bombers was recorded. All of the flak was inaccurate because of the window our bombers dropped to confuse the ground gunners' radar.

A feeble series of fighter attacks came, with 2 Me-109s, yellow nose types with gray tails, attacking from 9 o'clock high and breaking off at 6 o'clock low. Another came in from 3 o'clock high, and broke off at six o'clock low. Two FW-190s attacked us northwest of the target from 7 o'clock high, then broke off, and one FW-190 attacked at Conegliano from 5 o'clock level, then broke off down under. All fighters only made one pass. There was no reportable damage to our bombers due to enemy fighter fire.

159

Thirty of our B-24s dropped 34.98 tons of fragmentation bombs on the target (583 bombs) at 1111 hours, on an axis of attack of 342 degrees magnetic. The 1st Unit consisting of fifteen bombers, bombed from an altitude of 20,000 feet and the 2nd Unit of fifteen planes dropped from 18,000 feet. We flew at an indicated airspeed of 160 MPH, which was a true airspeed of about 224 MPH. Results were classified as good after analysts reviewed the strike photographs. Four bombers in the formation could not release their bombs because of release malfunctions and they returned their bombs to our air base. Fifty photographs were taken of the target by our photographers. The south aircraft dispersal area of the target was hit with a very good coverage of bombs.

The group returned to the base at 1318 hours and I logged 5:15 hours on the semi-milk run. All planes returned to base safely, none with reportable damage. This was the Group's tenth accredited mission in fifteen attempts and my fourth credited mission. I only had forty-six to go!

Although a milk run, it provided more needed formation flying practice and confidence in preparation for the big leagues, our tougher strategic targets in the underbelly of Europe that were to come later. Our formations were beginning to look much better and all, aircrews as well as ground support crews, were learning to do their jobs much better. We were developing into a more effective operating team.

Overall results, for all groups of the Fifteenth Air Force on the mission of March 18, were estimated by analysts to be a total of 162 enemy planes destroyed and another ten probably destroyed. Analysis of strike photos indicated that 106 enemy planes were destroyed on the ground, bombers claimed 23-7-9 in the air, and fighters claimed 33-3-3 in the air.

As we learned after the war, the number of pilots lost were more important than the number of planes lost. However, this mission restored our air superiority in northern

Italy. On this mission, a total of fifty-six enemy fighters and pilots were shot down in the air, with another 10 probables. There is no way of telling how many of these pilots were killed or wounded, nor how many pilots were casualties on the ground from our bombing. However, it certainly must have been a severe blow to their morale! This well designed mission involved 406 of our bombers and 186 fighters, the largest task force launched by the Fifteenth Air Force up to that time. A total of eleven Fifteenth Air Force planes were lost in this great showdown for air superiority over northern Italy, seven bombers, two P-47's, and two P-38's were shot down. This was an aggressive strike at the Luftwaffe. The Fifteenth was gradually coming of age, although this was only half the size of task forces the Fifteenth would be able to assemble for strikes a few months later when more planes arrived in Italy from the States.

What we in the air, on the mission didn't know, was that General Nathan Twining and some of his staff members had visited our 456th Bomb Group Headquarters at noon causing quite a flurry of activity. Offices were swept, grounds policed, and some even found clean trousers to put on. Thank goodness we missed it. I never learned the purpose of his visit, but it may have had something to do with the March 15 bombing of our own troops on the Cassino mission..

General Twining later sent a message to all units that participated in this raid of March 18 in the Udine, stating that "......strike photos show 106 enemy aircraft were destroyed on the ground (in lieu of the original estimated 56 on the ground), the most excellent bombing performance carried out by all units," and that "such losses to the enemy's already diminishing air force are invaluable to the success of our efforts."

March 19, 1944   Klagenfurt, Austria (Alternate Target).

Sunday and another bright spring day. My crew was passed over to fly on the Group's mission to bomb Steyr, Austria. Four of our bombers returned early, one with faulty controls, one with a gas leak on number two engine, one with an engine throwing oil and the three other engines backfiring, and one had to feather an engine in the traffic pattern after takeoff. This one turned out to be the toughest missions to date.

An alternate target, the airdrome at Klagenfurt, Austria had to be bombed instead of the primary target because of bad weather at Steyr. Our Group saw its P-38 escort fighters dogfighting with enemy Me-109s as it approached the target. Twenty-four enemy Me-109s succeeded in getting by our escort fighters, and they attacked our Group formation. Besides firing the usual 20mm cannon and machine guns at the Group, some fired rockets. Gunners on our Group's bombers claimed six enemy fighters shot down. S/Sgts Thomas S. Delaney and Carl Ezuk of my 746th Squadron flying in "Lassie Come Home," shot down one Me-109. Delaney reported seeing his tracer bullets go into the plane, then watched it go into a dive, never pulling out until it hit the ground and exploded. We lost one bomber to fighters over the target area, and four parachutes were seen to come from the plane. Delaney and Ezuk are both current members of the 456th Bomb Group Association.

Thirty of the 456th's Liberators dropped 72.5 tons of 500 pound general purpose and incendiary bombs on the target with fair results. Flying time for the mission was 5 hours and 50 minutes.

The plane shot down was a 745 Squadron plane, "The Paper Doll" flown by Lt. Edwin L. Feld's crew. It was hit by enemy fighter fire and seen to catch fire then explode in the target area. Six crewmen were killed and four successfully bailed out, captured, and put in prisoner of war camps. Those killed were the pilot, 2nd Lt. Feld; the navigator, 2nd Lt. Morris Turitz; nose turret gunner, S/Sgt Archie L. Rich; upper turret gunner, S/Sgt Reinaldo C. Garza; ball turret gunner, S/Sgt Albert W. Wilson; and tail turret gunner, S/Sgt William Lemanski. The four survivors were 2nd Lt. George O. Crawford, bombardier, and the copilot, 2nd Lt. Burt L. Talcott; T/Sgt John Exarhakos, radio operator; and S/Sgt Milton D. Plourde, engineer. Crawford and Talcott are currently members of the 456th Bomb Group Association.

One crew commanded by Lt. Edward L. Meyer distinguished themselves by electing to bring their aircraft back home, rather than play it safe and bail out, when their plane's hydraulic system had been shot out, fuel was leaking from a wing tank, and sparks and flames were seen in various places of the ship. Due to their valiant efforts, the entire crew and bomber were able to return to base and land safely.

The total Fifteenth Air Force effort for the day of March 19 was 234 bombers bombing the alternate Klagenfurt airdrome, and 76 B-24's bombing Graz. A total of 772 tons of bombs were dropped. For the day, the Fifteenth Air Force lost seventeen Liberators. Two Liberators were lost at Klagenfurt, twelve Liberators were lost at Graz, from enemy fighter attacks, and two were lost to flak. Another two Liberators were lost in a collision that day.

March 22, 1944   Bologna and Rimini, Italy.

Today was the first that weather allowed another mission be flown, and I flew as copilot on Boughner's crew to bomb the railroad marshaling yards at two cities, Rimini and Bologna, Italy. Thirty-three bombers took off but seven planes returned early because of malfunctions: one had a landing gear that would not retract, one had a runaway propeller, one had an oxygen leak, and four had turbo supercharger malfunctions on one or more engines.

Twenty-six bombers succeeded in dropping 67.5 tons of general purpose 500 pound bombs on both targets with good results. We had a total of twenty fighters as escort, P-38s and P-47s, and they were successful at keeping the enemy aircraft away from us. Flak was heavy and accurate over Bologna, and only light at Rimini. A few of our planes had flak damage. Flying time was 5 hours and 55 minutes and all aircraft returned to base safely. This was my fifth accredited mission and the group's twelfth accredited mission of seventeen missions flown in Italy.

As an example of the accuracy of our bombing, a typical result was the bombing at Rimini that was rated as good. Some missions had better accuracy, but some were not so accurate. Photo interpreters analyzed results of our bombing as having sixty-five percent of our bombs on the target, fifteen percent as inaccurate, and twenty percent could not be observed from the photographs.

March 23, 1944   Weather Abort, Steyr, Austria.

After another early morning wake-up, we attempted to bomb Steyr again, but we were recalled due to bad weather after we were airborne and on our way. I flew on that one and logged 1:10 hours, but no mission credit.

*March 24, 1944   Rimini Marshaling Yards, Italy.

My crew was scheduled to fly with the Group, the second day in succession, when the railroad marshalling yards at Rimini, Italy were hit again. My crew missed a true milk run, because we had to abort the mission fifteen minutes after we joined the group formation. We couldn't get the landing gear to stay up. My crew logged 2:00 hours, but naturally received no credit for the mission.

Thirty-seven of our bombers took off for the mission at 0800, but seven aircraft returned early, including our plane. The six other planes that returned early had these malfunctions: two aircraft had propeller governors malfunction, one plane had two engine oil leaks, one had a turbo supercharger malfunction, and one had the plane's interphone malfunction. Only twenty-nine of our bombers dropped 69.25 tons of general purpose 500 pound bombs on the target at 1207 hours from an altitude of 20,000 feet for the first unit and 18,000 feet for the second unit, hitting the target and part of the town. One aircraft had a bomb release problem at the target and didn't drop its bombs. No fighter escort accompanied the bombers, no enemy fighters were seen, flak was light and inaccurate, and movement through this railroad choke point was severely disrupted as a result of the bombing. None of our bombers were damaged by flak, and our group formation returned to base at 1341 hours. Flying time was recorded as 5:50 hours, and there were no aircraft losses. This was the Group's 13th accredited mission of the 19 missions flown in Italy.

March 25, 1944   Abort At Briefing for Milan, Italy.

After another early morning wake-up, we had a briefing to bomb marshalling yards in Milan, Italy. It was canceled during briefing when news arrived from higher headquarters that reconnaissance planes reported bad weather. The movie screen was lowered in the briefing room for an early morning showing of the movie "What A Woman" with Rosalind Russell.

In the evening, some went to the theater in Cerignola to hear the San Carlos Opera company present La Tosca.

**March 26, 1944 Airfield at Maniago, Italy (Alternate Target)*

Boughner's crew, with me as copilot, was selected to fly with the group to bomb Steyr, Austria. An impenetrable wall of clouds over the Alps caused the group to bomb its secondary target, the airdrome and aircraft dispersal area at Maniago, Italy. Nineteen enemy aircraft attacked our Group formation, and our gunners claimed two Me-109s destroyed, and one Me-109 and one FW-190 as probables.

Thirty-four bombers took off at one minute intervals, starting at 0810 hours, with my squadron commander, Major Paul T. Golden, in the lead ship of the 1st Unit and my tent mate, 1st Lt. Dave E. Tavel in the lead ship of the 2nd Unit.

Seven bombers aborted the mission in flight, and returned to our base prior to bombing. Two early returns happened because the pilots became ill, and another returned because a heating suit's electric circuit shorted. Two aircraft had engine problems because of supercharger malfunctions. One bomber had three generators go out of operation, and one Liberator, number 287 piloted by Lt. Hilbert I.Greenstone of the 747th Squadron, returned because of ear problems of his copilot, Lt. Merle H. Ross. Ross is a member of the 456th Bomb Group Association.

The route of flight took the Group formation from our air base to Tremiti Island, to Biseve Island, to Zirje Island, to the Initial Point (4522N/1510E), to the target on an axis of attack of 230 degrees magnetic. Weather was good enroute, with some scattered cumulus clouds below the formation and some high cirrus above it. The target area cleared, so that there were only four-tenths of cirrus above the formation with bases at 22,000 feet. Visibility was 10 miles in heavy haze, and the temperature at 18,000 feet was minus 25 degrees centigrade.

1. (a) Battle Order.   Date: 26 March 1944 736
   (Line Up)

1st Unit, 1st Box

Formation Leader: Golden, (Thomas) AP 763
No. 3: Smith (C)   AP 275   Dep Leader: Sinclair, (Mulligan) 279
                No. 4: Jones (C)   AP 281
No. 6: Powering   AP 187   No. 5: Johnson   AP 492

2nd Box

           Leader: Lee   AP 214
No. 3: Hillman (C) AP 285   Dep Leader: Terrell   AP 276
           No. 4: Rudd (C)   AP 295
No. 6: Desperock AP 212   No. 5: Barrasso   AP 233

3rd Box

          (Leader: Andrews   AP 284
No. 3: Riddle (C) AP 283   Dep Leader: Wallace   AP 638
           No. 4: Haviland (C) AP 470
No. 6: Ward   AP 595   No. 5: Mapa   AP 634
          No. 7: Greenstone   AP 257

2nd Unit, 1st Box

         Leader: Tavol, (Christian) AP 475
No. 3: Fleming (C) AP 217   Dep Leader: Miller   AP 268
           No. 4: Callin (C)   AP 312
No. 6: Pitkin   AP 472   No. 5: Passmore   AP 635
           No. 7: Fenhouse   AP 772

2nd Box

         Leader: Richards   AP 489
No. 3: Boughner (C) AP 199   Dep Leader: Sargent AP 480
           No. 4: Cutting (C) AP 442
No. 6: Snee   AP 231   No. 5: Randall   AP 436

3rd Box

         Leader: Douglas   AP 345
No. 3: Williamson (C) AP 487   Dep Leader: Meyer   AP 177
           No. 4: Laszowski (C) AP 207
No. 6: Little   AP 304   No. 5: Key   AP 334
           No. 7: Beck   AP 222

Only eight P-47s provided cover for us, and this was not sufficient to prevent nineteen enemy fighters from attacking our Group on the way to the target. First, four Ju-88s attacked our formation about seventeen minutes before we dropped our bombs. They attacked from the 6 o'clock position, then made a split "S" maneuver to escape. Two minutes later, five Me-109s attacked singly from the 4 to 8 o'clock positions, level, making several very aggressive passes. Near the target, four FW-190s attacked, making several passes in pairs from the 5, 6, and 7 o'clock positions, until we entered the flak cloud at the target. They were unwilling to enter their own flak at the target. Two of our planes were damaged from enemy aircraft fire. Flak was encountered at Fiume, Postumia, Trieste, and 20 miles east of Maniago. The flak was scattered and inaccurate, and none of our B-24s were damaged by it. Our gunners claimed two Me-109s shot down and one Me-109 and one FW-190 probably shot down.

Twenty-seven bombers of our formation were left to fly over the target. Twenty-six of these Liberators dropped 67.25 tons of M-17 incendiary bombs (269 clusters of 500 pounds each) on the secondary target at 1217 hours from an altitude of 20,000 feet for the 1st Unit and 18,000 feet for the 2nd Unit. The indicated airspeed was 160 MPH and the true airspeed was 219 MPH. The axis of attack was 230 degrees magnetic. Our bombs for this mission had nose fuse time delays of 34 seconds. One bomber in our formation had a bomb rack malfunction, could not release its bombs on the target, and jettisoned them into the Adriatic. Twenty-five photos were taken of the target area, and bombing results were later graded as poor. Although some bombs fell on the target, bomb falls were observed in fields west and north of the target.

Many of us had machine gun and cannon holes in our planes, more work for our hard working ground crews to patch up. Lt. George H. Gutting Jr.'s plane, of my 746th Squadron, had two huge cannon holes blasted near its tail. It was amazing that he was able to bring the crippled plane home.

Our Group formation of 27 planes returned to our base at 1431 hours, and I logged a combat flight time of 6:30 hours when we were on the ground. This was my sixth accredited mission, and the Group's fourteenth accredited mission of twenty missions flown in Italy.

I was astonished by the efficient and professional, fast job our ground crews did to get the our planes back in commission and ready for the next mission. Our ground crews swarmed on the bombers as soon as they were on the ground. We had no hangars for servicing the planes and they spent many hours working in very cold weather and throughout darkness of the night, outside, in very crude work conditions.

Some of our planes were so patched up that I'm sure that the extra drag induced by the many protruding patches on them increased the fuel consumption and reduced the available airspeed for a given throttle setting. We knew that planes with the olive green paint were about seven MPH slower because of the added drag induced by the paint, than new unpainted beautiful silver B-24's we later received as replacement aircraft.

The Russian Army has crossed the Dneister River and it was less than 200 miles from the oil fields of Rumania. The situation for the Germans is getting more desperate in the Balkans.

March 27, 1944   No Mission.

Weather was not good enough at any of our targets for a mission.

March 28, 1944 Verona East Marshaling Yards, Italy.

It wasn't my crew's turn to fly with the Group on this day. The mission bombed the Verona East Railroad Marshaling Yards in Italy. This rail center is the most important yard in Italy because it is the terminus of the vital Brenner pass railroad supply line running from Germany to Italy, Greece, Yugoslavia, and the vital Orient Express Line that supports German troops in the eastern front that were fighting Russians. Verona handles all of the Brenner Pass traffic. German lines of communication necessary to support troops fighting Russians in the eastern front were becoming a high priority because the Russian Army had the German Army in disarray.

There are two marshaling yards in Verona, the Main and Eastern marshaling yards. The Main yard was destroyed on a previous bombing. The 456th Bomb Group's target on this day's mission was the Eastern yard that carried a stock of 600 railroad cars. Our bombing halted rail traffic through this critical railroad choke point, a center for distributing German supplies, for many days afterward.

After a 0615 wake-up call, the crews had breakfast then attended a briefing at Group Headquarters at 0715. Aircraft stations time was 0830 hours, the lead aircraft started to taxi to the end of the runway at 0840, then took off at 0850 hours. Thirty-seven Liberators followed his off the dirt runway at one minute intervals.

There were four early returning B-24s, one because of a gasoline leak, one had both electric inverters malfunction, one had number one engine malfunction, and one had a propeller governor malfunction. In another major malfunction, eleven of the thirty four remaining B-24s in the formation that reached the target did not drop their bombs on the target. Of the eleven bomb release malfunctions at the target, four bombers had malfunctioning bomb racks that prevented bomb release, one had bomb bay doors that would not open, and the other six did not release their bombs at the target because their leader did not drop his bombs due to a bomb release malfunction. The other five bombers in that leader's Box did not release on the target because they did not see their leader release his bombs. All eleven bombers returned their bombs to our air base.

Our group was escorted by twenty-five P-38s enroute and P-47s provided coverage in the target area after the P-38s had to depart the area because of low fuel. Only two enemy aircraft succeeded in attacking our Group. One FW-190 attacked near the I.P. from the 11 0'clock high position, then dove under our formation and departed in the 5 o'clock position. One other Me-109 attacked during the formation's flight from the Initial Point to the target, coming from the 5 o'clock low position, then peeled away to the left of the formation. None of our planes reported damage from enemy aircraft and our gunners did not claim any fighters shot down. Seventeen of our planes were damaged by flak.

Weather enroute to the target area was fair, with six to seven-tenths coverage by stratocumulus clouds below the formation with their tops at 5500 feet. At the target area the stratocumulus cloud coverage reduced to three-tenths, tops at 7,000 feet, and the visibility was good. The temperature at 23,000 feet was minus 35 degrees centigrade.

Flak was intense, accurate, and heavy guns at Verona, evidently a heavily defended target. This was the first time our Group saw two different types of flak, one gray-white in color and the other the regular black type. The white bursts seemed louder and more effective, and they were probably from 105mm antiaircraft guns instead of the usual 88mm guns. No bombers were lost, but seventeen were damaged from flak. Ten of our bombers had severe damage from flak and seven had slight flak damage for our hard working ground maintenance crews to repair.

With the early returns and the planes that did not drop their bombs on the target due to malfunctions, only twenty-three of our bombers dropped their bombs at 1228 hours from an altitude of 24,000 feet, for the 1st Unit, and 22,000 feet for the 2nd Unit, on an axis of attack of 311 degrees magnetic. A total of 54 tons of general purpose 500 pound bombs (216 bombs) were dropped on the Verona East railroad marshalling yards at an indicated airspeed of 160 MPH, a true airspeed of 230 MPH. The target was well covered with bombs, but there were scattered bomb falls south and southeast of the target. Results were graded as fair after analysis of the twenty-eight photos taken by our photographers of the target area.

Second Lieutenant Paul F. Johnson, a pilot of my 746th Squadron, had his windshield blasted out by a flak burst, and he had to fly home in subfreezing wind blasts.

With seventeen Liberators damaged, the Group returned to our base at 1428 hours and logged 5 hours and 50 minutes combat flying time. There were many holes and damage for ground crews to repair. It was the Group's fifteenth accredited mission of the twenty-one missions flown in Italy.

On this day, March 28, the Fifteenth Air Force bombers dropped a total of 1,061 tons of bombs, mainly against enemy communications. This was the Fifteenth Air Force's first 1,000 ton day, marking a milestone in its continued growth, as more bomb groups became operational in Italy.

There was a general (General Edwards) visiting from higher headquarters, investigating the bombing of our own troops at Cassino on March 15. Lt. Col. Harmon Lampley Jr. was relieved of duty, and he has left the Group.

March 29, 1944 Marshaling Yards At Milan, Italy.

Today I earned my seventh accredited mission. We flew in the number three position of the 1st Box of the 1st Unit of the formation. We bombed the railroad marshalling yards at

Milan Lambrate-Serriate, Italy which was loaded with 5,000 pieces of railroad rolling stock. Although we were fired upon by antiaircraft guns enroute, at Ancone and Pesaro, it was scattered and inaccurate, and none of our planes had reportable damage. Thus, it was a milk run!

Thirty-six of our bombers took off for the mission. Major Paul Golden was in the lead ship, taking off at 0835 hours with the rest of the bombers following at 45 second intervals. Two of our bombers aborted their mission and returned early because of supercharger malfunctions.

We were escorted by twenty-five P-38s from landfall to the target area, then they left us because of low fuel. In the target area P-47s were waiting to cover us. No fighters attacked us and the flak was scattered and inaccurate. None of our planes reported damage. The weather was good, with thirty miles visibility and only two-tenths coverage by cumulus clouds below the formation to obstruct bombardiers' synchronization of their bombsights on the target. There was four-tenths coverage above us with cirrus clouds that didn't bother us.

After the two aircraft aborts, there were thirty-four Liberators left in our formation to fly over the target, and we dropped 84.5 tons of 500 pound general purpose bombs (337 bombs) at 1224 hours from an altitude of 21,000 feet for the 1st Unit and 19,000 feet for the 2nd Unit of the formation. One Liberator in the formation had three of its 500 pound bombs hang up in the bomb bay due to a bomb rack malfunction, and the bombs were returned to our air base.

ORDER NO. 69

<u>BATTLE ORDER</u>

DATE: 29 March 1944

<u>1st Unit: 1st Box</u>

Formation Leader: Golden, Thomas   AP 475
No. 3: Smith (C)   AP 275   Dep Leader: Abernathy, Meyer AP 345
                          No. 4: Griffin (C)   AP 214
No. 6: Terrell   AP 295   No. 5 : Jackson, W.L.   AP 233

<u>2nd Box</u>

No. 3: Ensign (C)   AP 486   Leader: Manlove   AP 492
                                  Dep Leader: Lehner   AP 199
                         No. 4: Richards, D.C. (C) AP 231
No. 6: Sagert   AP 480   No. 5: Johnson   AP 839
                         No. 7: Snee   AP 853

<u>3rd Box</u>

                     Leader: Callan   AP 217
No. 3: Laszowski (C) AP 749   Dep Leader: Douglass   AP 304
                         No. 4: Fleming (C)   AP 292
No. 6: Walker   AP 635   No. 5: Passmore   AP 312
                         No. 7: Palis   AP 487

<u>2nd Unit, 1st Box</u>

                              Jackson, C.Y.
                     Leader: Christianson,/   AP 279
No. 3: Boughner (C) AP 477   Dep Leader: Bowering   AP 189
                         No. 4: Greenstone (C) AP 661
No. 6: Wallace   AP 287   No. 5: Riddle   AP 633

<u>2nd Box</u>

                     Leader: Miller   AP 268
No. 3: Nunimaker (C) AP 501   Dep Leader: Jones   AP 291
                         No. 4: Lee (C)   AP 072
No. 6: Lambert   AP 276   No. 5: Hillman   AP 285
                         No. 7: Bock   AP 222

<u>3rd Box</u>

                     Leader: Clark, W.D.   AP 470
No. 3: Lane (C)   AP 638   Dep Leader: Andrews   AP 284
                         No. 4: Newhouse (C)   AP 283
No. 6: Loukuma   AP 634   No. 5: Van Leeuwen   AP 595

The railroad choke point, repair shops, the station and main area of the marshalling yard were thoroughly covered with bombs. Explosions were seen in the yards coming from rail cars that were evidently ammunition carriers, and a factory just north of the marshalling yards blew up. The raid destroyed thousands of pieces of railroad rolling stock. Analysis of the eighteen photos taken by our photographers indicated fair results.

Our thirty-four B-24s returned to Stornara at 1435 hours, and I logged 6:10 hours. This was the group's sixteenth credited mission of twenty-two missions flown in Italy. It was another milk run.

March 30, 1944   Industrial Center Of Sofia, Bulgaria.

I was able to fly again, for the second day in a row, to earn my eighth accredited mission. The target was the Industrial Center of Sofia, Bulgaria. This mission was made very bad by weather enroute and at the target. Only four Liberators of the thirty-nine launched on the mission were able to drop bombs on the target, and twenty-two of the Group's planes were riddled by flak. Six crewmen were injured by flak bursts.

We received wake-up calls in our tents at 0500 hours, had our C-ration breakfasts, then attended briefing up on the hill at 0615. Stations time at our aircraft was 0725, start engines time for the 1st Box of the 1st Unit was 0735, and the lead aircraft flown by Major John R. Sinclair took off at 0745 hours. Thirty-eight of our Liberators followed his, staggering off the dirt runway at 45 second intervals. The Group formation departed Giulia Air Base climbing at 250 feet per minute rate of climb and 160 MPH indicated airspeed, about 210 MPH true airspeed.

Three planes aborted the mission because of mechanical malfunctions. Two of these aircraft, one piloted by 1st Lt. Emil S.

BATTLE ORDER

No. 71

Date: 30 March 1944

1st Unit: 1st Box

Formation Leader: Sinclair(Demclik) AP 638
No. 3: Rudd (C) AP 275   Dep Loader: Golden   AP 477
                      No. 4: Townsend (C) AP 231
No. 6: Ensign   AP 486   No. 5: Desperock   AP 285
                      No. 7: Nunimaker   AP 268

2nd Box

Leader: Mulligan   AP 072
No. 3: Phifer(C) AP 501   Dep Leader: Lambert   AP 276
                      No. 4: Lee (C)   AP 799
No. 6: Mix   AP 233   No. 5: Amos   AP 214
                      No. 7: Barrasso   AP 290

3rd Box

   (C)   Leader: Clark, W. D.AP 470
No. 3: Strombum AP 634   Dep Leader: Chandler   AP 633
                      No. 4: Andrews (C) AP 772
No. 6: Leukuma AP 284   No. 5: Haviland   AP 661

2nd Unit: 1st Box

Leader: Reid(Taval) AP 499
No. 3: Bishop (C)AP 595   Dep Leader: Clark, MB(Nilsson) 297
                      No. 4: Phillips (C) AP 283
No. 6: Wallace AP 297   No. 5: Passmore   AP 635

2nd Box

Leader: Richards   AP 492
No. 3: Beck (C) AP 222   Dep Leader: Sanort   AP 480
                      No. 4: Cutting (C) AP 839
No. 6: Lehner   AP 199   No. 5: Boughner   AP 853
                      No. 7: Bowering   AP 189

3rd Box

   (C)   Leader: Gardner   AP 345
No. 3: Lasacwaki AP 749   Dep Leader: Monahan   AP 183
                      No. 4: Grimm (C) AP 487
No. 6: Lassitter AP 312   No. 5: Key   AP 292
                      No. 7: Little   AP 304

Laszewski of the 745th squadron, had number two supercharger become inoperative after forty-five minutes and he returned to base. Lt. Albert M. Lehner of my 746th Squadron returned after an hour and fifteen minutes enroute, also because of supercharger trouble. Both of these men are currently members of the 456th Bomb Group Association. A third plane also had engine trouble when the bearing of number four engine sheared just before reaching the bombing area.

We had P-38 escort for fifteen minutes in the target area, starting at 0910 hours, but no fighters were seen. This was probably because the weather was too bad for enemy fighters to take off and fly, and then find their bases again through the heavy weather conditions.

It was a messy mission because bad weather made problems for the entire mission. First, pilots had difficulty remaining in formation because cloud formations appeared on the Group's course. We had to fly around these clouds and in some cases the formation had no alternative but to fly through them enroute to the target. The formation had to fly through a weather front in Yugoslavia enroute to the target. There was a solid undercast of cumulus clouds with bases at 8,000 feet and tops at 12,000 feet over the mountains of Yugoslavia, and we flew under a solid overcast of cirrus clouds that had bottoms above us at 23,000 feet.

Navigators found it very difficult to keep track of our location because the leader had to keep changing course to avoid clouds, and navigators could not see the ground or the sun much of the time. Navigators had to do dead-reckoning navigation between the cloud formations. Because pilots had to continually change course to avoid clouds, it was a navigator's nightmare keeping track of the time and distance that a pilot flew on each aircraft heading, a necessary task for accurate dead reckoning navigation. Once the target area was found, the weather at the target was not too bad, with thirty to forty percent cloud coverage over the mountains, clear in the valleys, and visibility at the target of 20 miles. The temperature at 23,000 feet was minus 29 degrees centigrade.

Flak was encountered at twenty-one different locations enroute. Most of it, at fourteen locations, flak was of moderate intensity and accurate, fired from heavy guns. Four locations had an intense density of flak bursts, accurate firing, and from heavy guns. Germans were moving flak guns on railroad cars to position them along our normal flight paths in the area. They were tracking our formations with radar. The target, Sophia, had moderate, accurate, and heavy flak.

Twenty-two of our Liberators had flak damage, and six crew members were wounded. Lt. Dave E. Tavel's nose gunner, Sgt. Gordan H. Cotting of my 746th Squadron, received a serious hit in the ankle and awarded the Purple Heart. Others hit by flak on the mission and awarded Purple Hearts included an engineer hit in the leg, a tail turret gunner hit on the head, a bombardier hit on the left thigh, a copilot hit on the neck, and a navigator hit on the face and hand. A lucky crew member was Lt. Harold Dyer because a piece of flak went between his flak suit and his clothing and hit his belt buckle, preventing serious injury.

Only four aircraft were able to find and bomb the target. The rest never found the target. Four bombardiers found the target through breaks in the clouds and successfully dropped bombs at 1110 hours on the primary target from 21,000 feet on an axis of attack of 150 degrees magnetic. They dropped 10.25 tons of 500 pound general purpose bombs (36 bombs) with fair results. Crew members reported fires in the target area after our bombing and our planes took nine pictures of it.

One of our Group's bombers found an alternate target, Cara Lakatnik, and dropped five of its 500 pound bombs on it. It returned to Stornara with the rest of its bombs.

The rest of the Group's planes had varying reasons why they did not drop on the primary target. As noted above, three planes returned for mechanical problems before reaching the target. The rest of the aircraft could not find the target because of poor weather conditions enroute or at the target. Most of these returned to our base with their bombs on board.

Landing with bombs on board was acceptable if the aircraft was not subject to enemy inflicted damage. However, as we later decided, if the plane had been damaged from flak or fighters, it was not a good idea to risk landing with bombs aboard. Damaged aircraft could make the landing hazardous, not only to the crew in the landing aircraft, but to all others on the airfield. In such cases, bombs were usually jettisoned over the water.

Lt. Boughner's plane, in which I was flying as copilot, had considerable flak damage from the mission along with twenty-one other damaged planes in our Group. Thirty-six planes returned to our airfield by 1325 hours, and I logged 6:40 hours of combat time. This was my eighth accredited mission and the group's seventeenth accredited one of twenty-three missions flown in Italy.

On our longer missions, such as this one, we were given a "box lunch," which was a small box of dry "K" rations. The box was weather and waterproof, difficult to open, and it included a small piece of cheese, a chocolate bar, some small hard crackers, salt and pepper, a very small can of meat that required a can opener to open, and other things. This was before the era of quick-opening cans as we have today. The lunch box included a very small, less than an inch long, useful can-opener that had many uses. It was a can-opener, screwdriver, bottle opener (this was before twist-off bottle caps were invented), letter opener, seam ripper for enlisted men who wanted to replace their chevrons on promotion, among many other uses. Many of us attached this handy can-opener to chains that held our metal identification plates (known as "dog-tags"), and we carried them around our necks to keep them handy when needed.

March 31, 1944   No Mission.

Today was a day of stand-down, with no mission. Only a few training flights were conducted. The stand-down allowed flak holes to be patched and other much needed repairs to be made to our bombers. Many of us caught up on our letter writing. We wrote our letters on specially designed and handy "V"-mail stationery. To keep the locations of our bases secret, the government gave us a coded address for people to send their mail to, and ours was APO 520. Germans knew exactly where we were, but the use of APO numbers helped to facilitate the massive mail handling problem during wartime, with so many soldiers overseas. There is a note in the archives that a General Bourne is visiting our Group for a few days (mission unknown).

Note About the Growing Size of Fifteenth Air Force.

As concerns the growing size of the Fifteenth Air Force a pause here to explain what was happening to it. The Fifteenth received the rest of its heavy bomber groups and three additional fighter groups between mid-March and the tenth of May. This brought its heavy bombers up to full strength by May 10, a total of 21 heavy bomber groups, about 372 B-17s and 930 B-24s in Italy at any given time. Each heavy bomber group had an average of about 62 planes. There was then a total heavy bomber strength of about 1,302 planes. The precise number varied from day to day because of planes being shot down and replacements coming in regularly.

Fighters would not reach their full strength of 7 groups until June, 1944. Each fighter group had an average of about 70 planes. Thus, when the Fifteenth Air Force reached if full strength of fighters in June its 7 groups of fighters contained about 490 planes. Thus, by June the Fifteenth Air Force had 1,792 combat aircraft, not counting the specialized squadrons that were assigned to it.

The **5th Bomb Wing** contained all B-17 Flying Fortresses assigned to our Fifteenth Air Force in Italy. All other Wings of the Fifteenth Air Force were composed of B-24 Liberators. The 5th Bomb Wing was composed of six Groups (all B-17s), the 2nd, 97th, 99th, 301st, 463rd, and 483rd, and they were located in an area just north of Foggia, except for the 99th and 483rd Groups which were east of Foggia.

The **55th Bomb Wing** became complete, composed of the 460th, 463th, 465th, and 485th groups when the last of its groups, the 460th, became operational, flying its first mission on March 19, 1944. The 55th operated from an area that was a distance of about twenty-five to forty miles south of Stornara where our air base was located.

The **49th Bomb Wing** composed of the 451st, 461st, 484th Groups (all B-24s), with its aircraft located south and west of our base at Stornara, was complete when the 461st began its operations on April 2, 1944.

The **304th Bomb Wing**, of which I was part, was complete with four bomb groups, the 454th, 455th, 456th, and 459th Groups, and all its planes were located in an area about twenty miles southeast of Foggia.

The **47th Bomb Wing** was complete with its four groups, the 98th, 376th, 449th, and 450th (all B-24s), located near the heel of Italy's boot around Taranto.

181

In April the weather began to get better, but the best news that our bomber crews were to receive was that the first of the new fighter groups scheduled to be transferred into the Fifteenth Air Force in Italy, the 31st Fighter Group at San Severno, became operational with the new, long range ***North American P-51 B and C Mustang aircraft.***

These were needed to escort us on our long range missions deep into Germany, Austria, Hungary, Rumania, and Czechoslovakia. It wouldn't be until June that the conversion to P-51's and the build up to 7 fighter groups in the Fifteenth Air Force would be complete, but arrival of this first group of long range Mustangs, which proved to be the best propeller-driven fighter of the war, was very encouraging to us bomber crews. It appeared that we would now get more protection on our long range missions.

Until then, the fighter protection whereby we were supposed to be given fighter coverage at the target and coverage on withdrawal by P-47s and P-38s, was not adequate to keep our bombers from being attacked. German radar kept track of our escort fighters' progress and their limitations were well known by the enemy. Germans had close air control of their fighters, directing them to areas where our friendly fighters were not. They also took advantage of the limited endurance of our fighters in the target areas.

Three fighter groups, the 52nd, 332nd, and 325th, were located about thirty miles north of Foggia along the east coast of Italy, just west of the Italian boot's spur. A fourth fighter group, the 82nd, was located about twenty-five miles east of Stornara. Three more fighter groups, the 31st, 14th, and 1st, were located in an area about twenty miles north of Foggia.

All of these fighter groups had as a mission, in addition to bomber escort, bombing, strafing and Air-Sea Rescue of downed crew members. Many of the younger fighter pilots were more interested in making a kill than in protecting bombers, and they would follow enemy fighter decoys down to the ground, abandoning bombers, and making bombers clear for other groups of enemy fighters to attack. It was my personal experience that the P-38s were most consistent at remaining with the bombers, giving bomber protection their top priority, but when P-51s became numerous the Luftwaffe attacks diminished markedly.

April 1, 1944   Abort After Briefing, Vicenza Marshaling Yards, Italy

Another early morning briefing to bomb Vicenza marshalling yards in northern Italy, but the mission was canceled because of high winds and cumulous clouds.

Russian armies have split the German armies facing them on the eastern front, and this has now made our bombing of German lines of communications in the Balkans more important targets now.

April 2, 1944   Steyr, Austria

Palm Sunday saw my crew passed over for what turned out to be a rough mission. Today the Group, after many attempts, was finally successful at bombing the Daimler-Puch ball bearing manufacturing plant at Steyr, Austria. Steyr is about 100 miles west of the heavily defended Vienna. Our Group was scheduled to be provided a half-hour of fighter escort coverage at the target by 25 P-47s, and when they were out of fuel, 25 P-38s were supposed to provide another half-hour coverage. As stated below, the fighter escort provided little protection for our bombers.

After a 0500 hour wake-up call in the tents, breakfast, briefing started at 0615 hours. The intelligence briefing was conducted by Captain Lewis A. Stuck, Jr. of our group intelligence section, and he described, in addition to flak and enemy fighters expected, the importance of ball bearings that were produced at the Daimler-Puch ball bearing manufacturing plant at Steyr, Austria, the target for the day. Most mechanical equipment must rely on ball bearings as a vital part of their design, and without ball bearings equipment cannot operate.

file.
N. 75

BATTLE ORDER

Date: 2 April 1944

1st Unit: 1st Box

Jackson,C.Y.

Formation Leader: Sinclair/   AP 279
No. 3: Smith: (C)   AP 275   Dep Leader: Meyer(Abernathy) 345
No. 4: Miller (C)   AP 263
No. 6: Jackson,W.L.   AP 501   No. 5: Terrell   AP 276

2nd Box

Leader: Leo (Gruber) AP 214
No. 3: Hillman (C)   AP 285   Dep Leader: Desperock AP 212
No. 4: Jones (C)   AP 291
No. 6: Mix   AP 072   No. 5: Callan   AP 749
No. 7: Mapn   AP 311

3rd Box

Leader: Andrews   AP 364
No. 3: Strombom (C) AP 634   Dep Leader: Bishop   AP 470
No. 4: Lane (C)   AP 772
No. 6: Loukuma   AP 283   No. 5: Third   AP 284
No. 7: Ball   AP 287

2nd Unit: 1st Box

Demelik

Leader: Clark,R.R./   AP 768
No. 3: Fleming (C)   AP 183   Dep Leader: Haviland   AP 661
No. 4: Manlove (C)   AP 492
No. 6: Hundly   AP 853   No. 5: Young   AP 839
No. 7: Rawlinson   AP 633
(Movie Camera)

2nd Box

Leader: Townsend   AP 231
No. 3: Johnson (C)   AP 831   Dep Leader: Witkin   AP 477
No. 4: Bowering (C)   AP 189
No. 6: Lohner   AP 199   No. 5: Snee   AP 222
No. 7: Ensign   AP 486

3rd Box

Leader: Douglass   AP 487
No. 3: Palis (C)   AP 297   Dep Leader: Richards   AP 217
No. 4: Williamson (C) AP 177
No. 6: Walker   AP 304   No. 5: Lassiter   AP 312

Stations time at the aircraft was 0725 and start engines time for the first of the six Boxes was 0735. Major John R. Sinclair in the lead ship, took off at 0745 hours and thirty-seven Liberators followed his off the runway at 45 second intervals. After the Group formation was gathered around Sinclair's plane, the Group departed the Wing rendezvous point, Stornara, climbing on course at 160 MPH indicated airspeed and climbing at a rate of climb of 250 feet per minute headed for the first turning point at Andriaja Island.

A total of thirteen aircraft returned before reaching the target. Six planes in the last Box of planes to take off could not catch up with the formation after they were airborne, and all six had to abort the mission. Six additional planes returned early for the following reasons: gasoline leaks (three), supercharger out (one plane), oxygen system malfunction (one plane), and number two propeller runaway (one plane). One plane was severely shot up by enemy fighters before reaching the target and limped its way home as described below.

Weather started out with ceiling and visibility unlimited, and a cloud cover under the formation gradually increased enroute from three-tenths of altocumulus with tops to 10,000 feet to six-tenths coverage with tops at 16,000 feet. Then this condition gradually improved as the Group reached the target area to four-tenths coverage with tops at 10,000 feet. Visibility in the Target area was hazy and the temperature at 22,000 feet was minus 23 degrees centigrade.

There were 104 enemy aircraft encountered by our Group on the mission, including Me-109s, FW-190s, ME-110s, Me-210s, and JU-88s. Enemy attacks started in earnest at the Yugoslavian coast before our bombers reached the target, and the attacks continued until one hour after bombs away. The enemy fighter attacks were using many styles, including four abreast, two abreast, closing to within 300 yards, diving low, peeling off right and left, regrouping, and attacking again. The attacks came from many directions, high and low, including the 5, 6, 7, and 9 o'clock positions. Our group destroyed 9 of them, were credited with 8 more probably destroyed, and our gunners inflicted damage to 7 more enemy.

Our Group lost one bomber to enemy action, and three of our B-24s returned to base with damage from enemy aircraft fire. An additional fourteen of our B-24s had flak damage. This was the heaviest flak our Group had seen to date, and it was graded as heavy guns, intense, and accurate. At Steyr there were black, white, and red burst of flak. The flak was the heavy barrage type as well as tracking type. When our window confused the radar, and weather permitted visual sighting, as it did today, ground gunners could fire accurately by sighting our planes visually.

Twenty-five planes remaining in the Group's formation were able to reach the target despite fighter attacks and intense flak. These remaining bombers were able to drop 62 tons of M-17 incendiary bombs (248 clusters) on the target at 1231 hours from an altitude of 22,000 feet for the 1st Unit and 20,000 feet for the 2nd unit on an axis of attack of 330 degrees magnetic. The indicated airspeed was 160 MPH, a true airspeed of 225 MPH. Previous groups of our Wing had bombed the target before our Group reached it, leaving heavy smoke covering the target so our bombs had to be released into the smoke covered area. Seventeen photos of the target were taken by our photographers and all bombs fell within the smoke covered area. Results were later graded as very successful. One Liberator had two bombs hang up in its bomb bay, as the plane returned to our air base.

The Group formation of twenty-four planes arrived back over our base at 1449 hours. This was our Group's eighteenth accredited mission of the twenty-four missions flown in Italy, and 6:55 hours were logged.

187

We lost one B-24, "The Miss Zeke" flown by the crew of 2nd Lt. William R. Terrell of the 744th Squadron. Terrell's plane was flying in the number five position of the 1st Box of the 1st Unit of the Group's formation. The plane was listed as missing in action because it was last seen at about 10,000 feet, five minutes after bombs were dropped, descending, with one propeller feathered, gear down, and closely followed by enemy fighters. We learned later that eight crew members of Terrell's plane were able to bail out. Six of them were taken prisoner (two, F/O Claude McCrocklin, bombardier, and 2nd Lt. William R. Terrell, pilot, are currently members of the 456th Bomb Group Association), two evaded capture with the help of Yugoslavian Partisans and escaped. Two were killed in action. The two escapees, S/Sgt Herman Lipkin, radio operator, and S/Sgt Warren Stuckey, right waist gunner, were severely wounded and Sgt Lipkin's leg was amputated above the knee. Both evadees survived and were returned to Italy on June 27, 1944.

In addition to Terrell's lost crew, there were four other casualties. A radio operator on another crew was killed, a radio operator was wounded, and an engineer was wounded. Donald A. Allan, bombardier on Lt. Frank Powell's crew from the 744th Squadron was wounded in the left leg.

This mission on April 2 was part of a coordinated attack by Fifteenth Air Force groups, bombing about noon, the preferred bombing time that provided the best light for bombardiers to identify their targets. The targets were ball bearing and aircraft component manufacturing plants, and the airfield near Steyr. There were a total of 125 Fortresses and 325 Liberators engaged in the bombing, and they dropped a total of 1,093 tons of bombs on the area's targets with a loss of 20 bombers and 30 bombers were reported as damaged. Gunners of the bombers were credited with shooting down 84 enemy fighters and fighter escort downed 32 more. In addition, there were 43 enemy aircraft reported as probably destroyed and 16 enemy fighters damaged on the ground. At the same time, on another target, 63 B-24's and 29 B-17's dropped bombs on the airfield at Mostar, Yugoslavia, and marshalling yards at Bihac and Brod, Yugoslavia. The Fifteenth Air Force was getting much stronger confronting the Luftwaffe with much more strength.

On this April 2nd mission to Steyr, four fighter groups provided penetration and target coverage for the bombers for about 30 minutes each. This was the limit of their endurance. Luftwaffe fighters came in on the first bomber group at 10:15 to draw off escorting fighters while another formation of enemy fighters were hovering above 35,000 feet waiting their chance to attack the bombers unmolested after the USAAF fighters were drawn away. This was a tactic enemy fighters began to use more often as we began to get more fighter escort. On some missions the heavy bomber stream stretched over 100 miles long so it was difficult for our escort fighters to protect all of the bombers.

The four fighter groups that covered our bombers for thirty minutes each, before low fuel required them to return to Italy, was not sufficient to prevent enemy fighters from taking a heavy toll on some of our bomber groups. We didn't know it at the time, but sufficient fighter escort was on its way.

Some members of our Group attended church services for Palm Sunday at Group Headquarters, and the chaplain had real palm branches brought in from Cerignola for his services. Weather around our camp was getting very mild, and a few flowers were starting to bloom.

April 3, 1944   Marshaling Yards, Budapest, Hungary

I flew my ninth and tenth missions (a two-credit mission) with Boughner's crew to bomb the Ferencvaros marshaling yards at Budapest, Hungary, with Colonel Steed leading the formation. Purpose of the mission was to interrupt enemy rail transportation that was supplying the desperate German forces that were fighting in Rumania. The German Wehrmacht was trying to stop the strong Russian Army that had recently penetrated Rumania.

Russian Army advances to the north of Rumania had previously cut off German rail supply routes that supplied Wehrmacht troops in Rumania from the north. This meant that Germans had to rely solely on Hungarian and Rumanian railroads, the prewar "Orient Express" route, to supply their troops that were fighting in Rumania.

BATTLE ORDER

AS 76

Date: 3 April 1944

1st Unit: 1st Box

Formation Leader: Col. Steed (Thomas) AP 475
No. 3: Nix (C) AP 212   Dep Leader: Mulligan (Miller) 499
                No. 4: Grimm (C)   AP 437
No. 6: Monahan   AP 183   No. 5: Little   AP 304

2nd Box

Leader: Manlove   AP 231
No. 3: Snee (C) AP 477   Dep Leader: Ensign   AP 486
                No. 4: Richards (C)   AP 086
No. 6: Boughner   AP 189   No. 5: Sagert   AP 480
                No. 7: Randall   AP 839

3rd Box

Leader: Gardner   AP 345
No. 3: Meyer (C) AP 177   Dep Leader: Lagzowski AP 749
                No. 4: Wilsson (C)   AP 297
No. 6: Lassiter AP 312   No. 5: Key   AP 217

2nd Unit: 1st Box

Leader: Clark, F.B. (Tevel) AP 268
No. 3: Nunimaker (C)   AP 072   Dep Leader: Hydo(Lehner) AP 222
                No. 4: Rudd (C)   AP 295
No. 6: Johnson   AP 831   No. 5: Hundley   AP 853

2nd Box

Leader: Clark, W.D.   AP 311
No. 3: Strombom (C)   AP 634   Dep Leader: Ward   AP 661
                No. 4: Riddle (C)   AP 283
No. 6: Ball   AP 287   No. 5: VanLeouwen   AP 364

3rd Box

Leader: Phifer   AP 501
No. 3: Smith (C)   AP 275   Dep Leader: Lambert   AP 214
                No. 4: Jones (C)   AP 291
No. 6: Darrasso   AP 290   No. 5: Hillman   AP 235

Thirty-three of our Group's B-24s took off, starting at 0715 hours with Colonel Steed in the lead plane, and the rest of us following him off the runway in an orderly fashion at 45 second intervals. Major W. B. Clark and 1st Lt. Dave E. Tavel were in the lead plane of the 2nd Unit of the formation. Our target for the day was the north half of Budapest Main Marshaling Yard.

We were supposed to have twenty-five P-38s join us as air cover at 0935 hours, then they would leave us fifty miles south of Budapest where they were to be replaced by an escort of twenty P-47s that would cover us on the way into the target. There was to be no escort after leaving the target.

Four of our planes returned before reaching the target for the following reasons: one plane had two generators go out, one plane's engineer forgot his oxygen mask, one plane had a dangerous leak in its fuel transfer pump, and one plane had crippling damage by enemy flak before reaching the target and had to head home. This left twenty-nine of our 456th Bomb Group's B-24s left to bomb the target.

Only two enemy aircraft were encountered by our group, thus our fighter escort was doing its job of protecting us this day. No enemy aircraft were destroyed or damaged by our gunners.

As usual at Budapest, the flak was heavy, intense and accurate. Many hundreds of guns were firing at us from the ground. Flak destroyed one of our planes before reaching the target, as discussed below, and it damaged eighteen others. However, twenty-nine of our Group's bombers were able to fly their way through the thick black cloud of flak and drop 70 tons of general purpose 500 pound bombs (280 bombs) at 1108 hours from an altitude of 21,000 feet for the 1st Unit and 19,000 feet for the 2nd Unit. Two Liberators had bomb rack release problems, could not drop ten bombs on the target, and returned them to our air base. Results of the bombing were good, completely destroying this crucial railroad choke point at Budapest. Our bombing stopped the flow of rail traffic through it for some time.

The plane we lost was "The Texas Ranger," a 745th Squadron plane flown by 1st Lt. Emil S. Laszewski's crew. His navigator, Lt. Milton H. Halberstadt, was badly wounded when the plane was severely damaged by flak before reaching the target. When Laszewski's plane could not make it back to our base, the crew bailed out at 1400 hours 2 miles northwest of Orta Nova, Yugoslavia. The copilot, 2nd Lt. Howard N. Hartman and Sgt. Edward L. Dement, upper turret gunner (both current members of the 456th Bomb Group Association), as well as 2nd Lt. Edward C. Bonham, bombardier (now deceased), were taken Prisoner of War. The other crew members are listed as missing in action. Sgt. Frederick G. Abner, Jr., ball turret gunner, originally listed as missing in action is deceased and his wife, Mrs. Frederick Abner is currently a member of the 456th Bomb Group Association.

There were five casualties in addition to those of Laszewski's crew. A navigator on 1st. Lt. Gerald W. Nix's crew, 2nd Lt. Gerald L. Bush of the 744th Squadron, were killed by flak while over the target and one other navigator was seriously injured. Three other crew members were wounded, including a copilot, an engineer, and a nose turret gunner.

Our formation of twenty eight planes returned over our base at 1352 hours, and the flight time logged was 6:40 hours, giving me a total combat flying time up to this point of 50:25 hours. This was the Group's nineteenth accredited mission of the twenty-five missions flown in Italy.

April 4, 1944 Bucharest Marshaling Yards, Rumania.

The military way of expressing this date was 4/4/44. Another early morning wake-up call which usually meant a long mission. I was able fly again today, the second "two-fer mission" in a row, and it allowed me to get missions 11 and 12 logged. It was our Group's twentieth accredited mission in twenty-six attempts. It was a fairly rough mission because we were attacked by forty enemy aircraft, and we had to fight an air battle with fighters in addition to the ugly flak encountered.

We flew into the defensive hornets' nest at Bucharest, Rumania to bomb the marshalling yards. Bucharest was only thirty miles away from Ploesti, a target that I later bombed three times. This was the third most heavily defended area of Europe, only less heavily defended than Berlin and Vienna. The oil industry and supply lines in this area were absolutely vital to the German ability to wage war.

The Fifteenth Air Force had been given a new set of bombing priorities which included railroad facilities in Rumania and Bulgaria, and particularly the Orient Express route that Germans were relying upon to supply their troops that were in a desperate fight with invading Russians. The 456th Bomb Group's mission today was part of an overall Fifteenth Air Force effort involving 350 heavy bombers and an escort of 119 P-38's. The mission was designed to destroy all rail facilities in the Bucharest area and to engage and destroy as many German and Rumanian fighters in the air as possible.

After we took off, as we were flying in the local area maneuvering to join our group formation, I saw a large plume of smoke coming from the end of the 459th Group's runway. We later heard that one of their B-24's had crashed on takeoff, and there were rumors, again, that the crash was due to sabotage by an enemy spy. This was only one of many we saw at that airfield.

After our P-38 escort fighters left our formation, presumably because of low fuel, forty enemy aircraft attacked our Group while we were on our way to the target. It was a classic air battle and our gunners were credited with two enemy fighters probably shot down, and another five damaged. Enemy fighters used rockets, cannon fire, and dropped aerial bombs on some of the bomber formations of this raid.

S/Sgt Thomas S. Delaney, radio operator and waist gunner flying in "Peace-Maker" at the time, reported that he saw T/Sgt. Edward W. Broom, engineer on his plane (later my engineer, and killed in action later), get a probable Me-109. He said that he saw fire from Broom's guns hit the fighter square and it caused fire to spurt out of the enemy fighter. Delaney said that all gunners on his plane got shots at enemy fighters except the ball turret gunner, and they kept the enemy fighters out from our formation pretty far for about one-half hour. He said that our tight formation and our gunners' intense fire (we had tracer bullets making our fire visibly intimidating to the enemy, as well as providing aiming information for our gunners) kept enemy fighters from coming in too close to our formation. He said that the enemy pilots appeared rather green. He saw JU-88s and Me-210s attacking planes in the group that was flying ahead of our Group. The nose turret gunner of Peacemaker got off a few gun bursts at an Me-210. He said that seven enemy planes were seen hitting the ground and blowing up. Delaney reported that coming back, after dropping bombs on the target, an Me-110 followed our Group for about a half-hour, keeping out of range of our guns, and it seemed to throw a rocket. Twin-engine enemy fighters carry four rockets with a range of 1,000 yards, out of range of our guns.

Delaney got some gunnery practice firing at the Me-110 at long range. He also said that this was his first mission where his whole crew was able to fly together. Many times crew members had to fly as substitute members with other crews because of sickness, hospitalization for wounds, or other reasons why the regularly assigned members of the crew could not fly. This was Delaney's 9th and 10th missions.

As we approached the target, still fighting off enemy fighters, we saw what appeared to be an impenetrable black cloud of ugly 88mm and 105mm antiaircraft shells bursting over the target. Enemy aircraft refused to follow us into this cloud of shell bursts, their own antiaircraft fire. Although we were dropping considerable amounts of window in an attempt to confuse enemy radar that was being used to aim the 88mm and 105mm antiaircraft guns, the flak was graded as having an intense concentration of bursts, accurate, and with heavy, ugly black and white bursts. Somehow we were all able to fly through it and drop our bombs on the target. No bomb group of the Fifteenth Air Force was ever stopped from bombing its target by fighter attack or by intimidating heavy antiaircraft gun fire.

There was considerable smoke over the target, mostly from previous bombings, and it was difficult to assess bombing results until afterward. Bomb photos were later analyzed by intelligence personnel and 456th Bomb Group results were graded as good. The temperature at 21,300 feet was minus 24 degrees centigrade.

Twenty-seven of our bombers were reported to have dropped 65 tons of 500 pound general purpose bombs on the target. All of our aircraft returned to our base, but with many holes in them for our ground troops to repair. Flying time for the mission was 7 hours and 15 minutes. This was the Group's twentieth accredited mission, and the twenty-sixth mission flown in Italy.

For the total Fifteenth Air Force effort on that day, we were a part of 220 Liberators and 93 Fortresses that dropped 863 tons of bombs with excellent results, mainly on the Bucharest marshaling yards, but two groups of bombers bombed Otopeni Airdrome at Bucharest. Enemy fighter attacks against Fifteenth Air Force bombers were made by 100 ME-109's, in addition to some FW-190's, JU-88's, and Me-110's. Their attacks lasted for more than one hour and fifteen minutes as they attacked from all levels and angles, approaching to within fifty yards of the bomber formations. Luftwaffe and flak were able to shoot down ten Fifteenth Air Force bombers and damage many more.

Forty of the fifty enemy fighters that were claimed to be destroyed by Fifteenth Air Force planes on this mission, were destroyed by gunners of one Liberator group, the 449th. This Group failed to get fighter cover and it was attacked by more than one-hundred enemy fighters. Enemy radar and observational "shadowing planes" kept the enemy informed about the locations of our fighter escort, and directed their own fighters to attack undefended groups. In addition to being credited with shooting down forty of the enemy fighters, gunners of the 449th Bomber Group were also credited with probably getting thirteen more and damaging an additional six. It was some air battle! The 449th lost six B-24s to the fighters, but it successfully dropped its bombs on its target, the Bucharest marshaling yards. The Group was awarded a well deserved Presidential Unit Citation for this mission.

On this mission I noticed that fighters flown by Rumanian pilots were not as effective as those flown by German pilots, particularly when compared with the tactics of Hermann Goering's elite "Yellow Nose" fighters that we had encountered a few times before. Nicknamed the "Yellow Nose" squadron by us because they flew fighters that had their propeller spinners painted yellow, these elite, hand selected German pilots were much more aggressive and competent. They were all experienced pilots called in from the eastern front to defend against our growing Fifteenth Air Force threat.

Fighters had to point their noses in the direction that they were firing because their guns were fixed in their wings, and Goering's elite fighter pilots had their guns pointed at us, firing at us all of the time that they were in range of our bombers' guns. On this raid, I saw Rumanian pilots flying their ME-109 fighters parallel to our formation, in range of our guns, while they were unable to fire at us with their guns as they maneuvered their planes to get into position to fire at us. Our gunners shot many rounds of ammunition at them before they were able to respond with their own guns.

The Yellow Noses used aggressive head-on attacks many times so that the amount of time we were able to fire at them was cut to a minimum. This was due to the fact that the rate of closure from a head-on attack amounted to about 600 MPH. Yellow Nose pilots were so aggressive that they took their head-on attacks through our formations, missing our planes by only a few feet as they passed at high speed through our formations. When the Yellow Nose fighters attacked from the side of our formation, they used pursuit curves, continually turning, making it much more difficult for our gunners to hit them. Whenever we saw Yellow Nose fighters attacking us, particularly after they began flying the advanced, hot, FW-190 fighters, we knew we were in for a rough time. Many of the Luftwaffe's elite fighter pilots were credited with shooting down many more than 200 allied planes.

Luftwaffe pilots had an extremely hazardous and rough life. There was no such thing as rotating from hazardous combat duty to non-combat duty as pilots of our USAAF had the luxury of doing. Many Luftwaffe pilots had been on continuous combat duty for four years. Then during the year

1943, a total of 2,967 fighter pilots were killed, wounded, or missing in action, and during that time, the average number of pilots on duty who were in full or partially operational ready status at any given time was only 2,105. In other words, 141 percent of the pilots ready for duty were killed, wounded, or missing during 1943 on all fronts, including the Russian front. This amazing fact was researched by Williamson Murray for his book "Luftwaffe," The Nautical & Aviation Publishing Company of America, Baltimore, 1983 (Page 223). Thus, as our battles went on, the large number of fighters that the Germans were producing were becoming more and more difficult to fill with pilots. The Luftwaffe pilot training program had already been drastically reduced by lowering the number of flying hours that were required to become a Luftwaffe pilot in order to rush pilots into the combat planes. Still, pilot losses were more than Germans were able to train.

During the later part of April and most of May, when they were beginning to feel the shortage of pilots, Luftwaffe fighters were carefully controlled by ground controllers to make the most efficient use of their remaining fighter force. On one occasion, when we had no escort fighters, I saw a huge four-engine transport, a FW-200, that flew with us about twenty minutes out of range of our guns and parallel to our direction of flight. I assumed that the plane had high ranking Luftwaffe officers on board who were observing our bomber formations and/or they were directing Luftwaffe fighters that were attacking us. The defenseless transport FW-200 must have known that there were none of our escort fighter around to shoot it down.

Our intelligence people often flew along on our B-24s to listen to German fighter interplane radio conversations. Fighters were instructed by ground controllers to "only attack loose formations and straggling bombers that were unable to keep up with the main bomber formation."

This tactic was used to make the most efficient use of its dwindling fighter capability, against our growing bomber capability. By attacking stragglers and loose formations, enemy fighters would have fewer bomber machine guns firing at them when they made their attacks.

We would see Luftwaffe fighters cruising up and down our long formations looking for loose formations and stragglers. Knowing this, the veteran bomber groups would tighten up their formations, because we knew that Luftwaffe fighter pilots must have figured that good, tight formations not only meant that the group was experienced (which was a true indicator) and that there was a tight concentration of guns that would be firing at them if they attacked the group, but that the gunners of the group were more experienced and more accurate. However, on some occasions, the leaders of enemy fighter formations were heard to say, "There are no stragglers or loose formation and we are going to attack," and they responded to ground controllers' orders that told them not to do it with, "We cannot read you, your radio transmission is garbled. We are going to attack." Then they would attack aggressively.

A Note About The Cottontails.

A word must be said about the 450th Bombardment Group of Liberators whose two huge rudders were originally painted white, their Group's markings. Each bomber group had its own distinctive markings on their rudders. The 450th Group became known as the "Cottontails," and the they became famous throughout the Luftwaffe and throughout the Fifteenth Air Force because of an incident that was alleged to happen, and events that actually did follow afterward.

I didn't have a radio in Italy, but I was told by those that did have one, that Axis Sally said in one of her nightly radio broadcasts that if our bombers ever got into trouble, we could let our landing gear down as an indication that we were surrendering and Luftwaffe fighters would safely escort us to the nearest German airfield. Later, one of the Cottontail bombers was severely damaged as it came off the target at Regensburg, Germany and it could not keep up with the rest of its bomber formation. Luftwaffe fighters swarmed in for the kill when the pilot slowed his aircraft, put his flaps down, and dropped his landing gear, indicating surrender. All but two of the German fighters left the scene when they saw his wheels down, and the two remaining fighters put their flaps down and slowed up to fly close formation with the crippled Cottontail bomber, to lead it to the nearest Luftwaffe base.

It was alleged that the Cottontail pilot saw the two German fighters near his plane, sitting ducks for his gunners. With all the other fighters gone, he took advantage of the situation and ordered his gunners to shoot down the two remaining enemy fighters, which his gunners did easily. One of the enemy pilots was able to bail out and tell the story to Germans back home.

That night Axis Sally, at her regular 6:30 nightly broadcast, announced that Luftwaffe fighter pilots were going to destroy all planes with white tails for committing such a terrible act. From that time on, when Luftwaffe fighters cruised up and down our long line of Fifteenth Air Force heavy bomber groups looking for prey, while we were on our way to bomb our targets, they would pass up the rest of our bomber groups and zero in on the Cottontails with the intent of shooting the entire formation of white tails out of the sky. It was reported (by Donald R. Currier of the companion 449th group in his book "Fifty Mission Crush," Burd Street Press, 1992) that in six months the 450th Cottontails lost 110 planes while his 449th group flying along with them lost only 63 planes. This happened even though an attempted was made to throw the Luftwaffe off by changing the color of the Cottontail's rudder markings. Rudder markings of the entire 47th wing, the 98th, 376th, and 449th Groups as well as the 450th's were changed in an attempt to deceive the Luftwaffe. Thanks to the excellent German spy network, Axis Sally announced the new markings each time a change in rudder markings was made, and the Luftwaffe continued its concentrated attacks on the 450th.

Needless to say, the rest of us in other groups were glad to have the 450th Group along on any of our missions because it usually meant enemy fighters would pass us by until the 450th was completely destroyed. Unfortunately, there weren't many of our missions where the 450th Group was anywhere near to us, to help us out. They were in another wing, the 47th Bomb Wing, and they often had different targets than we did.

April 5, 1944   Group's Air Abort, Ploesti Marshaling Yards, Rumania.

The 456th was scheduled again, to return back into the hornets nest of defenses around Ploesti. Boughner's crew, with me on it, was scheduled to bomb Ploesti, but our group's mission was canceled due to weather a little while after we took off. I logged 2:40 hours, but of course we did not earn mission credit.

However, Fifteenth Air Force groups to our south, where the weather was better, were able take off and fly to the Ploesti marshaling yards and other marshaling yards at Nis and Leskovac in this area of heavy enemy defense. There were 95 B-17s and 135 B-24s that dropped 587 tons of bombs on Ploesti and 67 tons on the other targets with good results. One group, the 451st Bomb Group of Liberators stationed at Castellucio, Italy, was attacked by waves of enemy fighters totaling 85 planes while in Rumania. The group claimed 20 enemy aircraft destroyed, 12 probable, and 3 damaged. Five of their bombers were lost.

This attack proved the vulnerability to our bombers of this, the enemy's largest oil producing and refinery complex. Experience gained from this attack caused Fifteenth Air Force planners to make this complex a top priority target, and we soon destroyed it with a series of more raids.

April 6, 1944   No Mission.

This was a stand-down day, and we were kept busy with escape lectures by intelligence personnel. Afterward, a few of us went into town to get haircuts. Lieutenant Colonel Walter Cal Phillips, Group Executive Officer, proposed that an officer's club be built a hundred yards east of the headquarters mansion.

**April 7, 1944   Marshaling Yards, Bologna, Italy.*

I flew with Boughner's crew again to bomb the Stazione Nupia marshaling yards at Bologna, Italy. The mission turned out to be a true milk run.

Thirty-nine of our planes took off at 1010 hours, bankers hours, and we were given forty P-38s to escort us from Rimini to the target and they were scheduled to stay with us for twenty minutes after bombs were dropped. Two of our bombers returned early because of aircraft malfunctions. One plane returning early had a faulty landing gear and the other had a leak in a gas tank.

The weather at the target was CAVU (ceiling and visibility unlimited), with only ten percent scattered cloud coverage below us to obstruct the bombardiers' sighting of the target. The beautiful puffs of cumulus clouds below us looked like popcorn. Thin cirrus clouds were above us, about six-tenths cloud coverage with bases at about 23,000 feet. The temperature at 22,000 feet was minus 21 degrees centigrade.

On a day like this we couldn't help but have good bombing results and that is what we had, confirmed by thirteen photographs taken by our planes. Our bombs thoroughly covered the target area. Many bombs fell on the railroad choke point, but one crew reported seeing bombs fall about three miles short of the target, out of range of our photographs.

One bomber could not release its bombs on the target because of a short in the auxiliary bomb release toggle switch. Thus thirty-six of our planes were left to drop 66.9 tons of 100 pound general purpose bombs (1338 bombs) at 1324 hours from an altitude of 21,500 feet for the 1st Unit of the formation and 18,500 feet for the 2nd Unit, on an axis of attack of 311 degrees magnetic. The indicated airspeed was 160 MPH, about 226 MPH true airspeed.

No enemy fighters were encountered and we lost no bombers. The flak was classified as heavy guns, scattered bursts and inaccurate, and none of our planes reported significant flak damage. Someone on one of our planes reported that they saw only five guns on the ground firing at us.

With excellent weather, this was one of the few "joy rides" our crew was blessed to fly during my fifty-one missions. Even the temperature was warming up. However, we couldn't enjoy it properly until we had left the target area, were out of enemy territory, and safely on the ground because we knew that something unexpected and violent could always happen at any time.

There was another inadvertent drop of bombs from one of our Liberators due to a short in a bomb release auxiliary toggle switch, and it caused the release of two 100 pound bombs about two miles southwest of Stornarella on our return home, a near tragedy. Fortunately no one was hurt.

Our bomber formation of thirty-seven B-24s returned to our base at 1502 hours, and we logged 5:00 hours of combat flying time. This was my thirteenth accredited mission and the group's twenty-first accredited one of twenty-eight missions flown in Italy.

Flight crews and ground support personnel were getting to be old hands at it by now. The technical routine of maintaining, servicing, and loading the Liberators, crew wake-up, briefing, equipment loading, preflighting our bombers, taxi, takeoff, getting the bomb group formed, then flying in good formation to a target, bombing, flying home, and landing the formation safely was getting to be very efficient. Of course there was always a gnawing fear in all of our minds of being shot down, maimed, or killed, but we were getting very proficient at our jobs. I now had 62:40 hours of combat time and I was getting to feel like an old hand at it. I was wondering when, if ever, I would be able to get a crew of my own.

At the start of our mission, we saw another tall column of smoke rising from a plane on fire at the end of the runway of the 449th Group. It was another that had evidently crashed on takeoff. Rumors persist that it must be sabotage.

April 8, 1944 Weather Abort Enroute To Bad Voslau, Austria.

We had another early morning briefing for a raid on Bad Voslau, Austria, but were recalled shortly after the Group took off because of bad weather. We were recalled before we could assemble the group and I logged fifty minutes.

We were given special escape instructions for pick up in northern Italy to be used if we were ever shot down behind enemy lines. We were told to make it to a rendezvous point in an isolated, wooded area at the mouth of a very small river, the Cazzanelle. A boat was scheduled to call at the beach between 2300 and 0030 hours on April 17 and again on April 23 at the same time. We were instructed to flash the Morse Code for the letter "F" toward the sea at the appropriate time to get picked up. It sounded a little too complicated to me, but I tried to remember it. We weren't supposed to write it down.

April 9, 1944   No Mission, Easter.

Easter happened to be a stand-down day and we had an unusually good dinner because of the holiday. Some attended church services at Group Headquarters. The Italian troops that were working on our air base marched to confession early, all pressed and polished.

April 10, 1944   No Mission.

Another stand-down day because of bad weather.

April 11, 1944 No Mission For The Group (I Flew Training).

No Group mission again today. Boughner and I flew over to the replacement depot to pick up a replacement plane, and we logged 3:20 hours enroute. I was able to get some practice flying and landing the plane, in preparation for getting my own crew.

While in the officers' mess to get a good meal as a reprieve from our standard "C" ration fare at our base, I talked with a ferry pilot who had just ferried a plane in from the states. He told me that he collected $7.00 per day as per diem compensation for every day that he was away from his home base in the states, and that he was away from his base most of the time. He was a second lieutenant, the same rank as me, so we both made $225.00 per month as pay, but he was making more than me with an additional $210.00 per month in per diem. He was joy riding, seeing the world, and eating in good mess facilities, while I was being shot at, and eating and sleeping in marginal conditions. I determined that when I returned to the states I would try to get a job ferrying aircraft all over the world (which I did).

I knew that my situation was not a bad one when it was compared to the dog-face infantrymen near us at the front lines, living in foxholes in the rain, being shot at, being paid much less, and eating much worse food. Everything is relative, and life is not necessarily just.

April 12, 1944   Bad Voslau Airdrome, Austria

I was selected, with Boughner's crew, to fly what turned out to be a rough mission to bomb the Bad Voslau airdrome in Austria. Our target was the destruction of aircraft dispersed on the north side of the Bad Voslau airdrome in Austria. Bad Voslau is located between Vienna and Wiener Neustadt, seventeen miles from the heart of Vienna, with 300 antiaircraft guns and many Luftwaffe fighters protecting the area. Vienna was the second most heavily defended German target, second only to Berlin in importance. The Group was attacked by 100 enemy fighters that shot down 3 of our bombers, and damaged 8 more of our planes.

Thirty-nine of our Group's bombers followed Colonel Steed's lead plane off the runway when it took off at 0840 hours. We followed him off the dirt runway at 45 second intervals. After three bombers of the Group aborted the mission, this left thirty-seven of 456th planes to fly over the target.

Our plane, number 492 which was a last minute substitute plane, had generator problems an hour and a half after we took off, so we had to return to our base and abort this mission. We logged 3 hours and 10 minutes, and naturally received no credit for the mission. In addition to our plane, two other Liberators had to drop out of the Group formation and abort the mission. One bomber had a gasoline leak, and one had its top turret and nose turret Plexiglas blow off.

Although our Group was scheduled to have an escort of twenty P-38s, to provide protective "close cover" starting at 1120 hours, one hour before reaching the target, our Group's formation was attacked by 100 enemy fighters in the target area. At our morning briefing we were told that we "were going to have one group of P-38s rendezvous with our group over the Initial Point and provide close cover over the target and along the route back home to the limit of their fuel endurance." We were also told that, "one section of four aircraft will fly on each flank of the formation detailed to destroy shadowing Luftwaffe twin engine 'stool pigeon' fighters." I suspect that the Luftwaffe was tracking our fighter escort and positioned their attacking fighters where our escort was not, or they used decoy fighters to distract our escorting P-38s from their job of protecting our bombers. The Germans did this by radar and by using scout, or "stool pigeon," aircraft to track our escort. They knew that our fighters took off much later that our bombers and relied on a rendezvous with the bombers later. Another tactic used by the Germans was to attack our escort fighters early, to make them drop their external fuel tanks early, so their endurance would be reduced, and they would have to leave their bombers early.

DETAILED OPERATIONS BRIEFING

Battle Order: 12 April 1944

1st Unit, 1st Box

Formation Leader: Col. STEED, Thomas AP 817 or 475
No. 3: Smith (C)   AP 275   Dep Leader: Clark, W.B., Callan 34
                    No. 4: Miller (C) AP 268
No. 6: Haviland   AP 661   No. 5: Brabon   AP 799
                    No. 7: Johnson AP 831

2nd Box

Leader: Lee   AP 214
No. 3: Jackson, W.L. (C) AP 233   Dep Leader: Dosperock AP 501
                    No. 4: Jones (C) AP 291
No. 6: Nunimaker AP 285   No. 5: Lambert   AP 072
                    No. 7: Barrasso AP 290

3rd Box

Leader: Andrews AP 311
No. 3: Ward (C)   AP 637   Dep Leader: Lane   AP 283
                    No. 4: Chandler (C) AP 772
No. 6: Leukuma   AP 364   No. 5: Stromboa   AP 634

2nd Unit, 1st Box

Leader: Christensen, Jackson, C.Y. AP 279
No. 3: Witkin (C) AP 477   Dep Leader: Bishop   AP 470
                    No. 4: Williamson (C) AP 183
No. 6: Rawlinson AP 633   No. 5: Ball   AP 287

2nd Box

Leader: Richards AP 489
No. 3: Sagert (C) AP 480   Dep Leader: Bock   AP 222
                    No. 4: Townsend (C) AP 231
No. 6: Lehner   AP 006   No. 5: Boughner   AP 853
                    No. 7: Cutting AP 839

3rd Box

Leader: Douglass AP 334
No. 3: Moyer (C) AP 292   Dep Leader: Nilsson AP 304
                    No. 4: Grimm (C) AP 487
No. 6: Walker   AP 635   No. 5: Richards   AP 217
                    No. 7: Bowering AP 109

Luftwaffe fighters attacked our Group for forty minutes, unmolested by our P-38 escort fighters, and they used rockets as well as cannon fire. In the huge air battle that ensued we lost three bombers to enemy aircraft, all three were flying in the 3rd Box of the 2nd Unit, and nine other bombers were damaged from enemy fighter fire. Our bombers' gunners claimed twenty-two enemy aircraft destroyed, eight probables, and eight damaged.

With Colonel Steed leading, the Group fought its way to the target through fighters, then the heavy flak. Flak was classified as having heavy guns, moderate intensity, and accurate. Eight Liberators had flak damage, in addition to the fighter inflicted damage they had to endure. In addition to the normal black flak bursts of 88mm antiaircraft guns, huge white flak bursts of larger guns, probably 105mm were seen. The weather at the target was thirty to fifty percent coverage with cumulus clouds below the Group formation, tops at 7,000 feet, and fifty percent coverage by cirrus clouds that had bottoms at 22,000 feet, above the Group formation. The temperature at 20,000 feet was minus 25 degrees.

The Initial Point was the center of Lake Neusiedler. From there thirty-seven B-24s flew to the target and dropped 68.05 tons of 100 pound general purpose bombs (1361 bombs) at 1218 hours from an altitude of 21,000 feet for the 1st Unit of the formaion and 19,000 feet for the other, on an axis of attack of 292 degrees magnetic. Bombs were dropped at an indicated airspeed of 160 MPH which was a true airspeed of 219 MPH. Results were good. Smoke at the target prevented accurate observation, but nineteen photographs taken of the target area indicated that the target was well covered.

A 15th AF Liberator damaged by flak over Vienna, Austria. Photo courtesy of National Air and Space Museum, Smithsonian Institution.

Flak Damaged 15th A.F. Liberator Over Vienna

The Luftwaffe had constructed a bogus model of an airdrome, located five miles southeast of the real airdrome, but our competent navigators and bombardiers were not fooled. They reported their observation at the regular intelligence debriefing when they landed.

The three bombers that were shot down by fighters were all from the 745th Squadron. All downed planes were flying in the 3rd Box of the 2nd Unit of the Group formation. The "Missfit" piloted by 2nd Lt. Roger E. Walker was shot down when it could not stay up with the formation because of damage from fighters, and only two parachutes were seen to come from the plane as the plane was falling to the ground. However, three were later reported as prisoners of war, including the pilot, Walker, his bombardier, 2nd Lt. Albert G. Ranz, and the nose turret gunner, Cpl. William R. Sawyer. All of the rest of his crew were reported killed in action. Walker and Sawyer are currently members of the 456th Bomb Group Association.

The second plane lost, "Baby Dumpling" flown by the crew of 1st Lt. Norman O. Richards, was also victim of enemy fighters and three parachutes were seen to come from the plane before it disappeared from sight. When his damaged plane could not keep up with the rest of the formation, with his number four engine on fire, four Me-109s viciously attacked the plane until the whole right wing was seen to catch fire and tear lose from the plane. The "Baby Dumpling" spun violently to the ground. Later, two of his crew were reported as killed in action while nine others flying on the aircraft managed to bail out and they were taken as POW's. Two of the crew, 2nd Lt Kenneth C. Reimer, Navigator, and S/Sgt James H. Simmonds, radio operator, became members of the 456th Bomb Group Association after the war.

The third plane lost, flown by the crew of 2nd Lt. Edward J. Meyer, had ten parachutes reported coming from it. Two members of the crew, Meyer, and 2nd Lt Donald G. Adkins, his bombardier, are listed as missing in action. Eight were taken as POW's. Three of this crew, S/Sgt Leo A. Beaupre, engineer, S/Sgt Manuel W. Pacheco, ball turret gunner, and S/Sgt Dale E. Linebaugh, tail turret, became members of the 456th Group Association after the war.

The casualties for the day included, not only the regular size of three crews that were shot down with the three planes (normally thirty crewmen), but they also included an additional two cameramen who were on the planes. Thus, thirty-three men were initially reported as missing in action. Lt. George H. Gutting's nose turret gunner, Sgt Steve Kanuck who was flying as waist gunner on the mission, was injured in his hand by a 20mm fighter cannon burst and his shoes were also ripped by 50 caliber machine gun bullets.

We lost three B-24s and seventeen of our bombers were damaged by enemy fire. The remaining formation of thirty-four aircraft returned over our field at 1443 hours, and they logged 6:05 hours for the mission. This was the Group's twenty-second accredited mission of the twenty-nine missions flown in Italy.

Our 304th Wing had a total of 140 Liberators drop 259 tons of bombs on Bad Voslau, and the Wing lost a total of six bombers. The total Fifteenth Air Force effort for the day consisted of 446 bombers that dropped 1004 tons of bombs on targets in the same target area and a total of 8 bombers, including our three, were lost.

April 13, 1944 Tokol Airdrome, South Of Budapest, Hungary.

I earned my 14th and 15th accredited missions flying as copilot on this day, as usual, with Lt. Boughner's crew. It was a scary mission!

Our 456th Bomb Group was flying as part of a Fifteenth Air Force effort attacking four high priority targets in the same general area around Budapest. Six groups of B-17 fortresses from the 5th Wing attacked their target at 1400 hours, while a composite Wing of the 49th and 55th Wings attacked an adjacent target at 1410 hours. Our 304th Wing attacked a target on the same general area at 1420 hours. German defenses in the Budapest area had a busy day! Our Fifteenth Air Force saturation raids could not be stopped by the Luftwaffe, and it presented a difficult defense problem for the Germans as we were taking a heavy toll of their pilots. We were gradually gaining control of the air over central Europe.

Thirty-three of our Liberators took off starting at 0935 hours with Colonel Steed in the lead plane. The rest of our bombers followed his B-24 off the bumpy dirt runway at 45 second intervals. The Battle Order indicates that a Colonel Powers and 1st Lt. Dave E. Tavel were in the lead aircraft of the 2nd Unit. There was no Colonel Powers in our Group so he must have been a visitor or it was a typing error. Target for the day was the Tokol airdrome south of Budapest, Hungary. We were scheduled to have fifty-five P-38s as protective cover at the target. One of our bombers had to return home before reaching the target because it had two superchargers malfunction. That left thirty-two to fly over the target.

Although this was not my most dangerous mission, it was the first where I believed that it appeared inevitable that we were going to be blasted from the sky. It was the first time that I felt helpless, and it looked certain that we would be shot out within a few minutes. A huge swarm of 100 Luftwaffe fighters consisting of Me-109's, Me-110s, FW-190s, JU-88s, and Me-210s assaulted the bomb group that was flying just ahead of our group. They were in my plain view. We were flying in the number five position of the 2nd Box of the 1st Unit in our Group formation, and because

Boughner was flying at the time, I was able to watch the whole dramatic air battle unfold.

None of the fifty-five P-38 escort fighters that were supposed to give our 304th Wing target cover were anywhere in sight. I watched the huge air battle just ahead as the huge swarm of enemy fighters methodically blasted planes of the group flying ahead of us out of the sky, unmolested by any of our escort fighters that were no where around. They were concentrating all of their attention on the group ahead and ignoring our Group for the moment. Parachutes and exploding airplanes filled the air in front of us. Some of the planes were on fire in brilliant red-orange balls of fire and they were gyrating erratically out of control, some menacing our own formation by turning around and heading at us as we approached the Initial Point. We had to maneuver to avoid hitting many parachutists that filled the air in our flight path. The entire scene was awesome, and I felt pity for the airmen of the group ahead of us, but I also realized that we were next in line for the same treatment.

As the few remaining planes of the besieged bomb group in front of our Group entered the flak area to make their bomb run, enemy fighters as usual were not willing to follow them into their own heavy flak bursts. The huge swarm of fighters then turned their attention on us, the next group in line. They began to maneuver their fighters to start an attack on our formation. Two JU-88s attacked from 5 o'clock high and peeled down and away. Seven Me-109s came in from 2 to 5 o'clock low then peeled off to the right and down. Three Me-110s abreast made one pass at 5 o'clock high, then peeled to the right and down. One FW-190 came in at 3 o'clock and peeled away. One JU-88 fired two rockets at 100 yards, then dived under our formation at 900 yards.

We expected to be blasted out of the sky as the group in front of us had been, until the last minute. Then, as I had seen many times in Hollywood movies when the United States Cavalry led by Errol Flynn arrives at the last minute to rescue people in covered wagons from relentless Indian attacks, our scheduled escort fighters finally arrived over the target area to chase the enemy planes way. All enemy fighters dove for the ground in a matter of seconds, unwilling to engage our escort fighters. Our fighters were too late to help the bomb group ahead of us, but they were just in time to save our group.

There is no way to describe the patriotic feeling, the pride in our own USAAF escort fighters, nor the tremendous relief from tension when we saw the stars and strips painted on the fuselages of our own fighters as they passed dangerously close to our planes, and flying across our path directly in front of my plane which was near the front of our formation.

Our fighter pilots were either unaware of their own peril, or they chose to ignore their own safety as they aggressively flew by the front of our formation in hot pursuit of some of the enemy fighters that had just flown by the front of our formation. Our fighters came dangerously close to being shot down by our own nervous gunners. As soon as I saw the stars and stripes painted on our little friends, I shouted over our plane's interphone system that the fighter planes were ours and to withhold fire.

After all enemy fighters had left, we saw the usual dark cloud of black flak over the target ahead of us and we entered it with trepidation to make our bomb run. Flak was classified as heavy guns, moderate concentration, and accurate at the target and some red flak bursts were seen enroute to the target. Eight of our planes suffered flak damage, including my plane.

Typical of the experience and emotion of other crews, was the experience recorded in the diary of S/Sgt Thomas S. Delaney, radio operator of "SQUAT 'N DROP IT (

DONALD DUCK)" who was manning a gun in the waist of his plane. His bomber was flying in the 2nd Box of the 1st Unit, number six position. He reported, "....our formation ran into a barrage of flak, and we found a few big holes in our plane. I found out after we hit the ground that flak came through the waist and hit my gun support. The ground crew found the piece of flak at the bottom of the support! Our pilot kept it as a souvenir. I was lucky again, the Lord was with us, and I pray he will be with us always. My rosary beads were hanging up again and seemed to give me courage! Lt. (James J.) Duston, our bombardier got hit by flak on his helmet! The helmet saved him! The pilot and copilot had trouble with the plane, 2 turbos were out, and oil was leaking from number 2 engine. Flak also broke the oxygen tubing going to the tail gunner's turret. Almost a "milk run." Oh yes, the photographer got a real scare. Flak busted right by his head! On our return from the target a rocket was shot at us from the ground!" (Delaney and Duston, both excellent men, were later assigned to my crew when I was given one.) These were emotions and experiences often endured by many aircrews on our missions.

As our formation approached the target, the weather was good, with only thin cirrus above us, nothing below us, and 12 to 17 miles visibility to the ground. The temperature at 20,500 was minus 24 degrees centigrade.

Thirty-two of our Group's B-24s were able to make their way through the dense cloud of exploding flak bursts to the target. Four planes had bomb rack malfunctions and couldn't drop their bombs on the target. The remainder of the formation was credited with dropping 60.25 tons of 100 pound general purpose bombs (1205 bombs) at 1258 hours from an altitude of 21,000 feet for the 1st unit of our group formation and 19,500 feet for the 2nd unit on an axis of attack of 6 degrees magnetic. Bombing results were excellent. Our planes took 19 photographs covering the target area and they indicated that a large percentage of our bombs hit the target. Out of 66 enemy aircraft dispersed on the airdrome, 44 were destroyed (5 single engine, 36 twin engine, 2 transport, and 2 gliders) and 14 others received damage. Our Group's bombardiers were getting much more accurate, particularly when the visibility was as good as it was for this day's bombing.

Four planes of our formation that flew over the target with us had bomb rack malfunctions. Three of these bombers returned fourteen of their bombs to base and the other one jettisoned them. The bombardier that jettisoned the bombs, salvoed them because he "pressed the charging switch and one bomb went away, he hit the toggle switch and none went away, he hit the salvo lever and five (bomb) stations went away, then the pilot shook the ship three seconds after the normal bombs away time and they all fell out, beyond the target." We have had some Liberators experience problems with the bomb release mechanisms on almost every mission.

Our group formation of thirty-three planes returned over our field at 1535 hours and I logged 6:00 hours for my fourteenth and fifteenth missions (a two-fer). It was our Group's twenty-third accredited mission of the thirty missions flown in Italy.

We lost no aircraft from our group, only eight damaged bombers from this mission. We were only a part of the total Fifteenth Air Force mission which consisted of 342 B-24's and 163 B-17's that were bombing in a coordinated attack on airdrome, aircraft component manufacturing plants, and a repair base in the Budapest area. A total of 985 tons of bombs were dropped in the area. For the day, eighteen bombers, primarily from the group in front of ours, and three escort fighters were shot down by the enemy. Total Fifteenth Air Force air claims were 43 enemy fighters destroyed, thirteen 13 probables, and 15 damaged for the mission. Many more were destroyed on the ground, because our Group alone destroyed 44 enemy fighters on the ground and damaged 14 others.

The Fifteenth Air Force was beginning to assert its air power on a consistent basis and the Luftwaffe was feeling the crunch. It could not prevent it. The Luftwaffe was less willing to hang around to dogfight our escort fighters. As soon as our escort fighters arrived, enemy fighters dove for the deck to get away to conserve their limited number of available fighter pilots.

April 14, 1944 Weather Abort Enroute To Budapest, Hungary.

After another early morning briefing to bomb Budapest again, we took off, but the mission was canceled while we were enroute to the target. I logged 2:30 hours of flying time, but naturally, no mission credit.

Today, Major Leonard A. Weissinger, our group adjutant issued a memorandum about malaria prevention and control for our Group. The malaria season was approaching. Among other provisions, all buildings and structures used by troops at night were to be screened where practical, and all personnel were to sleep under bed nets beginning 15 April 1944. Head nets and mosquito gloves were issued to those who wanted to use them. Personnel outdoors between dark and dawn, were ordered to wear hats, keep their shirts buttoned, wear trousers tucked inside boots or leggings, and apply quartermaster issued insect repellent at four hour intervals.

The memorandum said that after April 15, 1944 all personnel must take one Atabrine tablet a day after the evening meal under the supervision of an officer before they leave the mess hall.

Amid rumors that B-24s were blowing up on takeoff due to sabotage, a new security system is being organized at our air base. Captain Percy R. Follis is in charge of the system. Each aircraft has a 24 hour guard on it, and a big problem is controlling Italians in their wanderings around the base.

April 15, 1944   Nis, Yugoslavia (Alternate Target).

The 456th attempted to bomb Bucharest again, but weather prevented it. Thirty-five bombers dropped 93.5 tons of 500 pound General Purpose bombs on a target of opportunity, the marshalling yards at Nis, Yugoslavia. Escort was provided by fifty P-38's. No enemy aircraft attacked our Group, but a few Me-110s, JU-88s and Me-109s were seen. A few gunners got off some bursts at them but they remained out of practical range of our guns. All aircraft returned safely, undamaged, to our air base. Flak was graded as scant, inaccurate, and heavy. There was a good pattern of bombs falling on the marshaling yards, and they obliterated the important railroad choke point. This was the Group's twenty-fourth accredited mission of the thirty-one missions flown in Italy. Flying time was 7:00 hours, and I missed another true milk run.

The malaria season was officially opened because we were each given an atabrine tablet at dinner. We were told to close the mosquito nets of our tents and bunks at night, use insect sprays, and use insect repellent. Trucks came around our tent cities in the evening spraying insect spray.

April 16, 1944 Turnu-Severin Airdrome, Rumania (Alternate).

I missed another milk run this day. Aircrews received wake-up calls in their tents at 0415 hours. After an early breakfast and briefing at 5:30 hours, the intelligence portion briefed by Major Dickerson, stations time at the aircraft was 0700 hours. Major John R. Sinclair in the lead plane took off at 0730 hours followed by thirty-two other B-24s at 45 second intervals. Capt. Kenneth W. Gruber and 1st Lt. Dave E. Tavel were in the lead aircraft of the 2nd Unit. The target for the day was the Brasov marshaling yards in Rumania, but weather required the Group to bomb the secondary target, Turnu-Severin airdrome, also in Rumania. Two bombers returned early, one because of gas siphoning out of its number two tank and the other had a leak in a right wing tank.

This was a landmark mission in that the Group's fighter escort was scheduled to be provided by thirty of the new P-51s and thirty P-38s. This is the first mission where we had P-51s as our fighter escort instead of the shorter range P-47s. However it turned out that they were not needed. Our gunners were briefed to look for the scoops on bellys of P-51 fighters because this was the most notable difference, and one of the only ways to tell the P-51 from the Me-109. The P-51 and the Me-109 look almost the same from a distance.

C O N F I D E N T I A L

BATTLE ORDER

Date: 16 April 1944

1st Unit: 1st Box

Formation Leader: Demelik, Sinclair AP 768
No. 3: Smith (C)   AP 291   Dep Leader: Mulligan   AP 279
                    No. 4: Phifer (C) AP 501
No. 6: Nix   AP 233   No. 5: Randal   AP 189

2nd Box

Leader: Lee   AP 214
No. 3: Lunt (C)   AP 752   Dep Leader: Desperock AP 285
                    No. 4: Jackson, W.L. (C) AP 295
No. 6: Nunimaker   AP 268   No. 5: Brabon   AP 799

3rd Box

Leader: Lane   AP 311
No. 3: Ward (C)   AP 637   Dep Leader: Bishop AP 661
                    No. 4: Clark (C) AP 772
No. 6: Ball   AP 284   No. 5: Malinowski AP 912

2nd Unit, 1st Box

Leader: Tavel, Gruber AP 499
No. 3: Hundley (C) AP 853   Dep Leader: Witkin AP 477
                    No. 4: Riddle (C) AP 290
No. 6: Leukuma   AP 283   No. 5:   AP

2nd Box

Leader: Manlove AP 492
No. 3: Boughner (C) AP 086   Dep Leader: Ensign AP 486
                    No. 4: Richards (C) AP 489
No. 6: Cutting   AP 831   No. 5: Sagert   AP 480

3rd Box

Leader: Gardner AP 345
No. 3: Little (C} AP 334   Dep Leader: Nilsson AP 297
                    No. 4: Douglass (C) AP 749
No. 6: Fleming   AP 589   No. 5: Phillips   AP 183

Stations: 0705   456th HEADTOP TWO FOUR

Engines: A 0710 B 0710 C 0720   Penetration: CARTLOAD ONE
         D 0720 E 0735 F 0735
                                   Target Area: CARTLOAD TWO
Take-off: 0730
                                   Withdrawal: CARTLOAD THREE and
E.T.R.: 1400   CARTLOAD FOUR.

C O N F I D E N T I A L

There was no flak at the target and no enemy aircraft were seen. The target weather was very good with only a high cirrus cloud coverage above our group at about 23,000 feet, and visibility to the target was twelve miles. The outside air temperature at 15,000 feet was minus 12 degrees centigrade. Window was thrown from our bombers to confuse the enemy radar.

Our Group again demonstrated its bombing accuracy when thirty of its bombers dropped 74.75 tons of 500 pound bombs on the Turnu-Severin airdrome at 1050 hours from an altitude of 18,000 feet for the 1st Unit of our formation, and 15,000 feet for the 2nd Unit on an axis of attack of 281 degrees magnetic. Nine photos were taken of the target area. Bombing results were excellent with a good pattern of bombs covering the target area, especially the hangar area, and numerous fires were seen and one big explosion was observed.

One bombardier in the formation did not drop his bombs on the target because he was on the flight deck, away from his bomb sight, repairing a leak in his oxygen mask when the group dropped its bombs on the target. He brought his ten 500 pounders home.

Weather enroute was good, with only one stretch where there were some altocumulus clouds covering seven-tenths of the area

Another bomber had one 500 pound bomb hang up on its rack, and it was brought back to our base.

The formation of thirty-one Liberators returned to our base at 1308 hours and the logged flying time was 5:45 hours. There were no enemy fighters or flak, so this was a true milk run that I missed. All aircraft returned home safely. This was the group's twenty-fifth accredited mission of thirty-two missions flown in Italy.

April 17, 1944   Marshaling Yards At Sophia, Bulgaria.

This was another mission to the marshalling yards at Sophia, Bulgaria. I participated in it as copilot with Boughner's crew to get my sixteenth accredited mission. We were able to sleep in a little later because of the shorter mission, and after a 0600 hour wake-up call we attended briefing at 7:12 AM with Major Dickerson, Group S-2, briefing the intelligence portion. We had an aircraft stations time of 0910 hours, with start engine time of 0915 for the 1st Box and each of the five other Boxes started engines at five minute intervals after the first. Captain Louis M. Abernathy, in the lead ship, took off at 0930 hours and thirty-seven B-24s followed him off the runway at 45 second intervals. After we formed the Group formation around Abernathy's plane, he led us over Giulia Airfield at 4,000 feet to rendezvous with the other groups of the 304th Wing. We flew in a formation of groups with the other groups of the 304th Bomb Wing, echeloned left, in the order, 454th, 455th, 456th, and 459th. We departed Giulia Airfield climbing on course at an indicated airspeed of 160 MPH, climbing at 250 feet per minute rate of climb to bombing altitude. The 304th Wing was attacking two different targets in the same area to divide fighter opposition. My plane was flying in the number five position of the 3rd Box of the 2nd Unit in our Group formation.

Six bombers returned early before reaching the target for the following reasons: one had a gas leak, one had two generators malfunction, one elevator trim tab became lose, one had number two engine go out, one had its elevator control become inoperative and one plane had its pilot and bombardier become sick .

C O N F I D E N T I A L

BATTLE ORDERS

Date: 17 April 1944

1st Unit: 1st Box

Formation Leader: Thomas, Abernathy AP 768 Clark,R.R.
No. 3: Desperock (C) AP 501   Dep Leader: Witkin/   AP 477
                              No. 4: Lee (C)   AP 214
No. 6: Strombos   AP 634   No. 5: Ball   AP 284

2nd Box

                    Leader: Andrews   AP 912
No. 3: Hapa   (C)   AP 311   Dep Leader: Newhouse   AP 283
                              No. 4: Leukuma (C) AP 772
No. 6: Haviland   AP 661   No. 5: Malinowsky   AP 637
                              No. 7: Rawlinson   AP 287

3rd Box

                    Leader: Miller, Reid   AP 268
No. 3: Jones   (C)   AP 291   Dep Leader: Van Dyke   AP 872
                              No. 4: Rudd (C)   AP 295
No. 6: Hillman   AP 285   No. 5: Griffin   AP 752
                              No. 7: Brabon   AP 799

2nd Unit: 1st Box

                    Leader: Jackson,C.Y.,Christensen AP 499
No. 3: Barrasso (C)   AP 290   Dep Leader: Townsend   AP 231
                              No. 4: Gardner (C) AP 487
No. 6: Palis   AP 183   No. 5: Bowering   AP 189

2nd Box

                    Leader: Richards   AP 489
No. 3: Bock   (C)   AP 492   Dep Leader: Sagert   AP 480
                              No. 4: Cutting (C) AP 086
No. 6: Ensign   AP 486   No. 5: Boughner   AP 853
                              No. 7: Johnson   AP 831

3rd Box

                    Leader: Grimm   AP 345
No. 3: Fleming   (C)   AP 589   Dep Leader: Callan   AP 749
                              No. 4: Nonahan (C) AP 334
No. 6: Williamson   AP 165   No. 5: Phillips   AP 297
                              No. 7: Little   AP 304

Stations: 0910   456th CONAY TWO THREE

Engines: A 0915 B 0920 C 0925   Fighters: RINGWAY
         D 0930 E 0935 F 0940

Take-off: 0930

E.T.R.: 1400   C O N F I D E N T I A L

Weather enroute was good, with only one stretch where there were some altocumulus clouds covering seven-tenths of the area below us. When we reached the target area there were no clouds below us, only four-tenths of high cirrus above the formation, but visibility was reduced to 3 to 5 miles, air to ground, because of smoke and haze caused by fires from previous bombings by groups ahead of us. Outside air temperature at 19,100 feet was minus 16 degrees centigrade.

On entering the bomb run flak was graded as the inaccurate, barrage type, rather than the accurate tracking type. We were seeing more barrage type of flak because our "chaff," or "Window" as the British called it, was working. Chaff was made up of long strips of aluminum or lead tinsel, the type many people use on their Christmas tree decorations. Our two waist gunners dropped large amounts of it out open waist windows of our B-24s. A chaff dispenser was installed later to drop it in controlled amounts and all Liberators of our formation would begin dispensing it as soon as we entered a flak area to confuse the radar used to aim antiaircraft guns on the ground. Massive amounts of chaff floating down in the sky confused enemy radar so that ground radar operators could not get our altitude, speed, and course, to accurately shoot us down. However, if the weather was such that gunners on the ground could see us, as was the case this day, they could visually aim their guns at us.

Thirty-two of our Group's bombers dropped 63.7 tons of 100 pound general purpose bombs on the Sophia marshaling yards at 1221 hours from an altitude of 20,000 feet for the 1st Unit and 19,000 for the 2nd Unit. The axis of attack was 131 and 154 degrees magnetic, for each. We flew at an indicated airspeed of 160 MPH, which was a true airspeed of about 220 MPH. The bombardiers' bomb release interval setting was set at 60 feet. Two of our bombers had some bombs hang up in their racks after release at the target and they had to jettison them manually on the way home. This usually meant that someone had to put on a portable oxygen mask and walk out into the bomb bay, with bomb bay doors open, cold air swirling around, and hack the bombs off their shackles with a fire ax.

Twenty-two photos were taken of the target area with five K-20 and six K-22 cameras. Bombing results were fair and we had a good pattern of bombs on the target. Our bombs caused severe damage to the central part of the marshalling yards, including the rail choke point. The target was full of dust and smoke from the bombing of other groups.

As usual, after bombs away, our formation made a descending turn, this time to the right to 210 degrees, to evade the flak. We had to avoid flying over the town of Pernik nearby because it also had some flak guns.

Our scheduled escort fighters did not prevent us from being attacked by enemy fighters after we had released our bombs on the target. Nine enemy aircraft attacked our Group soon after bombs were dropped and our gunners were credited with one destroyed and one probably destroyed. First, at 1225 hours, four minutes after bombs away at the target, one Me-109 attacked from the 6 o'clock low position, broke off to 3 o'clock in the target area. Next, seven Me-109s and an Me-110 came in flying four abreast, then peeled off to regroup to attack singly from the 4 and 6 o'clock positions. Four minutes after that, one of the Me-109s fired rockets from the 3 o'clock position at 1229 hours.

We lost no planes, but two of our B-24s were damaged. Our formation of thirty-two planes arrived over home at 1441 hours. We logged 5:15 hours flying time. It was the Group's twenty-sixth accredited mission of the thirty-three missions flown in Italy.

To the delight of everyone, news came down from headquarters that there will be no mission tomorrow. A

Major Hayes from our Wing administration section visited our headquarters, and gave instructions about making out mission reports. (Reviewing the archives for this book, I can see where it was badly needed.)

April 18, 1944   No Mission

This was another stand-down day. We also received news that tomorrow would be another stand-down day, and everyone was jubilant until we learned that there would be a personal inspection and that we would have to march in parade. We had to take our dress uniforms from our foot lockers, and polish our shoes. Many were busy polishing shoes and trying to get the wrinkles out of their dress winter uniforms that hadn't been worn much in Italy. Dress was usually very casual.

April 19, 1944   Parade, No Flying.

The group had an inspection and parade. Major General Twining, Commanding Officer of the 15th Air Force, presented medals to some of our people. Colonel Fay R. Upthegrove, Commander of the 304th Wing, also attended. Lt. Benjamin Smalley, lead bombardier in my 746th Squadron, received the Silver Star for his heroic efforts. A few, including 1st. Lt. Arthur F. Bowering of my 746th Squadron (shot down less than three weeks later) received the Distinguished Flying Cross. Along with hundreds of others, I earned an Air Medal with two Oak Leaf Clusters, but there was no formal presentation of Air Medals. I wasn't notified of it until much later.

Our Group Commander, Colonel Steed, made a speech telling us that we were doing a superior job, both in the air and on the ground.

We had a spit and polish inspection before we marched by a reviewing stand to the tune of military music played by a visiting marching band. The hearts and minds of most

228

aircrews were not in the inspection exercise because we felt we had more important life and death concerns to deal with. But when the music began playing most of us felt a patriotic fervor that sent chills up our spine and put a spring in our steps.

Awards presented included: Distinguished Flying Crosses, 5; Silver Stars, 4; Soldiers Medal, 1; Purple Hearts, 25; Air Medals, 578; Bronze Oak Leaf Clusters to the Air Medal, 294; and Silver Cluster to the Air Medal, 1.

April 20, 1944   Aurisina Marshaling Yards, Italy (Target of Opportunity).

I flew with Boughner's crew on this mission to bomb Opicina, Italy, but weather forced us to bomb a target of opportunity. We flew in the Number 4 Position of the 2nd Box of the 1st Unit in the Group formation.

We felt like bankers because we were allowed to sleep in our tents until 0730 hours this day. We attended a briefing at 0845 hours with the busy Lt. Gilbert Smith conducting the intelligence portion. Start engines time for the first Box was 0940 hours, and Colonel Steed in the lead ship started to taxi to the end of the runway at 0950. Captain Chester Ladd and 1st Lt. Dave E. Tavel were in the lead ship of the 2nd Unit of the formation. Colonel Steed in the lead ship took off at 1000 hours, and thirty-nine of our Liberators followed his off the runway at 45 second intervals. One bomber returned early because of engine trouble.

Fighter escort was provided by P-38s and P-51s. The Fifteenth Air Force bomber groups were scheduled to attack three targets in the same general area to divide the enemy fighter opposition. However, bad weather interfered with these plans.

Weather at our primary target, Opicina, prevented bombing it, so we went to a target of opportunity, the marshaling yards at Aurisina, Italy. The weather at Aurisina

229

was almost as bad as that at the primary target. Aurisina had eight-tenths cloud coverage by cumulus clouds that had bottoms at 8,000 feet and tops at 14,000 feet. Temperature at 18,400 feet was minus 18 degrees centigrade.

Although there was no flak at the target area, there was scant and inaccurate flak encountered on the way to the target at Pola, Muggia, and Brioni. One vessel in the harbor of Trieste fired a few bursts at us.

We were scheduled to be escorted by P-38 and P-51 fighters at our primary target. None were around us at this alternate target. Sixteen enemy aircraft attacked us as we approached the target of opportunity at 1255 hours, two minutes before we dropped our bombs. There was no flak at the target to keep enemy fighters from following us all the way to the target. Four Me-109s painted with black tops and silver bellies made two aggressive attacks from the 5 and 6 o'clock low positions, and they broke off their attacks from under our formation, and then another three FW-190s attacked from the 3 o'clock low position, made one pass then peeled to the right and away in the 2 o'clock direction. Next, three more Me-109s made one pass from 4 o'clock level across our formation's tail, then it dove down under our formation just as our bombardiers were releasing their bombs on the target of opportunity at 1257 hours. Our gunners destroyed three enemy fighters and we lost no bombers.

C O N F I D E N T I A L

BATTLE ORDER

Date: 20 April 1944

1st Unit, 1st Box

Demelik
Formation Leader: Col. Steed/ AP 475   Callan
No. 3: Riddle (C) AP 772   Dep Leader: Clark, W.B./ AP 345
No. 4: Manlove (C) AP 492
No. 6: Hundley   AP 853   No. 5: Peterson   AP 309

2nd Box

Leader: Townsend AP 231
No. 3: Witkin (C) AP 477   Dep Leader: Johnson AP 831
No. 4: Boughner (C) AP 480
No. 6: Snee   AP 839   No. 5: Bowering   AP 189
(Movie Camera)   No. 7: Ensign AP 486

3rd Box

Leader: Douglass AP 749
No. 3: Fleming (C) AP 165   Dep Leader: Nilsson AP 297
No. 4: Gardner (C) AP 589
No. 6: Little   AP 183   No. 5: Wilkinson   AP 334
No. 7: Malinowski AP 284

2nd Unit, 1st Box

Tavel
Leader: Ladd / AP 499   Hyde
No. 3: Wallace (C) AP 311   Dep Leader: Lehner/ AP 489
No. 4: Mulligan (C) AP 872
No. 6: Brabon   AP 799   No. 5: Lunt   AP 752
No. 7: Rawlinson AP 633

2nd Box

Leader: Clark, W.D. AP 912
No. 3: Lane (C)   AP 287   Dep Leader: Bishop   AP 661
No. 4: Strombom (C) AP 634
No. 6: Ward   AP 637   No. 5: Jennings   AP 364
No. 7: Newhouse AP 283

3rd Box

Phifer
Leader: Reid,/ AP 501
No. 3: Rudd (C)   AP 295   Dep Leader: Nix   AP 214
No. 4: Jackson, W.L. (C) AP 285
No. 6: Nunimaker   AP 268   No. 5: Lambert   AP 290
No. 7: Parks, (Smith) AP 291

Stations: 0835   456th BETTY TWO

Engines: A 0840 B 0840 C 0850   14th FG KEYWORD TWO
D 0850 E 0905 F 0905

Take-off: 0900   C O N F I D E N T I A L

Only thirty-four B-24s successfully released their bombs on this target, dropping 85 tons of 500 pound general purpose bombs with poor results from an altitude of 20,000 feet for the first unit, and 18,000 feet for the second one, on an axis of attack of 165 degrees magnetic. The indicated airspeed was 160 MPH, a true airspeed of 215 MPH. Because of the poor weather conditions, and the difficulty of synchronizing on the target, most bombs were reported to have fallen in an open field north of the marshaling yards. Fourteen photographs were taken of the target area to confirm it. This was one of those days!

Five bombers traveled with the formation to the target, but did not drop their bombs. The reason that bombs were not dropped by the five planes were: two of them had bomb rack malfunctions, two other bombardiers could not see the target, and another bombardier did not see his leader drop so he didn't drop.

Our formation returned over the field at 1500 hours and I logged 5:10 hours combat flying time after we were on the ground. I recorded my seventeenth accredited mission and a total of 78:05 combat hours. It was the Group's twenty-seventh accredited mission of the thirty-four flown in Italy.

Weather in Italy was getting more agreeable and we were able to fly more combat missions, but we were still dependent on weather over targets outside Italy to enable us to bomb our highest priority targets. We no longer had to wear heavy winter clothing while on the ground. The temperature at 18,400 feet for this mission was minus 18 degrees centigrade, so the air was warming up considerably from what we had to endure on missions during February and early March. We noticed a great difference, and we were kept much more comfortable in our flying suits.

April 21, 1944 Bucharest Marshaling Yards, Rumania.

Today was my second mission to bomb Bucharest marshaling yards during April, and it was the toughest of the two. Three of our Liberators were shot down and two more were so critically damged that, though the pilots heroically flew them back to Italy, the Liberators would never fly again. It was also my second flight in two days. Bucharest and nearby Ploesti, thirty-five miles away, were heavily defended by Germans because the oil and transportation facilities in the area were vital to their ability to continue the war. We always expected heavy flak and many enemy fighters when we went to that area. We were attacked by 65 enemy fighters. There was a disastrous communications mix-up concerning all Fifteenth Air Force Liberators and the new P-51 Mustang fighters.

After a morning wake-up call at 0600 hours, breakfast, ride in the back of six-by-six trucks to our Headquarters up on the hill and briefing at 0700, our stations time at our aircraft was 0815 hours, start engine time was 0820 for all aircraft in the 1st Box of the formation, 0825 for the 2nd Box, 0830 for the 3rd Box, 0835 for the 4th Box, 0845 for the 5th Box, and 0850 for the 6th Box. We were scheduled to have the usual two Units in our Group formation, two "V" formations of Boxes with each Unit containing 21 Liberators for this day's mission. Colonel Steed in the lead plane started to taxi out to the end of the runway at 0835 hours then he took off one minute early at 0844 hours. One plane had a mechanical malfunction that caused it to abort before takeoff, so only forty-one bombers were able to get off the ground, following him off the runway with 45 second takeoff intervals between planes.

After takeoff, we gathered the Group's planes into our usual fighting formation, then our Group rendezvoused with the 459th Bomb Group over its airfield at Giulia at 3000 feet before departing on course. Giulia Airfield was an air base about fifteen miles east of Stornara, home of the 459th Bomb Group. The 459th Bomb Group followed our Group's lead, flying in trail with us, and we followed the 454th and 455th groups to the target. We departed Giulia climbing on course at 0945 hours at a rate of climb of 200 feet per minute to our bombing altitude. Our climbing indicated airspeed was 160 MPH, a true airspeed of about 200 MPH.

Three Liberators aborted the mission prior to reaching the target area; one returned because cowling tore loose on an engine, and two returned early because they were crippled by enemy fighter attack.

We now had an alternate method of bombing in our Group formation, a radar-equipped B-24 called the "Pathfinder" that some called "Mickey." Fred Riley, a former bombardier in my 746th Squadron, notes that the Mickey operator and the bombardier worked together to aim and release the bombs. This radar had not been perfected yet so it was not reliable enough to be used as the primary bombsight in place of the Norden visual bombsight. Pathfinder was officially designated H2X, an American modification of the British H2S airborne radar that the British had used as early as October 1943. If weather at the target was overcast to the extent that visual bombing could not be accomplished, the Pathfinder's crew would drop its bombs on the target through the clouds using its radar bomb sight and the other bombardiers of the Group would release their bombs at the same time they saw the Pathfinder release its bombs. The Group was briefed to bomb by "Pathfinder" aircraft on this mission if weather prevented visual bombing of the target.

The other three groups of our 304th Bomb Wing, the 454th, 455th, and 459th, were also scheduled to bomb the same marshaling yards at Bucharest. The B-17 Fortresses of the 5th Bomb Wing were scheduled to bomb Ploesti, a target near ours, only thirty-five miles away. This tactic was planned to saturate the area, and to dilute the attention of

C O N F I D E N T I A L

BATTLE ORDER

21 April 1944

1st Unit, 1st Box

Thomas

Formation Leader: Col Stood/ AP 817   Andrews
No. 3: Monahan (C)   AP 334   Dep Loader: Clark, R.R./ AP 470
                    No. 4: Richards (C) AP 489
No. 6: Gutting   AP 231   No. 5: Sagert   AP 480
                    No. 7: Fleming AP 589

2nd Box

Leader: Manlove   AP 492
No. 3: Ensign (C)   AP 486   Dep Loader: Lohner AP 931
                    No. 4: Snee (C) AP 839
No. 6: Boughner   AP 549   No. 5: Hundley   AP 853
                    No. 7: Beck   AP 222

3rd Box

Leader: Grimm   AP 345
No. 3: Wilkinson (C) AP 165   Dep Leader: Douglass AP 749
                    No. 4: Laszewski (C) AP 309
No. 6: Palis   AP 183   No. 5: Peterson   AP 297
                    No. 7: Little   AP 304

2nd Unit, 1st Box

Tavel

Leader: Christensen/ AP 499   Gruber
No. 3: Malinowski (C) AP 772   Dep Leader: Miller/ AP 268
                    No. 4: Riddle (C) AP 283
No. 6: Smith, Parks AP 275   No. 5: Van Dyke   AP 872
                    No. 7: Strombom AP 634

2nd Box

Leader: Lee   AP 214
No. 3: Jackson, W.L. (C) AP 501   Dep Loader: Griffin AP 752
                    No. 4: Jones (C) AP 291
No. 6: Lambert   AP 295   No. 5: Barrasso   AP 290
                    No. 7: Hillman (C) AP 285

3rd Box

Leader: Lane   AP 912
No. 3: Ward (C)   AP 637   Dep Loader: Haviland AP 661
                    No. 4: Loukuma (C) AP 364
No. 6: Mapa   AP 311   No. 5: Jennings   AP 098
                    No. 7: Ball   AP 284

Stations: 0815   456th FRUITTART THREE ONE

Engines: A 0820 B 0825 C 0830   Penetration: CONWAY ONE
         D 0835 E 0845 F 0850
                                   Withdrawal: CONWAY TWO
Take-off: 0845

E.T.R.: 1500   Top Cover: SHORTBREAD

C O N F I D E N T I A L

enemy fighters because all groups were to be bombing in the same area about the same time.

We were scheduled to have P-38 fighter escort from the point that we entered enemy territory to the limit of endurance of the P-38 fuel supply, then two groups of P-38s were scheduled to provide cover as we withdrew from the target after we released our bombs. A new group of long-range P-51 Mustangs, the 31st Fighter Group which had first become operational five days before, was scheduled to escort the B-17s to their target nearby at Ploesti. Thus there should be plenty of fighter protection for us bombers in the area. Unfortunately, this is not the way it turned out for us!

This mission was a terrible mix-up for the Fifteenth Air Force. All groups were recalled by higher command, using a pre-arranged, secret, coded radio transmission while we were enroute to the target. For the first time that I can remember, we were not given a secret code word that would be used to recall our formation if higher headquarters decided to abort the mission. For the first time, our mimeographed briefing sheets that were given to us at our morning briefing (see the attached) did not have a recall code word on it, and I don't remember ever receiving one. Whether we never received the secret code, and failed to return to Italy because we didn't recognize it, or we just couldn't hear the message, our Group and all the rest of the B-24 groups flying on this mission continued on the mission as briefed.

Advance, stripped-down, high-speed reconnaissance planes had been sent to fly over the target area ahead of the bombers, and they reported that bad weather existed over the entire land mass east of the Adriatic, including our targets at Bucharest and Ploesti. We were all ordered to return to our bases by a radio message, using the secret recall word, transmitted by Fifteenth Air Force Headquarters. This order came after my 456th Group and all the other B-24 bombers of the Fifteenth Air Force had already crossed the Adriatic.

Unfortunately, only the B-17 groups and our scheduled P-38 escort, which were to the rear of our bomber stream and took off later than our B-24s, received the recall code word and returned home. All of the 304th Bomb Wing's B-24s and all of the other B-24s continued on course in an attempt to bomb the target as ordered, in spite of the terrible weather, because they didn't know about the recall message.

The new 31st Fighter Group, consisting of thirty-six P-51s, and scheduled to escort the B-17s, did not hear the recall message either. They continued to the target by flying around the bad weather. The P-51s spotted a swarm of enemy fighters headed for our B-24 bomber stream, and three dozen P-51s engaged the enemy fighters. In the gigantic dogfight that followed, P-51s displayed their performance superiority by claiming seventeen enemy aircraft destroyed, seven probables, and ten damaged. Only two Mustangs and their pilots were lost in the air battle. Though we never saw them, they did help out one of our other Liberator groups of the 304th Wing that was about to be attacked.

It was the first important action of the long-range P-51s of the Fifteenth Air Force, a milestone of things to come. Later, when the word was passed around the Luftwaffe about the potent Mustangs enemy pilots would seldom remain to dogfight with them. In future battles, as soon as the P-51s appeared, enemy fighters would disappear, diving to the ground to get away. The problem for the Luftwaffe, however, was that the Mustangs could dive faster than any of their fighters and it was difficult for them to get away. We were glad to have the long range P-51s escorting us!

While this activity was in progress, my Group's formation was being attacked by 65 enemy fighters (some estimated it to be 100 fighters) as we neared the target area. Two of our B-24s were so severely crippled by the attacking fighters that they could not keep up with our formation, and they turned around before reaching the target area. Aircrews of my Group of bombers never saw any of our escort fighters that were supposed to be protecting us, so it was another classic air battle consisting of our bombers' gunners against the 65 enemy fighters. During the melee, our gunners destroyed three enemy fighters, claimed four more probables, and damaged five.

We lost five B-24s on the mission, three shot down before they could return to Italy, and two more returned to Italy so badly damaged that they were never flown again. At least two of these Liberators were lost as a result of flak fire. The other three bombers were lost by enemy fighter attack and/or a combination of flak and fighter fire. An additional six of our Group's bombers were damaged by fighter fire before we reached the target, and another seven of our Liberators were damaged by flak. Thus, we had a total of five B-24s lost as a result of this mission and an additional thirteen were damaged by enemy fire.

While our formation was flying around, trying to find breaks in the cloud buildups and an alternate target, dropping to an altitude as low as 15,000 feet to avoid clouds, our Group's formation was being pummeled by antiaircraft guns at Belgrade, Imotski, and Vrsac. As noted above, seven Liberators were damaged by flak, and one B-24, flown by 2nd Lts. John W. Wallace and Arthur Malinowski, as discussed below, was shot down by a direct hit from flak.

In trying to reach the primary target our leader had to guide our formation of Liberators around huge buildups of cumulonimbus clouds that obstructed our flight path. Finally, we learned that our formation was unable to get to the target because a solid wall of clouds blocked the way in front of us. Clouds reached up to 25,000 feet and we were flying at 21,000 feet, so no bombs were dropped on the primary target and we soon found out that the secondary target had the same foul weather. Pathfinder radar could not be used because our bomber formation couldn't reach the target where it could be used. We could only get to the targets by flying through the high build up of clouds, which we couldn't do with our formation of bombers. Weather covered all possible alternative targets, so no bombs were dropped except that eleven ships jettisoned their bombs into the clouds to lighten their loads because of damage to their planes or because they were low on fuel.

Six of these eleven Liberators jettisoned their bombs because the bombers had been so badly crippled from enemy action that they had to get rid of their bombs and lighten their aircraft to stay in the air. Another five aircraft were so low on gas, in addition to being crippled, they jettisoned their bombs to save fuel. Twenty-four bombers brought their bombs back to our base and landed with them. Two of our B-24s had to land at friendly fields because they couldn't reach Stornara..

The temperature at 21,000 feet was minus 24 degrees centigrade, but the Group's formation varied its altitude, flying as low as 15,000 feet to avoid clouds.

Our aircrew casualties for the mission included two crews missing in action and eleven crew members taken prisoners of war. In addition, four of our airmen had serious wounds, including two tail turret gunners, a radio operator, and an engineer. Slightly wounded were a pilot, a bombardier, and a navigator.

One of the five planes lost was piloted by 2nd Lts. John W. Wallace and Arthur Malinowski, copilot, of the 747th Squadron. The diary of Werner "Judge" Foss, bombardier flying on Lt. Stanley A. Sagert's crew, indicates that Wallace and Malinowski's plane took a direct flak hit that caused the plane to blow up, knocking the plane's tail off. He notes that no parachutes were seen to come from the plane as it dropped into the clouds below. The Group formation was flying at 15,000 feet at the time. Group's official records show that this happened at 1414 hours near Belgrade. The entire crew was listed as missing in action and we have not heard from any of the crew since then.

Another plane lost, "The Flying Fliver" piloted by 1st Lt. Norman E. Grimm of the 745th Squadron, lost two engines and was last seen dropping into the clouds over Yugoslavia. The entire crew was later reported as Prisoners of War. Five members of Grimm's crew are currently members of the 456th Bomb Group Association: Grimm, the pilot; 2nd Lt. Joseph J. Howard Jr.; navigator; T/Sgt Gilbert L. Muddel; engineer; S/Sgt John M. Tononi, tail turret gunner; and S/Sgt Charles Lind, photographer. The wife of S/Sgt Charles E. Stone, ball turret gunner, is also a member.

One plane piloted by Lt. John S. Mapa of the 747th Squadron returned to Italy with five of his crew injured by fighter attack, and the plane was so riddled by enemy fire that it had to be scrapped. Mapa is currently a member of the 456th Bomb Group Association.

A fourth plane lost with its crew, also from the 747th Squadron, was flown by an unknown pilot who substituted for Lt. Lewis T. Phillips at the last minute because Phillips had a sinus problem. Thus, Phillips survived. The copilot is also unknown. The crew is still listed as missing in action, except for T/Sgt Edward R. Moran, engineer who survived. Both, Phillips and Moran are members of the 456th Bomb Group Association.

A fifth Liberator destroyed was that flown by Lt. Rex Wilkinson. Lt. John Dupont who was copilot on Lt. Rex Wilkinson's plane told us of his experience, in the 456th Bomb Group Association's history book. He stated that his plane was heavily damaged by enemy fighters and it had two engines out so they jettisoned their bombs. As they were crossing the Adriatic, it appeared that they were going to have to ditch their plane in the sea because they were losing altitude. When the pilot called to the crew to alert the aircrew to the fact that they were about to ditch the plane, there was a frantic call on the interphone saying that the ball turret gunner, Sgt. Kenny Mayberry, was stuck in his turret because he could not align it properly. He could not get out. After some frantic moments, while the plane continued to lose altitude, the pilot was able to keep it at 200 feet above the water until reaching the Italian coast and the ball turret gunner was pulled from his turret. Their plane made an emergency landing on an airfield near the coast. The plane never flew again due to extensive structural damage.

Two of our planes, one piloted by Lt. Emil S. Laszewski and the other piloted by Lt. Rex Wilkinson, both of the 745th Squadron, landed at friendly fields because of fuel shortages, plane damage, and/or wounded on board. A major hospital was located at Foggia, near a runway, so planes with severely wounded aboard would land there to get their wounded immediate, high level medical attention.

We were stretching the limits of endurance for the B-24 when flying close formation and dodging clouds for such a length of time. Close formation flying consumed more fuel than would be consumed if we were flying at a steady, normal cruise, when we could keep constant throttle settings. In formation, throttles had to be constantly adjusted to remain in formation and this burned more fuel. Pilots flying at the rear of the formations usually had to make the greatest movements of their throttles because it was like a whiplash position. A small movement of the position of planes in the front of the formation required a much larger adjustment and movement of planes in the rear of the formation to stay in tight formation.

Our formation returned home at 1615 hours and we logged 7:30 combat hours for the mission. Though we could not drop our bombs, the Group was given credit for the mission presumably because of the aerial combat and because of the recall mixup. Thus, I logged my missions

241

number eighteen and nineteen, and it was our Group's twenty-eighth credited mission of thirty-five missions flown in Italy.

A reason for differences in fuel consumption between planes of our group, in addition to the whiplash effect of flying at the tail end of the formation, was that some pilots were not as smooth as the rest at jockeying the throttles to keep their positions during close formation flying. Our longer missions required pilots to carefully control the amount of fuel consumption by smooth operation of the throttles, by keeping the propeller RPM's at a minimum for a given manifold-pressure setting on the engines, and by keeping the fuel mixture controls at the minimum (leanest air to fuel ratio) for the conditions. Carelessness at managing any of these factors by the pilot would cause fuel shortages on our longer missions.

There was a "V" mail letter from my mother waiting for me when we finally reached our tent area. It contained a message telling me that my draft notice came to my home. I had turned twenty-one years old on January 20, 1944, so I was now eligible to be drafted into the armed forces. The draft notice ordered me to appear before my draft board for evaluation to be inducted into the military service. I told my folks in my next "V" mail letter home, to tell the draft board that I couldn't appear before them until I finished my fifty missions. I only had nineteen missions completed and I had thirty-one more to go.

Rain came that night, but it was a welcome sight because it helped settle the dust that was getting bad. In general, weather in Italy was becoming more agreeable.

My 746th Squadron now had a decent privy dug by the Italian soldiers and one shower head for the entire squadron was built by one of our pilots, the talented Lt. Harry J. Ragland. A steady supply of fresh water became available to use for washing and to keep clean. Italian women were coming around our tents on a regular basis to take our laundry. Post Exchange supplies were becoming plentiful, and the food was also made decent because our food preparers gained more experience. All personnel were now housed in the larger, more comfortable pyramidal five-man tents. Spring was finally here, and we were flying missions more frequently.

I did get to travel around southern Italy, on my days off, to such places as Naples, Bari, Foggia, and of course into Stornara and Cerignola. British, U.S. Army, and Red Cross canteens were the main places to visit, other than ordinary sight-seeing, because the Italian economy was so depressed. Many cities had been thoroughly bombed out, or they were so economically depressed and primitive that they weren't interesting sight-seeing targets, except for the big city of Naples that we visited a few times. As discussed later, a few of my crew and I went to rest camp on the Isle of Capri for a few days. That and the few visits to Naples were high points of my sight seeing. I did visit Benghazi, Libya, and the Island of Sardinia on business flights, but other than that my sight-seeing was from the air. I was never able to visit Rome during World War II because Germans continued to occupy it the entire time I was in Italy.

A late model B-24G that I was assigned to fly later had bubble side-windows for the pilots to stick their heads into to look down and back from the airplane, and I spent some time with high powered binoculars looking down on the countryside as we flew over it, when the other pilot was flying. We were deliberately routed, many times, to fly close to a number of industrial areas to make workers quit work and run to bomb shelters, so that many man-hours of productive work would be lost from their factories. Of course we would avoid flying over towns that had flak guns. We would make a feint, flying directly at the towns, as though we were going to bomb them, then we would fly past them. It was interesting, and also sad to watch through the binoculars, the scrambling for cover in the streets of picturesque towns below. However, they had started the war and their armies had perpetrated dastardly atrocities. War is hell!

Malaria was getting to be more of a concern, because mosquitoes were becoming plentiful now that the weather was hot. We had to keep mosquito nets tight around our sleeping cots, and we used mosquito repellent on the exposed parts of our bodies. Our tent areas and tents were sprayed with insect bombs when we closed the tent flaps at night.

The number of reported malaria cases detected in our Group for the following months of 1944 were: June, one case; July, seven cases; August, eight cases; September, five cases; and October, one. My squadron, the 746th, had six cases of malaria reported during that period.

April 22, 1944   No Mission.

It was a cloudy, cool day and night, and no mission scheduled for this day. I guess we needed the time to repair our Liberators from yesterday's mission. A couple of us went into Cerignola to get shaves and haircuts. I still didn't have enough whiskers to shave very often, so I just got haircuts to avoid the embarrassment of asking for a shave. I shaved myself whenever it became necessary.

*April 23, 1944   Bad Voslau Airdrome, Austria.

I was scheduled to fly with Boughner's crew again on this one, another rough one. We lost three Liberators. Our target was Bad Voslau Airdrome, Austria, and bombing results were superior. Our Group was attacked by 66 enemy aircraft and we lost 3 Liberators.

After a late wake-up and a quick breakfast, we rode up to the headquarters hill to attend the mission briefing. The intelligence part of the briefing was conducted by Lt.

Alfred Levine, and a Lt. Col. Williams from our 304th Wing Intelligence participated in the briefing. The Colonel stressed that we should drop no bombs on Yugoslavia unless it was a briefed target. Evidently, some crews had been jettisoning their bombs on Yugoslavia and there were complaints. We had the late stations time of 1005 hours for being at the aircraft, banker's hours compared to the early hours to which we were accustomed. Start engines time for my plane, which was in the 5th Box of the 2nd Unit, was 1030. Our lead plane for this day was flown by Major Louis M. Abernathy and he started to taxi his Liberator to the end of the runway at 1020 hours. We started to taxi our plane at 1035 hours. We had to watch for the plane ahead of us in our fifth Box to taxi by our hardstand parking ramp position, then we followed him in the taxi line, waiting for our turn to takeoff. There were thirty-three Liberators lined up on the taxiways waiting their turn to takeoff. Major Louis M. Abernathy of the 745th Squadron, in the lead plane, took off at 1030, and thirty-five of our group's B-24s followed his plane, taking off at forty second intervals. We were reducing the spacing between each plane's takeoff to save fuel and assembly time. Captain F. Weston Hyde, Jr. my 746th Squadron operations officer was in the lead plane of the 2nd Unit of the formation, leading the three Boxes.

After taking off, Boughner's crew discovered a gasoline leak on our plane and we had to return to the base. I logged twenty minutes flying time, and unfortunately no mission credit. However, this turned out to be a very rough mission so it may have been fate at work causing us to miss it.

Seven bombers, in addition to ours, also returned early. They returned for the following reasons: four planes had malfunctioning engines or superchargers that wouldn't work properly, one plane had a gushing oil leak, one had a fire in its bomb bay, and one had its electrical system become inoperative.

C O N F I D E N T I A L

DETAILED OPERATIONS BRIEFING

(a) Battle Order.
    (Line Up)

Date: 23 April 1944.

1st Unit: 1st Box

Demelik

Formation Leader: Abernathy / AP 768   Andrews

No. 3: Riddle   AP 287   Dep Leader: Clark, R.R./ AP 470
                     No.4: Rudd   AP 295
No.6: Brabon   AP 799   No.5: Ball   AP 633

2nd Box

Leader: Clark, W.D. AP 912
No.3: Newhouse   AP 283   Dep Leader: Haviland   AP 661
                     No.4: Bishop   AP 284
No.6: Leukuma   AP 364   No.5: Jennings   AP 637

3rd Box

Leader: Phifer   AP 501
No.3: Nix   AP 233   Dep Leader: Desperoak   AP 290
                     No.4: Jones   AP 291
No.6: Nunimaker   AP 275   No.5: Lunt   AP 752

2nd Unit, 1st Box

Jackson, C.Y.

Leader: Hyde, /   AP 279
No.3: Hillenbrand   AP 486   Dep Leader: Mulligan   AP 214
                     No.4: Townsend AP 231
No.6: Strombom   AP 634   No.5: Hundley   AP 839

L   **2nd Box**

Leader: Richards   . AP 489
No.3: Gutting   A P 222   Dep Leader: Sagert   AP 480
                     No.4: Boughner AP 549
No.6: Bowering   AP 189   No.5: Johnson   AP 831
                     No.7: Witkin   AP 492

3rd Box

Leader: Callan   AP 487
No.3: Phillips   AP 309   Dep Leader: Douglass   AP 749
                     No.4: Gardner   AP 589
No.6: Nilsson   AP 297   No.5: Palis   AP 304

Stations: 1005   456th DAYLONG FOUR FOUR

Engines: A 1010 B 1015 C 1020   P-47's "SANDSAIL"
         D 1025 E 1030 F 1035
                                     P-38's "SEEDCAKE"
Take-off: 1030
                                     Recall signal: "NEG"
E.T.R.: 1730

C O N F I D E N T I A L

After our Group formation had finished assembling around Abernathy's plane, he led us over Stornara at 4,000 feet to rendezvous with the 455th Group. Our two groups then departed Stornara to join the rest of the 304th Wing bombers at 1115 hours to form a trail type cruising formation consisting of the 459th Group first, then the 454th, 455th, and our 456th last. Our Wing was the fourth wing flying in the Fifteenth Air Force bomber stream of Wings this day, all flying to the same target area around Vienna. Our groups were attacking four high priority targets in the same general area to divide the fighter opposition. Six groups of B-17s from the all Flying Fortress 5th Wing dropped their bombs at 1400 hours, a composite wing of 49th and 55th Wings dropped their bombs at an adjacent target at 1410 hours, and our 304th Wing and the 47th Wing dropped bombs on nearby targets at 1420 hours. It was a formidable challenge to the Luftwaffe, and a devastating blow to Luftwaffe strength in the Vienna area.

Our 304th Bomb Wing's bombers were scheduled to be escorted by P-38s, P-47s, and the new P-51s. Groups of the 304th Wing were supposed to rendezvous with P-47s at 1308 hours, about 1:12 hours before the scheduled target time. That is not what happened! Our fighter escort did not prevent sixty-six enemy fighters from attacking the 456th Bomb Group enroute to the target. Evidently, as we had been told, shadowing enemy aircraft had located the position of our bomber formation and our fighter escort location, then Luftwaffe controllers directed their fighters to attack bombers where our escort was not. Enemy radar on the ground assisted in this process. Reading Luftwaffe records after the war, I learned that German fighters tried, many times, to locate their attacks on bombers where our escort fighters were not, and if fighters were around they would try to keep the bomber formations between the escort fighters and themselves. Another tactic used by Luftwaffe fighters was to send a decoy of Luftwaffe fighters to attack our fighter escort early, requiring them to drop their external fuel tanks early for a dogfight, reducing their endurance time, then their main Luftwaffe fighter force would attack the bombers when our escort had to leave us because of low fuel.

In any case, as outlined below, our escort fighters were busily engaged in a huge air battle of their own.

Our Group was first intercepted at Lake Balaton, Hungary by sixty-six Me-109s and FW-190s, and their attacks continued through and beyond the target area in Austria. At Lake Balaton the attacks were from directions all around the clock, high, low, and level because our escort fighters were not in sight. Luftwaffe fighters were having a free hand to do what they wanted. Some Me-109s came in from 6 o'clock, closed to within fifty yards, then peeled off right and left. Our gunners noted that the Me-109s were using belly tanks under the center of their fuselages, and they now looked like our P-51s from a distance.

Northwest of Lake Balaton six Me-109s came in to attack frontally in elements of three aircraft. Other enemy aircraft came in from the 6 o'clock position and made perpendicular approaches from below, then turned over and lobbed rockets from 300 to 400 yards.

Near the 456th Group's Initial Point, Donnerskirchen, Austria, Me-109s attacked from 6 o'clock level and closed to within fifty yards firing 20mm cannon, then they scattered in all directions. Two waves of Me-109s, one a wave of 8 fighters and the other a wave of 9 fighters, came in from 12 o'clock high, head on, then dived through our bomber formation and away after attacking. Rockets were lobbed into our formation by FW-190s and Me-109s from 300 to 400 yards out. Aerial bombs were dropped on the Group formation from above by Me-109s, but they were ineffective. Other fighters were seen sitting out of range of our Group's guns, then they suddenly attacked in trail formation from all levels and angles.

The FW-190s had yellow spinners, Hermann Goering's elite fighters, and they were painted with fuselages that had blue tops and silver bottoms. The Me-109s were painted silver with red wing tips.

Finally, P-38s arrived to save the day and bust up the attack. They quickly cleared the air of enemy fighters!

Our Group lost two B-24s to enemy fighters at 1405 hours, seventeen minutes before we reached the target. Fighters in the target area critically damaged two more bombers, and four more received lesser damage from fighter fire. In addition to damage inflicted on our Group by Luftwaffe fighters, flak severely damaged another of our planes and slightly damaged eight more on the bomb run.

A Liberator on fire after being hit by enemy fighter fire over Austria. Photo provided by the San Diego Aerospace Museum.

Liberator On fire Over Austria

Enemy fighters broke off their attacks to avoid their own antiaircraft fire. We knew that there were at least 300 antiaircraft guns to fire at us in the Vienna area. Flak was graded as having heavy guns, moderate in concentration, and accurate. Our B-24 gunners claimed 13 fighters destroyed, 6 probable, and 10 damaged.

The flak bursts were larger than usual, possibly 105mm guns rather than the usual 88mm ones we had previously seen firing at our formation. Aircrews reported that they saw five white flak bursts, different than the others, as our formation entered the main flak area. It appeared that they were a signal for enemy fighters to stop attacking because of the impending heavy flak fire.

From our Group's Initial Point, Donnerskirchen, Austria the bomb run was made on an axis of attack of 287 degrees magnetic through the menacing ugly flak bursts. We were briefed to bomb at an altitude of 23,000 feet for the first unit, and 22,700 feet for the second unit, higher than we had been bombing previously. Bombs were actually released from 22,000 feet and 19,000 feet respectively, because there were cirrus clouds above the Group formation with bases at 23,000 feet that prevented bombing from a higher altitude. The outside temperature at 20,000 feet was minus 25 degrees centigrade. Below our Group's formation, to obscure the target, there were five-tenths of altocumulus clouds in target area with bases at 10,000 feet and tops at 15,000 feet.

Bombs were released on the target at 1422 hours, only two minutes later than scheduled. The bombing speed was 160 MPH indicated airspeed, about 230 MPH true airspeed. Our target was the airdrome at Bad Voslau, Austria and twenty-five of our planes were reported to have dropped 61.25 tons of 500 pound general purpose bombs (245 bombs) on it with superior results. One bomber in the Group had a bomb rack malfunction and could not drop its bombs on the target. Bombing results were superior. Six hangers, their contents, and some surrounding buildings were destroyed. There was a superior concentration of bombs on the target. Five pictures were taken of the target by photographers aboard our bombers. The temperature at 20,000 feet was minus 21 degrees centigrade.

Later, Major General Nathan F. Twinning, Commander of the Fifteenth Air Force, stated of the bombing at Bad Voslau that "No better job has been done by any bombardment organization."

Casualties for the 456th Bomb Group this day were reported as 26 aircrew members missing in action, one top turret gunner seriously wounded on a returning bomber, and three returning crew members were slightly wounded, including a waist gunner, an engineer, and a photographer. The formation of twenty-five Liberators arrived back over Stornara at 1638 hours. Flying time was 6:15 hours. This was the Group's twenty-ninth accredited mission of the thirty-six missions flown in Italy.

One of the bombers that was lost before reaching the target at 1403 hours, while over Hungary, was from my 746th squadron. It was "Towney's Tavern," flown by the crew of Captain John C. Townsend, pilot. Towney was on his twenty-third mission. He was flying the number four position in the 1st Box of the 2nd Unit. He only had nine crew members aboard because one was grounded and didn't make the flight. Nine parachutes were seen coming from his crippled plane as it went down. Capt.Townsend was originally listed as MIA and his copilot, 2nd Lt Gordon L. Graham, was reported as having been taken POW. However, Captain Townsend was captured, put in solitary confinement for 21 days in Budapest before being transferred to Stalag Luft III, southeast of Berlin. Stalag Luft III was a prison camp that was especially designed by the Germans to be more escape proof than all other prison camps. Towney and

Graham are current members of the 456th Bomb Group Association. All of the other members of his crew are either MIA or deceased. Those other crew members still listed as missing in action are: S/Sgt Glenn E. Duncan, upper turret gunner; T/Sgt Leslie C. Kensinger, engineer; and S/Sgt Douglas L. Marston, radio operator.

The other bomber lost to enemy aircraft fire before reaching the target area was flown by the crew of 2nd Lt. Warren G. Haviland of the 747th Squadron. Nine parachutes were seen to come from his doomed plane. Three of the crew who had been taken as POWs and put into Stalag Luft 17B are current members of the 456th Bomb Group Association: S/Sgt Fred G. Best, turret gunner; S/Sgt Harry D. Cofman, turret gunner; and S/Sgt Eugene E. Domulevicz, engineer. Two others of the crew, turret gunners, were taken POWs in the same Stalag Luft 17B, S/Sgt Merton H. Shores, and S/Sgt John J. Janicezak (now deceased). One, T/Sgt Olaf B.Styrwoll, radio operator, was killed in action. All of the others are listed as MIA.

The third plane lost on the mission was flown by the crew of 1st Lt. James Gardner of the 745th Squadron. It was so seriously damaged that it didn't appear capable of flying all the way back to our base. The planes' rudders were so severely shot up, six of his crew members bailed out when they saw how much damage their plane had suffered. They couldn't talk to the pilot because communication with the rest of the plane had been destroyed by enemy action, the plane's hydraulic system failed, and the aircraft was losing altitude.

Lt. Gardner was able to get his plane free from twelve attacking Me-109s by diving his ship to within 150 feet above the ground and one fighter followed him down. That remaining fighter was shot down by S/Sgt Paul L. Fleener, currently a member of the 456th Bomb Group Association. Lt. Gardner somehow managed to bring his crippled plane back to our base. Because many controls had been shot out, including the ability to lower flaps, a belly landing at the base was determined too dangerous. The four remaining crew members aboard his bomber bailed out, and they landed safely by parachute on our field. Gardner headed his plane out toward the Adriatic before he bailed out and it was seen by Royal Air Force people to crash and sink. Three of Gardner's crew members who had bailed out at the target area, are now members of the 456th Bomb Group Association. They are 2nd Lt. Thomas C. Norris, bombardier who became a POW; S/Sgt Robert E. Field, radio operator, who became a POW; and S/Sgt Arthur S. Rosenthal, tail turret gunner who was listed as MIA. Sgt. Paul J. Spurgeon, ball turret, and S/Sgt Frank Coube, engineer were listed as MIAs, and S/Sgt Robert J. Sciaqua, nose turret, was taken POW, and is now deceased.

Our mission on April 23 was part of a Fifteenth Air Force effort that consisted of a total of 956 bombers and fighters airborne to Austria to bomb four targets that were in the Vienna area near each other. A total of 456 heavy bombers participated on the mission, the rest were fighters. Bombers dropped 1292 tons of bombs on the Me-109 assembly plant at Bad Voslau, the nearby He-219 aircraft assembly plant, the jet aircraft works at Schwechat, and the airdrome and Me-109 assembly plant at Wiener Neustadt, also nearby. The strategy of this mission was to drop bombs on these high priority targets in the same general area within a twenty minute period, between 1400 and 1420 hours to divide the high concentration of enemy fighters known to be there, so that no one bomber group would receive the full brunt of enemy fighter attacks.

Participating were 285 B-24s and 171 B-17s. Two B-17s and eleven B-24s were lost on the mission and three escort fighters were lost. In addition to damage inflicted on targets on the ground by the bombs dropped, total claims in the air battle by Fifteenth Air Force planes for the day were 51 destroyed, 16 probables, and 32 damaged. Among them were Me-109s, FW-190s, Me-210s, and Ju-88s.

One reason our Group wasn't protected by escort fighters on the mission was that there was another huge air battle in the area that day. In addition to the bombers' air battles, seventy-six P-38s of the 1st Fighter Group that were escorting our 304th Wing's bombers to Bad Voslau engaged about one-hundred enemy fighters. The P-38s claimed nine enemy destroyed, three probables, and fourteen damaged. None of the P-38s were lost.

With 956 aircraft on this mission, the Fifteenth Air Force was growing fast and making its strength felt.

April 24, 1944   Bucharest Marshaling Yards, Rumania.

A slight rain fell prior to takeoff but it did not prevent the mission. The cloud ceiling was such that it allowed our group to collect the formation then proceed to the target that was reported to have good weather. Boughner's crew was not selected to fly with the group today, so I didn't fly on the mission. The target this day was another return to the Bucharest Marshaling Yards.

Wake up call came at 0630 hours, briefing at 0730, stations time at the aircraft at 0835, start engines time for the 1st Box at 0840, 2nd Box at 0845 and the 3rd Box at 0850. There were only enough planes, twenty-two planes, available to launch three Boxes this day, because of the heavy damage sustained by our Group's Liberators on yesterday's mission.

The standard bomber formation was reduced to one "V" of three Boxes instead of the normal two "Vs" made up of six boxes. There were three spare aircraft standing by for the mission, but they were only to be used if necessary. Major John R. Sinclair was in the lead aircraft and he took off at

0900 hours with the other twenty-one bombers following him off the runway at 45 second intervals.

The group gathered over Giulia Airfield at 4,000 feet after takeoff and then departed Giulia at 0932 hours, after being joined by the 459th Group. The groups climbed on course at 160 MPH indicated airspeed, a true airspeed of about 215 MPH and a rate of climb of 200 feet per minute until bombing altitude was reached. There were four 456th Group bombers that aborted the mission and returned early, one for a fuel leak in the bomb bay, one with a faulty supercharger, one with an electric system that failed, and one with the left inboard engine siphoning gas.

Escort was provided by one group of P-38s that rendezvoused with the bombers about one hour and fifty minutes before bombs away at 1044 hours. When they withdrew due to fuel shortages, another group of P-38s provided target cover starting at fifteen minutes before target time, at 1219 hours. These were joined by another group of P-38s at 1223 hours to help with target cover and withdrawal cover, and finally, about sixteen minutes after bombs away, a group of P-47s picked up the withdrawal cover from the P-38s at 1245 hours. They did a good job on this mission because no fighters were allowed to attack our Group.

The Initial Point was Clejani and the Bucharest marshaling yards were attacked on a heading of 60 degrees magnetic from that town. The weather over the target was clear with unlimited visibility. The temperature at 23,000 feet was minus 25 degrees centigrade. After four aircraft aborted the mission earlier, as described above, this left eighteen bombers able to drop 45 tons of 500 pound general purpose bombs on the target at 1234 hours from an altitude of 23,000 feet, a higher altitude than normal. Bombing was at an increased indicated airspeed of 165 MPH, about 240 MPH true airspeed. The axis of attack was on a heading of

060 degrees magnetic. The weather over the target was clear with unlimited visibility. Eleven photographs were taken of the target and bombing results were confirmed as being good. Almost all bombs fell in the center of the marshaling yard, hitting the railroad tracks and buildings. After bombs were away the formation made descending left turn to avoid flak.

_ C O N F I D E N T I A L _

Battle Order   24 April 1944

1st Box

Thomas)
Formation Leader: Maj Sinclair) Ap 475
Miller
No. 3: Van Dyke   Ap 872   Dep Leader: Capt Ladd/: Ap 279 ¨¨

No. 4: Lambert   Ap 072

No. 6: Bowering   Ap 189   No. 5: Lehner   Ap 853

No. 7: Manlove   Ap 492

2nd Box

Gruber
Leader: Mulligan/: Ap 227

No. 3: Smith   Ap 275   Dep Leader: W.L. Jackson Ap 501

No. 4: Lee   Ap 214

No. 6: Hillman   Ap 233   No. 5: Barfosso   Ap 290

No. 7: Snee   Ap 839

3rd Box

Leader: Andrews   Ap 470

No. 3: Newhouse   Ap 283   Dep Leader: Lane   Ap 912

No. 4: Bishop   Ap 098

No. 6: Leukuma   Ap 364   No. 5: Ward   Ap 637

No. 7: Beck   Ap 222

Spares: Witkin   Ap 831   Nilsson Ap 297   Jenning Ap 287

Stations: 0835   456th RUBBISH FIVE THREE

Engines: A C840 B 0845 C 0850   Penetration Escort "FLYWHEEL ONE"

                    WITHDRAWAL "FLYWHEEL TWO"
Take-off: 0900   "FLYWHEEL THREE"

                  Target cover: "LARGECUP"

           Recall Signal "PRO"

C O N F I D E N T I A L

Only four fighters were seen, one FW-190 and three Me-210s, but they didn't attack our Group. The flak was the barrage type, indicating that our chaff was successfully confusing their radar as we wanted, so that accurate tracking-type, radar-guided flak could not be fired at our planes. Flak was classified as intense, inaccurate, and heavy. Only one of our planes had slight flak damage, and none had damage from enemy fighters.

The Group's formation of eighteen bombers returned safely over our field at 1553 hours. Flying time was 6:45 hours. This was the Group's thirty-seventh mission flown in Italy, and its thirtieth accredited one.

April 25, 1944   Aircraft Factory At Turin, Italy.

Target for the day was the aircraft factory at Turin, Italy. I flew on the mission as copilot on Boughner's crew. The mission turned out to be a fairly rough one as we were attacked by 14 fighters. We lost one aircraft and nine other Liberators were damaged by enemy fire.

After a wake-up call in our tents at 0600 hours, our usual C-ration breakfast, we rode up to the hill we attended our crew briefing at 0715 hours. Lt. Howard I. Neff gave the Intelligence portion of the briefing, then we rode out to our planes for a time at stations by our bombers, 0830 hours. Start engines time for our plane which was flying in the 1st Box of the 1st Unit this day was 0835 hours, and Liberators of each of the other six Boxes of our formation started their engines at five minute intervals after that. The lead aircraft, with Major Louis M. Abernathy flying it, taxied out at 0850 hours and took off at 0900 hours. Thirty-two aircraft followed him off the runway at 45 second intervals.

C O N F I D E N T I A L

BATTLE ORDER

Date: 25 April 1944

1st Unit, 1st Box

Formation Leader: Abernathy, Domolik   AP 268
No. 3: Desperock (C) AP 214   Dep Leader: Clark, R.R.   AP 470
              No. 4: Boughner (C) AP 549
No. 6:   AP   No. 5:   AP

2nd Box

Leader: Manloye AP 831
No. 3: Ensign (C) AP 442   Dep Leader: Lehner   AP 477
              No. 4: Snee (C) AP 839
No. 6: Hundley   AP 853   No. 5: Bowering   AP 189
      (Movie Camera)

3rd Box

Leader: Callan   AP 227
No. 3: Peterson (C) AP 297   Dep Leader: Phillips AP 309
              No. 4: Little (C) AP 304
No. 6: Rawlinson   AP 798   No. 5: Wilkinson   AP 475

2nd Unit, 1st Box

                              Gruber
Leader: Jackson, C.Y./ AP 279   Mulligan
No. 3: Brabon (C) AP 799   Dep Leader: Randall/ AP 222
              No. 4: Jones (C) AP 291
No. 6:   AP   No. 5: Ball   AP 633

2nd Box

                              Phifer
Leader: Maj. Reid/ AP 872
No. 3: Barrasso (C) AP 290   Dep Leader: Nix   AP 233
              No. 4: Rudd (C) AP 275
No. 6: Nunimaker   AP 072   No. 5: Lunt   AP 752

3rd Box

Leader: Clark, W.D. AP 912
No. 3: Ward (C)   AP 637   Dep Leader: Newhouse AP 283
              No. 4: Riddle (C)AP 364
No. 6: Strombom   AP 634   No. 5: Jennings   AP 287

Stations: 0830   456th FRUITTART

Engines: A 0835 B 0840 C 0845   Fighter: FIRTREE
         D 0850 E 0855 D 0900
                              Recall: CRA

Take-off: 0900

ETR: 1600

C O N F I D E N T I A L

Three B-24s returned prior to bombing the target. Two returned early because of supercharger failures and they could not keep up with the formation. The other early abort of the mission was Number 442, Lt. Robert Ensign of my 746th Squadron, because it was hit by flak over Arezzo, Italy at 1143 hours, before reaching the target and had to return to our airfield. Flak knocked out the plane's ailerons, hydraulic system, and number three engine. Its alarm bell sounded and the bombardier and nose gunner bailed out. Before the rest of the crew could bail out, the aircraft was brought under control and the pilot returned the bomber safely to our base with the rest of the crew.

After takeoff, our bombers gathered around Louis Abernathy's plane forming the Group's six box combat formation, then he led the formation over our base at Stornara to assemble at 3,000 feet where the 455th Group rendezvoused with our Group. We departed Stornara at 0945 hours, climbing on course at 160 MPH indicated airspeed, about 215 MPH true airspeed, at 200 feet per minute rate of climb.

Weather enroute to the target was fair, with from twenty to forty percent of cloud cover below our formation with tops at 15,000 feet and eighty percent cirrus cloud coverage above our formation with bases at 23,000 feet.

We encountered flak at Prato, Figline, Arezzo, Pistoria, and Florence on the way to the I.P. First Lieutenant Joseph Desperock's plane was hit by flak near Florence, as described in more detail below, and dropped out of the formation. Flak over the target was moderate to intense, accurate, and heavy. On the way home our formation encountered more flak at Sienna that was rated as moderate intensity, accurate, with heavy guns. Beside Desperock's plane that was lost to flak near Florence, nine of our bombers had flak damage. The flak was made up of both the tracking type of flak and the barrage type.

Although we were supposed to have P-38 and P-47 fighter escort starting at 1146 hours, about an hour and ten minutes before our scheduled bombs away time, our Group was attacked by eighteen enemy fighters. Two them, Me-109s, attacked us at 15 miles west of Asti, Italy from 12 to 2 o'clock high, made one pass and then peeled off. Then fourteen Me-109s attacked a little later from 12 o'clock low and level positions. Next, near the target, two FW-190s attacked from the 3 o'clock position, made one pass and peeled off to our left. Three Me-109s in trail formation came from the 10 o'clock high position, made one pass then peeled at 2 o'clock low. Next, six FW-190s came in high at 6 o'clock then dove under our formation. One FW-190 fired two rockets from 2 o'clock high, then ten Me-109s attacked from 4 and 10 o'clock positions, 2 abreast, then peeled off to our left. Four enemy aircraft were claimed to be destroyed by our gunners and three fighters were claimed to be damaged. We lost no bombers to fighters.

As we approached the target, the cloud coverage below our formation improved to only twenty percent cumulus clouds, and the cirrus above us dropped to twenty percent coverage. It was good weather for visual bombing. The temperature at 22,000 feet was minus 24 degrees centigrade and the air to ground visibility was ten miles.

The remaining twenty-nine of our aircraft that were able to fly over the target, and twenty-seven dropped 69.75 tons of 500 pound general purpose bombs (279 bombs) on the target at 1312 hours from 22,000 feet for the 1st Unit and 21,000 feet for the 2nd Unit at an indicated airspeed of 165 MPH, a true airspeed of 235 MPH. Two of the aircraft in the formation that flew over the target could not drop bombs on the target and jettisoned them. One of the bombers had trouble with its bomb-bay doors and jettisoned its bombs later at 1341 hours, and the other bomber jettisoned its bombs before reaching the target, at 1140 hours, because its damaged plane could not keep up with the formation and the pilot had to lighten its load.

A good pattern of bombs hit the target area, including machine shops, assembly shops, and hangars. Results were classified as fair. The axis of attack was 356 degrees magnetic.

The aircraft lost on the mission to flak was a plane from the 744th Squadron piloted by 1st Lt. Joseph Desperock, the "Leap Year Lady." It was hit by flak near Florence at 1143 hours, had engine trouble on the way to the target, and was forced to ditch in the Adriatic near Fossacesia, Italy. The B-24 had notoriously bad ditching characteristics because the weak bomb bay doors would collapse on impact with the water and that would allow the plane to rapidly fill with water, then sink. Italian fishermen rescued three of the crew: 2nd Lt Nathan Hoffman, copilot; T/Sgt Clifford Adams, radio operator; and T/Sgt Thomas R. Cable, engineer, who is currently a member of the 456th Bomb Group Association. Eight of the rest of the crew, originally reported as missing in action, were later determined to have been killed in action and they are interred in the Florence Cemetery, Italy.

Casualties for the day were eight killed in action and two missing in action. Our formation of twenty-nine Liberators returned over our base at 1616 hours. This was our Group's thirty-first accredited mission of thirty-eight missions flown in Italy. This was my twentieth accredited mission and I logged 7:10 hours. I was experienced and much more confident in my ability now. Like many of my friends, I was superstitious about dwelling on how many missions I had left. I knew that it was a long way off and anything could happen before the magic fifty was reached.

Among the different crew comments recorded at the intelligence interrogation after we were on the ground were: "three electric suits went out today (on our plane)"; "good mission, good leader"; "lead very poor"; "wing formation was bad"; "too much talk on B-channel of VHF radio," and "P-38s were fired on by the rear gunners of the formation." Evaluation of the quality of lead sometimes depended on where you were flying in the formation. Liberators at the end of the formation had to make large, exaggerated corrections for each small correction made by the lead aircraft. Planes at the front of the formation only had to make small adjustments.

April 26, 1944   No Mission.

Rain began before the early morning briefing was over, and weather looked bad in general. A stand-down was announced. It was a good day to catch up on our chores around our tent, catch up on the gossip and rumors, writing letters, and reading. I took a " French bath," out of my steel helmet with water patiently heated over our gasoline heater. I even shaved!

A group intelligence officer, Lt. Alfred D. Levine, came down to the squadron area and lectured on Russian aircraft because we were bombing close to Russian lines and could encounter them.

There were no movies for us to attend in the evening, in our group briefing room, because the projector broke down last night.

April 27, 1944   No Mission

Today's mission was canceled again when rain began at daybreak and clouds were hanging heavy and low. The movie projector was fixed and the announced movie was "Madam Curie," a movie about Madame Marie Curie, the Nobel Prize winner who discovered radium and experimented with radio activity, with her husband Pierre Currie in Paris. She died from leukemia as a result of over exposure to radiation

264

April 28, 1944   Porto San Stefano, Italy.

My crew was selected to attend the late morning briefing at 0945 hours. Again, bankers' hour as far as we were concerned because we were allowed to sleep until 0800 hours this morning. Late briefings usually meant milk run missions. It did turn out to be a milk run.

After being allowed to sleep late, have a leisurely C-ration breakfast in mild spring weather, we took our usual trip up to the hill in the back of Army six by six trucks for the briefing to bomb Porto San Stefano, Italy. We had a late time to be at our aircraft, 1120 hours. Start-engines time for the 1st Box was 1125 hours, with the other five Boxes in the day's formation starting their engines at 5 minute intervals. We were flying as number four position, in the 2nd box. We were bombing this target on our own, not accompanied by any other 304th Wing Group.

Thirty-seven bombers took off on schedule starting at 1145 hours with Major John R. Sinclair of the 744th Squadron in the lead ship, other planes following at 45 second intervals. One plane returned early because of a runaway propeller. We assembled our formation, then the Group departed Stornara at 4,000 feet over our air base, climbing on course to the Initial Point at 1235 hours, at an indicated airspeed of 160 MPH, about 200 MPH true airspeed. We climbed on course at the low rate of climb, 200 feet per minute, so that all planes could easily maintain their positions in the formation during the climb. We were not flying in formation with other groups of our wing on this mission, so there was not the usual rendezvous with other groups. Once at our bombing altitude of 21,000 feet, we cruised at 165 MPH indicated, or about 235 MPH true airspeed to the Initial Point of Manciano, Italy.

C O N F I D E N T I A L

BATTLE ORDER

28 April 1944

1st Unit, 1st Box

FORMATION LEADER: Maj. Sinclair, Thomas AP 817
Dep Leader: Christensen, Miller AP 268
No. 3: Fleming (C)   AP 304
No. 4: Gutting (C)   AP 499
No. 5: Ball   AP 595
No. 6: Stromben   AP 634

2nd Box

Leader: Harlow.   APP 426
Dep Leader: Lehror   AP 853
No. 3: Pitkin (C)   AP 477
No. 4: Boughner (C) AP 549
No. 5: Johnson   AP 831
No. 6: Sagert   AP 480
No. 7: Bowering   AP 189

3rd Box

Leader: Douglass   AP 749
No. 3: Williamson (C) AP 227   Dep Leader: Nilsson AP 297
No. 4: Monahan (C) AP 334
No. 5: Marlar   AP 309
No. 6: Palis   AP 183

2nd Unit, 1st Box

Clark, W.B.
Leader: Mulligan,/   AP 279
No. 3: Beck (C)   AP 222   Dep Leader: Griffin AP 799
No. 4: Jones (C)   AP 291
No. 5: Jennings   AP 287
No. 6: Hillenbrand   AP 839

2nd Box

Leader: Clark, W.D. AP 912
No. 3: Andrews (C)   AP 470   Dep Leader: Ward   AP 637
No. 4: Bishop (C)   AP 777
No. 5: Rawlinson   AP 098
No. 6: Loukuma   AP 633
No. 7: Riddle   AP 283

3rd Box

Leader: Leo   AP 752
No. 3: Van Dyke (C) AP 872   Dep Leader: Smith   AP 275
No. 4: Jackson,E.L. (C) AP 290
No. 5: Hillman   AP 285
No. 6: Lambert   AP 233

Stations: 1120

Engines: A 1125 B 1130 C 1135
D 1140 E 1150 F 1155

Take-off: 1145

456th RETAIN-THREE-ONE
82 FG AIRSLUG TWO
325 FG AIRSLUG THREE
Recall signal: KIND

We had two groups of P-38s, one from the 82nd Fighter Group with call sign "Air Slug Two," and the other from the 325th Fighter Group with a call sign "Air Slug Three," providing fighter cover starting at 1420 hours, about twenty minutes before bombs away time. The escort fighters also provided coverage over the target and coverage of our withdrawal from the target to the extent of their endurance. Our escort did their job well because no enemy fighters attacked us, although we saw fifteen FW-190s circling above us at Lake Bolsena at 1429 hours, twelve minutes before bombs away, and another eight Me-109s at Manciano at 1458 hours, seventeen minutes after bombs away.

Our call sign on VHF channel "B" was "RETAIN-THREE-ONE," our recall sign was "KIND."

Weather was not perfect for our mission. We had to climb our Liberator formation through and in-between clouds on our way to bombing altitude. We had two to three-tenths of cumulus clouds, bases at 4,000 and tips at 10,000 feet on the way out, and this became six to eight-tenths coverage by altocumulus clouds at the spur of Italy with bases at 9,000 feet and tops at 9,500. After reaching a clear (CAVU) area over the Adriatic Sea, cloud coverage increased as we turned over land across Italy, increasing to five to nine-tenths cloud coverage, with bases at 10,000 and tops at 13,000 feet. Finally, on reaching the target area, the cumulus cloud coverage had reduced to three-tenths below our formation with bases at 6,000 and tops at 12,000 feet. The air to ground visibility was fifteen miles with slight haze. The outside air temperature at 20,200 feet was minus 26 degrees centigrade

Two bomb runs had to be made by our formation over the target, through the flak, because some aircraft did not see the target through the clouds on the first pass. This was much to the disgruntlement of some pilots and crews, because the flak was heavy, moderate, and accurate. Crews complained because we had no chaff to drop to confuse enemy radar, so the enemy flak fire was accurate. Seven of our planes had flak damage, one of them was so severely damaged that it had to land at another base on return to friendly territory.

On the first pass over the target, 24 bombers dropped 69.75 tons of 500 pound general purpose bombs (239 bombs) at 1441 hours on an axis of attack of 235 degrees magnetic from 21,000 feet at an indicated airspeed of 160 MPH, a true airspeed of 227 MPH. The Bombardiers' bomb interval setting was 75 feet for bombs dropped by each plane.

On the second pass over the target, 11 bombers dropped 25.25 tons of the bombs (101 bombs) at 1451 hours on an axis of attack of 130 degrees magnetic, same altitude and airspeed. In addition to the one aircraft that returned early, another plane had a supercharger malfunction and had to jettison its bombs in an open field before reaching the target to reduce its weight enough to be able to stay in the formation. In addition, one plane had one bomb hang up in its bomb bay due to a rack malfunction, and it returned the one 500 pound bomb to our air base with the formation

Thus, only 35 bombers were left to drop on the target. Although most bombs were reported to fall in the vicinity of the target, many bombs fell in the water, and results were graded as poor. Nineteen photos were taken of the target area. After bombs were dropped, our Group formation made a descending right turn to avoid flak fire.

The one B-24 that had severe damage from flak, and had to jettison its bombs in order to stay with the formation, was damaged so badly that it was forced to land for repairs at a B-25 base near Mt. Vesuvius on the way home. It was reported to be the plane of Lt. Joseph Leukuma of the 747th Squadron. A B-25 crew at that base ferried his crew back to our base. There were no casualties.

(Seventy-five B-25s were destroyed a short time later at that base by an eruption of Mt. Vesuvius that suddenly rained rocks on the parked planes near the base of the mountain.)

Our formation returned to Stornara at 1735 hours, minus the one plane that landed at the B-25 base near Naples. Flight time was 5:40 hours and this was the group's thirty-ninth mission in Italy, and the thirty-second accredited mission. This was my twenty-first credited mission, and I now had 98:25 combat hours.

At the intelligence interrogation after our flight, crews made the following comments for the record: (1) "too fast rate of climb by the lead ship;" (2) "red flare was fired too late on the first bomb run, to signal the I.P.;" (3) "the course was good, but too fast;" (4) "poor leadership of the formation, jeopardized lives of all crews by making a second run over the flak area;" (5) "we had no chaff;" (6) "poor bombing, lead bad, good fighter escort."

Because our high priority strategic long range targets had bad weather much of the time, targets in Italy were often bombed. A total 464 Fifteenth Air Force heavy bombers dropped 1248 tons of bombs in Italy this day. For the Fifteenth Air Force in its entirety this day, 168 Liberators (including our 35) dropped a total of 418 tons of bombs on the San Stefano Port area, 108 Liberators dropped 267 tons of bombs on the Orbetello Port area, and 188 B-17s dropped 563 tons of bombs on the Piombino Steel Works and Port.

April 29, 1944   Weather Abort Enroute To Toulon, France.

I was briefed with Boughner's crew to bomb Toulon, France but after taking off, the formation was turned back at Naples due to weather. I logged 2:10 hours, but of course we were not credited with a mission. The intelligence briefing was conducted by the omnipresent Lt. Gilbert Wheatland Smith. My friends and I had become acquainted with him

269

on our trip from the States and in our close living quarters in the pink farm house before we moved to our air base at Stornara, and he established himself as unique character, highly intelligent, very resourceful with a great sense of humor.

Today was a Post Exchange ration day, and personnel lined up to collect their weekly rations. We each had ration cards that were punched as we received our rations for cigarettes, cigars, candy, toilet articles, and other such items. I didn't smoke cigarettes, only an occasional cigar, but I realized the barter value of cigarettes on the Italian economy, and among my friends who were smokers, so I took my full ration. We could barter for light bulbs, stovepipe, laundry, and such. In addition, they could be used as tips for good or extra service from Italian soldier-laborers.

April 30, 1944   Lambrate Marshaling Yards, Milan, Italy.

I was wakened at 0530 hours to fly with Boughner's crew. This was another early morning wake-up call for briefing at 0700 hours, but this turned out to be an exception to our expectations that early morning briefings meant tough missions. It turned out to be another milk run. We had no fighters attack us and only one plane had slight damage from flak. Our target was the Lambrate marshaling yards at Milan, Italy, and we were scheduled to be escorted by forty-eight hot new P-51s of the 31st Fighter Group. This was a boost to morale of aircrews because we had already seen these great new fighters and had heard about their superiority. On this mission we saw eleven enemy fighters, Me109s and FW-190s in the target area, but none had the courage to attack us with P-51s around. We also saw P-38s in the area.

C O N F I D E N T I A L

BATTLE ORDER   Date: 30 April 1944

1st Unit, 1st Box

Christensen
Formation Leader: Demelik,/ AP 817   Clark,
                        AP 285   Dep Leader: Callen,/ AP 227
No. 3: Nunimaker   No. 4: Phifer   AP 501
No. 6: Fleming   AP 475   No. 5: Bowering   AP 189

2nd Box

Leader: Lane   AP 470   (C)
No. 3: Newhouse   AP 284   Dep Leader: Andrews /AP 912
                        No. 4: Bishop (C) AP 777
No. 6: Jennings   AP 287   No. 5: Ward   AP 637

3rd Box

Maj. Reid
Leader: Lee, / AP 872
No. 3: Nix .   AP 233   Dep Leader: Barrasso AP 290
                        No. 4: Rudd .   AP 291
No. 6: Brabon   AP 799   No. 5: Lunt   AP 275

1st Unit, 1st Box

Leader: Jackson, C.Y. AP 279
No. 3: Smith ,   AP 549   Dep Leader: Witkin AP 477
                        No. 4: LeVally   . AP 633
No. 6: Williamson AP 810   No. 5: Boll   AP 595

2nd Box

Leader: Richards   AP 839
No. 3: Gutting   AP 222   Dep Leader: Sagert AP 480
                        No. 4: Boughner   AP 486
No. 6: Johnson   AP 831 (C)   No. 5: Hundley (C) AP 853

3rd Box

Leader: Laszewski AP 309
No. 3: Phillips   AP 183   Dep Leader: Nilsson AP 297
                        No. 4: Little (C) AP 304
No. 6: Peterson   AP 334   No. 5: Wilkinson   AP 749

Stations: 0805.   456th: "CARTLOAD TWO THREE"

Engines: A 0810 B 0815 C 0820   31st FG - P-51's, "MAYFLOWER TWO"
          D 0825 E 0830 F 0835
                              RECALL SIGNAL: "PUTRED"

Take-off: 0830

E.T.R.: 1300

At the morning briefing, the intelligence portion conducted by Lt. Alfred D. Levine, we were told that our "A" Force agents (whoever they are) were now operating in northern Italy, from the Po valley down to the allied lines. These agents had organized cells of "Helpers," usually poor farmers or other peasants who can be contacted in cafes in small villages. These "Helpers," who have organized young boys and girls to be watchers and guides, have instructions to pass along aircrews who are evading capture to other cells of "Helpers" to a point where they can be guided to the 8th Army lines. There at the lines, one-hundred individuals are engaged in the business of smuggling bodies across the lines to freedom.

In the event of bailout, we were told to contact a poor farmer in an isolated spot, be inconspicuous, wear civilian clothes if obtainable, and remember that it's difficult to arrive at a point 10 miles from the battle lines without finding "A" Force assistance.

Our Group's VHF radio recall signal for this mission was "PUTRED."

We were also told by our intelligence briefer, Lt. Levine, that most of the flak positions around the area were unoccupied, and that little, if any flak would be encountered. For once they were right!

Station time at our aircraft was 0805 hours, start engine time for the first box was 0810 hours, with the other five boxes starting their engines at five minute intervals. Taxi out time for the first aircraft was 0820 hours. My crew was flying in the fourth aircraft position of the 2nd Box of the 2nd Unit of the formation, thus we were the 28th Liberator to take off and our start engines time was 0830 hours. Captain Andrew A. Demelik of the 747 Squadron in the lead ship took off at 0830 hours. The rest of the bombers, thirty-five planes, followed him with 45 second intervals between planes. Captain Demelik was a transfer from the 8th Air

Force where he had flown on fifteen missions, flying from England before joining our Group.

Three planes returned early. Reasons for early returns were: one aircraft had all its radios become inoperative, one had its number three engine's propeller-governor run away, and one bomber had a spark plug wire burn a hole in an oil line on number one engine that caused an oil leak.

After our Group's Liberators had formed our combat formation around Demelik's plane, he led our Group formation over Giulia Airfield at 4,000 feet where we were joined by the 459th Group. With the 459th Group following our Group in trail formation, we joined the rest of the 304th Wing groups to cruise to the target. We flew in a trail type of cruising formation that was in the order, 454th, 455th, 456th, and the 459th last. Our formations of Liberators departed Giulia climbing on course at 0911 hours climbing at 200 feet per minute at 165 MPH indicated airspeed, a true airspeed of about 210 MPH, to the Initial Point of Lodi, Italy.

Weather enroute to the target was not ideal, and the Group formation had to fly around and through various layers of cumulus and altocumulus clouds with from three to four-tenths coverage and with bases from 4,000 feet to 14,000 feet until we reached bombing altitude. In the target area, there were four-tenths of cumulus cloud coverage below the formation with bases at 8,000 feet to tops around 15,000 feet. Above us, there was a coverage of four-tenths of cirrus clouds. Visibility from air to ground was 10 miles, with light haze. The temperature at 20,000 feet was minus 21 degrees centigrade.

Only thirty-three of our Group's B-24s flew over the target after the three planes aborted the mission. They dropped 78.75 tons of 500 pound general purpose bombs on the target (313 bombs) at 1214 hours from 20,000 feet, indicated airspeed of 160 MPH, a true airspeed of

220 MPH, on an axis of attack of 345 degrees magnetic. The bombardiers' bomb release interval setting was 120 feet. Two of our Liberators returned seven bombs to our air base because they could not release them from their bomb bays due to rack malfunctions. The slow bombing indicated airspeed, 160 MPH, was used to enable a very tight formation over the target so that the pattern of bombs hitting the ground would be tight.

Thirty-four photos of the target were taken by our bombers, and they showed a good concentration of bombs falling in the marshalling yards. There was no flak at the target, but some flak was encountered over Castano, Genoa, Calliate, Asenstico, Rimini, and Pistola. Some of the flak appeared to be mobile flak on railroad cars. Only one of our planes had slight damage from flak.

The Group's 33 bombers returned over Stornara at 1500 hours on a nice spring day. I logged 6:30 hours, it was my twenty-second credited mission, and the Group's thirty-third accredited one of the forty missions flown in Italy.

Today is exactly four months since the Group's air echelon departed from the United States. Much has been accomplished in that short time. The weather turned colder this evening and the wind increased its velocity.

A Summary Of The Bombing Accuracy For Groups Of The 304th Wing.

Our 304th Wing bombing accuracy as reported in the official reports is contained in the chart on the next page. It indicates that the 456th Bomb Group had the best record of the four groups of the Wing. It also shows the state of high altitude bombing technology.

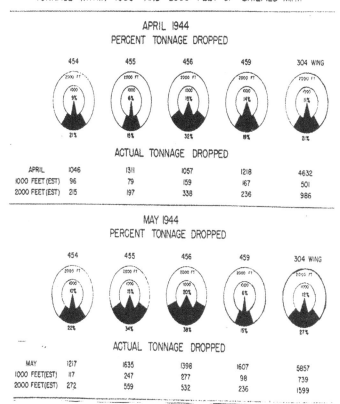

304TH BOMB WING (HV)
STATISTICAL ANALYSIS
APRIL-MAY INCLUSIVE

BOMBING ACCURACY

TONNAGE WITHIN 1000 AND 2000 FEET OF BRIEFIED M.P.I.

APRIL 1944
PERCENT TONNAGE DROPPED

	454	455	456	459	304 WING
APRIL	1046	1311	1057	1218	4632
1000 FEET (EST)	96	79	159	167	501
2000 FEET (EST)	215	197	338	236	986

MAY 1944
PERCENT TONNAGE DROPPED

	454	455	456	459	304 WING
MAY	1217	1635	1398	1607	5857
1000 FEET(EST)	117	247	277	98	739
2000 FEET(EST)	272	559	532	236	1599

Extract of a 304th Bomb Wing (HV) report. It shows improvement in bombing
accuracy from April to May 1944, and the comparative accuracy of the groups.
Source: The National Archives.

Summary Of Bombing Accuracy

Our Group Lost 35.5% of its Assigned Aircraft In Less Than Three Months.

From February 10 to May 1, 1944 our Group had already lost 22 of its 62 assigned Liberators. Of course, we had a continuous flow of replacement aircraft and crews into our Group to replace them, so that we kept an averaged 62 planes on any given day. However, these numbers indicate the odds that crews in the Group faced on their missions before finishing the magic fifty that allowed them to go home. We could expect many more loses in coming months because the good flying weather of May, June, July, and August were still ahead, when we could bomb our tougher long range strategic targets more often.

May 1, 1944   Abort Enroute Because of Weather, Graz, Austria.

We attended a briefing to bomb Graz, Austria. The intelligence portion of the Group briefing was given by Lt. Howard Neff of my 746th Squadron intelligence. Shortly after we were airborne, the mission was canceled. I logged 4:05 hours, and of course no mission credit.

Mayday, a new month, and with its arrival everyone expected favorable bombing weather to be more consistent. Of course, we at group level were not aware of the secret time table for gaining air superiority over Europe by June, in time to allow Operation Overlord, the invasion of Europe from England to come off as scheduled. This date was tightly kept, so that only a few top planners in England and possibly our top commanders knew the date and the tight time schedule. That date for the invasion, set by the allied powers, was only one month away! The Luftwaffe was still very strong in central Europe, but the U.S. Army Air Forces in Europe were getting stronger every day as additional bombers and fighters were constantly arriving from the United States.

May 2, 1944   Abort Enroute Due to Weather, Verona Marshaling Yards, Italy.

Group mission number forty-one was briefed by Major Joseph T. Dickerson of group intelligence to bomb the Verona East marshaling yards. Planes began taking off at 0835 hours, but returned at 1128 due to bad weather, before reaching the target.

May 3, 1944 Abort After Briefing, Ploesti Marshaling Yards, Rumania.

We attended a briefing to bomb Ploesti marshaling yards for a takeoff at 1030 but a stand-down was announced before planes took off. Evidently, our fast weather reconnaissance aircraft that were sent out ahead of us came back with a bad weather report.

An officer from the base censorship office in Naples, Lt. John Langhan, gave a talk to our Group and Squadron intelligence personnel regarding censorship. All officers had as an additional duty, at times, to read and censor mail being sent out by group personnel. Some of the letters were very interesting, and there were times we had to black out some information that was included in the mail. Most of us did not enjoy the censorship duty.

May 4, 1944   Abort Enroute Due To Weather, Ploesti Marshaling Yards, Rumania.

Captain Lewis A. Stuck Jr. of intelligence briefed crews again for a mission to bomb Ploesti marshaling yards, the planes took off, but they had to return early because of bad weather. Weather was good enough to allow some practice flying in the local area.

The group did lose one plane during a practice flight. A B-24 from the 745th Squadron, "Calamity Jane" piloted by 2nd Lt. Clifford E. Wages, lived up to its name. While over the Adriatic, two of its engines had runaway propellers and Wages had to ditch his plane in rough seas. During the belly landing on the rough water, the left wing struck a wave, tearing it off, and the plane sank rapidly. As mentioned earlier, B-24s usually sank rapidly anyway, because their bomb bay doors were so weak that they collapsed on hitting the water allowing water to gush into and fill the fuselage with water.

Italian fishermen rushed to the scene of Wages' plane and succeeded in rescuing five members of his crew: 2nd Lt Armando Bruno, one of two copilots on the flight; 2nd Lt Robert D. Moriarty, navigator; S/Sgt Robert Carlson, radio operator; S/Sgt George G. McFadden, engineer; and Pfc

Thomas L. O'Flaherty, upper turret gunner. Moriarty and Carlson are currently members of the 456th Bomb Group Association.

Five other members of the crew, including Wages, were killed. A sixth member of the crew, S/Sgt Edgar R. Agren, nose turret gunner, is listed as missing in action because his body was never recovered.

May 5, 1944   Ploesti Marshaling Yards And Military Installations, Rumania.

My crew was not scheduled to fly on this mission. We missed a very tough one, to bomb the Ploesti Marshaling Yards again, and our Group lost three bombers.

The wake-up call in our tents at 0730 hours and briefing at 0845 hours was unusually late for such a long, seven hour mission. The target was the Ploesti Oil Refinery and Military Installations in Rumania.. The Group was briefed to bomb by "Pathfinder" aircraft, if weather prevented visual bombing of the target.

Station time, after the usual breakfast and briefing was 0955 hours, start engine time for the 1st Box was 1000 hours, with other five Boxes starting their engines at five minute intervals. Taxi out time was 1015 for the leader, Colonel Steed, who took off at 1025 hours with thirty-eight other bombers following at 45 second intervals. Assembly of the Group formation was over Giulia Airfield at 3,000 feet, where the 459th Group joined our Group, to follow Colonel Steed's lead to the target, in trail formation. Four of our B-24s returned early for the following reasons: one, number 839 piloted by Lt. William H. Snee of my 746th Squadron, had loose cowling on number three engine; one, number 183 piloted by Lt. Joseph W. Palis of the 745th Squadron, had two generators go out; one, number 297 piloted by Lt. Blair Nilsson of the 745th Squadron, had malfunctioning controls, and one, number 487 piloted by Lt. Paul T. Marler of the 745th Squadron, had a gas leak in its bomb bay.

After the Group's Liberators had organized themselves around Col. Steed's lead plane, he led them over Giulia at 3,000 feet, where our Group was followed by the 459 Group. The two-group formation departed Giulia at 1122 hours, climbing on course to the I.P. at 160 MPH and a climb speed of 200 feet per minute. Fighter escort was to be provided by P-38s on penetrating enemy territory, P-51s over the target, and P-38s for withdrawal protection after the bombing.

Weather enroute to the Initial Point, Targoviste, was not too bad, with from thirty to fifty percent cloud coverage from cumulus and altocumulus clouds below the formation, having tops at 13,000 feet, and forty to fifty percent coverage from thin cirrus clouds above the formation with their bottoms at about 18,000 feet. The cirrus clouds at 18,000 feet delayed our Group's climb to reach bombing altitude, but that was no serious problem. The fact that our Group was supposed to have fighter escort did not prevent enemy fighters from attacking our Group's bombers!

C O N F I D E N T I A L

BATTLE ORDER   5 May 1944.

1st Unit, 1st Box

                                    Thomas
        Formation Leader: Col. STEED AP 817   Abernathy
                                    Dep Leader: Mulligan/ AP 791
No. 3: Barrasso   AP 290
            No. 4: Webster (c) AP C98
No. 6: Newhouse   AP 284   No. 5: Ashman   AP 912

2nd Box

                    Leader: Phifer   AP 501
                                    Dep Leader: Lambert   AP 752
No. 3: Jackson,W.L.AP 285
            No. 4: Jones   (c) AP 291
No. 6: Parks,Smith AP 275   No. 5: Van Dyke   AP 872
                No.7: Brabon   AP 799

3rd Box

                    Leader: Clark, W.D. AP 470
                                    Dep Leader: Bishop   AP 777
No. 3: Leukuma   AP 287
            No. 4: Lane   (c) AP 595
No. 6: Ward   AP 637   No. 5: Riddle   AP 633
                No. 7: Strombom   AP 634

2nd Unit, 1st Box

                    Leader: Reid,Tavel AP 227
                        Dep Leader: Lehner   AP 235
No. 3: Johnson   AP 831
            No. 4: Leszewski (c)AP 309
No. 6: Hillenbrand AP 549   No. 5: Peterson   AP 499
                No. 7: Wilkinson   AP 807

2nd Box

                    Leader: Richards   AP 486
                                    Dep Leader: Sagert   AP 480
No. 3: Bowering   AP 189
            No. 4: Gutting (c) AP 492
No. 6: Hundly   AP 853   No. 5: Snee   AP 839
                No. 7: Beck   AP 222

3rd Box

                    Leader: Douglass   AP 749
                                    Dep Leader: Monohan   AP 334
No. 3: Williamson AP 810
            No. 4: Little (c) AP 304
No. 6: Nilsson   AP 297   No. 5: Marlar   AP 487
                No. 7: Palis   AP 183

Stations: 0955   456th: BETTY TWO ONE
                            Penetration: BARTEND ONE
Engines: A 1000 B 1005   "   "   BARTEND TWO
         C 1010 D 1015   Target and withdrawal: BARTEND THREE
         E 1020 F 1025   BARTEND FOUR
                                        BARTEND FIVE

Take-off: 1025
                    Recall signal: "OBTAIN"
                C O N F I D E N T I A L

Enemy fighters were very aggressive. Targets in this area were among the most critical that the Third Reich had to defend, and it was the third most heavily defended target, only behind Berlin and Vienna in defense capability. As our Group approached the target area, four FW-190s attacked at 1407 hours, five minutes before bombs away. They made one head-on pass from the 12 o'clock position. Next, at 1409 hours, three minutes before bombs away three Me-109s attacked from the 4 o'clock high position. One minute later, at 1410 hours, one Me-109 came in from the 4 o'clock position. Next, one minute after that, at 1411 hours, two FW-190s came in again on a head-on attack from the 12 o'clock low position. No enemy fighters were shot down by gunners of our Group and we lost no bombers to enemy fighters.

Weather in the target area had forty to fifty percent cloud coverage from alto cumulus clouds having tops at 13,000 feet. Temperature at 20,300 feet was minus 18 degrees centigrade. It was getting warmer. Aircrews could feel the difference and welcomed it.

Lt. Fred Riley, currently president of the 456th Bomb Group Association, was the lead bombardier on this day, and he was under great pressure to perform well. He only had a few minutes to find the target between the clouds, then synchronize his Norden bombsight on it. He ususally coordinated closely with the Pathfinder crew to identify the target through cloud coverage. As usual for the Ploesti area, flak was heavy, intense, and accurate and three planes were lost to the flak.

While Fred Riley was synchronizing his bombsight on the target, three bombers went down between the I.P. and the target. Two of them went down at 1410 hours, two minutes before reaching the target, and the third Liberator went down in a bizarre accident (described below). Both of the two bombers that went down before reaching the target were from my 746th Squadron, one was flown by 1st Lt. Albert M. Lehner's crew and the other was flown by my friend, our Squadron's Assistant Operations Officer Lt. Richard E. Beck a West Pointer. Beck's plane, number 42-52222, "Deuces Wild" exploded violently and crashed in the target area. Lehner's plane, number 42-78235 "Yo-Yo," was on fire and crashed in the target area.

A third bomber, number 499 flown by Lt. Lawrence E. Peterson from the 745th Squadron, was lost in a ghastly accident when struck by an airman floating down in his parachute from Lehner's plane (described further below), and Peterson's Liberator went down just after its bombs were released. Peterson's plane was able to drop its bombs on the target, so a total of thirty-three of our Group's bombers were able to drop bombs on the target when Lt. Riley dropped his bombs in the lead plane of the formation.

Fred Riley, working with the Pathfinder navigator to locate the target through the clouds, visually spotted a half row of oil tanks through an opening in the clouds. He set the cross hairs of his Norden bombsight on the target, and bombs went away. There was a good concentration of bombs on the marshaling yards, oil storage tanks, and the Concordia Vega oil refinery. Three huge fires resulted, with smoke rising almost as high as the Group's bombing altitude. Thirty-six photos of the target area were taken.

With Riley's lead, our Group's thirty-three Liberators dropped 80.5 tons of 500 pound general purpose bombs on the target (322 bombs) on an axis of attack of 85 degrees magnetic from an altitude of 20,000 feet for the 1st Unit, and 19,000 feet for the 2nd Unit at 1412 hours. Indicated airspeed was 160 MPH, 222 MPH true airspeed. After bombs were released, the formation made a rapid descending turn to the left to evade radar-guided flak.

Thirty-two planes returned to our field at 1738 hours, and logged 7:35 hours by the time they were on the ground, a long mission. This was the group's forty-second mission in Italy, and its thirty-fourth accredited one.

More about the fate of the crews that went down was learned later. All of Lehner's crew became prisoners of war, except S/Sgt Bill P. Garcia, his substitute waist gunner who was killed in action in a unique accident explained below. Of Lehner's crew, six are currently members of our 456th Bomb Group Association: Lehner; S/Sgt James W. Childress, upper turret; S/Sgt William G. Clark, tail turret; 1st Lt Raymond Hollerbach, navigator; T/Sgt Reinhardt Dickwisch, engineer; and S/Sgt Kenneth T. Jenkins, also an engineer.

**Ploesti bombing smoke rises to flight altitude.
Photo courtesy of National Air and Space Museum,
Smithsonian Institution.**

Ploesti Smoke Rises To Flight Level

Beck's crew was less fortunate. No parachutes were seen to come from the small bits of Beck's plane that remained after the explosion. No one had hopes of any of the crew getting out alive. We didn't learn until much later that two crew members on Beck's plane were able to get out and became prisoners of war, 2nd Lt. John Teune, copilot and a current member of the 456th Bomb Group Association, and 2nd Lt. Harold E. Dyer, bombardier who has deceased since. Teune was miraculously thrown out of the plane after it exploded and disintegrated, and he woke falling through space over the target, pulled the rip cord, and settled to earth. He spent a month in a hospital near Ploesti and then went to a prison camp in the Carpathian Mountains.

All other members of Becks crew, including my friend Lt. Beck, were killed in action, except his navigator who was listed as missing in action. There were only nine crew members on his plane for this mission. The navigator on Beck's crew, 2nd Lt. Glenn A. Coleman, was another close personal friend of mine, and he was listed as missing in action because his body was never found and he wasn't reported as a prisoner of war. All of us believed that he had been killed because of the violence of the explosion. However, as I was registering at the University of California, Berkeley sixteen months later after the war (Fall of 1945), I saw Glenn "Rock" Coleman standing six places ahead of me in the school's registration line. I was pleasantly shocked, as it was like seeing a ghost. He said that the nose section of his aircraft, where he was sitting at the time of the explosion, was blown away from the rest of the parts of the disintegrated aircraft, and he blacked out. The nose section where he was located rapidly tumbled through the air toward the earth. He said that he doesn't know how it happened, but he next remembers waking up as he was floating down to earth with his parachute open, about one-thousand feet above the ground. He said that he could see soldiers on the ground waiting for him to land. On landing, he was immediately captured by Rumanian soldiers and put in a Rumanian prisoner of war camp. He had only minor injuries.

Peterson's plane was a victim of a bizarre accident. Peterson's plane went down as a result of Lehner's plane crash. A substitute waist gunner from Lehner's plane, S/Sgt Bill P. Garcia, flying ahead and above 1st Lt. Lawrence E. Peterson's plane bailed out of his plane in the 1st Box of the 2nd Unit. Garcia floated down in his parachute directly into the path of Peterson's plane. He struck the right wing tip of Peterson's plane and the impact of Garcia's body sheared off the wing tip outside of the number four engine. The plane spun wildly out of control to the ground. When Peterson's plane flipped over on its back, it was photographed by T/Sgt George L. Dancisak of the 745th Squadron as it spun upside down toward the earth. Garcia was killed instantly and all members of Peterson's crew, from the 745th squadron, were killed. Peterson's crew is interred at Jefferson Barracks, Missouri, except two who are still listed as missing in action: Sgt Charles V. Carter, ball turret; and Sgt Henry G. Kuntz, tail turret.

Our 456th Bomb Group mission to Ploesti, Rumania was a part of a massive Fifteenth Air Force attack on Ploesti and its vicinity. A total of 640 heavy bombers dropped 1,650 tons of bombs, setting a new Fifteenth Air Force record for tonnage dropped. Nineteen of Fifteenth Air Force's heavy bombers were lost on the day, while eighteen enemy fighters were claimed to be destroyed. Considerable damage was done to oil installations, pumping stations, marshalling yards, tracks, rolling stock, and troop concentrations. Huge fires were left as bombers returned home.

May 6, 1944 Campina Marshaling Yards, Rumania (Near Ploesti).

I was awakened by an orderly very early in the morning to fly, knowing that such early wake-up calls usually meant a long tough mission to a strategic target. Sure enough, this was another mission to the hotbed of enemy defenses around Ploesti. When we saw the length of the red yarn on the map on the wall at the end of our briefing room, we were all fearful. It was the second consecutive day that our Group bombed in the Ploesti area. We were all aware that three bombers were lost on the mission the day before, and that it had been a long one, 7:35 hours. The target this day was the Campina Marshaling Yards, about thirty miles from the heavily defended Ploesti.

Again, we had a radar-equipped Pathfinder plane as a backup to our Norden bombsights in the event that the target was covered by too many clouds to allow visual bombing.

After our wake-up call at 0515 hours, a C-rations breakfast, we rode up to an early briefing at 0630 hours. Lt. Howard I. Neff of the 746th Squadron intelligence section gave the Group intelligence portion of the briefing. He told us that yesterday's bombing in the Ploesti area by Fifteenth Air Force heavy bombers had destroyed most of the lines supplying the German front, where they were fighting the tough Russian Army. He said that the only major railroad facility left that was capable of handling the critical traffic was our target for this day, the Campina Marhsaling Yards.

Neff also gave us escape and evasion instructions to be used if we were to bail out. We were told to go west toward Belgrade. In the vicinity of Belgrade there are Partisan occupied areas east, north, and south. Don't ask for either Partisans or Chetniks. Ask for Allied Missions only. The Partisans are distinguished by the red star on their caps, and by their salute which is the clenched fist brought to the temple. They wear a variety of uniforms. The Chetniks

288

wear Yugoslav or German uniforms with the royal Yugoslav insignia on their caps. When you are with the Partisans do not discuss politics or other controversial matters. Above all, don't call them Communists.

After briefing we had a 0740 station time at our planes, my plane's start engine time was 0750 hours for our 2nd Box of the 1st Unit of the formation. Taxi out time for the lead plane was 0755. The lead bomber, with Major John R. Sinclair flying it, took off at 0805 hours. Thirty-six bombers followed Sinclair's plane off the runway at 45 second intervals.

C O N F I D E N T I A L

BATTLE ORDER

6 May 1944

1st Unit, 1st Box

Domelik
Formation Leader: Sinclair/ AP 817   Andrews
No. 3: Wilkinson   AP 807   Dep Leader: Clark, R.R./ AP 470
                    No. 4: Monahan   AP 334
No. 6: Hillenbrand AP 492   No. 5: Smith, E.W.   AP 549

2nd Box

Witkin
Leader: Hyde/ AP 486
No. 3: Dowering   AP 189   Dep Leader: Johnson AP 831
                    No. 4: Boughner AP 430
No. 6: Hundly (C) AP 853   No. 5: Snee   AP 839

3rd Box

Leader: Douglass   AP 749
No. 3: Phillips   AP 487   Dep Leader: Palis   AP 183
                    No. 4: Nilsson AP 810
No. 6: Marlar   AP 239   No. 5: Solcher (C) AP 304
                    No. 7: Brabon   AP 799

2nd Unit, 1st Box

Jackson, C.Y.
Leader: Gruber/ AP 279
No. 3: Jackson, W.L. AP 072   Dep Leader: Miller AP 268
                    No. 4: Strombom AP 634
No. 6: Aschmann   AP 964   No. 5: Ball   AP 595

2nd Box

Leader: Lee (C)   AP 872
No. 3: Rudd   AP 295   Dep Leader: Griffin AP 077
                    No. 4: Jones   AP 291
No. 6: Nunimaker   AP 501   No. 5: Nix   AP 233
                    No. 7: Lunt   AP 752

3rd Box

Leader: Clark, W.D. (C) AP 912
No. 3: Webster   AP 637   Dep Leader: Bishop (C) AP 777
                    No. 4: Newhouse AP 284
No. 6: Jennings   AP 287   No. 5: Leukuma   AP 633

Stations: 0740.   456th PU'PUP ONE-FOUR.
                                   Penetration FG-BELLBUOY ONE.
Engines: A. 0745 B. 0750 C. 0755   Over Target: KEYWORD ONE
         D. 0800 E. 0805 F. 0810

Take-off: 0805.
                    Recall signal: "AFFORD"

Three Liberators aborted the mission and returned early. One, number 492 flown by Lt. John R. Hillenbrand of my 746th Squadron, had a gasoline leak in the bomb bay. Another Liberator, number 077 flown by Lt. Ralph O. Griffin of the 744th Squadron had a gasoline leak in the main fuel tank. The third bomber, number 487 flown by Lt. Phillips of the 745th Squadron, returned early because its number two engine was vibrating.

After our Group's Liberators had formed their six Box combat formation around Sinclair's plane, he led our Group to our bomber rendezvous point over Stornara at 4,000 feet, where we followed the lead of the 455th Group. We departed Stornara at 0845 hours. The cruising formation for groups of the 304th Wing was in the order of 459th, 454th, 455th, and last, the 456th. We left climbing on course at a speed of 160 MPH and a 200 feet per minute rate of climb to our 1st Unit's bombing altitude of 19,000 feet. Fighter escort, P-38s, were supposed to rendezvous with our Wing over the target and give us withdrawal coverage as we left the target.

Again, fighter escort did not prevent thirty-three aggressive Me-109s from attacking our Group formation. In the classic air battle that followed, our gunners claimed three enemy fighters destroyed, one probable, and two damaged. We lost no Liberators on this mission.

Our 456th Bomb Group Association's history book recorded the following two comments of our gunners about their destruction of two of the attacking enemy fighters. These two reports of gunners are typical of those made to intelligence personnel at each mission's debriefing when we were safely on the ground. Usually, many gunners are able to confirm a gunner's claimed kill because many eyes are warily tracking attacking fighters. In huge dogfights, when many enemy fighters are attacking at the same time, and flying through our formation, more than one gunner

291

may think he hit the same fighter. Intelligence personnel attempt to sort out such possible claims. Intelligence people usually required that each gunner's claim be confirmed by another crew member's sighting of the event. Wyrick and Brace claims were typical claims that were confirmed and recorded as enemy fighters destroyed.

S/Sgt Cecil G. Wyrick, Jr., ball gunner of the 747th Squadron said, "As we rallied from the target our flight was momentarily separated from the formation. Four Me-109's in train made a direct attack, coming in at 6:30 o'clock low; they each broke away at 600 to 700 yards. One Me-109 came in low firing 20mm cannon shells. I fired approximately 250 rounds of 50 caliber shells at him. He started to smoke and went into a spiral dive, seemingly out of control. He caught on fire and was seen to hit the ground and burn, blazing fiercely."

S/Sgt Earl F. Brace, nose turret gunner of the 747th Squadron, reported, "Two Me-109's came in at 11:30 o'clock at about 16,000 feet, as they closed I fired a burst of about 20 rounds at them. I then concentrated on the closest one and followed him, firing approximately 45 rounds. As he closed, I lined him up dead center and fired another burst. I noticed my tracers go into the nose of the enemy aircraft, he went up momentarily and over in a straight spin. He then continued to spin downward and finally struck the ground and exploded."

Thirty-three of our group's bombers dropped 80 tons of 500 pound general purpose bombs at 1130 hours on an axis of attack of 106 degrees magnetic from the Initial Point, which was at Badeni, flying at an altitude of 19,000 feet and 160 MPH indicated airspeed. The bomb release interval was 50 feet. Results were graded as fair. Six bombs hit the main railroad tracks, there were numerous hits on sidings and branches, and many direct hits on the Astra Romana Machine Factory. Flak was graded as heavy, moderate, and accurate. Our Group formation made a descending turn to the right after bombs away to evade the flak. We lost no aircraft and there were no casualties, but some bombers had damage. This was our Group's forty-third mission in Italy, with thirty-five of them accredited. I was able to record my twenty-third and twenty-fourth accredited missions. Flying time was 7:00 hours, giving me a total of 111:55 combat hours.

This was a milestone day for the Fifteenth Air Force. It was the first day when 1,500 tons of bombs were dropped. All bombs were dropped by 640 heavy bombers in the Ploesti area on marshaling yards, oil pumping stations, oil installations, and troop concentrations. Huge fires were started in the oil facilities. Nineteen heavy bombers were shot down and eighteen enemy fighters were claimed to be destroyed.

May 7, 1944 Bucharest Marshaling Yards, Rumania (Near Ploesti).

This was the group's third day in a row of flying into the hornets' nest of enemy defenses in the Ploesti area, and I was not among those selected to fly on it. The target for this day was the Bucharest Marshaling Yards, Rumania, about forty miles from Ploesti. As it turned out, it was one of our less stressful missions, like a milk run. Evidently the enemy was getting worn down or critically damaged from so many planes attacking on consecutive days.

Again, the Group had a Pathfinder plane available to bomb by radar if weather was too bad for visual bombing at the target.

Early morning briefing was at 0630 hours, stations time at 0745, start engines time for the first box was at 0750 and each of the other five boxes started their engines at five minute intervals. Taxi out for the first bomber was at 0800 hours, takeoff of the lead plane with Major Louis

Abernathy of the 745th Squadron flying was at 0807 hours, two minutes late. Thirty-three bombers followed him at 45 second intervals.

Eight of the Group's Liberators aborted the mission and returned to our airfield early. Evidently our planes were becoming battle weary. One plane returned early because its airspeed indicator did not work, one returned early because three of its generators were fluctuating erratically, two bombers had supercharger regulators malfunction, one plane had a gasoline leak in its main tank, one had no fuel pressure on one engine and was leaking oil, and one because of a gasoline leak. Two aircraft had late takeoffs because of preflight discrepancies and they could not catch the Group formation.

C O N F I D E N T I A L   MAY 7, 1944

· · BATTLE ORDER

1st Unit, 1st Box

Thomas
Formation Leader: Abernathy,/ AP 768   Hyde
No. 3: Smith,G.T.   AP 275   Dep Leader: Witkin /   AP 279
     No. 4: Nilsson   AP 297
No. 6: Wilkinson   AP 334   No. 5: Smith,E.W.   AP 189

2nd Box

Leader: Richards   AP 489
No. 3: Draughnor   AP 495   Dep Leader: Robert   AP 480
     No. 4: Gutting   AP 831
No. 6: Snee   AP 839   No. 5: Hillenbrand   AP 853

3rd Box

Leader: Laszewski   AP 749
No. 3: Little   AP 304   Dep Leader: Williamson AP 239
     No.4: Palis   AP 183
No. 6: Phillips   AP 807   No. 5: Solcher   AP 810

2nd Unit, 1st Box

Leader: Reid, Tavel   AP 227
No. 3: Webster   AP 634   Dep Leader: Phifer   AP 501
     No. 4: Rudd   AP 295
No. 6: Jennings   AP 287   No. 5: Blackwell   AP 912

2nd Box

Leader: Andrews   AP 470
No. 3: Lane   AP 777   Dep Leader: Leukuma   AP 633
     No. 4: Riddle   AP 284
No. 6: Ward   AP 637   No. 5: Goretti   AP 098
     No. 7: Ball   AP 595

3rd Box

Leader: Mulligan   AP 872
No. 3: Lunt   AP 752   Dep Leader: Brabon   AP 799
     No. 4: Jackson,W.L. AP 290
No. 6: Munimaker   AP 268   No. 5: Lambert   AP 072
     No. 7: Jones, E.C. AP 077

Stations: 0745   456th: SEARCHLIGHT FOUR THREE.

Engines: A 0750 B 0755 C 0800   Penetration: (1st FG) BETTY ONE.
     D 0805 E 0810 F 0820
     Target cover: (14th FG) BETTY TWO.
Take-off: 0805   (31st FG) BETTY THREE.

E.T.R. 1400   Withdrawal: (82nd FG) BETTY FOUR.

Recall signal: DANDY.

After the Group's combat formation of six Boxes were formed around Abernathy's plane, he led the formation to the bomber rendezvous point that was at Giulia at 4,000 feet. The 459th Group joined us and followed our 456th Group's lead, then the formation departed Giulia at 0850 hours, climbing on course at 160 MPH indicated airspeed and a rate of climb of 200 feet per minute to the bombing altitude of 21,000 feet for the 1st Unit of the formation. The 2nd Unit bombed at 20,000 feet this day. Four fighter groups composed of P-38s, P-47s, and the hot new P-51s were scheduled to give our bombers cover on penetration of enemy territory, over the target, and withdrawal from the target

The Group had no enemy fighter attacks, although fourteen fighters were seen. Ten Me-109s, two FW-190s, and two JU-88s were seen, but they didn't have the courage to attack us with our escort fighters around. Our fighter escort was doing an efficient job of protecting the Group bombers. Flak was heavy, moderate, and inaccurate, and we lost no planes. Our chaff did its job of confusing the enemy radar that aimed the flak guns

The Initial Point was Lunguletul and our bombers attacked the target on axis of attack of 118 degrees magnetic. There were no clouds below the Group's formation at the target to interfere with visual bombing. Above the formation there was a solid overcast of cirrus clouds, bases at 22,000 feet. Visibility from air to ground was bad due to a heavy haze, from fires due to previous bombings. The temperature at 20,000 feet was minus 18 degrees centigrade, and winds were from 280 degrees at 36 knots.

At 1131 hours twenty-five of the twenty six bombers that made it to the target dropped 62 tons of 500 pound general purpose bombs on the marshalling yards at Bucharest, Rumania, from an altitude of 21,000 feet for the 1st Unit and from 19,000 feet for the 2nd Unit. One bomber had jettisoned its bombs before reaching the target because it had engine trouble that required the pilot to lighten its load in order to keep up with the Group formation.

The indicated airspeed was 160 MPH, and the true airspeed was 222 MPH at that temperature and altitude. The bomb release interval was 100 feet. Practically all bombs that were dropped by the main formation fell in the target area. They scored two direct hits on the approach to the railroad overpass, hits on railroad tracks and sidings, rolling stock, and facilities. Twenty photos covering the target area were taken by photographers using eight cameras on our planes. They had three K-21s and five K-22 type cameras. After bombs had been released, our formation made a descending right turn to evade flak gunners.

The formation of twenty-six B-24s returned to Stornara at 1506 hours. This was the group's forty-fourth mission in Italy, and its thirty-sixth credited mission. Flying time was 7:00 hours.

May 8, 1944   Abort Due to Weather After Briefing, Ploesti, Rumania.

Crews were briefed to bomb Ploesti again but a stand-down was announced before takeoff. Weather would not permit bombing. This was a much needed stand-down because the Group had flown into the tough defenses around the Ploesti area the last three days in succession, and ground crews needed the time to make necessary patches of flak and cannon holes and repairs to airplanes. I heard rumors that I may finally be getting a crew, and that I was to get a flight check tomorrow.

May 9, 1944   No Mission, My Flight Check.

There was no mission, again, today because of obvious poor weather at potential targets, but today was the day that I was given my own crew! I heard that it would be Lt. Warren T. Randall's crew, as he was having some kind of trouble.

My 746th Squadron commander, Major Paul T. Golden, a San Francisco native, took time to take me up for a 1:10 hour flight check. He checked my flying procedures, my emergency procedures, and three landings as my final check out so that I could take command of a crew of my own. Finally, something I had been patiently waiting for came to pass! I had 24 accredited missions, 111:55 hours of combat flying, and a total of 593 flying hours as a pilot. Of these, a total of 362 hours were in the B-24. I was twenty-one years old. Members of my new crew were:

> 2nd Lt Robert S. Capps, pilot
> 2nd Lt Sydney H. Brooks, copilot*
> 2nd Lt James G. Vaughn, navigator
> 2nd Lt James J. Duston, bombardier
> T/Sgt Edward W. Broom, engineer
> S/Sgt Carl Ezuck, tail turret gunner
> S/Sgt Thomas S. Delaney, radio operator
> and waist gunner*
> S/Sgt William E. Halper, nose turret
> gunner
> S/Sgt Andrew R. Smyth Jr., ball turret
> gunner
> S/Sgt Robert M. Gafner, waist gunner

(Brooks and Delaney are currently members of the 456th Bomb Group Association.)

The next day, without any notice that would allow us to freshen up, to look neat for the picture, we were ordered from our tents to the nearest aircraft hardstand to have our pictures taken for the Group archives. The nearest plane happened to be "Lassie Come Home," because our new plane had not arrived. "Lassie" was later shot down with its crew.

298

Today was the official day for discarding our winter uniforms and to start wearing summer, cotton suntan uniforms, but it was so chilly that many flight jackets were worn over them. Many put their woolens back on in the afternoon to keep warm.

Lt. Capps (standing on the left) and crew. Copilot Sydney H. Brooks is standing next to him. Lt. James J. Duston, bombardier is standing far right. S/Sgt. Thomas Delaney is kneeling on the left. T/Sgt Edward W. Broom is kneeling, second from right. Photo taken by Sgt. Phillip N. Savage of the 746th Squadron Intelligence. Photo provided by Richard C. Hood. Savage and Hood are current members of 456th Bomb Group Association.

Lt. Capps And His New Crew Near Friend's Place

299

Chapter 4
COMPOSITE DIARIES
OF THE GROUP'S
NEXT 34 MISSIONS
(From May 9, 1944 to July 7, 1944)

May 10, 1944 Wiener Neustadt, Austria. (The Group's First Presidential Distinguished Unit Citation Was Earned On This Mission).

This was the day after I was checked out as a commander of an aircrew, and my new crew had not been put together long enough. Thus, I was not scheduled for this mission, and I missed a momentous mission in the history of the 456th Bomb Group. The Group earned a Presidential Distinguished Unit Citation for "outstanding performance of duty in armed conflict against the enemy" when it bombed the aircraft factory, Werk Two, buildings 16 and

17, at Wiener Neustadt, Austria. It was a rough mission and six bombers were lost.

The mission started off like any of our other missions to that area. As the citation states, in General Order 22 issued by the War Department in Washington D.C. on 2 April, 1944, "the Group was notified to prepare a maximum effort for the mission, and ground personnel (as usual) worked feverishly, enthusiastically, and with untiring intensity to get all type B-24 aircraft in the best possible mechanical condition to insure the success of the operation." Forty bombers were prepared for this mission.

Our Wing's bombers were scheduled to have a fighter escort of P-38 Lightnings provided by the 14th and 82nd Fighter Groups, and P-47 Thunderbolts provided by the 325th Fighter Group. Fighter coverage was scheduled to begin 1 hour and 43 minutes before target time and continue through the target, through the bombers' withdrawal until they left enemy territory.

After an early morning wake-up call of 0430, crews were briefed at 0545 hours. The intelligence briefing told crews about escape procedures to be used in the event of bail out. They were told, "In Austria escape is due south, with the objective in mind of reaching Yugoslavia. First, hide your chute, get water, and hide out for a day, in this order. Then travel only at night. In the event of capture make every effort to escape before reaching a prison camp. In Yugoslavia (if you make it that far), ask to see the Allied Commission. Remember that Partisans are identified by soldiers wearing a red star on their cap. Any soldier wearing a steel helmet belongs to the German side and should not be approached."

Stations time at the aircraft was 0655, start engines time for all aircraft of the 1st Box was 0700, and crews of the other five Boxes started engines of their bombers at five minute intervals afterward. Taxi out from the B-24 parking stands started at 0710, then the lead aircraft took off at 0721 hours with Major John R. Sinclair flying it. Thirty-nine B-24s followed him at 45 second intervals. Captain Kenneth W. Gruber and Lt. Dave E. Tavel were in the lead aircraft of the 2nd Unit. There were twenty bombers scheduled to fly in each of the two Units of the formation.

After our Group had assembled its formation, our Group made a rendezvous with the other three groups of our 304th Wing over Stornara at 3,000 feet. The 304th Wing formation of four groups departed Stornara climbing on course at 0810. The climb was made at an indicated airspeed of 160 MPH, a true airspeed of about 200 MPH, and a rate of climb of 200 feet per minute.

Eight of the 456th's bombers returned early before reaching the target for the following reasons: four planes had supercharger malfunctions, one feathered #3 engine because it was leaking oil, one bomber had a runaway propeller on #4 engine, one had a leak in the pilot's oxygen system, and one aborted after 1 hour and 32 minutes because a sick man was aboard.

Two of the 304th Wing's group formations returned to their bases when they encountered bad weather that caused them to lose sight of the two groups ahead of them. This left the 456th Group and one other group to continue on to the target by themselves.

The citation about the 456th Group continues to read. "The group met the other units of the 304th Bombardment Wing at the point of rendezvous and proceeded towards the target on course. Adverse weather conditions were encountered over the Adriatic Sea and the weather began to close in with the ceiling 3,000 to 5,000 feet and visibility from 5 to 10 miles. Increasingly severe weather conditions forced the wing formation to become broken up and the groups were separated. Clouds obscured the 456th Bombardment Group (H) from the lead group. For 1 hour and 30 minutes the 456th Bombardment Group (H) flew on

302

course still hampered by heavy cloud formations. A break in the weather permitted the two groups to close up the gap and resume their position as the first combat wing of the briefed formation. The other two groups, separated during the ascent through heavy cloud formations, were forced to return to their home bases. Thirty minutes from the target, the weather showed a marked improvement. However, 80 to 90 enemy fighter airplanes began making aggressive attacks on the formation as the group penetrated the target area. The fighters made a well coordinated and vicious attack, and in the ensuing bitter air battle, enemy aircraft used rocket, guns, cannon, aerial flak, and heavy caliber machine-gun fire in an effort to disrupt the operation. Upon reaching the initial point of the bombing run, the group encountered heavy, intense, and accurate flak. The leading aircraft of the group, though hit by flak and forced to feather two engines, led the formation through for a highly successful bombing run which virtually obliterated the strategic enemy manufacturing center. Turning from the target, the formation was again attacked by successive waves of enemy fighters. In the savage engagement, the gunners of the 456th Bombardment Group (H) accounted for the destruction of eight enemy fighters, probably destroyed two others, and damaged another. Fifteen minutes after leaving the target area, the group was met by an escort and was covered from enemy attack until reaching friendly territory. The group lost four aircraft in the target area, two being hit by antiaircraft fire and two by enemy fighters. Another aircraft was missing in action and one crashed in friendly territory. All remaining aircraft, though riddled by flak and fighters, returned safely. The heroic leadership, determination, and combat efficiency of the crews, together with the professional skill and intense devotion to duty of the ground personnel, enabled the officers and enlisted men of the 456th Bombardment Group (H) to carry out a highly successful mission, thereby reflecting great credit on themselves and the armed forces of the United States."

DECLASSIFIED
> 11652, Sec. 3(E) and 5(D) of (E)

OSD letter, May 3, 1972
_____ NARS Date /-B-74

BATTLE ORDER

10 May 1944

1st Unit, 1st Box

Formation Loader: Sinclair, Miller   AP 817   Lane
                                     Dep Leader: Clark, R.R./ AP 894
No. 3: Nix   AP 233
                    No. 4: Jennings   AP 287
No. 6: Aschmann   AP 633   No. 5: Van Dyke   AP 872
                    No. 7: Rawlinson AP 964

2nd Box

                    Loader: Leo   AP 077
No. 3: Barrasso   AP 290   Dep Leader: Griffin AP 752
                    No. 4: Jones   AP 291
No. 6: Brabon   AP 799   No. 5: Smith, G.T.   AP 275
                    No. 7: Rudd   AP 295

3rd Box

                    Loader: Clark, W.D. AP 912
No. 3: Riddle   AP 777   Dep Leader: Bishop AP 768
                    No. 4: Strombom   AP 634
No. 6: Leukuma   AP 637   No. 5: Newhouse   AP 284
                    No. 7: Ball   AP 595

2nd Unit, 1st Box

                    Loader: Gruber, Tavol AP 227
No. 3: Phillips   AP 177   Dep Leader: Bowering AP 189
                    No. 4: Monahan   AP 334
No. 6: Smith, E.C. AP 549   No. 5: Marler   AP 304
                    No. 7: Blackwell AP 098

2nd Box

                    Loader: Manlove   AP 492
No. 3: Hillenbrand AP 480   Dep Leader: Johnson AP 831
                    No. 4: Boughner   AP 486
No. 6: Gutting   AP 489   No. 5: Hundley   AP 853
                    No. 7: Snee   AP 839

3rd Box

                    Loader: Douglass AP 749
No. 3: Palis   AP 183   Dep Leader: Laszewski AP 309
                    No. 4: Flemming   AP 487
No. 6: Williamson   AP 239   No. 5: Selchor   AP 810
                    No. 7: Wilkinson AP 807

Stations: 0655   456th "FRONTROOM TWO TWO"

Engines: A 0700 B 0705 C 0710   Penetration: 82nd FG "SHAPELY ONE"
         D 0715 E 0720 F 0725   Target cover: 14th FG "SHAPELY TWO"

Take-off: 0720.   Withdrawal: 325th FG, "SHAPELY THREE"

The fighter attacks were made by Me-109s, FW-190s, and JU-88s. Many of the planes had yellow spinners, markings of Goering's elite fighter squadron. The flak at the target was very accurate, and there were red, white, and black flak bursts. Returning crews reported that the flak over the target was the heaviest and the most accurate they had ever seen or encountered. In addition to the aircraft lost, as reported in the citation above, twenty-six of the bombers had flak damage, each had from 3 to 100 holes in it.

Thirty-one of our Group's bombers were able to drop 74 tons of high explosive RDX 500 pound bombs (296 bombs) at 1121 hours from an altitude of 21,000 feet for the 1st Unit and 20,000 feet for the 2nd Unit at an indicated airspeed of 160 MPH, a true airspeed of 226 MPH. The bomb release interval setting was 70 feet, and the axis of attack was 278 degrees magnetic from the Initial Point, Saint Margarethen. Although there was a solid undercast of clouds enroute to the target, with many cloud buildups to fly around, the weather at the target improved significantly. The target had one-tenth coverage by cumulus clouds below the formation with bases at 7,000 feet, and seven-tenths coverage above the formation by cirrus clouds, bases at 24,000 feet. The air temperature at 21,000 feet was minus 22 degrees centigrade. Twenty-seven photographs were taken by our bombers of the target area. A good pattern of bombs were reported on the target.

Bombs hit buildings 13, 15, 16, and 17, some of which appeared to burst into flames. There was   much smoke in the area from the bombing, as the 456th was the second group over the target. After bombs away, the formation rallied by making a descending left turn at a slow airspeed of 155 to 160 MPH indicated airspeed, about 215 to 226 MPH true airspeed. The slow speed was maintained to enable the Group's pilots to keep a tight formation, the best defense against enemy fighters. The formation continued its left turn to a heading that took it to the town of Cankova, then it flew from there to Soline before heading home.

Twenty-six damaged bombers returned over its Stornarella base at 1403 hours, and the recorded flying time was 6 hours and 45 minutes by the time it was on the ground. As noted above, of the 26 bombers that returned to the base, 25 had damage. One plane that was severely damaged made an emergency crash landing at Foggia and had to be scrapped. This was the thirty-seventh credited mission for the Group in forty-five missions. At the time of the mission, fifty-three personnel were reported as missing in action, one killed, and one a ball turret gunner very seriously wounded.

Three of the planes lost were flying in the 1st Box of the 1st Unit, flown by pilots 1st Lt. Lyle W. Lane, 2nd Lt. John F. Jennings, and 2nd Lt. Harold N. Aschmann, all of the 747th Squadron. Two of the planes lost were flown by pilots 1st Lt. Arthur F. Bowering and 1st Lt. Donald C. Manlove, both from my 746th Squadron. Beside the 53 crewmen flying on the planes lost, the ball turret gunner on Capt. William H. Snee's crew, S/Sgt Leo V. Dietrich, was badly injured in the right leg by a 20mm fighter cannon, and he received the Purple Heart for his wound.

Lane's crew, flying in the deputy lead position of the 1st Box of the 1st Unit with the 747th Squadron commander, Captain Richard R. Clark flying as his command pilot, was hit by flak on the bomb run. Fire started in the bomb bay of Lane's plane and in its #1 engine. Eight parachutes from his plane were seen to open as the ship went down in the target area. After the war it was learned that four were killed in action, four listed as missing in action (now believed to have been killed), and three were made prisoners of war in Stalag Luft IV. There were two navigators on board. The three POWs, believed to be the only survivors, were T/Sgt David O. Bowlan, S/Sgt James K. Allen (both members of the 456th Bomb Group Association) and S/Sgt Edward J. Curry, since deceased.

Jennings crew, flying "Fat Ass" in the number four position of the 1st Box of the 1st Unit, had six members killed, and Jennings and three others of his crew are missing in action. Those killed are buried in the American Military Cemeteries at Lorraine, France and Rhone, France.

Aschmann's crew, the third crew of the 747th Squadron that was lost flying in the number six position of the 1st Box of the 1st Unit, had difficulty staying with the formation enroute to the target because of a faulty supercharger. His plane took a direct flak hit at the target which tore a massive hole in the right wing and caused a dangerous fuel leak. The pilot was unable to keep up with the Group formation and his plane was being stalked aggressively by enemy fighters. The plane was reported to have been hit by rockets of an Me-109 at 10,000 feet and no chutes were seen to open. However, after the war it was learned that the crew was forced to bail out over Hungary near Yugoslavia. All of the crew were captured and taken as POWs, except the radio operator who was killed in action and is interred in the American Military Cemetery in Florence. Italy. They were held as POWs in Stalag Luft IV. Two of these members, Sgt. Paul L. Zimmerman, nose turret gunner, and Sgt. Chris R. Togarelli, tail turret, are current members of the 456th Bomb Group Association.

Bowering's plane, "Squat and Drop," one of the two 746th Squadron's planes lost, was flying in the deputy lead position of the 1st Box of the 2nd Unit. The plane was struck in the nose by a flak burst that wounded the navigator and the bombardier. Both suffered chest injuries. The pilot, Bowering, was struck in the palm of his right hand. Fuel lines in the bomb bay were severed and raw gasoline formed puddles on the catwalk. Number three engine was on fire and all of the controls were gone except for a slight bit of aileron control that remained. Fiery pieces were flying off the engine so the crew bailed out and they were taken as POWs. Bowering, who has since deceased, related his experiences after the war. Three of the crew, copilot 2nd Lt. Paul F. McKeown, upper turret gunner M/Sgt. Abraham J. Mozzor, and engineer M/Sgt Martin S. Reidy are current members of the 456th Bomb Group Association.

Lt. Donald C. Manlove's plane, "Curly Top," was seen to turn out of the Group formation at 1010 hours to return to base because of difficulty, and when the Group's staff made its report to higher headquarters, his plane had not been seen or heard from since. It was missing. However, we learned much later that Manlove and his crew were able to bail out, evade capture, and return to Italy. He and four other members of his crew are currently members of our 456th Bomb Group Association: 1st. Lt. Kenneth A. Bein his bombardier, 2nd Lt. Donald D. Fuller his copilot, M/Sgt Juney Lee Patterson his radio operator, and 1st Lt. Arthur Serafinski his navigator. Later they were able to relate the story, of what had happened. Their plane had been leaking oil and two engines, numbers one and two, had been shut down on one side of the plane. They were over water of the Adriatic so Manlove turned back toward Yugoslavia so they would be over land for bail out of the crew. When they were finally over the island of Kornati, Croatia, the crew bailed out. Lt. Manlove, being the last to leave, had some difficulty because the plane was again over water by the time he was able to try exiting the plane. He had to climb back into the cockpit and turn his plane back toward land. By the time he was over land again, the plane had descended to 500 feet, and he bailed out. He landed on the island of Zut, Croatia. Manlove's crew was immediately picked up by Tito's Partisans on Kornati and returned to Italy. Manlove was found two days later by Partisans and taken to the island of Vis. He arrived back in Bari, Italy, several days after his crew.

For the entire 15th Air Force that day, May 10, 1944, 174 B-17s and 126 B-24s (of which the 456th Group was a part) were able to make it to the target area and they dropped 795 tons of bombs on the Messerschmidt factory at Wiener Neustadt, with good results. This was in addition to a total of 102 B-24s that dropped 212 tons of bombs on the airdrome at Wiener Neustadt. A total of twenty-eight Fifteenth Air Force bombers and three escorting fighters were lost, fifty enemy fighters were claimed destroyed, twenty-two claimed as probables, and twenty-three damaged.

May 11, 1944   No Mission.

This day was a stand-down day, with good cause. Six planes were lost yesterday, in addition to the fact that 25 of the returning 26 bombers from yesterday's mission had battle damage. Furthermore, 7 planes had returned from the mission early because of mechanical malfunctions and they needed repair. This stand-down was a much needed reprieve. The ground crews needed time to repair our planes. I used the day to get acquainted with my new crew.

Since we didn't have to fly, I visited some of our wounded friends in the Foggia Hospital. While we were talking at the bedside of one friend, the famous movie actress Madeleine Carroll came around and we got to meet her. She was more beautiful than she appeared in her moving pictures. My new radio operator, S/Sgt Thomas Delaney who was also visiting wounded friends in the Foggia Hospital, said that Madeleine Carroll came to S/Sgt Leo Dietrichs bed while he was there. She told Leo that she was a good friend of General Dwight D. (Ike) Eisenhower, Supreme Commander of the Allied Armed Forces in Europe, and that she was going to ask Ike to have S/Sgt Leo Dietrich, ball turret gunner on Capt. Snee's crew, who was badly wounded in his right leg on the

May 10 mission, flown home. Shortly afterward, Leo was flown home.

May 12, 1944 Dock Installations and Railroad Bridge at Chiavaria, Italy (Alternate Target)

I was anxious to fly a mission with my new crew and I got my chance on this day. I felt more than adequately prepared for it. Two short missions were planned for this day by the 304th Wing Headquarters, one in the morning and one in the afternoon. Representatives from the 304th Wing visited our Group last night, on the 11th, and delivered the mission order. However, the afternoon mission was canceled because of a bad turn in the weather after the early morning mission was flown.

This was the day that our crew was assigned to the new silver B-24G, "Porky," and we were proud of it, but it was not ready for us to use on this, our first mission. We were given another crew's plane, named "Peace-Maker."

The morning mission was briefed to bomb the marshaling yards at Fidenza, Italy, the primary target. Cloud cover at the primary target prevented it from being bombed, and an alternate target, the dock installations and railroad bridge at Chiavaria, Italy had to be bombed. There was no flak or enemy aircraft encountered. We didn't lose a plane on the mission, but one bomber was originally listed as missing in action because no one knew what had happened to it. It turned up the next day, having made an emergency landing at Corsica.

Our Group mission was a part of the Fifteenth Air Force's first 1,000 plane raid on this day. A total of 1,143 aircraft were sent to northern Italy in support of our allied ground forces. A total of 1,912 tons of bombs were dropped.

Our ground crews worked very hard all night and produced 42 planes that were pronounced ready for this mission. An early takeoff, at 0515 hours, was originally scheduled to enable us to have enough daylight remaining to fly the second mission scheduled for the afternoon.

With 42 planes ready, there were six Boxes planned for our Group formation. We had a very early wake-up call for a briefing at 0400 hours, stations time of 0450, start engines time for the first Box at 0455, and the remaining five Boxes started their engines at five minute intervals after the first Box started its engines. Taxi out began at 0505 hours and the first aircraft, with Major John R. Sinclair and 1st Lt. Richard Witkin of my 746th Squadron in the lead plane, took off at 0515 hours. The other forty-one planes followed at 45 second intervals. Our Group rendezvoused with other groups of the 304th Wing over Stornara at 4,000 feet, then we departed climbing on course at 0615 hours.

I was flying in the number 5 position of the 2nd Box of the 2nd Unit, off the right wing tip of my former crew, Boughner's crew, that was flying in the number 4 position. Captain William B. Clark, newly appointed commander of the 747th Squadron who had replaced Capt. Richard R. Clark (who was shot down on the May 10 mission), was in the lead aircraft of the 2nd unit. Because no flak was expected at the target, we could bomb at a lower altitude than normal, 15,000 feet for the 1st Unit and 14,000 for the 2nd Unit. This was expected to make the bombing more accurate.

Two aircraft returned early. One returned because of a faulty landing gear, and another returned early for some unknown reason and it never made it back to our base to make its report. It was last seen at 0821 hours, near the town of Piombino, a little northeast of the island of Elba, and it was listed as missing. It turned up the next day, and its crew reported that it had made an emergency landing at another allied base on Corsica because of mechanical problems.

311

BATTLE ORDER   Date: 12 May 1944

1st Unit: 1st Box

Formation Leader: Maj SINCLAIR/ AP 768 (C)   Thomas   Witkin
Dep Leader: Maj REID/ AP 227

No.3: Brabon   AP 233
No. 4: Jackson, W.L. AP 268
No.6: Blackwell (C) AP 964
No. 5: Strombom   AP 634
No. 7: Phillips (C)   AP 304

2nd Box

Leader: Andrews   AP 470
Dep Leader: Bishop (C) AP 912

No.3: Newhouse   AP 284
No. 4: Riddle (C)   AP 777
No.6: Leukuma   AP 637
No. 5: Ball   AP 595
No. 7: Webster   AP 098

3rd Box

Leader: Phifer   AP 501
Dep Leader: Lambert AP 072

No.3: Smith,G.T. AP 275
No. 4: Jones,W.W.   AP 291
No.6: Hillman   AP 295
No. 5: Barrasso   AP 290
No. 7: Lunt (C)   AP 752

2nd Unit, 1st Box

Leader: CLARK,W.B./ AP 279   Mulligan   Jones
Dep Leader: GRIFFIN/ C AP 077

No.3: Monohan (C) AP 334
No. 4: Williamson (C) AP 810
No.6: Wood   AP 477
No. 5: Gullick   AP 299
No. 7: Fleming   AP 239

2nd Box

Leader: Richards   AP 489
Dep Leader: Cutting C AP 442

No.3: Johnson (C) AP 831
No. 4: Boughner   AP 934
No.6: Smith (C)   AP 549
No. 5: Capps   AP 486
No. 7: Ragland   AP 201

3rd Box

Leader: Douglass (C) AP 749
Dep Leader: Gardner AP 203

No.3: Wilkinson   AP 113
No. 4: Palis   AP 183
No.6: Nilsson   AP 297
No. 5: Savage (C) AP 807
No. 7: Marlar   AP 487

312

Weather at the primary target was too bad for visual bombing. The target was completely covered with stratocumulus clouds.Our formation went to the secondary target at Chiavaria, Italy. It wasn't much better, as it had nine-tenths coverage by stratocumulus clouds that had bases at 4,500 feet. Chiavaria also had nine-tenths coverage with altocumulus clouds with bases at 12,000 feet. Nevertheless, 37 of our planes were able see the target sufficiently to drop 92.5 tons of 500 pound general purpose bombs (370 bombs) at 0942 hours, flying at an indicated airspeed of 160 MPH, a true airspeed of 203 MPH. The bombardiers' bomb release interval setting was 30 feet, and bombs were dropped on an axis of attack of 37 degrees magnetic. The outside air temperature was a relatively warm minus 10 degrees centigrade because we were bombing from such a low altitude. The bridge at Chiavaria received direct hits, and bombs hit the Chiavaria dock installations, railroad bridges, and railroad marshaling yards. Twenty-six photos were taken of the target area by eleven K-22 cameras and three K-21s cameras that were carried aboard our bombers. Results were graded as fair, which was a good effort considering the poor weather over the target.

Three planes in the formation had mechanical release problems and they were unable to release their bombs on Chiavaria. Two of them dropped their bombs later on the marshaling yards at La Spezia, Italy, and the third bomber that had a release problem at Chiavaria succeeded in dropping its bombs on marshaling yards at Lerici, Italy. Results of the bombing by these three planes were also rated as fair, and marshaling yards at La Spezia and Lerici received hits.

Our formation of 40 bombers returned to our base at 1205 hours. When the afternoon bombing was canceled because of weather, we had the whole afternoon off. The Group recorded its 38th accredited mission of the   46 missions it had flown in Italy. I recorded my 25th combat mission and logged 6 hours and 55 minutes of combat flying time.

My new crew performed very well together, they all appeared very competent at their jobs, and they all had very good "can do" attitudes. I was particularly impressed by the competence of my new engineer, T/Sgt Edward W. Broom who had an exceptional knowledge of the B-24, but the copilot Brooks, the navigator, bombardier, and all of the gunners also seemed very competent too. I was happy to have them on the crew.

S/Sgt Thomas S. Delaney, radio operator and waist gunner of our new crew, kept a very good diary of events. His notes for this mission read, "We flew our first mission with Lt. Capps, our new pilot. Gee it was another beautiful milk run, no fighters, no flak! Lt. Capps sure flew a wonderful formation. Our bombs hit right in the marshaling yard. It was the "Peace-Maker's" (number 486) 42nd mission! Our crew has been assigned a new silver colored plane. The name was "Porky", number 306."

May 13, 1944 Marshaling Yards at Borgo Panigale, Italy.

My crew was assigned to fly our new silver B-24G, "Porky", on this mission for the first time. The crew chief for our new Liberator was Sgt. Candelario R. Aguilar Jr. and he appears to be very interested in his work and competent. We were very glad to learn that he would be assigned to care for Porky. Except for some bothersome weather enroute and a little flak, this mission turned out to be another milk run for the Group, and the bombing results were excellent because the weather at the target was excellent, for a change. The target was the railroad marshaling yards at Borgo Panigale, Italy.

Individual crews were assigned to specific Liberators that our Group owned on a more or less permanent basis so that they could become familiar with their plane's characteristics. This also allowed the crews to become familiar with their planes' ground crews. Each B-24 had some features, good and bad, that others did or didn't have. Crews were expected to monitor the planes assigned to them and to keep in touch with their plane's status. Whenever the crew flew, and their assigned plane was in commission, they would fly their assigned plane. This did not preclude other crews from flying their plane if their assigned crew was not selected to fly on the mission that day.

This was the first mission that my crew was able to fly in our new, beautiful, silver assigned plane. It was a sleek new silver, non-painted aircraft, a B-24G Model NT named "Porky," aircraft number 42-78306. It was manufactured for Consolidated Aircraft Corporation of San Diego by the North American Plant located in Dallas, Texas. Only twenty-five B-24Gs were built. It was one of our first new B-24s that was not painted with olive-drab camouflage paint. The Army Air Force decided that paint was no longer needed. The crew that flew the plane over from the United States had paid seventy dollars while they were in North Africa, enroute to Italy, to have the name "Porky" and giant shark's teeth and large eyes painted on the plane's nose section. The crew was very disgruntled because the plane was taken away from them, and assigned to my 456th Bomb Group. They were assigned to a different organization. The crew that paid seventy dollars for the paint job was separated from its plane. Such are the exigencies of war! My crew was glad to get such an unusually decorated plane.

C O N F I D E N T I A L

13 May 1944

1st Unit, 1st Box

Formation Leader: Col. STEED, Miller AP 768
No. 3: Fleming   AP 239   Dep Leader: Ladd, Nilsson AP 279
                               No. 4: Palis   AP 183
No. 6: Voshell   AP 201   No. 5: Wood   AP 442

2nd Unit

Leader: Snee   AP 831
No. 3: Hundly   AP 853   Dep Leader: Boughner   AP 256
                               No. 4: Capps   AP 306
No. 6: Gullick   AP 299   No. 5: Ragland   AP 934
                               No. 7: Scott   AP 477

Leader: Laszowski AP 749
No. 3: Wilkinson AP 304   Dep Leader: Williamson AP 810
                               No. 4: Gardner   AP 203
No. 6: Solcher   AP 487   No. 5: Marlar   AP 113
                               No. 7: Savage   AP 807

2nd Unit, 1st Box

Leader: Gruber, Tavel   AP 227
No. 3: Smith,B.V. AP 549   Dep Leader: Hyde, Ensign AP 486
                               No. 4: Rudd   AP 295
No. 6: Nix   AP 233   No. 5: Cerotti   AP 912

2nd Box

Leader: Lee   AP 268
No. 3: Hillman   AP 285   Dep Leader: Brabon   AP 799
                               No. 4: Jones,F.S. AP 291
No. 6: Jones,E.C. AP 077   No. 5: Van Dyke   AP 872
                               No. 7: Lunt   AP 752

3rd Box

Leader: Bishop   AP 470
No. 3: Webster   AP 098   Dep Leader: Loukuma   AP 637
                               No. 4: Riddle   AP 777
No. 6: Ball   AP 595   No. 5: Strombom   AP 634
                               No. 7: Blackwell AP 964

Stations: 0945.   456th "RINGWAY TWO FOUR"

Engines: A 0950 B 0955 C 1000   1st FG "KEYWORD TWO"
         D 1005 E 1010 F 1015
                                        Recall Signal: "MUDPIE"
Take-off: 1015.

316

Our crew picture was taken with Porky a few days later, on a day off for my crew, May 15, 1944. It is shown on page.325. Unfortunately, "Porky" was destined to fly only twenty-six missions before it was violently destroyed in the air as described in Chapter 5."Porky" performed delightfully on this mission! We were all happy with it, and I never had to abort a mission because of mechanical failure, or for any other reason, while I flew it. In fact, I never had to abort any mission I was assigned to fly while I was an aircraft commander in Italy.

Wake up was at 0730 hours, briefing at 0830, stations time at our new aircraft, "Porky," was 0945. Start engines time was scheduled for 0950 hours for the planes in the 1st Box, and the other five Boxes started their engines at five minute intervals after that. I was flying in the 2nd Box of the 1st Unit, number 4 position, so I was scheduled to start Porky's engines at 0955 hours. However, there was a fifteen minute delay for some reason that I never discovered. The lead plane started to taxi out to the end of the runway at 1020, then Colonel Steed in the lead bomber took off at 1030 hours, instead of the 1015 hours that we had been briefed. The rest of us, thirty-nine more B-24s, followed his plane at 45 second intervals. Captain Kenneth W. Gruber and 1st Lt. Dave E. Tavel, my tent-mate until he moved his living quarters up to Group headquarters, were in the lead plane of the 2nd Unit.

Eight aircraft returned to our airbase early, before bombing, for the following reasons: four had turbo-superchargers that malfunctioned, two had engines malfunction, one became separated from the formation as it went through a cloud bank over Foggia, and one had its oxygen system go out.

After he took off, Colonel Steed flew his Liberator in a race track pattern while the rest of our planes caught up with him to assemble our Group formation over Giulia at

5,000 feet. Colonel Steed then led us to rendezvous with the 455th Bomb Group over San Giovanni, before climbing on course to reach our target. We climbed at 165 MPH, a true airspeed of about 220 MPH, and 200 feet per minute rate of climb. Our route took us over Isernia, but no enemy aircraft attacked our Group.

Weather at the target was excellent, with ceiling and visibility unlimited except for a moderate haze. Temperature at 21,300 feet was minus 21 degrees centigrade. Flak was scant, inaccurate, with ugly, heavy black bursts, but none of our aircraft reported damage. Three crews could not release their bombs on the target because of release malfunctions, but 29 bombers were able to release 87 tons of the huge 1,000 pound bombs (174 bombs) on the primary target at 1422 hours. The formation was flying at 160 MPH indicated airspeed, about 226 MPH true airspeed, and we bombed from an altitude of 21,000 feet for the 1st Unit and 19,000 feet for the 2nd Unit. The axis of attack was 40 degrees magnetic. There was an excellent pattern of bombs that hit the target. Three K-21 and seven K-22 cameras on planes of our formation took pictures of the target. This mission illustrated the quality of bombing that can be accomplished when the weather is excellent. The formation made a descending turn to the right after bombs away to confuse the flak gunners on the ground who were shooting at us.

Thirty-two B-24s in our formation returned to our base at 1605 hours, and I recorded 5 hours and 40 minutes after landing. This was the Group's 39th credited mission in 47 missions. It was my 26th mission. It was an excellent mission for my crew to get thoroughly acquainted with one another. This was an enjoyable shakedown flight for "Porky!" If we had known the outcome of the mission before we took off it would have been much more pleasant and enjoyable because we wouldn't have been so jittery and constantly watchful throughout the mission. We never knew, as past experience had taught us, when something violent and life-threatening was going to occur on any of our missions, particularly while we were in enemy territory. We had to keep alert at all times.

Our new radio operator, also a waist gunner, who was experienced with twenty missions flying with other crews before he joined my crew, recorded in his diary, "Well we christened our new plane 'Porky.' It sure is a wonderful plane! We went on a sweet "milk run" in Italy, just a little flak and no fighters. Lt Capps flew a wonderful formation! The bombardier really blasted the target! I watched the bombs (1,000 pounders) hit......... The smoke from the bombing came up to our (flight) level."

May 14 Airdrome at Reggio Emilia, Italy.

Now that I had my own crew and had been assigned to a sleek new plane, "Porky", I was anxious to fly it as often as possible. However, we learned that Porky could not make this mission because it was being repaired. Instead, we were given another crew's plane to fly, number 486 "Peace-Maker." My crew was selected to fly for the third day in succession. It was another beautiful day for flying and bomb results were good.

Again, the Fifteenth Air Force launched all 21 of its heavy bomber groups to bomb targets in northern Italy in support of our Allied ground forces, and to continue its mission of destroying the Luftwaffe in Italy. The mission was designed to severely cripple German railroad transportation facilities in northern Italy to prevent their supplying German ground troops. The two airdromes we were bombing this day had been used as transit stopover bases for Luftwaffe bombers that threatened our ground troops, in addition to threatening our U.S. Army Air Force airfields in Italy. Recent reconnaissance photography showed a heavy concentration of fighter-bombers at these bases. The Fifteenth Air Force dispatched all of its bomb groups to bomb marshaling yards at Ferrara, Vicenza, Padua, Treviso, Mestre, and airdromes at Piacenza, and Reggio Emilia.

The target for my 456th Bomb Group was the airdrome at Reggio Emilia, in coordination with one other group of our 304th Wing that was bombing at the same target, the 459th Bomb Group. The 306th Fighter Wing provided P-38 Lightning and P-51 Mustang fighter cover for us, starting with our penetration of enemy territory, then continuing over the targets and throughout withdrawal of our heavy bomber formations from their targets. They did a good job of protecting us because my Group encoutered no enemy fighters on this mission.

Again, our great ground crews worked to prepare forty bombers for the mission. Only two planes aborted the mission early after takeoff on this day, a tribute to the growing efficiency to our ground crews. There hadn't been much aircraft damage inflicted on our bombers by enemy action for a few days, for our ground crews to repair, so they could concentrate on doing a good job of loading our planes and getting them ready for this mission. One of the planes that returned early had an engine malfunction and the other had a gasoline leak.

C O N F I D E N T I A L

Date: 14 May 1944

1st Unit, 1st Box

Witkin

Formation Leader: Sinclair,/ AP 227   Smith, G.T.

No. 3: Marlar   AP 113   Dep Leader: Reid,/ AP 268
               No. 4: Wilkenson AP 304
No. 6: Scott   AP 256   No. 5: Voshell   AP 201

2nd Box

Leader: Gutting AP 442

No. 3: Hundley   AP 853   Dep Leader: Johnson   AP 831
               No. 4: Capps   AP 306
No. 6: Wood   AP 477   No. 5: Doan   AP 934
               No. 7: Gullick   AP 299

3rd Box

Leader: Douglass AP 749

No. 3: Monahan   AP 334   Dep Leader: Gardner   AP 309
               No. 4: Nilsson AP 297
No. 6: Phillips   AP 183   No. 5: Roak   AP 239
               No. 7: Solcher   AP 810

2nd Unit, 1st Box

Clark, W.D.

Leader: Mulligan,/ AP 768

No. 3: Smith, B.V. AP 549   Dep Leader: Webster   AP 098
               No. 4: Lambert AP 072
No. 6: Ragland   AP 489   No. 5: Lunt   AP 752
               No. 7: Savage   AP 807

2nd Box

Leader: Andrews AP 470

No. 3: Ball   AP 595   Dep Leader: Riddle AP 777
               No. 4: Strombom AP 634
No. 6: Corotti   AP 912   No. 5: Newhouse   AP 284
               No. 7: Blackwell AP 964

3rd Box

Leader: Rudd   AP 295

No. 3: Nix   AP 291   Dep Leader: Griffin   AP 077
               No. 4: Jackson, W.L. AP 275
No. 6: Brabon   AP 799   No. 5: Hillman   AP 285
               No. 7: Van Dyke AP 872

Stations: 0845   456th "PLAYFAIR FOUR THREE"

Engines: A 0850 B 0855 C 0900   Fighter: "GOWAY THREE"
       D 0905 E 0910 F 0915
                         Recall: "DANDY"
Take-off: 0915

C O N F I D E N T I A L

Wake-up calls came in our tents at 0630 hours, and after breakfast and a ride up to Group headquarters in open Army six by six trucks, briefing started at 0730. Stations time at the aircraft was 0845, start engines time for the first Box at 0850, and the other five Boxes of our formation this day started their engines at five minute intervals after the first Box. My plane was number 4 in the 2nd Box of the 1st Unit, so I started at 0855. Taxi out started at 0905 hours, and the first plane, with Major John R. Sinclair and Lt. Richard Witkin of my 746th Squadron flying, took off at 0915 hours followed by our 39 other B-24s that took off at 45 second intervals afterward. After our formation was assembled, we rendezvoused over Giulia at 4,000 feet with the three other groups of the 304th Wing. The 456th Group was leading all other groups of the 304th Wing today. We departed Giula climbing on course at 1013 hours at 160 MPH indicated airspeed, a true airspeed of about 200 MPH, and 200 feet per minute rate of climb. Once at bombing altitude, the cruise speed was increased to 165 MPH, a true airspeed of about 230 MPH.

Weather was excellent for the entire trip with only three to seven-tenths of thin cirrostratus clouds above our bomber formation enroute to the target and at the target. The air temperature at 18,600 feet was a relatively warm minus 13 degrees centigrade at the target. Our true airspeed for the bomb run was 220 MPH, an indicated airspeed of 160 MPH. Thirty-seven bombers were able to drop 49.2 tons of 20 pound fragmentation bombs (4,980 bombs) on the primary target at 1253 hours from 18,000 feet, bombing on an eighteen ship front. This was an unusual formation with the two Units of our Group formation flying abreast. That meant that six Boxes were flying abreast when bombs were released. The axis of attack was 250 degrees magnetic from the initial point of Camposanta.

Two bombers in the formation had bomb rack malfunctions and couldn't release on the target. Flak was scant, inaccurate, but with heavy black shells bursting around us. Although threatening and worrisome, none of our planes reported damage. The formation made a left descending turn after bomb release to evade flak. Again, with good weather, bombing results were good. A very good pattern of bombs dropped on the target area covering runways and hangers. Twenty-five photos were taken of the target area by seven K-22 and three K-21 cameras.

Our formation of 38 bombers returned to our base at 1527 hours, and I logged 6 hours and 15 minutes. It was my twenty-seventh mission, and the Group's fortieth credited mission of forty-eight missions flown in Italy. No planes were damaged and there were no casualties.

S/Sgt Thomas S. Delaney of our crew recorded the following in his diary, ".....Blasted the airdrome with fragmentation bombs. I saw them hit right in there, destroying hangars and field! It was another "milk run"! Lt. Capps flew another wonderful formation.....".

May 15, 1944   No Mission Today.

Without advance notice, someone came around to my crew's tents to ask us to go out to our new plane, "Porky," to have a crew picture taken. The resulting picture is shown on a the following page. The short notice did not allow us to look pretty for the picture. We rushed out from our tents to have our photos taken beside our wonderful "Porky." Two of my crew members were not present for the picture, 2nd Lt. James G. Vaughn, navigator, and S/Sgt Carl Ezuck.

Lt. Capps and crew in front of their new Liberator,"Porky," a B-24G. Two crew members are missing. Lt. Capps is standing, second from the right next to Lt. James Duston on the right and Lt. Sydney Brooks on the left.

Lt. Capps And Crew Near New Plane, "Porky"

Our Group Headquarters Intelligence Detachment held some lectures on the hill where crew members of another Bomb group talked about their experiences behind enemy lines after they had been shot down. An officer named Lt. Fassonlis told of his experiences behind German lines after being shot down on September 2, 1943, and was finally able to make his way to allied territory eight months later. A Lt. Thompson from Group also told of his experiences while escaping from Yugoslavia after bailing out of his crippled ship. Both men emphasized the necessity of having a good knife and a good pair of shoes for survival purposes when you bailed out.

May 16 and 17, 1944 Two More Stand Down Days.

Weather over potential targets must be bad. A light rain did fall on our base at 1500 hours on the 17th, then when the sun finally came out a few hours later, everything smelled clean and fresh.

In their spare time, many personnel were donating their time to help work on the headquarter's enlisted mens' club, to help out Italian laborers, so the job could be finished in time for the scheduled opening tomorrow night. Walls of the headquarters officers' club are about finished and the roof and floor has to be started. Progress is being made on our club, in my 746th Squadron, thanks to the energetic driving force being provided by pilot Lt. Harry J. Ragland whose genius and sweat built our only shower in the Squadron.

**May 18, 1994 Ploesti.*

Another mission to Ploesti today and my new crew was scheduled to fly. Our ship "Porky" was still being repaired, so we had to fly another crew's Liberator, number 831 "Man-O-War." I had been on missions to the Ploesti area three times before, to Bucharest twice, which was about thirty-five miles from Ploesti, and to Campina marshaling

CONFIDENTIAL

13 May 1944

BATTLE ORDER

1st Unit, 1st Box

	Formation Leader: Sinclair,Callan AP 279 Webster
No. 3: Smith	AP 275 Dep Leader: Clark,W.B./ AP 768
	No. 4: Hillman AP 285
No. 6: Voxhell	AP 486 No. 5: Blackwall AP 964

2nd Box

	Leader: Bishop AP 470
No. 3: Cerretti	AP 912 Dep Leader: Rawlinson AP 098
	No. 4: Riddle AP 777
No. 6: Tosalli	AP 293 No. 5: Ogden AP 225
	No. 7: Ball AP 595

3rd Box

	Leader: Phifer AP 501
No. 3: Kix	AP 233 Dep Leader: Brabon AP 799
	No. 4: Lambert AP 072
No. 6: Van Dyke	AP 872 No. 5: Lunt AP 752
	No. 7: Jones,E.C. AP 077

2nd Unit, 1st Box

	Leader: Gruber, Tavel AP 227
No. 3: Addis	AP 256 Dep Leader: Jones, W.W. AP 268
	No. 4: Laszewski AP 309
No. 6: Wood	AP 477 No. 5: Roak AP 239
	No. 7: Ashley AP 442

2nd Box

	Leader: Richards AP 489
No. 3: Hundley	AP 853 Dep Leader: Smith,B.W. AP 549
	No. 4: Capps AP 831
No. 6: Scott	AP 299 No. 5: Ragland AP 201
	No. 7: Dean AP 934

3rd Box

	Leader: Douglass AP 749
No. 3: Williamson	AP 810 Dep Leader: Phillips AP 882
	No. 4: Fleming AP 334
No. 6: Savage	AP 807 No. 5: Miller AP 203
	No. 7: Palis AP 183

Time at stations: 0705.   456th: BETTY THREE TWO.

Start engines: A 0710. B 0715. C 0720. Penetration: SHAPLEY ONE # 52nd FG
D 0725. E 0730. F 0735. SHAPLEY TWO.

Taxi out: 0720. Take-off: 0730.   Target cover: 14th FG SHAPLEY FOUR
                                       31st FG SHAPLEY THREE.

Recall: "KEEPER"   Withdrawal: 1st FG SHAPLEY FIVE
                                   82nd FG SHAPLEY SIX.

yards which were thirty miles from Ploesti. Today our target was the Ploesti Dracia Romano Refinery. We were expecting a tough battle as usual for this target area. It was heavily fortified by the Nazis because it was so vital to their continued ability to fight the war, and it had many fighter aircraft and 168 guns to fire at us. This was the first direct attack on the oil refineries of Ploesti since the Fifteenth Air force was formed. We had bombed marshaling yards and airdromes all around Ploesti that supported the oil industry there, and 163 B-24s had attacked Ploesti from Africa on August 1, 1943, before the Fifteenth Air Force was formed. However, this was the first concerted effort by the USAF to completely destroy the oil producing facilities at Ploesti. Oil is a controlling factor in military operations and Ploesti produced 27 percent of all Axis petroleum products.

Seven-hundred heavy bombers were launched on this day by the Fifteenth Air Force for its first direct assault on the oil refineries themselves at Ploesti. Bad weather allowed only 206 of the bombers to get through, and we dropped 493 tons of bombs on the refineries. My 456th Bomb Group, with 36 bombers, were part of the 206 that successfully flew around the weather and dropped their bombs on Ploesti refineries. A total of fourteen heavy bombers of this Fifteenth Air Force bomber fleet were lost and 23 enemy fighters were destroyed. While many other bombers on the mission were unable to bomb Ploesti through the weather, they were able to find alternate targets at marshaling yards in Nis, which received 131 tons of bombs, and 280 tons were dropped on marshaling yards at Belgrade.

Wake-up calls for my Groups came early in our tents, at 0500 hours, briefing was held at 0600, stations time at our aircraft was 0705, start engines time for my Box, which was the 2nd Box of the 2nd Unit where my crew was flying in the #4 position, was 0725 hours. The lead bomber started to taxi out toward the end of the runway at 0720, and Major

John R. Sinclair who was flying it took off at 0730. There were 36 B-24s that followed his plane off the runway at 45 second intervals. Captain Kenneth Gruber and Lt. Dave E. Tavel of my squadron were in the lead plane of the 2nd Unit. After our Group's six Boxes were assembled, Major Sinclair led our formation for a rendezvous over Stornara at 3,000 feet with the 455th Bomb Group. Our two groups left to bomb the same target. Only one of our 456th Group's B-24s returned early and it was because of a gas leak. This was another tribute to the growing efficiency of our hard working ground crews.

The two other groups of our 304th Wing, the 459th and 454th were ordered to bomb another target in the Ploesti area, the Ploesti Redeventa Refinery. Those two groups had a rendezvous over the nearby Giulia at 4,000 feet. Our two groups departed Stornara at 0825 and the other two groups that had rendezvoused at Giulia departed from a 1,000 feet higher altitude three minutes after us, a 0828 hours. With the 455th Group in the lead of the Wing formation of groups, we flew to the target area with the 456th Group second, then came the 459th followed by the 454th. A Pathfinder capability was available in the lead bombers of all groups as at back-up mode of bombing by radar, if needed. Each aircraft had five cartons of window to dispense when we neared the briefed flak area.

We were told that a very close formation would be necessary for maximum fighter cover, and that accurate routes and timings at our targets would be essential. There were many groups bombing many targets in a small area, and heavy fighter opposition was expected. Each group was flying at a minimum of 1,000 feet above or below the nearest group that would be in the area, to avoid collision while flying around, and through expected clouds.

Our Wing had one group of P-51 Mustangs for fighter cover on penetration of enemy territory which started at

1000 hours. Another group of P-51s relieved them at 1048 hours, then a group of P-38 Lightnings arrived at 1054 hours to assist them. After bombs away, another group of P-38s joined the fray at 1109, followed by another group joining our Wing formations at 1140.

The weather was not very good for keeping the formations. The Adriatic was clear at first, then it got worse. Starting at the east side of the Adriatic Ocean, cloud cover below our formation increased to seven-tenths of altocumulus, bases at 8,000 feet and tops at 14,000 feet. There were also five-tenths coverage by cirrus clouds above us, bases at 22,000 feet. Occasional cumulus cloud build ups required our formation to fly around them. Poor weather conditions continued to the target. The target area was obstructed by six-tenths coverage from altocumulus clouds, bases at 6,000 feet, tops at 10,000 feet. There were two-tenths coverage by cirrus clouds above us, bases at 23,000 feet, but that didn't bother us much. The temperature at 21,500 feet was minus 20 degrees centigrade.

We saw some enemy fighters, but none attacked us, thanks to our friendly fighter cover, and the fact that we had become very proficient at flying a very tight bomber formation which discouraged enemy fighter attacks. Tight formations provide maximum concentration of fire power from our bombers' fifty caliber machine guns to fire on any enemy fighters coming in their range. We knew enemy fighters selected loose bomber formations and straggling bombers that couldn't keep up with their formations as their priority targets. One other group, discussed below, was selected by 100 enemy fighters for an all-out attack on this day.

Flak was a different story. We attracted flak for many miles around the target area while we were flying to and from Ploesti. Flak was particularly heavy near Campina and near the Turnu-Severin airdrome in Rumania. In spite of the massive amounts of window we dropped, the flak was intense, accurate, heavy, and both black and white type bursts were seen. Twelve of our planes, including mine, had flak damage, but all of us were able to bring our damaged planes home.

Radio operator on our "Porky," S/Sgt Thomas S. Delaney recorded in his diary, "Hit the Ploesti oil refineries in Rumania! Gee the flak was darn accurate, and they had 168 guns tracking us. We got about 8 flak holes in our plane! Number 3 engine started to throw a lot of smoke from a burst of flak, so we feathered it......"

Because of cloud coverage at the target and effective smoke-screening of the oil fields by Rumanians, bombing had to be made through clouds using our Pathfinder radar. Many called this radar "Mickey." Thirty-six bombers in our 456th Group's formation were able to drop 87 tons of 500 pound general purpose bombs (348 bombs) through the clouds on the Ploesti Dacia Romano Oil Refinery at 1122 hours from 21,000 feet for the 1st Unit and from 20,000 feet for the 2nd unit. The axis of attack was 200 degrees magnetic, and the bomb release interval setting was 50 feet. The bombardier of one of our bombers had to jettison his bombs because of a failure of his intervalometer.

With clouds covering much of the area, and the very effective smoke screening, bombing results could not be accurately observed, but it was the belief of the crews that bombs hit in the target area. Smoke clouds were observed rising high from oil fires on the ground. Sixteen photos of the target area were taken by seven K-22 cameras and two K-21s. After bombs were released, our Group rallied by making a descending 30 degree left turn then a right turn on our course home.

Near our target, only one mile away from us at the Ploesti Romano Americano Oil Refinery, thirty-five B-17s of the 463rd Bomb Group, part of the 5th Wing on the mission, was attacked by 100 very aggressive enemy fighters. Enemy fighters continued their attack until friendly escort fighters arrived. In the huge air battle that followed, the 463rd lost seven B-17 bombers, and B-17 gunners claimed 28 enemy fighters destroyed, 30 probables, and 2 damaged.

Our 456th Bomb Group formation had to dodge some tall thunderheads on the way home, with tops at 30,000 feet. Only 35 bombers in our Group returned to our home base at 1502 hours because one plane made an emergency landing at Giulia Field,, home of the 459th Group. It was forced to land there because of flak damage that caused it to feather #1 engine. It had a propeller governor malfunction, and its fuel pressure system was inoperative.

S/Sgt Delaney's diary states, ".... We came all the way back to the base on 3 engines. Lt. Capps made a beautiful landing on 3 engines. Our gas was real low too."

The Group logged its forty-first credited mission of forty-nine missions flown. I logged my twenty-eighth and twenty-ninth missions, a "two-fer," and logged 7 hours and 45 minutes combat flying time. My plane ("Man-O-War") had quite a few flak holes, along with eleven other planes of our Group, but there were no significant casualties and no planes were lost.

The headquarters detachment opened its enlisted mens' club with a christening party that included music provided by the Group band. Some Women's Army Corps members were invited to the party, but none showed up. There were many types of alcoholic beverages served (low quality), and they provided many headaches for the participants in the morning.

May 19, 1944 Alternate Target, Leghorn Harbor and Dock Installations.

This day saw a Group mission to bomb Italy's Genoa Harbor, but it was overcast so the Leghorn harbor and dock Installations were bombed as an alternate. My crew was

C O N F I D E N T I A L

19 May 1944

BATTLE ORDER

1st Unit, 1st Box

Formation Leader: Thomas, Col. STEED AP 768   Ladd
                              Dep Leader: Gardner/ AP 227
No. 3: Toselli   AP 284
                  No. 4: Barrasso   AP 291
No. 6: Lunt   AP 752   No. 5: Ball   AP 995
                  No. 7: Ragland   AP 299

2nd Box

                  Leader: Lee   AP 268
No. 3: Brabon   AP 799   Dep Leader: Nix   AP 233
                  No. 4: Rudd   AP 295
No. 6: Jones, E.C. AP 077   No. 5: Zurney   AP 285
                  No. 7: Van Dyke   AP 872

3rd Box

                  Leader: Newhouse AP 470
No. 3: Cerretti   AP 912   Dep Leader: Webster AP 098
                  No. 4: Riddle   AP 777
No. 6: Ogden   AP 225   No. 5: Rawlinson   AP 293
                  No. 7: Blackwell AP 637

2nd Unit, 1st Box

                  Leader: Jackson, C.Y., Hydo AP 279
No. 3: Ashley   AP 835153   Dep Leader: Smith, G.T. AP 275
                  No. 4: Flemming   AP 239
No. 6: Wood   AP 477   No. 5: Miller   AP 203

2nd Box

                  Leader: Ensign   AP 489
No. 3: Voshell   AP 201   Dep Leader: Johnson AP 831
                  No. 4: Smith, E.W. AP 549
No. 6: Addis   AP 256   No. 5: Scott   AP 442

3rd Box

                  Leader: Nilsson   AP 304
No. 3: Williamson AP 810   Dep Leader: Selcher AP 113
                  No. 4: Laszewski AP 309
No. 6: Phillips   AP 882   No. 5: Wilkinson   AP 807
                  No. 7: Palis   AP 183

Time at stations: 0550.   456th: THICKRUG ONE
Start engines: A 0555. B 0600. 0 0605
               D 0610. E 0615   F 0620   14th FG CREENHFRD

Taxi out: 0605   Take-off: 0615

Recall: LOVEBIRD   C O N F I D E N T I A L

not selected to fly on it. Takeoff was unusually early for a mission in Italy. For what was expected to be a milk run, 13 bombers had flak damage. I believe our commanders were hoping to fly a second mission this day, after this one, but weather discouraged it.

Wake up time for the crews came at 0345 hours in their tents, mission briefing started at 0450 with Capt. Howard I. Neff giving the intelligence part of it, then stations time for being at the aircraft was set at 0550 hours. Start-engines time for the 1st Box of Liberators began at 0555, and then the other 5 Boxes of today's formation followed by starting their engines at 5 minute intervals. The lead bomber, with Colonel Steed flying, started to taxi out to the end of the runway at 0605 hours, then it took off at 0615 hours. The other 39 planes in today's formation followed his plane off the runway at 45 second intervals. Captain F. Weston Hyde Jr., my 746th Squadron's operations officer, was in the lead aircraft of the 2nd Unit. The weather over the base was beautiful for flying, but it deteriorated as we went north.

Two planes returned early, one because of an oil leak, and one because it had to feather an engine. During our early missions, when we had 40 planes scheduled to fly in the formation, 6 or 8 bombers would abort the flight early for mechanical reasons. Recently, less than two of our bombers were returning early because of mechanical malfunctions. This was an indication that our ground crews were becoming much more proficient as they gained experience! In addition, flight crews were becoming much more knowledgeable about their aircraft, and would not abort the mission for some of the minor problems, such as indicator gage malfunctions or fuel cap leaks, that would have causeed them to return early on past flights. Caps on fuel tanks were more carefully checked by our flight engineers during their preflight inspection of our aircraft, and that eliminated one common reason that had caused early abort of missions in the past when fuel would be seen leaking, and siphoning

333

out around the loose caps after takeoff. After Colonel Steed had assembled our Group formation, he led the Group over to Stornara at 3,000 feet where our Group was joined by the 459th Group. The formation of two groups departed on course climbing at 0703 hours. Climb speed was 160 MPH indicated airspeed, a true airspeed of about 200 MPH, and a rate of climb of 250 feet per minute. The Group was using a higher rate of climb than the 200 FPM used in the past.

There were no enemy fighters seen, and the Group had P-38 Lightnings and P-51 Mustangs for escort in case any were to come around. As the Group formation approached the target area, flak was moderate, accurate, with heavy black bursts. It was the tracking type of accurate radar-controlled flak. The Group flew through flak at Genoa, Leghorn, and again at La Spezia in search of targets to bomb. Thirteen bombers received flak damage.

Weather was good enroute, with only high cirrus above the formation until an undercast of altocumulus clouds developed as the formation flew north toward the target. Genoa had a complete undercast of altocumulus clouds hiding it with tops at 18,000 feet. Turning to Leghorn the weather improved, and only one-tenth coverage with cumulus clouds were seen over that target, enabling it to be bombed. The temperature at 21,000 feet was minus 22 degrees centigrade.

Turning at the I.P. two of my 746 Squadron planes collided, as described below. Thirty-five of the remaining thirty-six planes were able to drop 87 tons of 500 pound general purpose bombs (348 bombs) on the Leghorn Harbor at 1027 hours from 19,000 feet for the 1st Unit and 18,000 feet for the 2nd Unit, on an axis of attack of 180 degrees magnetic. The indicated airspeed was 160 MPH, a true airspeed of 216 MPH. The bomb release interval setting was 50 feet. One plane had a bomb rack malfunction, so it did not drop on the target. The rally after bombs were released was a sharp descending right turn at an indicated airspeed of between 155 and 160 MPH to keep the formation tight to guard against fighter attack.

Twenty-four photos of the target area were taken by six K-22 cameras, and they revealed a good concentration of bombs falling on Leghorn Harbor. Several ships were hit, as well as warehouses, railroad tracks, and the general dock area.

Thirty-seven bombers returned safely home at 1246 hours, with one bomber that was originally reported as missing and described below, but it had safely landed at another base. This was the Group's forty-second credited mission of a total fifty missions flown. The flying time was 6 hours and 30 minutes.

Two 746th Squadron planes in the Group collided as the formation turned for the final approach to the target at the Initial Point. Both planes and crews survived. One, #201 piloted by Lt. LaVerne M. Voshell, continued on with the formation and landed safely with it. The other bomber, with part of its wing tip knocked off left the formation at 1010 hours and made an emergency landing at a fighter base at Marciana, Italy.

The collision occurred when Lt. Eugene W. Smith, Jr. flying in aircraft #549 in the #4 position of the 2nd Box of the 2nd Unit was caught in the propeller wash of bombers that were flying ahead of his plane in the formation. The prop wash made his plane veer erratically. This caused his left wing to smash into the right wing of the aircraft that was flown by Voshell in the #3 position of the same Box. Voshell's plane was flying ahead, above, and to the left of Smith's plane. Smith's plane hit aircraft #201 piloted by Lt. LaVerne M. Voshell. The collision sheared off nine feet of Smith's left wing and it made a deep gash in the trailing edge of Voshell's right wing between his #3 engine and #4 engine. Voshell jettisoned his bombs, but he was able to stay with the formation. Smith's engineer, Sgt. Phillip N. Hickey who was in the waist of the plane, looked out and told Smith that he believed they had lost 3 to 4 feet of their plane's wing tip as a result of the collision. Smith could not see the damage from his position in the cockpit, and believed that the damage was less than the actual nine feet that he had lost.

Lt. Smith left the formation, jettisoned his bomb load, and started to head home, but he soon discovered that his navigation instruments were out of operation. The navigator decided to use dead reckoning navigation as best he could to lead the plane home. To simplify the navigation they decided to follow the Italian coast down to friendly territory, but they encountered flak as they passed Genoa. By this time the hole in the wing caused them to lose a great deal of gas so they decided to land at the nearest Allied airfield. They saw the fighter base at Marciana, Italy, and began to land. As they approached the small fighter strip, Smith's #1 and #2 engines, on the side of the wing that had been lost, cut out. He landed with his two good engines, and the torsion that was caused by the unbalanced condition on his landing tore up part of the fighter strip's steel matting. There were no injuries and the ship was able to be repaired and put back into service at a much later date. Smith and his crew caught a plane ride back to our base the same day. Smith said, "If I had known that we had lost nine feet of wing, not three or four as we thought, I would have really sweat it."

I got to know a very colorful member of the group headquarters intelligence staff, 1st Lt. Gilbert W. Smith. He was a very enterprising young officer. Three other buddies and I became acquainted with him long before bombers arrived at our airfield. We all lived in close quarters on our sea voyage to Italy, and again when we were still living together in the pink Italian farm house where we had been billeted with the rest of the officers of the headquarters detachment, while waiting for our airfield to be built. It became apparent to us that he was not the run-of-the-mill intelligence officer,

A 15th Air Force B-24D splashing through water in "sunny" Italy on steel
matting. Photo Courtesy of National Air and Space Museum,
Smithsonian Institution.

B-24 Taxiing Through Water In Sunny Italy

In addition to his other normal intelligence duties, Lt. Smith kept busy much of the day handling the Italian civilians and troops on our base who were working at many different jobs. Whenever Italians come to our base for any reason, they were usually referred to Lt. Smith.

May 20, 1944   No mission this day.

It rained last night and there was a light drizzle this morning. The temperature is very mild and pleasant, in spite of the rain. It was poor flying weather.

Our 304th Wing commander, Colonel Fay R. Upthegrove, gave our group a commendation this day for the excellent and consistent bombing accomplished on our last four missions. He said, "The fighting spirit displayed at Weiner Neustadt, under adverse circumstances proves that this Group can't be stopped. The excellent bombing since evidences high morale and air discipline to a degree which no single day's losses can upset. Please convey my admiration and appreciation to all the combat crews and maintenance personnel. Such a standard is an inspiration to the Groups of this Wing and the Air Force as a whole."

Security of the airdrome was strengthened considerably this day, as Captain Percy R. Follis, who was made Group Security Officer on May 18, 1944, was put in charge of a squadron of colored soldiers who had arrived and who will do guard duty. Our Group will now have an Officer of the Day and a Group Officer of the Guard.

I wonder if this move for tightened security was a reaction rumored about sabotage of B-24s that I had been hearing. Recently, while writing this book, I talked to Captain Follis and he told me that though he had only heard rumors of sabotage of some B-24s, he never saw written reports about it. He said that he received orders at this time to have 24-hour guards put on all of our B-24s. Up to then, there had been no guards on duty.

In the afternoon all available bombardiers in the squadrons went up to Group Headquarters to study high priority targets.

May 21, 1944   Another Stand Down Day.

Weather was too poor for flying again this day. The wind blew hard, so hard that it blew over Sgt. William Debreczeni's house, which was a stone house that he and his mates paid $100 to build. Everyone asked him if he had insurance.

The industrious Lt. Gil Smith keeps receiving Italian visitors at Group Headquarters. Everyone from beggars to the Mayor of Stornara paid him a visit. Yesterday, the nuns of Stornara stopped by to see him and today they sent him about two dozen roses which he put in a bucket of water on his desk. Eye witness accounts report that the nuns were very pretty.

338

The staffs of group and squadron headquarters were given an intelligence briefing by Group Intelligence about the latest development in the war, covering all fighting fronts. Captain Samuel Parks gave an interesting talk about his trip to visit the 5th Army.

May 22, 1944   Weather Abort After Takeoff.

We were given a morning briefing, the intelligence part given by Capt. Lewis A. Stuck, to bomb the Borgo Panigale railroad junction in Italy. Then, the target was changed due to weather reports, and we were sent to bomb La Spezia Harbor installations, Italy. We took off, but very bad weather made us turn back. No planes were lost, and I logged 3 hours and 10 minutes on the mission. Of course, no credit was given for this one.

Lt Gilbert W. Smith was kept busy today paying off his Italian employees as it was their payday.

**May 23, 1944   Troop Concentration in the Marino Area, South of Rome.*

This was a sad day for me, because I lost two of my close buddies on the mission, and our Group lost two bombers. Our regular plane "Porky" was still being repaired so we flew "Man-O-War," number 831, again on this mission.

Wake-up calls came to our tents at an early 0430 hours and briefing started at 0530 hours. The target was a large German troop concentration in the Marino area, just south of Rome. Stations time at our aircraft was 0645, and start engines time for my Box of the formation, the 2nd Box of the 1st Unit where I was flying #4 position, was 0655 hours. Taxi out started at 0700 hours and Major John R. Sinclair in the lead bomber took off at 0710. There were 38 bombers that followed his takeoff, each leaving the runway at 45 second intervals. There were only two early returns this day, one because of a faulty engine and one because of an oil leak, thanks again to our hard working ground crews.

C O N F I D E N T I A L

BATTLE ORDER

23 May 1944

1st Unit, 1st Box

Sinclair

Formation Leader: Miller, R.E./ AP 889

| No. 3: Addis | AP 256 | Dep Leader: Webster | AP 227 |
| No. 4: Wilkenson AP 334 |
| No. 6: Vosholl | AP 8275 | No. 5: Ashley | AP 486 |

2nd Box

Leader: Snee   AP 489

No. 3: Poker	AP 477	Dep Leader: Hundley	AP 853
No. 4: Capps	AP 831
No. 6: England	AP 299	No. 5: Scott	AP 442
No. 7: Dean	AP 934

3rd Box

Leader: Gardner   AP 304

| No. 3: Miller | AP 203 | Dep Leader: Phillips | AP 832 |
| No. 4: Douglass AP 749 |
| No. 6: Blewitt | AP 113 | No. 5: Roak | AP 183 |
| No. 7: Solcher | AP 310 |

2nd Unit, 1st Box

Leader: Jackson, C.Y. AP 279

No. 3: Savage	AP 807	Dep Leader: Palis	AP 098
No. 4: Hillman	AP 285
No. 6: Bruce	AP 2275	No. 5: Cerretti	AP 912
No. 4: Zurner	AP 295

2nd Box

Leader: Jones, W.W. AP 291

| No. 3: Brabon | AP 799 | Dep Leader: Nunimaker | AP 212 |
| No. 4: Jackson, W.L. AP 752 |
| No. 6: Van Dyke | AP 872 | No. 5: Jones, E.C. AP 077 |
| No. 7: Lambert | AP 072 |

3rd Box

Leader: Andrews AP 284

No. 3: Toselli	AP 595	Dep Leader: Rawlinson	AP 293
No. 4: Ward	AP 637
No. 6: Ogden	AP 225	No. 5: Leathers	AP 777
No. 7: Blackwell AP 964

Time at stations: 0645.   456th: "GOWAY THREE"

Start engines: A 0650. B 0655. C 0700. P-38's: "CRAWFORD".
                D 0705. E 0710. F 0715.

Taxi out: 0700. Take-off: 0710.   Recall: "PENCIL".

S E C R E T
**Copy of the Original
456th Bomb Group Battle Order
Source:NationalArchives,Wash. D.C.**

After our Group formation was assembled around Major Sinclair's plane, he led us over Giulia at 4,000 feet where we were joined by the 459th Group. The order of the 304th Wing formation for the day was the 454th Group in the lead, followed by the 455th, 456th and the 459th last. We departed Giulia at 0802 hours, climbing on course at the standard 160 MPH indicated airspeed, about 200 MPH true airspeed, with a rate of climb of 200 feet per minute until we reached our bombing altitude of 20,000 feet.

The weather was very messy. Our massive formation had to dodge build ups of clouds enroute. On the way to the target we encountered two layers of cloud cover. First, there was four-tenths of cumulus cloud cover, bases at 7,000 feet, tops at 11,000 feet. Next, there was a layer of four-tenths of coverage by altocumulus clouds, bases at 10,000 and tops at 18,000 feet. Weather over the target was not much better. We ran into seven to ten tenths cumulus cloud cover over the target with tops at 18,000 feet and visibility 6 miles with haze. Temperature at 19,200 feet was minus 17 degrees centigrade. We could see the ruins of Cassino to our south that were still on fire. Our target was just north of the Anzio beachhead landing area.

Flak was scant, inaccurate, with heavy black bursts. None of our planes had flak damage and none had damage from enemy aircraft because we saw none. We had P-38s and P-47s for escort in case they were needed.

Only 16 bombers, planes in 1st Unit of the formation of which my plane was a part, were able to see the target sufficiently through the clouds to drop their bombs, and we dropped 39 tons of 500 pound general purpose bombs (156 bombs) from 20,000 feet at 0958 hours on an axis of attack of 140 degrees magnetic. The indicated airspeed was 160 MPH, a true airspeed of 222 MPH. The bomb release interval was set at 100 feet. One aircraft in our 1st Unit, number 810 flown by Lt. Kemp D. Solcher of the 745th Squadron, had a bomb rack malfunction and his bombardier jettisoned their bombs over the Adriatic. Results of the bombing could not be observed because of the cloud cover. The rally after bomb release was a descending right turn at an indicated airspeed of 155 MPH to allow the formation to remain tight.

The rest of the bombers, the entire 2nd Unit of the formation consisting of 18 bombers, were unable to find the target through the clouds by the time their Unit flew over it, and they returned to our base with their bombs. This turned out to be hazardous, as discussed below. A total of 35 planes arrived over Stornara from the mission at 1100 hours, a short mission, and I logged 4 hours and 5 minutes. It was my 30th credited mission and the Group's 43rd credited mission of 51 missions flown.

A tragic accident occurred in the air over our airfield during the Group's landing procedure. Two of our bombers collided in a midair collision at about 1,500 feet directly over our field. The collision resulted in twenty crewmen being killed and one seriously injured.

Our landing procedure after we arrived over the home base was for each box to fly over our runway, then peel off one Box at a time, in order to enter the traffic pattern for landing in a controlled manner. Boxes of the 1st Unit landed first, since they had taken off first and were lowest on fuel, then Boxes of the 2nd Unit of the formation would follow. I was in the 1st Unit. of the formation to land. After I had landed my plane, parked the B-24 on the steel matted hardstand, cut the engines and got out of my plane, Boxes from the 2nd Unit were still landing. I saw our plane's crew chief pointing excitedly into the air. I and the rest of my crew looked up in time to see two B-24s that had collided and both began to tumble down to the ground, out of control, in a horrible flaming crash in front of us. One plane, with its tail almost gone, made a wide sweeping turn, and we didn't know where it would hit the ground around us. The other crashed down in front of us. Both planes hit the ground going almost straight down, in a huge fiery ball and explosion. There were some very anxious moments until we were certain the planes would not land on us because we were so near. One of the planes crashing injured a ground crewman.

From radio conversations heard by crews that were aboard other planes in the air at the time, it appears that the plane flying in #4 position of the 2nd Box of the 2nd Unit in "Salvo Susie," aircraft number 42-9799 flown by 1st Lt. William L. Jackson, had heard instructions saying that his Box leader, 1st Lt. William W. Jones, was taking his Box around for another circle of the base again before landing because the traffic pattern was still too full of planes from the Box ahead of his that hadn't landed yet. The plane flying formation with him, on his left wing in the #6 position of the 2nd Box, flown by 2nd Lt. John W. Van Dyke in "Blue Booties," aircraft number 42-94872, apparently did not hear the message about going around the base again before entering the landing traffic pattern.. Both planes were from the 744th Squadron. When Jackson turned with the rest of his box to make another circle around before entering the landing pattern, Van Dyke flew his plane into the tail of Jackson's plane. Both B-24s were critically damaged by the collision so that they spun to the ground directly over our base from the point that they would normally have peeled off to enter the traffic pattern, at about 1,500 feet.

I didn't know at the time that my two close buddies, copilot 2nd Lt. Gail J. Scritchfield and bombardier 2nd Lt. Edward J. Heffner, both on Jackson's plane, were on board one of the aircraft that I was watching, nor did I know that both planes had their full load of bombs on board because they didn't drop on the target. There was only one survivor of the crash, S/Sgt Robert Gullet, tail gunner, and he is currently a member of the 456th Bomb Group Association.

343

Gullet miraculously survived with only bruises and a broken back and burns.

One member of Van Dyke's crew, the ball turret gunner S/Sgt Donald K. Switzer, was not aboard the plane because he had been injured previously by flak and was not able to fly with his crew on the mission. He survived his crew's fate. However, Switzer was shot down later, on July 2 while flying with another crew, and he was made a POW in Stalag IV. Switzer is also currently a member of the 456th Bomb Group Association.

Crew comments at the intelligence debriefing after we were on the ground, included criticisms by two different pilots saying that the let down over the field to land was too fast, better than 1,500 feet per minute rate of descent. Another pilot commented that the Group should start a school to instruct new men in formation flying before they were sent on a combat mission.

That evening, many of us experienced another exciting adventure. I went up to the Group briefing room to see a movie, to get some relaxation after the sad experience of the day. That wasn't what I got! The briefing room that we used as a movie theater had only one small entrance door. there was no other exit. My friends and I were sitting in the front, far away from the door, so that we could see the small, dim movie screen better. While the movie was being shown, and it had our entire attention, we suddenly heard some ear-shattering explosions that sounded as though it was just outside the briefing room. It sounded as though we were being bombed. Everyone's nerves were already on edge because of the day's events, but the explosions, one after another, caused everyone to panic and rush to the one entrance door to get out of the small briefing room and find a bomb shelter. Luckily, my friends and I were far away from the door, because in front of us were bodies piled one on top of another from the floor to the ceiling. Airmen had scrambled over each others' backs, in alarm, as they tried to reach the door. My friends and I at the front of the room couldn't get within thirty feet of the door because bodies were stacked one on top of the other all the way to the roof, as the men clawed their way to the door, trying to get out, as more bombs explode

When things calmed down, someone realized that the exploding bombs were caused by demolition crews exploding bombs found in the wreckage of the two planes that had crashed that day on our airfield. Some had brought their bombs back.

If that were not enough bad news and excitement for the base that day, a fire had broken out in the base tailor shop in the afternoon, and it caused many clothes to be burned or damaged.

May 24, 1944 Munchendorf Airdrome, Vienna, Austria.

After yesterday's excitement on the base, there was a numbed reaction to the routines necessary to continue work. The day's mission, for which my crew was not selected , was a rough one to bomb the Munchendorf Airdrome, Vienna, Austria and we lost two bombers to flak.

There was a very early wake-up call at 0345 hours, briefing at 0455. Time for crews to be at their aircraft was 0555 hours. The 1st Box started engines at 0600, and the other five Boxes started their engines at five minute intervals after that. Major John R. Sinclair was in the lead aircraft and he taxied out at 0610, then took off at 0620 hours. Thirty-seven bombers followed him off the runway at 45 second intervals. Four bombers returned before reaching the target for the following reasons: one had bomb bay doors malfunction, one had a supercharger go out, one had to feather a bad engine, and one had the strap around its bundle of fragmentation bombs break and they fell loose -- he jettisoned them and returned to base.

C O N F I D E N T I A L

24 May 1944

BATTLE ORDER

1st Unit, 1st Box

Witkin

Formation Leader: Sinclair, / AP 889

No. 3: Addis	AP 256	Dep Leader: Mulligan AP 212
No. 4: Williamson AP 297		
No. 6: Wood	AP 477	No. 5: Scott AP 442

2nd Box

Leader: Richards AP 489

No. 3: Ecker	AP 934	Dep Leader: Sagert AP 8275
No. 4: Smith	AP 831	
No. 6: Ashley	AP 853	No. 5: Ragland AP 486
No. 7: Voshell	AP 299	

3rd Box

Leader: Douglass AP 749

No. 3: Solcher	AP 882	Dep Leader: Laszewski AP 309
No. 4: Fleming	AP 334	
No. 6: Roak	AP 304	No. 5: Marlar AP 203
No. 7: Savage	AP 807	

2nd Unit, 1st Box

Clark, W.D.

Leader: Gruber, / AP 279

No. 3: Zurney	AP 072	Dep Leader: Jones, W.W. AP 291
No. 4: Ward	AP 637	
No. 6: Ball	AP 595	No. 5: Leathers AP 912
No. 7: Blowitt	AP 113	

2nd Box

Leader: LouKuma AP 284

No. 3: Toselli	AP 364	Dep Leader: Rawlinson AP 293
No. 4: Riddle	AP 777	
No. 6: Ogden	AP 225	No. 5: Mapa AP 098
No. 7: Blackwell AP 964		

3rd Box

Leader: Phifer AP 501

No. 3: Brabon	AP 799	Dep Leader: Nix AP 233
No. 4: Minimaker AP 285		
No. 6: Bruce	AP 2275	No. 5: Jones, E.C. AP 077
No. 7: Lunt	AP 295	

Stations: 0555.   456th "FOOTHOLD ONE-TWO"

Engines: A 0600 B 0605 C 0610 Fighters: BREWER   .
          D 0615 E 0620 F 0625

                              Recall Signal: "PARTIAL"
Take-off: 0620.

C O N F I D E N T I A L

After our Group assembled its formation, Major Sinclair led it to rendezvous over Stornara at 3,000 feet with the 455th Bomb Group. The 455th Group was leading the 304th Wing formation this day, the 456th was in the second position, followed by the 459th, and the 454th was the last group in the formation of groups flying in trail. Climb-out on course started at 0720 at 160 MPH indicated airspeed, about 200 MPH true airspeed, and a rate of climb at 200 feet per minute toward the Initial Point, Neu Lengbach, Austria.

Fighter escort, P-38s and P-51s, picked the Wing formation up at 0933 hours and the fighters were scheduled to provide escort in relays from the time the bomber formation penetrated enemy territory, through the bombing of the target, and during withdrawal from enemy territory, as long as the fighters' fuel held out. Although some Me-109s were seen by the aircrews in the target area, none attacked the Group formation and none of the Group's planes were damaged by enemy fighter. However, flak was the most destructive to the Group's bombers this day!

Anytime we went to the Vienna area, where there were 300 guns on the ground firing at our formation, we expected heavy damage. As noted earlier, Vienna was the second most heavily defended Axis target, second only to Berlin. There were also many enemy fighters in the area but our fighter escort successfully took care of them. Two lonely straggling enemy fighters made unsuccessful passes at the Group formation. The flak was very heavy, moderate intensity, and accurate with ugly black and red bursts. We lost two bombers to the flak and three bombers reported flak damage.

Weather was clear until the formation reached the Yugoslavian coast, then a solid undercast developed with altocumulus clouds reaching up to 17,000 feet, and thin cirrus clouds covered the air above the formation. At the target, there was seven-tenths coverage with altocumulus clouds that had bases at 16,000 feet and tops at 19,000 feet. The ground could be seen through holes in the clouds, and smoke screens could be observed on the ground in the vicinity of the target. The temperature at 20,000 feet was minus 23 degrees centigrade.

Thirty-four B-24s were able to find the Munchendorf airdrome through the clouds and flak. They dropped 79.05 tons of 20 pound fragmentation bombs with instantaneous fuses (7,905 bombs) at 1028 hours from 20,000 feet altitude on an axis of attack of 115 degrees magnetic. The indicated airspeed was 160 MPH, a true airspeed of 220. The bomb interval release setting was 250 feet. Bombing results could not be accurately assessed because of the cloud cover, but crew members reported bombs falling on the target area. The rally from the target after bombs away was a descending 30 degree right turn.

As explained below, one bomber failed to return with the formation. Thirty-three B-24s returned to our base at 1255 hours. One of the returning Liberators had to be scrapped because of extensive damage. This was the Group's 44th credited mission of 52 missions flown. It took 6 hours and 35 minutes.

The bomber that did not return to our airbase, and was lost, was aircraft #42-52291 flown by Lt. William W.Jones of the 744th Squadron. He had taken over the lead of the 2nd Unit of the formation when the Unit leader, Capt. Kenneth Gruber, had to abort the mission and leave the formation. Jones' plane was struck by six direct hits of flak, most on the left wing during the bomb run, and there was a hole between the #1 and #2 engines large enough for a man to pass through it. Jones' crew was able to drop its bombs on the target after being hit. After bombs away, gas was seen leaking from the trailing edge of the left wing and there was a gas leak in the bomb bay. Jones continued to lead the 2nd

Unit of the formation until reaching Yugoslavia, then he dove out of the formation, and headed for home.

Losing gasoline, Jones tried to reach Vis, Yugoslavia where other planes had made emergency landings before him, and where there were friendly Partisans to help. Fuel was nearly exhausted, with three engines coughing from lack of gas, and the navigator told the crew they were over friendly territory. Eleven crewmen bailed out and they landed about 15 miles northwest of Tirane, Albania. Friendly peasants arrived almost immediately and hid them from Germans who were in the area.

Jones and T/Sgt Donald E. Rothrock, his radio operator, were united two days later at Preze. Two days after that, on May 28, they were joined by S/Sgt Wesley Stroup, upper turret gunner, and S/Sgt Joseph Morin, nose turret, who had been cared for by local peasants. On May 30 they reached an Allied mission where they stayed until June 15 when they joined another party going to an evacuation point for returning to Allied territory, and they were returned to Italy on July 7, 1944.

Albanians indicated that the rest of Jones' crew were taken prisoner by the Germans, except for one man who had landed in an open field and had been machine-gunned by Germans as he attempted to escape. One of those taken prisoner is believed to have suffered a broken leg. The present status of those on Jones' crew is unknown, and it is unknown how many of those that weren't evacuated with Jones had survived.

May 25, 1944   Piacenza Airdrome, Italy.

My crew was selected to fly on this Group mission to bomb Piacenza airdrome in northern Italy. Our plane "Porky" was still being repaired, so we flew another crew's Liberator, number 831 again, "Man-O-War." I expected it to be a milk run, but we were attacked, unexpectedly, by

C O N F I D E N T I A L

25 May 1944

BATTLE ORDER

1st Unit, 1st Box

Formation Leader: Mulligan, AP 791   Callan
No. 3: Webster   AP 098   Dep Leader: Clark, W.B./ AP 768
                  No. 4: Munimaker AP 501
No. 6: Mapa   AP 964   No. 5: Leathers   AP 595

2nd Box

                  Leader: Lee   AP 077
No. 3: Brabon   AP 799   Dep Lumt   AP 295
                  Jr. 4: Hillman   AP 285
No. 6: Bruce   AP 275   No. 5: Lambert   AP 233

3rd Box

                  Leader: Newhouse AP 284
No. 3: Toselli   AP 364   Dep Leader: Ward   AP 637
                  No. 4: Riddle   AP 777
No. 6: Ogden   AP 225   No. 5: Coratti   AP 912

2nd Unit, 1st Box

                  Leader: Taval   AP 227
No. 3: Ecker   AP 934   Dep Leader: Fleming AP 334
                  No. 4: Little   AP 304
No. 6: Ashley   AP 477   No. 5: Blewitt   AP113

2nd Box

                  Leader: Gardner AP 749
No. 3: Williamson AP 297   Dep Leader: Phillips AP 882
                  No. 4: Palis   AP 183
No. 6: Miller   AP 309   No. 5: Reicher   AP 807
                  No. 7: Marlar   AP 203

3rd Box

                  Leader: Ensign   AP 486
No. 3: Smith E.W. AP 442   Dep Leader: Sagert AP 8275
                  No. 4: Capps   AP 831
No. 6: Wood   AP 489   No. 5: Hundley   AP 853
                  No. 7: Voshall   AP 299

Stations: 0935   456th "ENCORE FOUR ONE"

Engines: A 0940 B 0945 C 0950   Fighters: "EXCEED"
         D 0955 E 1000 F 1010
                                  Recall signal: "LOOSELIP"
Take-off: 1000

C O N F I D E N T I A L

53 enemy fighters. This happened despite the fact that we were supposed to have a group of P-51 Mustangs providing fighter cover for us from the time we penetrated enemy territory, over the target, and through our withdrawal from the target.

We were allowed to "sleep in" until 0730 hours this morning, briefing was conducted at 0830 and Lt. Alfred D. Levine gave the intelligence briefing. Stations time at our aircraft was set for 0935 hours. My start engine time, because I was in the last Box scheduled to start engines, the 3rd Box of the 2nd Unit, was 1010 hours. Capt. Walter F. Mulligan, Jr. of the 744th Squadron was in the lead plane of the 1st Unit and Lt. Dave E. Tavel of the 746th Squadron was in the lead plane of the 2nd Unit. Captain Mulligan started to taxi his lead bomber out to the end of the runway at 0950 and took off at 1000 hours. Thirty-seven Liberators followed his plane off the runway at 45 second intervals.

After we had gathered the Group formation together in flight, Mulligan led the formation over Giulia at 3,000 feet to rendezvous with the other groups of the 304th Wing. Our 456th Group led all groups of the 304th Wing to the target, in the order, 456th, 459th, 454th, and 455th Groups. We departed Giulia at 1051 hours climbing on course toward the initial point, Fidenza, at 160 MPH indicated airspeed, about 200 MPH true airspeed, and a rate of climb of 200 feet per minute. Two of our B-24s returned early, one because its flaps could not be retracted, and one had engine trouble.

The weather enroute to the target was not bad at our flying altitude, but there was five-tenths of cumulus cloud coverage below us with tops at 9,000 feet. Over the target, there was six-tenths coverage by cumulus clouds below our formation to obscure visual sighting of the target. Their bases were at 10,000 feet with tops at 12,000, but as we approached the target clouds cleared enough for bombardiers to see it. The temperature at 18,000 feet was minus 17 degrees centigrade.

We cruised over the Adriatic Sea as far as possible to avoid flak areas, but as we made land fall in northern Italy seven yellow-nose FW-190s attacked the 2nd Box of the 1st Unit from the front, then the FW-190s reformed and attacked them aggressively from the rear, closing to within 300 yards. We were told at our morning briefing that we would have P-51 fighter escort, but they were no where around. Near Fidenza, which was the initial point, 15 to 20 Me-109s attacked our rear Boxes, where I was flying, and their attacks continued into the target area. Ten Me-109s attacked my Box from the 3 o'clock position. Next, flying six abreast in a head-on attack, Me-109s attacked our formation, then they broke away. They returned to attack my Box in pairs from the rear. Seven Italian Macchi 202s were seen in the target area, but they didn't attack. During the bomb run, 20 Me-109s closed for another attack, ignoring the scant, inaccurate flak. The FW-190s had yellow spinners with checkerboard cowling, indicating Goering's elite fighters. The Me-109s were painted black with silver under their fuselages. As my radio operator notes below, there were P-38s flying above us all the time that we were being attacked, but they didn't do anything to prevent it. As we spread our formation out for the bomb run so that we had six Boxes flying abreast, we were much more vulnerable to fighter attack.

I read that the Luftwaffe was withdrawing many of its fighters from the eastern front that were fighting the Russians, to defend the German, Austrian, and Hungarian homeland targets that we were destroying.

S/Sgt Thomas S. Delaney, radio operator and waist gunner on my crew, recorded his observations in his diary. "It was a rough day for crew 4 (we were flying in the number 4 position of the 3rd Box of the 2nd Unit)! ....We got jumped by 12 enemy fighters. Three attacked us at 3 and 5 o'clock. Four attacked at the 6 o'clock level (postion). The crew got a few probables. Everyone of the gunners got shots for the first time! Twenty millimeter shells were exploding all around us! Plane 299 (Lt. LaVerne M. Voshell's plane from our 746th Squadron) on our right wing, got hit with a 20mm. One of the waist gunners got hit in the leg, but will be all right! Pieces of the 20mm got him! <u>God sure saved us again!</u> FW-190s were the fighters attacking us! They would make a pass, and throw their armor plating belly at us! Me-109s were also attacking us! We had an 18 plane front on the bomb run, which left us hang out by ourselves! Plane 279 (possibly plane 297 flown by a Lt. Williamson) lagged behind too (much) and got hit! This was the 22nd straight mission without return for "Man-O-War" number 831 (the plane we were then flying). Two more missions for "Man-O-War" and it will be a 15th Air Force record! Lt. Capps and Lt. Brooks flew a wonderful formation! It was my halfway mark on missions! The funny part of it was that when the Jerries were attacking us, the P-38s were above us. Maybe they didn't see them or something, they fooled around for about a half hour! Lt. Sagert's plane (Lt. Stanley A. Sagert of our 746th Squadron flying above us to our right) got hit with a 20mm also and his hydraulic system and flaps were out! He brought the plane in for landing, and had the crew throw parachutes to stop it! The plane had no brakes, all in all it was pretty rough! We sure have a lot to thank God for! Everybody's prayers helped us, I know for sure!"

Our Group's gunners claimed 6 enemy fighters destroyed, 4 probables, and 2 damaged. Flak was encountered at Bologna, Modena, Ferrara, Fidenza, and the target, Piacenza. Most was scant, inaccurate with heavy black bursts, but some were accurate and came close to our planes. Only two of our planes were seriously hit by the flak. None of our planes were lost, only damaged. The waist gunner on a crew that was just assigned to my 746th Squadron, piloted by Lt. LaVerne M. Voshell, was hit in the leg by enemy fire. A few other crew members had minor shaves by enemy shells.

To fully cover the target on this mission, all six of the Group's Boxes were ordered to fly over the target abreast, fanned out by flying on an 18 ship front. This formation left us more vulnerable to enemy fighter attack because our guns were not concentrated, as they would have been if we flew our normal formation. The box that I was flying in, the 3rd Box of the 2nd Unit was extended way our to the right of the formation by itself. Thirty-six planes flew over the target, but only 35 succeeded in dropping 79.26 tons of their 20 pound fragmentation bombs (7,926 bombs) on Piacenza at 1327 hours from 18,000 feet on an axis of attack of 280 degree magnetic. The indicated airspeed was 160 MPH, a true airspeed of about 215 MPH. The bomb release interval setting was 250 feet. Bomb results were graded as good, and a good pattern of bombs covered the target, including the airdrome runways, and dispersal areas. Thirty-three photos were taken of the target area by nine K-22 cameras. The rally after bombs away was a descending left turn at 155 MPH indicated airspeed to keep the formation tight for best defense against the fighters.

Lt. Stanley Sagert's bombardier, Lt. Werner C. "Judge" Foss, could not open the right front bomb bay door of his plane because of battle damage, and his were the bombs not released over the target. As Sagert's navigator Lt. Paul J. Crisafuli tried to crank the bomb bay doors open on the lower flight deck, an enemy 20mm cannon shell barely missed his head and it splattered his face with debris. Lt. Steve Hansen, copilot, took over the job, opened the doors, then Foss walked out on the bomb bay catwalk when the plane was over the Adriatic and manually kicked out the bombs. Bomb bay doors could also be cranked closed.

A 304th Bomb Wing B-24 showing how its crew used parachutes to stop after a no-flap, no-brakes landing when the plane's hydraulic system was shot out. Lt. Sagert's crew used this method after the May 25, 1944 mission to Piacenza. Photo courtesy of National Air and Space Museum, Smithsonian Institution.

Liberator Stopped By Parachutes After Landing

<u>Lt. Stanley Sagert's Crew after its no-flap, no-brake landing.</u> (May 25, 1944). F/O Werner C. "Judge" Foss, who flew as bombardier on my crew for nine missions, is upper right in the window, next to Lt. Paul Crisafulli, navigator. Sagert, pilot, is standing fourth from the right, and copilot, Lt. Steven E. Hansen is the tallest. Photo courtesy of Richard C. Hood of the 746th Squadron.

Lt. Sagert's Plane and Crew After Landing

This was only the beginning of trouble for Sagert's crew because a 20mm cannon shell had knocked out their plane's hydraulic accumulator and its entire hydraulic system, so they had no brakes for landing and the copilot had to manually crank down flaps and landing gear before they could land. Foss had remembered reading earlier about a crew that deployed two parachutes out the waist windows of their Liberator to slow up their plane after landing with brakes inoperative, by anchoring the chutes to the waist guns. Foss, with the help of the rest of his crew did just that, and the plane was landed safely and brought to a safe stop within the length of the runway, thanks to the drag of the two parachutes. The crew's picture is attached, taken by Philip N. Savage of our 746th Squadron. Also attached is a picture of a 456th Bomb Group plane illustrating how the parachutes were deployed.

Thirty-six B-24s returned to our base at 1525 hours and I logged 5 hours and 35 minutes. It was my 31st credited mission, the Group's 45th credited mission, and the 53rd mission flown.

After we landed we saw that our plane had a few enemy fighter-inflicted holes, but my crew pointed to some bullet holes that came from wild fire from guns of our own B-24s. Fifty-caliber machine guns sprinkled across our rudder. Evidently, some enthusiastic gunner from another Liberator in our formation kept firing at an enemy fighter as he passed behind "Porky", and hit its rudder.

At the intelligence interrogation after we had landed, the following comments by crew members were among those recorded: "(electric) heating suits are no good," "radio procedure is terrible," "while enemy fighters were attacking the formation, some 7 or 8 P-38s were overhead and made no attempt to help," "there was no food on the trip," "there was a good formation," " there was a good bomb pattern," and "no bombsight was in aircraft #364." (That plane was flown by Lt. Ernest Toselli, and I wonder why he didn't correct the problem before taking off.)

For some unexplained reason, my former crew, 1st Lt. Kenneth L. Boughner's crew, was mysteriously sent home to the United States this day, before it had flown its fifty missions. One other crew was also sent home with his. I heard rumors that they were being sent home to become instructors to train combat crews, but it remains a mystery to this day. Lt. Boughner died a few years ago.

May 26, 1944   Marshaling Yards at Grenoble, France.

My crew was not selected to fly on this milk run. The weather was very good, there was no flak, and no fighter attack. Fighter escort kept the 18 enemy fighters that were seen away from our Group. There were no planes lost or damaged. It was a mission that bombed one of the most important marshaling yards in southern France, at Grenoble. Fifteenth Air Force bombers were sent to bomb fourteen of the most important marshaling yards in the south of France for the next few days.

There was an early morning wake-up call at 0345 hours, briefing at 0445. Lt. F. T. Neff conducted the intelligence briefing. Stations time at the aircraft was 0555, start engines time for the first Box at 0600, taxi out at 0610, and the first bomber, with Major John R. Sinclair flying the lead airplane, took off at 0625 hours and 32 bombers followed him off the dirt runway at 45 second intervals. After the Group formation had gathered, Our Group rendezvoused over Stornara at 4,000 feet with other groups of the 304th Wing. The 456th flew last in the 304th Wing formation today. The groups flew to the target in trail formation with the 459th Group first, followed by the 454th, 455th, and 456th. The formation departed Stornara at 0715, climbing on course at an indicated airspeed of 160 MPH, about 200 MPH true airspeed, and rate of climb of 200 feet per minute.

Two aircraft returned early because one had an electrical shortage, and the other plane had a gas leak on #2 engine. Weather was excellent with ceiling and visibility unlimited for the entire route. Only a thin overcast of cirrus clouds were above the formation with cloud bases at 22,000. Temperature at 20,000 feet, the cruising altitude, was minus 16 degrees centigrade.

Ten Me-109s and 8 FW-190s were seen, but our Wing's escort of P-38 Lightnings kept them away. There was no flak. Thirty B-24s were able to drop 73.5 tons of 500 pound general purpose bombs (294 bombs) on the Grenoble marshaling yards at 1045 hours, from 20,000 feet altitude for the 1st Unit and 19,000 feet for the 2nd Unit. Bombing speed was 160 MPH indicated airspeed, a true airspeed of 223 MPH, and the axis of attack of 10 degrees magnetic. One B-24 had problems with bomb bay doors that would not open, among other troubles, so that it couldn't drop its bombs on the target. The pilot, Lt.. Richard W. Nunimaker of the 744th Squadron, radioed to the lead ship that he was making an emergency landing at the Island of Corsica.

Thirty pictures of the target area were taken with nine K-22 cameras aboard the bombers. Bombing results were rated as fair. Crews reported a good pattern of bombs falling in the marshaling yards and vicinity.

The Group's formation of 30 bombers returned to over our base at 1405 hours. The trip took 7 hours and 30 minutes of flying time by the time planes were on the ground. It was the Group's 46th credited mission of 54 missions flown in Italy.

Crew comments that were recorded at the regular intelligence interrogation, after planes had landed, included the following: "very good lead," "men should be briefed on the procedure for dropping chaff (window) -----(they) even dropped it way out over water," "lead navigator and bombardier did a good job," "crew felt that the mission was worth double credit (it was only a single credit mission)," " too slow on climb to get to altitude for target bombing."

While the crews were flying the mission, those that weren't flying the mission attended a lecture by a Colonel Dixon, flak expert from Naples, about flak and how it worked. During his lecture, the base had a red alert, warning of an air raid, but it was called off a few minutes later.

C O N F I D E N T I A L

26 May 1944

BATTLE ORDER

1st Unit, 1st Box

Miller, R.E.

Formation Leader: Sinclair,/ AP 839   Hillman

No. 3: Blackwell   AP 364   Dep Leader: Hyde,/ AP 235

No. 4: Numismaker AP 338

No. 6:   AP   No. 5: Ball   AP 595

2nd Box

Leader: Bishop   AP 284

No. 3: Rawlinson AP 293   Dep Leader: Ceretti AP 912

No. 4: Riddle   AP 777

No. 3: Ogden   AP 225   No. 5: Mapa   AP 964

3rd Box

Leader: Phifer   AP 501

No. 3: Nix   AP 233   Dep Leader: Jones AP 077

No. 4: Lambert   AF 319

No. 6: Lunt   AP 295   No. 5: Zurney   AP 275

2nd Unit, 1st Box

Leader: Jackson, C.Y. AP 227

No. 3: Addis   AP 256   Dep Leader: Webster AP 098

No. 4: Wilkinson AP 334

No. 6: Walker   AP 203   No. 5: Gullick AP 477

No. 7: Reicher   AP 882

2nd Box

Leader: Snee   AP 489

No. 3: Rugland   AP 486 .   Dep Leader: Hundley AP 853

No. 4: Smith   AP 831

No. 6: Scott   AP 934   No. 5: Wood   AP 442

3rd Box

Leader: Douglass AP 749

No. 3: Roak   AP 487   Dep Leader: Laszewski AP 309

No. 4: Little   AP 304

No. 6: Solcher   AP 297   No. 5: Savage   AP 807

No. 7: Marlar   AP 183

Time at stations: 0555.

Start engines: A 0600 B 0605 C 0610
D 0615 D 0620 E 0625

Take-off: 0615.   456th SENILE FOUR-FOUR
          1st FG RADCLIFF FIVE

Recall: FUEL

May 27, 1944   Montpellier Frejergues Airdrome, France.

My crew was selected to fly on this long, eight-hour mission to bomb in southern France. Our ship "Porky" was not out of the repair docks yet, so we were assigned to fly number 831, "Man-O-War" again. The plane broke the Fifteenth Air Force record with 24 straight missions without an abort. We flew in the 2nd Box of the 1st Unit.

It was the second day in a row that the Fifteenth Air Force bombers were sent to bomb targets in southern France. Although it was a long mission, it was only worth single-mission credit because enemy opposition was not strong in the area. Our target for the day was the Montpellier Frejergues airdrome. Although we were supposed to have one group of P-51 Mustangs for fighter cover from the time we penetrated the coast of France, they didn't prevent enemy fighters from attacking us. We were attacked by eleven enemy fighters. Two ships were originally listed as missing, but one was later reported to have made an emergency landing at an Allied airbase on the Island of Corsica.

It was another early morning wake-up call at 0315 hours, briefing at 0415, and a sleepy stations time at our planes at 0530 hours. It was a beautiful, mild spring morning. The 1st Box of Liberators started their engines at 0540 and planes of the remaining five Boxes started engines at five minute intervals after that. The first ship taxied out at 0550, and it took off at 0600 followed by 36 more B-24s at 45 second intervals. Two planes returned early, one plane had an engine cowling tear off of #4 engine, and one plane had an engine burn out.

During the beautiful sunrise we gathered our Group's B-24s around the lead plane, then the formation flew to Stornara at 4,000 feet, the rendezvous point for forming our Wing formation of groups. The Wing formation departed Stornara at 0642 hours, climbing on course at 160 MPH indicated airspeed, about 200 MPH true airspeed, and a rate of climb of 200 feet per minute.

The weather enroute was very good. Above us, we had high thin cirrus clouds with two-tenths cloud coverage, bottoms at 24,000 feet, tops at 25,000 feet. Below our formation, enroute to the target, there were scattered cumulus clouds with only one to two-tenths cloud coverage, bases at 5,000 feet and tops at 7,000 feet. Over the target there was the same cirrus coverage above our formation, but no clouds below our formation. It was excellent bombing weather. The temperature was minus 13 degrees centigrade at 21,000 feet, reasonably warm, and the visibility was good, from 15 to 20 miles.

Again, we were briefed to have P-51 fighter escort that was scheduled to rendezvous with us at the coast of France, but I never saw them, and they didn't keep enemy aircraft from attacking us. Seven Me-109s attacked our Group in the target area, 3 of them coming in from the 11 o'clock position level and they closed to 500 yards. Four Me-109s came in from the 6 o'clock low position and they fired rockets. Four FW-190s assaulted our formation at 1026 hours, after the target run, and they attacked from 10 o'clock, singly. My waist gunner, also our radio operator, noted, ".....Three FW-190s gave us (our Box) a little trouble, but all of us kept them well out of range, especially the nose turret gunner and the Sperry ball turret gunner! The enemy fighters were afraid to come close! (Our 50 caliber machine guns had tracer bullets in them so that, with a massive number of white tracers coming at them clearly visible to the enemy pilots, they were very intimidating!) We were flying in Baker-2 (officially the deputy lead plane of the 2nd Box of the 1st Unit)."

Flak was rated as moderate, accurate, with heavy, ugly black bursts, but for our particular Box in the formation, it appeared intense, accurate, and heavy. Two planes in our

Box were hit by flak and had to make forced landings. Lt. George H. Gutting's plane flying in the number 5 position of our Box, and the plane flying in the number 6 position, "Ice Cold Katie" were hit. Gutting's plane made an emergency forced landing on the Island of Corsica and "Ice Cold Katie" left the formation at 0950 hours before reaching the target, and it was last seen headed home at 0950 hours. It was losing altitude but it seemed to be under control. We later learned that it made an emergency landing at a fighter base in Italy. Thus, no aircraft were lost on the mission. However, four other Liberators of our Group were damage and were able to return to our base with the formation. My plane didn't get hit on the mission.

Of the 34 bombers that were left to fly over the target, two had bomb rack malfunctions that prevented them from dropping their bombs on the target. Therefore, 32 planes were left to drop 62.5 tons of 100 pound general purpose bombs (1,252 bombs) on the Montpellier Frejergues airdrome at 1024 hours from 21,000 feet altitude, 160 MPH indicated airspeed, a true airspeed of 229 MPH, on an axis of attack of 246 degrees magnetic. The bomb interval release setting was 50 feet. The rally after bomb release was a descending left turn at 155 MPH indicated airspeed.

Bombing results were graded as good, and 17 photos were taken of the target area by seven K-22 cameras. Crews reported a good pattern of bombs falling on the target area, hitting the motor transport pool, hangars, barracks, and other installations of the airdrome. My gunner, S/Sgt Thomas S. Delaney recorded in his diary that, "The Lord was with us again as usual! We really smashed the airdrome at Montpellier, France. The flak was heavy, intense, and accurate....we didn't get hit"

Thirty-three B-24s returned home with the formation at 1335 hours. By the time we were on the ground we had logged 8 hours for the mission, a very long one. It was my longest mission to date and it was my 32nd accredited one. The attacking fighters, flak, and the length of this mission made it a rougher one than many where we were given double credit. It was the Group's 47th accredited mission of the 55 missions flown in Italy.

Crew comments at the intelligence debriefing after landing included: "gunners fired at our own escort, mistaking P-51s for Me-109s," "good bombing pattern, good coverage of the target," "let down was too fast," "double credit for such long missions is desirable," "interrogators recommend that navigators be instructed to maintain better logs. Many logs are very incomplete, lacking valuable information."

A whole family of Italians were observed to be waiting outside of Lt. Gilbert Smith's office this morning, as usual, waiting to get passes that would allow them on the post.. The Group's acknowledged expert with the Italian language, the talented Gil Smith, was always kept very busy with many talkative Italian civilians each wanting something.

A little before the crews arrived for their interrogation from the mission, an Army weapons carrier was passing another weapons carrier near Stornara when it hit a bump in the road. It side swiped the other carrier, causing it to turn over. Several personnel were injured, and Corporal Maunch was killed.

That evening, at 1845 hours, another red alert was sounded to warn of an air raid. An all clear signal was given 15 minutes later.

May 28, 1944   An Alternate, Genoa Harbor and Dock, Italy.

My crew was not selected to fly on this mission. It was expected to be another milk run, to northern Italy to bomb the Turin South marshaling yards. However, six of our Group's B-24s had damage from the flak they encountered.

Due to poor weather at the primary target the Genoa harbor installations were bombed as an alternate.

Wake up time was at an early hour again, 0415 hours, briefing was at 0530, and stations time at the aircraft was 0640. Start engines time was 0650 for B-24s in the 1st Box, and each of the other five Boxes started at five minute intervals afterward. Again, Major John Sinclair was in the lead plane, and he taxied out at 0700 and took off at 0710 hours. Lt. Dave E. Tavel was flying the lead ship of the 2nd Unit. Thirty-five bombers followed Sinclair's lead plane off the runway at 45 second intervals. There were no early returning aircraft, a testimonial to the increasing proficiency of our hard working ground crews. After our Group formation was assembled, the Group flew over Stornara at 3,000 feet to rendezvous with other groups of the 304th Wing. The 456th Group followed the 455th Group in the Wing formation, and they departed Stornara at 0800 hours climbing at 160 MPH indicated airspeed, a true airspeed of about 200 MPH, and a rate of climb of 200 feet per minute.

Rendezvous with P-51 fighter escort was at 0953 hours but only 3 enemy fighters were encountered and there was no damage to our bombers by enemy fighters.

Weather was too poor for visual bombing at Turin, so the formation went to bomb the Genoa harbor and dock installations. Flak was moderate and accurate with heavy bursts. Six of our Group's bombers had flak damage, but none of our planes were lost and there were no casualties. As our Group formation flew over the Genoa Harbor target, 29 bombers were able to see the target well enough to drop 71 tons of 500 pound general purpose bombs (284 bombs) on it at 1113 hours from an altitude of 21,000 feet on an axis of attack of 295 degrees magnetic, with good results. The bombing indicated airspeed was 160 MPH, a true airspeed of 226 MPH. The weather closed in too much for 7 bombers to see the target, so they did not drop and brought their bombs back home.

The Group formation of 36 bombers returned to our airfield at 1400 hours. Flying time was 6 hours and 50 minutes. It was the Group's 48th credited mission, and its 56th attempt.

C O N F I D E N T I A L

28 May 1944

1st Unit, 1st Box

Formation Leader: Sinclair, Witkin AP 889

No. 3: Voshell   AP 442   Dep Leader: Mulligan   AP 279
                       No. 4: Wilkinson   AP 437
No. 6: Selchor   AP 810   No. 5: Walker   AP 203

2nd Box

Leader: Sagert   AP 8275
No. 3: Ragland   AP 256   Dep Leader: Smith   AP 831
                       No. 4: Ecker   AP 489
No. 6: Wood   AP 853   No. 5: Dean   AP 934

3rd Box

Leader: Lassewski   AP 309
No. 3: Savage   AP 807   Dep Leader: Phillips   AP 882
                       No. 4: Monohan   AP 304
No. 6: Reicher   AP 113   No. 5: Marlar   AP 297

2nd Unit, 1st Box

Leader: Tavel   AP 227
No. 3: Leathers   AP 912   Dep Leader: Griffin   AP 338
                       No. 4: Nunimaker   AP 501
No. 6: Lunt   AP 295   No. 5: Rawlinson   AP 293

2nd Box

Leader: Newhouse   AP 284
No. 3: Tosalli   AP 364   Dep Leader: Ward   AP 637
                       No. 4: Riddle   AP 777
No. 6: Ogden   AP 225   No. 5: Hull   AP 485
                       No. 7: Corette   AP 964

3rd Box

Leader: Hillman   AP 285
No. 3: Jones   AP 077   Dep Leader: Nix   AP 947
                       No. 4: Brabon   AP 799
No. 6: Bruce   AP 290   No. 5: Whittaker   AP 319
                       No. 7: Zurney   AP 493

Stations: 0640   456th: GREENHERD TWO

Engines: A 0650 B 0655 C 0700   325th FG: PUSSCAT ONE
         D 0705 E 0710 F 0715
                                  1st FG: PUSSCAT TWO
Take-off: 0710

Recall signal: HOTSEAT

C O N F I D E N T I A L

29 May 1944

1st Unit: 1st Box

Formation Leader: Col STEED, Thomas   AP 791
No. 3: Goza   AP 493   Dep Leader: Lee, Parks   AP 227
              No. 4: Webster   AP 098
No. 6: Blackwell AP 964   No. 5: Corrotti   AP 777

2nd Box

Leader: Phifer   AP 501
No. 3: Bruce   AP 285   Dep Leader: Lunt   AP 338
              No. 4: Braben   AP 799
No. 6: Whitaker   AP 319   No. 5: Powell   AP 947

3rd Box

Leader: Bishop   AP 284
No. 3: Ogdon   AP 225   Dep Leader: Hall   AP 912
              No. 4: Napa   AP 435
No. 6: Shotterly AP 293   No. 5: Toselli   AP 364

2nd Unit, 1st Box

Leader: Jackson, C.Y.   AP 279
No. 3: Blewitt   AP 113   Dep Leader: Hunimaker AP 077
              No. 4: Williamson   AP 810
No. 6: Reicher   AP 334   No. 5: Dean   AP 934

2nd Unit

Leader: Ensign   AP 486
No. 3: Ashley   AP 442   Dep Leader: Smith   AP 831
              No. 4: Addis   AP 489
No. 6: Scott   AP 8275   No. 5: Food   AP 853
              No. 7: Voshell   AP 290

3rd Box

Leader: Gardner   AP 749
No. 3: Wilkonson A P 297   Dep Leader: Fleming AP 309
              No. 4: Liddle   AP 882
No. 6: Roak   AP 307   No. 5: Walker   AP 203

Stations: 0605.   456th "SANDSAIL FOUR"

Engines: A 0615 B 0620 C 0625   Recall signal: "PEPPER"
          D 0630 E 0635 F 0640

Take-off: 0648.

May 29, 1944 Zegar, Zavalje, and Drvar Yugoslavia.

This was another milk run for the Group, one on which my crew was not selected to fly. It was a mission to bomb three different targets in Yugoslavia, Zegar and Zavalje in the morning and Drvar in the afternoon. They were all troop concentrations. No flak or fighters were encountered, there were no planes lost, and no Group casualties.

The ubiquitous, Lt. Gilbert Smith gave the intelligence briefing for the morning flight at 0500 hours, stations time at the aircraft was 0605, start engines time for the 1st Box was 0615. The lead plane, with Colonel Steed in command, taxied out at 0638 and he took off at 0648 hours. Thirty-six B-24s followed his plane at 45 second intervals. For the second day in a row, there were no early returning aircraft, another great tribute to the increasing efficiency of our ground crews. After our Group assembled, our Group rendezvoused over Stornara at 4,000 with the 455th Group and our Wing formation departed Stornara at 0743 hours, climbing on course. There was no fighter escort and none were needed this day.

Of the 1st Unit's 18 Liberators, 17 dropped 30.7 tons of 100 pound general purpose bombs (614 bombs) at 0912 on Zegar from 16,000 feet with fair results. One plane in this formation had a bomb rack failure that prevented it from dropping its bombs. That plane returned its bombs to our airfield.

The 2nd Unit, consisting of 19 bombers dropped 37.5 tons of 100 pound general purpose bombs (750 bombs) on Zavalje with fair results. In the afternoon, 35 bombers dropped 69.7 tons of bombs on Drvar, again with fair results. After bombs were released, the formation's rally was a descending turn to the left at 155 MPH indicated airspeed. All 37 of the morning's bombers returned to our airfield at 1033 hours for a flying time of 3 hours and 45 minutes.

All 35 bombers returned safely from bombing Drvar in the afternoon's mission. They dropped 69.7 tons of 100 pound general purpose bombs on the troop concentrations with fair results. Flying time was 3 hours and 30 minutes for the afternoon mission. No flak or fighters were seen, and there were no casualties for the day. No aircraft lost or damaged.

The morning mission was the Group's 49th accredited mission, and the afternoon was the Group's 50th accredited one. These were the Groups 57th and 58th mission attempts.

On 26, 28, and 29 May, 1944 a total of 593 heavy bombers of the Fifteenth Air Force dropped 1,077 tons of bombs on troop concentrations in Yugoslavia.

May 30, 1944   Wels Airdrome, Austria.

This was a mission to bomb the Wels airdrome, about 15 miles southwest of Linz, Austria. My crew was not selected to fly on it. Except for three planes that received slight flak damage, this turned out to be another milk run. No enemy planes attacked the formation, there were no casualties, and all of our planes returned safely to our airfield. Of course, the crews flying on the mission expected it to be much worse than it turned out, because of the dangerous area they were attacking.

After another early morning wake-up call at 0400 hours, briefing was at 0515, stations time at the aircraft was 0625 hours, start engines time for the 1st Box was 0635, and the other five Boxes started their engines at five minute intervals following the 1st Box. Captain Louis M. Abernathy of the 745th Squadron was in the lead B-24 and he started to taxi out to the end of the runway at 0645 then he took off at 0655 hours. Thirty-six bombers followed him off the dirt runway at 45 second intervals. Only one plane returned early because it had an engine go out. Our planes were becoming much more reliable, again thanks to the effort of our ground crews.

371

C O N F I D E N T I A L

30 May 1944

1st Unit: 1st Box

Formation Leader: Abernathy/Cullan AP 791

No. 3: Leathers   AP 912   Dep Leader: Mulligan   AP 279
           No. 4: Webster   AP 093
No. 6: Goza   AP 493   No. 5: Whitaker   AP 319

2nd Box

Leader: Loukuma   AP 225
No. 3: Shetterly   AP 364   Dep Leader: Ward   AP 637
           No. 4: Rawlinson   AP 293
No. 6: Ball   AP 777   No. 5: Blackwell   AP 964
           No. 7: Ragland   AP 442

3rd Box

Leader: Hillman   AP 285
No. 3: Jones   AP 077   Dep Leader: Lunt   AP 501
           No. 4: Nix   AP 338
No. 6: Powell   AP 947   No. 5: Hula   AP 290
           No. 7: Zurney   AP 268

2nd Unit: 1st Box

Leader: Gruber, Clark, W.D.   AP 768
No. 3: Miller   AP 183   Dep Leader: Monahan   AP 334
           No. 4: Wilkinson   AP 487
No. 6: Marlar   AP 297   No. 5: Gullick   AP 934

2nd Box

Leader: Snee   AP 831
No. 3: Vaughell   AP 201   Dep Leader: Hundley   AP 853
           No. 4: Ecker   AP 486
No. 6: Addis   AP 489   No. 5: Scott   AP 8275
           No. 7: Doan   AP 256

3rd Box

Leader: Laszowski   AP 309
No. 3: Blewitt   AP 749   Dep Leader: Selchor   AP 810
           No. 4: Phillips   AP 882
No. 6: Savage   AP 807   No. 5: Fulker   AP 203

Stations: 0625

Start engines: A 0635 B 0640 C 0645
              D 0650 E 0655 F 0700

Takeoff: 0655

456th: RINGWAY TWO THREE
Fighters - Penetration SHAPELY
Channel "A" WELLS Area 52nd FG
FALSETEETH ONE
14th FG FALSETEETH TWO

Recall: PENCIL

After our Group assembled its formation around Abernathy's lead plane, our formation rendezvous was over Stornara at 4,000 feet with the 455th Group. We joined the other groups of the 304th Wing, flying in the order, 454th first, then the 459th, 456th, and the 455th last. The groups departed climbing on course at 0745, at the standard 160 MPH indicated airspeed, about 200 MPH true airspeed, and a rate of climb of 200 feet per minute.

Some Me-109s and FW-190s were seen in Austria, but the Group's escort of P-51s and P-38s that provided penetration, target, and withdrawal cover, kept them away from our bombers.

Weather enroute and at the target was clear, visibility was 10 miles with smoke and haze. It was perfect weather for visual bombing. There were some thin cirrus above our Group's formation enroute with bases at 23,000 feet, but that vanished as the target was reached. The temperature at 21,000 feet was minus 16 degrees centigrade.

Flak was encountered along the route at Klagenfurt, Linz, St. Michael, Hieflau, Steyr, and Bruck. At the target, there were scant, inaccurate, heavy black bursts of flak. Three bombers had slight damage from the flak.

Some aircraft in the formation had bomb rack malfunctions that kept them from dropping their bombs on the target, but 34 bombers did drop 75.78 tons of 20 pound fragmentation bombs (7,578 bombs) on the Wels airdrome at 1047 hours from an altitude of 22,000 feet for the 1st Unit and 21,000 feet for the 2nd Unit on an axis of attack of 175 degrees magnetic. The bombing airspeed was 169 MPH indicated, a true airspeed of 230 MPH. Crews reported a good pattern of bombs on the target. Twenty-nine photos were taken of the target area by seven K-22 cameras, and bombing results were graded as excellent. The Group's rally after bombs away was a descending left turn at 155 MPH indicated airspeed. Of 61 enemy aircraft on the field at Wels, the Wing destroyed 25 and damaged 12, in addition to considerable damage to the airdrome.

All 36 aircraft in the formation returned safely over our airfield at 1314 hours. There were no reported casualties. Only 3 planes had flak damage. Flying time was 6 hours and 20 minutes. It was our Group's 51st accredited mission of 59 missions flown.

There was a major change in capability of our fighter escort that had taken place in the last few weeks. The Fifteenth Air Force now had three fighter groups equipped with the new long range P-51 Mustangs. In addition, the Fifteenth's Lightnings groups were now equipped with the new P-38J aircraft that had a one-third increase in its internal fuel capacity compared to the old models. This meant that our fighter escort could accompany our bombers to and from our longer strategic targets more easily, and we wouldn't have to rely on precise timing of fighter rendezvous as much as we had in the past.

May 31, 1944   Ploesti, Unirea Sperantza Oil Refinery, Rumania.

My crew was selected to fly on this mission with the Group to bomb Ploesti's Unirea Sperantza Oil Refinery in Rumania. We expected a rough mission, as usual at Ploesti, and it turned out to be fairly rough. We lost one plane, shot down, and a total of thirteen aircraft, including mine with five holes, were damaged by enemy fire. I was scheduled to fly our beloved "Porky' on this mission, but it did not check out in time for this mission, so we had to fly an alternate plane provided by the 745th Squdron, "Big Butch," number 203, a very good plane. My crew flew in deputy lead.

374

C O N F I D E N T I A L

31 May 1944

1st Unit: 1st Box

	Formation Leader: Col STERN Witkin AP 862 Reid
No. 3: Smith AP 201	Dep Leader: Munimaker/ AP 791 or 768
	No. 4: Palis AP 183
No. 6: England AP 256	No. 5: Reicher AP 862

2nd Box

	Leader: Sagert AP 831
No. 3: Addis AP 489	Dep Leader: Capps AP 306
	No. 4: Ecker AP 853
No. 6: Gullick AP 934	No. 5: Scott AP 442

3rd Box

	Leader: Gardner AP 749
No. 3: Savage AP 807	Dep Leader: Little AP 334
	No. 4: Williamson AP 810
No. 6: Roak AP 487	No. 5: Marlar AP 309
	No. 7: Delwitt AP 203

2nd Unit: 1st Box

	Leader: Tavel, Ladd AP 227
No. 3: Leathern AP 912	Dep Leader: Hillman AP 268
	No. 4: Jones AP 319
No. 6: Ogden AP 435	No. 5: Huls AP 290

2nd Box

	Leader: Phifer AP 501
No. 3: Bruce AP 275	Dep Leader: Draben AP 799
	No. 4: Lunt AP 338
No. 6: Gozm AP 493	No. 5: Powell AP 072

3rd Box

	Leader: Newhouse AP 284
No. 3: Tessolli AP 364	Dep Leader: Rall AP 777
	No. 4: Rawlinson AP 293
No. 6: Blackwell AP 964	No. 5: Hall AP 328
	No. 7: Cerrotti AP 098

Stations: 0540

Start engines: A 0540 B 0545 C 0550
              D 0555 E 0600 F 0605

Take-off: 0600

456th GREENHEAD TWO ONE
Route cover: 82nd FG: MAYFLOWER ONE
Penetration: 52nd FG: MAYFLOWER TWO
Target Cover: 1st FG: MAYFLOWER FOUR
Withdrawal: 14th FG: MAYFLOWER FIVE

Recall: MESSY

There was a very early morning wake-up call in our tents for crews participating in the mission. It came at about 0315 hours. After our usual hasty C-ration breakfast, a cool ride in open six-by-six trucks up to the hill, briefing started at 0430 hours. As we entered the briefing room sleepy-eyed, we saw the long yarn on the map at the end of the room which lead for the first time to Ploesti. If anyone hadn't awakened sufficiently by that time, that long yarn did the job. We had bombed in the Ploesti vicinity many times before, but this was the first time we would be bombing the oil production facilities. This was my fourth trip to bomb in the Ploesti area, and we usually ran into stiff enemy opposition each time we went. It was the third most heavily defended Axis target.

After briefing, we rode in the back of Army six-by-six trucks to our aircraft for stations time at 0540 hours. Most of us arrived at our planes much earlier than the stations time, as usual. We had to give our planes a quick preflight check to make sure everything was good enough for us to bet our lives on it. My preflight check of the plane was merely a double check of the flight engineer's and ground crew's work, which had been completed before we arrived. We also had to give the rest of the crew a quick briefing about the mission, put on our Mae Wests, flak suits, and parachutes before getting aboard the huge bombers. The emergency first-aid kits with morphine in them were delivered and signed for by designated crew members. This day, I was flying in the deputy lead position, #2 position, of the 2nd Box of the 1st Unit, so my start engines time was set for 0545 hours, five minutes after Liberators of the 1st Box started their engines. Everything was done in radio silence, and members of the operations staff fired colored flares to signal the proper times. Colonel Steed led the formation this day, and he started his taxi out to the end of the runway at 0550, then he coaxed his laboring, heavily laden Liberator off the bumpy, runway at 0600. Lt. Richard Witkin of my 746th Squadron was flying with Colonel Steed, as were Capts.Robert Carlin and Allen Trobaugh from Group to do the navigating and aim the bombs. Thirty-five B-24s followed him off the runway at 45 second intervals. We flew at about 170 or 180 MPH indicated airspeed to catch him and take our assigned places in the Group formation.

Five B-24s returned early, one because it had a gas leak, one because three of its gun turrets were inoperative, two because they had engines become inoperative, and one because it had a faulty landing gear. This was an unusually high abort rate, but I believe crews were willing to fly missions that were milk-runs with many minor aircraft malfunctions that they would not fly with on tougher missions.

After we joined Colonel Steed and assembled our Group formation, he led the formation to the 304th Wing's rendezvous point which was over Stornara at 3,000 feet where we joined other groups of the 304th Wing. Our Group was in the lead of the Wing formation this day. We departed Stornara at 0648 hours, climbing on course at 160 MPH indicated airspeed, a true airspeed of 200 MPH, and a rate of climb of 250 feet per minute. We maintained this higher rate of climb this day until we reached 15,000 feet of altitude, a slight increase form the normal 200 FPM. After reaching 15,000 feet the rate of climb was reduced to 150 FPM until we reached a bombing altitude of 20,000 feet for the 1st Unit. The 2nd Unit of our formation bombed at 19,000 feet of altitude. Our route to the target took us over Pecenisca, Pesteana, Sinaia, and then to our Initial Point, Homoraciul for our bomb run on Ploesti's Unirea Sperantza Oil Refinery. (Names of many of these cities was changed by the Communists when they took control after the war.) Our route was carefully controlled by our navigators so that we avoided known flak areas as much as possible. Long range fighters, P-38Js and P-51s, joined us starting at 0805 hours to provide our Wing with fighter cover, in relays, on penetration, over the target, and during withdrawal from enemy territory.

This escort of P-38s and P-51s didn't prevent twelve enemy fighters from attacking our Group aggressively, and our gunners claimed two of them destroyed and one damaged. S/Sgt Thomas S. Delaney, radio operator of my crew, noted in his diary, "...Ten Me-109s threw plenty of 20mm (cannon shells) at Fox Flight (the 3rd Box of the 2nd Unit)! I saw them bursting all around them!.....The Luftwaffe seemed to be getting much weaker! The P-38s chased the Me-109s away!...." Our gunners claimed two enemy fighter destroyed and one damaged from this attack.

Flak in the target area was heavy, intense, and accurate, as usual for this area. Our radio operator, S/Sgt Delaney, recorded, "....The flak was the worst I have ever seen in all of my missions! Red, white, and black flak, heavy, intense, and very, very accurate! We counted five holes in our plane, but the Lord guided us through with flying colors...." The navigator on the lead aircraft of our Box (the navigator on 1st Lt. Stanley A. Sagert's crew that was leading the Box, Lt. Paul J. Crisafulli) was seriously wounded by flak. We were flying as his deputy lead, off his right wing, so our navigator gave him the magnetic heading home." Crisafulli was hit in the back by a two inch piece of flak and a small piece in his rear end. His plane had six flak holes in it.

One of our planes was hit critically over the target. It was lost as described below, and thirteen planes, including mine with five flak hits on it, were damaged by the accurate flak. The target was obscured by an enemy smoke screen, and it could not be seen sufficiently to bomb visually. The Group's Pathfinder radar, "Mickey" as some called it, dropped bombs on the target and the rest of the planes in the formation dropped their bombs when they saw bombs fall from the radar-guided lead plane. One bomber in our formation had a bomb rack malfunction that prevented it from dropping its bombs, and its bombs were returned home.

Thirty bombers of our Group formation were able to drop 73.5 tons of 500 pound general purpose bombs (294 bombs) on the Ploesti's Unirea Sperantza Oil Refinery from 20,000 feet for the 1st Unit of the formation, and from 19,000 feet for the 2nd Unit. Indicated airspeed was the usual 160 MPH, and 222 MPH true airspeed. The axis of attack was 175 degrees magnetic and the bombardier's bomb release interval setting was 100 feet. Result of the bombing could not be observed because the target was obscured by smoke, but smoke from the target came up to our flight level, indicating severe damage to the refinery. The Group rallied after bombs away by making a descending left turn at 155 MPH to foil flak gunners that were firing at us, and the speed was kept low to allow the Group's formation to keep tight in defense of attacking enemy fighters.

On return to Italy, one plane of the formation, Lt. Sagert's number 831 "Man-O-War," landed at Foggia because it had wounded aboard. "Man-O-War" was about to break a Fifteenth Air Force record of thirty missions flown without an abort, as it recorded twenty-nine missions with this one. It only had one more to go! When there were crew members aboard who were critically wounded, it was our standard procedure to land at Foggia where the airstrip was near the Foggia Hospital that could provide more immediate expert attention.

Our crippled formation of twenty-nine B-24s arrived over our field with tired aircrews from the long mission at 1308 hours, and I logged 7 hours and 50 minutes. I now had 163 hours and 25 minutes of combat flying time. This was my 33rd and 34th credited mission. It was the Group's 52nd accredited mission of 60 missions flown in Italy.

379

The bomber "Big Stud" from the 744th Squadron, piloted by 1st Lt. Douglas W. Hillman, was hit in the tail over the target, had three of the crew bail over the target, including the nose gunner, navigator, and bombardier. All three were in the nose of the aircraft. However, the pilot was able to nurse his shot-up plane, with rudder controls shot out and other damages, back to our airfield where the rest of the crew successfully bailed out over our airfield. It was too dangerous to try to land the crippled plane. The abandoned plane then crashed about two miles south of the base. The three who bailed out in the target area, bombardier 1st Lt. Albert W. Anderson, navigator 2nd Lt. John F. Daniel, and gunner T/Sgt Howard L. Haught, were originally reported as missing in action, but it was later learned that they had been taken as POWs. The entire crew survived the war. They include: Hillman, pilot; 1st Lt. Albert W. Anderson, bombardier; S/Sgt James A. Antonucci, gunner; T/Sgt Robert B. Crumpton, engineer; 2nd Lt. John J. Daniel, navigator; T/Sgt Howard L Haught, gunner; 2nd Lt. Robert L. McElroy, copilot; S/Sgt Patrick P. Rizzotti, engineer; S/Sgt Edward J. Rausch, gunner; T/Sgt Richard T. Jensen, engineer. Hillman, Anderson, and Daniel are currently members of the 456th Bomb Group Association, and the others have not been heard from since and their whereabouts are unknown.

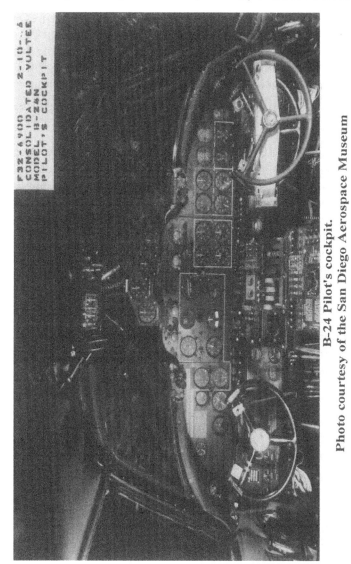

B-24 Pilot's cockpit.

Photo courtesy of the San Diego Aerospace Museum

Pilot's Instrumental Panel In Liberator

A British liaison officer, Captain Clark, gave lectures at 1430 and 2030 hours on this day in our Group headquarters concerning the Balkan situation. He explained the role that the Fifteenth Air Force would play, and is playing, in its outcome. The Fifteenth Air Force is playing a vital role in the outcome of the war in that area by bombing of enemy troop concentrations, transportation facilities that supply the area, and the enemy oil supplies.

The Allies were nearing the magic date for Operation Overlord, the invasion of Europe from England, and control of the air over Europe by Allied air power was almost accomplished. During the month of May 1944 the Luftwaffe lost 50.4 percent of the operational fighter force that it had at the beginning of the month, on April 30, 1944, according to a study by Williamson Murray in his book "Luftwaffe" (The Nautical and Aviation Publishing Company of America, Baltimore, Maryland, 1985). The Luftwaffe had lost a comparable amount of its fighter force the month before. We in the 456th Bomb Group noticed a decided reduction in the number of planes the Luftwaffe was able to launch against us and a decided degradation in the quality of enemy fighter pilots.

June 1, 1944   No Mission Today.

Weather was too bad everywhere for flying our formations.

Lt. Col. Joseph G. Russell was assigned to Group Headquarters as Deputy Group Commander. Information came down from higher headquarters that major targets for June were to be rail communications, oil production facilities, aircraft factories and assembly plants, in that order of priority.

June 2, 1944 Miskolc Marshaling Yards and Repair Facilities, Hungary.

My crew was selected to fly on this two-credit mission into Hungary to bomb the Miskolc marshaling yards, rolling stock, and repair facilities. We were finally able to fly this mission with our beloved "Porky," with a new nose wheel. We flew in the number 4 position of the 1st Box of the 1st Unit. An intelligence officer flew with us on this mission, I believe it was our friend Lt. Gilbert W. Smith, and T/Sgt Delaney our radio operator notes in his diary that our crew had fun with him. Smith lost his helmet!

We also had bombardier F/O Werner "Judge" Foss fly with us for the first time (the first of nine times) because his pilot, Lt. Stan Sagert was flying deputy-lead of our formation beside Capt. Weston Hyde our Squadron Operations Officer. They used a lead bombardier, Lt. Fred Riley (currently president of our 456th Bomb Group Association) for the mission. Our navigator had been wounded and was in the hospital and our regular bombardier, Lt. James J. Duston was also a navigator, so Foss filled out our crew. Foss noted that since we had an S-2 Intelligence officer volunteer to fly with us, it defined the mission as a two-fer milk run. That is not quite what it turned out to be, and although we had no fighter attacks, we did have some flak that damaged three of our Liberators. The Intelligence officer listened to enemy radio transmissions and he told us some interesting things about the Luftwaffe ground control of their planes.

We expected strong opposition as usual in this area, but no enemy aircraft attacked our Group formation so the Luftwaffe must be getting weak. We had no planes lost. We were briefed to have two groups of P-38s that were to give our Wing target and withdrawal escort fighter cover, but we never saw them. However, they must have done a good job of protecting us or they were out dogfighting somewhere.

C O N F I D E N T I A L

BATTLE ORDER

2 June 1944

1st Unit, 1st Box

Callan

Formation Leader: Abernathy, / AP 791   Hyde

No. 3: Leathers   AP 912   Dep Leader: Sagert, / AP 227
                    No. 4: Capps   AP 306
No. 6: Wood   AP 489   No. 5: Voshell   AP 201

2nd Box

Leader: Gutting   AP 442

No. 3: Ragland   AP 256   Dep Leader: Hundley   AP 853
                    No. 4: Smith   AP 831
No. 6: Ashley   AP 486   No. 5: Doan   AP 934
                    No. 7: Walker   AP 203

3rd Box

Leader: Lesnewski   AP 309

No. 3: Miller   AP 807   Dep Leader: Solcher   AP 810
                    No. 4: Flemming AP 334
No. 6: Blewitt   AP 113   No. 5: Wilkinson   AP 329
                    No. 7: Phillips AP 304

2nd Unit, 1st Box

Monahan

Leader: Clark, W.D., / AP 768

No. 3: Webster   AP 098   Dep Leader: Rudd   AP 295
                    No. 4: Mapn   AP 485
No. 6: Powell   AP 947   No. 5: Gosa   AP 493

2nd Box

Leader: Bishop   AP 284

No. 3: Satterly   AP 777   Dep Leader: Chandler   AP 328
                    No. 4: Ward   AP 637
No. 6: Tosalli   AP 364   No. 5: Strombom   AP 293
                    No. 7: Ogden   AP 225

3rd Box

Leader: Lee   AP 279

No. 3: Bruce   AP 275   Dep Leader: Nix   AP 290
                    No. 4: Jones, E.C. AP 799
No. 6: Whitaker   AP 319   No. 5: Huls   AP 072

Stations: 0505.   456th "ROADTLAMB FOUR"

Engines: A 0510 B 0515 C 0520   Fighters: 1st FG - "FRONTROOM"
         D 0525 E 0530 F 0535   82nd FG - "PULPWOOD"

Take-off: 0530B.

Copy of the Original
456th Bomb Group Battle Order
Source: National Archives, Wash. D.C.

384

There was an early 0300 hour wake-up call in our tents, after our hasty C-ration breakfast, briefing began at 0400, and stations time at our aircraft was 0505. I was flying in the #4 position of the !st Box of the !st Unit, so my start engines time was 0510 hours and the other five Boxes of the formation started their engines at 5 minute intervals after the 1st Box. Captain Louis M. Abernathy of the 745th Squadron was in the lead aircraft, and he taxied out at 0520, then took off at 0530 hours. Thirty-four of our B-24s followed him off the runway at 45 second intervals. Two bombers returned to our base before bombing because one had an oxygen leak, and one had a supercharger malfunction. This was a low abort rate. Both planes returned their bombs to our base.

After assembly of our Group formation, we rendezvoused with the 455th Group over Stornara at 4,000 feet. The battle order for our Wing formation this day had the 459th group and the 454th group flying in a lead element of groups, in that order, to bomb the Miskolc South Marshaling Yards. The 455th and 456th Groups, flying in that order, bombed the Miskolc East Marshaling Yards. Our groups departed Stornara at 0630 hours, with the groups climbing on course at 160 MPH indicated airspeed, a true airspeed of about 200 MPH, and the rate of climb of 250 feet per minute to 15,000 feet altitude, then the rate of climb was reduced to 150 feet per minute until the 1st Unit reached its bombing altitude of 21,000 feet. Our route of flight took us over Sipan Island, Podgrab, Sotin, to the Initial Point of Polgar (Communist rule after the war changed many of these names) for our bomb run on the Miskolc East Marshaling Yards.

Weather over Italy was clear, but it gradually became worse as we flew north. Cloud coverage, by altocumulus clouds below us, gradually increased to five-tenths coverage, with cloud bases at 9.000 feet and tops at 15,000 feet. As we flew further north the weather over the target area became worse. The target was obscured by seven to nine-tenths cloud coverage with altostratus clouds, bases at 16,000 feet and tops at 19,000 feet. Temperature at 21,500 feet was minus 17 degrees.

As expected for the area, flak was scant, accurate, with heavy black bursts. Flak was encountered at Szeged, Szentes, and the target area. Only three of our bombers were hit by flak. No fighters we seen, a further indication of Allied domination of the sky over Europe just prior to the scheduled invasion of Project Overlord. From an I.P. of Polgar, thirty-three of our Group's B-24s were reported to drop 81.5 tons of 500 pound general purpose bombs (326 bombs) on the Miskolc East Marshaling Yards at 0915 hours from an altitude of 22,000 feet for the 1st Unit, and from 21,000 feet for the 2nd Unit. The indicated airspeed for the bomb run was the usual 160 MPH, about a true airspeed of 230 MPH. The axis of attack was 321 degrees magnetic, and the bombardiers' bomb release interval setting was 60 feet. On "Porky", our intervolemeter did not work, and we salvoed the bombs on the target in a bunch.

The rally after bombs away was a descending left turn at 155 to 160 MPH indicated airspeed, at 220 to 230 MPH true airspeed. We had six K-22 cameras taking pictures, but the target was obscured with clouds so that bomb results could not be evaluated.

All 33 bombers of our Group formation returned safely to our airbase at 1225 hours and there were no casualties. I logged 7 hours by the time "Porky" was on the ground. This was our Group's 53rd credited mission of 61 missions flown in Italy. It was my 35th and 36th accredited missions and I now had a total of 170 hours and 25 minutes combat flying time.

June 3, 1944 No Mission Today.

The weather was bad everywhere.

June 4, 1944 Genoa Harbor and Marshaling Yards, Italy.

My crew wasn't selected to fly on this mission, but we flew another crew to the aircraft depot to pick up another bomber for our Group. I logged two flights this day, one going and one coming, each took 1 hour and 10 minutes.

This was the day that the Allies occupied Rome, indicating that the ground forces were on the move north.

The Group was briefed to bomb Alessandria Marshaling Yards (about 55 miles northwest of Genoa), but bad weather at this primary target required the Group to bomb a target of opportunity, the Genoa Harbor and Marshaling Yards instead. No enemy aircraft were encountered and the flak was scant, accurate, with ugly, heavy black bursts. Four of the Group's bombers were damaged by flak, but no planes were lost, and there were no casualties. Bomb results were good. There were bomb hits on the north choke-point of the railroad, the center of the marshaling yards, and hits were scored on considerable rolling stock, tracks, and buildings. Many hits were also made on the Ansaldo Steel Plant.

It was another early morning wake-up call for aircrews, at 0400 hours, briefing was conducted at 0515, stations time at their planes was set for 0625, start engines time for the 1st Box at 0630, taxi out at 0640, and takeoff at 0650 for the first B-24 and 36 bombers followed the leader off the runway at 45 second intervals. Three aircraft returned before reaching the target, one because of a fuel leak, one had a malfunctioning propeller governor, and one lost generators while the Group was enroute to the target and it had to turn back.

Thirty-four bombers flew over the target but only 33 were able to drop their bombs because one plane had a bomb rack malfunction that prevented it from dropping its bombs.

387

That plane returned its bombs to our airbase and landed with them. Thus, 33 planes dropped 80 tons of 500 pound general purpose bombs (320 bombs) on the Genoa Dock and Marshaling Yards at 1057 hour from 20,000 feet for the 1st Unit and from 19,000 feet for the 2nd Unit. Bombs were dropped at an indicated airspeed of 160 MPH, which was about 226 MPH true airspeed.

Thirty-four B-24s returned safely over the field in the Group formation at 1322 hours. Flight time was 6 hours and 35 minutes. It was the Group's 54th credited mission of 62 missions flown in Italy. There were no aircraft lost, only four damaged, and no casualties.

June 5, 1944   No Mission.

Weather was too bad all around to allow a mission today.

June 6, 1944   Brasov Marshaling Yards, Rumania. (Today Was Also The Allied Invasion of the Normandy Peninsula in France from England.)

This was the day of the famous Operation Overlord, the invasion of France from England, and the Allies had overwhelming air superiority over the battlefield. Only a token showing by two Luftwaffe planes was all the Germans could muster to oppose the massive armada and thousands of planes that participated in the invasion. The Allies had won the battle for control of the air over Europe! Six months ago it didn't appear to aircrews in the heavy bomber groups as though it would happen. Although we would continue to see sporadic groups of enemy fighters attack us occasionally on our future missions, the Allies now had undisputed control of the air over Europe. Our long range fighter escort, the P-38J Lightnings and P-51 Mustangs, coupled with the massive numbers of heavy bombers that kept coming was more than the Luftwaffe could handle.

My crew wasn't selected to fly on this day's mission
to bomb the Brasov Marshaling Yards in Rumania. Brasov
was about 65 miles north of Ploesti, so stiff opposition was

C O N F I D E N T I A L

6 June 1944

BATTLE ORDER

1st Unit: 1st Box

Formation Leader: Ladd, Witkin AP 889   Griffin
No. 3: Toselli   AP 364   Dep Leader: Lambort/ AP 791
            No. 4: Strombom   AP 912
No. 6: Whitaker   AP 493   No. 5: Blackwell   AP 284

2nd Box

            Leader: Newhouse   AP 777
No. 3: Leathers   AP 637   Dep Leader: Hall   AP 328
            No. 4: Webster   AP 098
No. 6: Ogden   AP 225   No. 5: Rawlinson   AP 293
            No. 7: Coretti   AP 485

3rd Box

            Leader: Rudd   AP 338
No. 3: Luther   AP 501   Dep Leader: Bruce   AP 275
            No. 4: Jones,E.C.   AP 077
No. 6: Powell   AP 947   No. 5: Hula   AP 285
            No. 7: Dean   AP 934

2nd Unit: 1st Box

            Leader: Tavol,Ecker   AP 227
No. 3: Savage   AP 807   Dep Leader: Nix   AP 233
            No. 4: Palis   AP 487
No. 6: Ragland   AP 256   No. 5: Blewitt   AP 113
            No. 7: Voshell   AP 201

2nd Box

            Leader: Johnson   AP 831
No. 3: Addis   AP 489   Dep Leader: Hundley   AP 853
            No. 4: Smith   AP 486
No. 6: Scott   AP 442   No. 5: Gullick   AP 306
            No. 7: Wood   AP 8275

3rd Box

            Leader: Lessewski   AP 309
No. 3: Wilkinson   AP 329   Dep Leader: Flemming   AP 749
            No. 4: Little   AP 334
No. 6: Solohor   AP 810   No. 5: Phillips   AP 882
            No. 7: Miller   AP 203

Stations: 0450.   456th, "FALSETEETH ONE"

Engines: A 0455 B 0500 C 0505   Penetration: RETAIN
        D 0510 E 0515 F 0520
                              304th Wing Escort: RINGWAY
Take-off: 0520.
                              Recall Signal: LOOSELIP

expected. Although the Group was attacked by two Me-109s, none of our bombers were lost and only one B-24 had damage from flak. There were no reported casualties.

Crews were awakened at the early hour of 0230 hours, briefing was held at the early hour of 0340, and stations time at the aircraft was 0450 hours. Captain Chester R. Ladd was in the lead aircraft. He started his engines at 0455, taxied out at 0510, and took off at 0520 hours. Thirty-eight B-24s followed him off the runway at 45 second intervals. Only one B-24 returned to our airfield prior to bombing because it lost an engine enroute to the target.

After the Group's bombers had been assembled in its six Box formation, they were joined at 3,000 feet over Stornara by the 455th Group that followed our Group's lead to the target. The Wing formation of groups departed Stornara climbing on course at 0615 hours, at 160 MPH indicated airspeed, about 200 MPH true airspeed, and 250 feet per minute rate of climb to 15,000 feet. When it reached 15,000 feet, the formation began to climb at a reduced rate of climb, 150 feet per minute, until the bombing altitude of 19,000 feet for the 1st Unit was reached.

The route to the target took the formation through Yugoslavia to the initial point, Sercaia (Name changed by Communist rule after the war). Cruising speed of the formatiion was 165 MPH indicated airspeed, about 226 MPH true airspeed. Weather enroute was clear all the way to the target. Below the formation at the target there was three-tenths of altostratus cloud coverage, bases at 10,000 feet and tops at 11,000 feet. Above the formation there was a thin cirrus, one-tenth coverage, bases at 22,000 feet and tops at 23,000 feet. The temperature at 19,500 feet was minus 14 degrees centigrade.

Fighter cover was provided by P-38s and P-51s starting at 0845 hours. This did not prevent two Me-109s from attacking our Group formation at 0907 hours, over the target area. The Me-109s came in from the 6 o'clock position and lobbed rockets. The Me-109s were olive-drab in color with red cowling around their engines. Next, two FW-190s (painted olive drab with yellow stripes around their fuselages) and three Me-109s (painted olive-drab with yellow wing tips) were seen at 0925 hours, then two JU-88s were seen later, but none of these later enemy fighters attacked our Group.

Flak was scant, inaccurate, with heavy black bursts. Only one of our bombers was slightly damaged. Thirty-eight bombers flew over the target, but four planes had accidental releases of their bombs over the I.P., before the target was reached. The leader of the 2nd Box of the 1st Unit accidentally released his bombs at the I.P., and three other planes in his box, seeing him drop his bombs, dropped theirs also. Thus, only thirty-four B-24s dropped their bombs on the Brasov Marshaling Yards at 0912 hours from 19,000 feet on an axis of attack of 131 degrees magnetic. They dropped 81 tons of 500 pound general purpose bombs (324 bombs) at 160 MPH indicated airspeed, a true airspeed of 222 MPH. The Group made a descending right turn after dropping its bombs, to confuse flak gunners on the ground, and it flew at a reduced airspeed of 155 MPH indicated, a true airspeed of 210 MPH, to keep the formation tight to defend against enemy fighters.

Twenty-four photos of the target area were taken by six K-22 cameras aboard aircraft in the formation. Bomb results were good. There was a good coverage of the target and one big explosion was observed in the marshaling yards.

Thirty-eight B-24 returned in the Group formation over our airfield at 1237 hours. It was the Group's 55th accredited mission of the 63 missions flown in Italy. Combat flight time logged was 7 hours and 25 minutes by the time planes had landed. No planes lost, one was damaged, and there were no casualties.

391

June 7, 1944 Sovona Marshaling Yards, Italy (Alternate Target).

My crew drew another true milk run this day when it was briefed to bomb Sestri Ponente, Italy, but poor weather over the primary target required the Group to bomb a target of opportunity, the marshaling yards at Savona, Italy which is a couple of miles south west of Genoa. No enemy aircraft were seen, and only scant, inaccurate, heavy black bursts of flak were encountered as we passed near the Island of Elba, famous for a place where Napoleon had been exiled. No damage to aircraft or casualties were reported as a result of this mission. Our beloved "Porky" was being repaired from damage it sustained, and we had to fly "Yo Yo," Lt. Albert M. Lehner's plane from our 746th Squadron. F/O Judge Foss, who had been promoted to 2nd Lt. on June 4, 1944, flew with us as bombardier.

Crews were awakened at 0400 hours, briefing was held at 0500, and stations time at our aircraft was 0600 hours. Captain Louis M. Abernathy of the 745th Squadron was in the lead bomber of the formation, and he started his engines at 0605 hours. The rest of us started engines at five minute intervals, for each Box, afterward. My crew was flying in the #2 position, deputy lead position, of the 2nd Box of the 1st Unit. My copilot 2nd Lt. Sidney H. Brooks and I started our engines at 0610, five minutes after Abernathy's. Abernathy taxied out at 0620 hours, then took off at 0630. Thirty-nine bombers followed his plane off the runway at 45 second intervals. One B-24 returned early because it had a supercharger malfunction.

After the Group formation had gathered around Abernathy's plane, Abernathy led the formation to rendezvous with 455th Group over Stornara at 4,000 feet. Our Group followed the lead of the 455th. The Wing formation departed Stornara at 0725 hours, climbing on course at 160 MPH indicated airspeed, about 200 MPH true

C·O·N·F·I·D·E·N·T·I·A·L

BATTLE ORDER

7 June 1944

1st Unit, 1st Box
Callan
Formation Leader: Abernathy, / AP 889
No. 3: Wood   AP 853   Dep Leader: Mulligan AP 279
No. 4: Williamson AP 810
No. 6: Dean   AP 934   No. 5: Gullick   AP 486

2nd Box
Leader: Gutting AP 442
No. 3: Ragland AP 256   Dep Leader: Capps AP 199
No. 4: Addis   AP 489
No. 6: Scott   AP 8275   No. 5: Ashley   AP 201
No. 7: Blackwell AP 284

3rd Box
Leader: Gardner AP 309
No. 3: Walker   AP 203   Dep Leader: Solcher AP 487
No. 4: Nilsson AP 749
No. 6: Roak   AP 329   No. 5: Blewitt   AP 882
No. 7: Marlar   AP 807

2nd Unit, 1st Box
Gruber
Leader: Clark, W.D./ AP 768
No. 3: Jones, E.C. AP 077   Dep Leader: Monohan AP 334
No. 4: Brabon   AP 799
No. 6: Leathers AP 364   No. 5: Strombom   AP 912

2nd Box
Leader: Lambert AP 072
No. 3: Powell   AP 947   Dep Leader: Nunimaker AP 501
No. 4: Lunt   AP 338
No. 6: Goza   AP 493   No. 5: Luther   AP 233
No. 7: Whitaker AP 319

3rd Box
Leader: Bishop AP 777
No. 3: Rawlinson AP 293   Dep Leader: Mapa AP 485
No. 4: Ward   AP 637
No. 6: Ogden   AP 225   No. 5: Hall   AP 328
No. 7: Shetterly AP 098

Stations: 0600   456th "ENCORE TWO FOUR

Engines: A 0605 B 0610 C 0615   Fighters: PUSSCAT
D 0620 E 0625 F 0630
Recall signal: PENCIL
Take-off: 0630.

airspeed. The rate of climb for the Wing formation was 250 feet per minute until we reached 15,000 feet altitude, then the climb rate was to 150 feet per minute until we reached the bombing altitude for the 1st Unit, 21,000 feet. Our route to the target took us over San Felice Circeo, Pianosa Island (near Elba), Rogliand, then to the Initial Point which was a set of coordinates in the water south of Genoa. The formation cruised to the Initial Point at an indicated airspeed of 165 MPH, about 238 MPH true airspeed.

The weather was not very good enroute to the target, nor at the target. There was nine to ten-tenths cloud coverage below our formation, consisting of altocumulus clouds, bases at 15,000 feet and tops at 18,000 feet. There was five to ten-tenths of thin cirrus above our formation with bases at 20,000 feet. This cloud coverage below our formation prevented the primary target from being seen, so we went to a nearby target of opportunity, marshaling yards at Savona, Italy which had good weather and clear visibility. The temperature at 21,000 feet was minus 12 degrees centigrade.

Thirty-nine B-24s of our Group formation flew over the target, but two bombers had bomb rack release malfunctions that prevented them from dropping their bombs on the target. Thus, 37 aircraft were able to drop 109 tons of huge 1,000 pound general purpose bombs (218 bombs) on the Savona Marshaling Yards from 20,000 feet at 1020 hours at an indicated airspeed of 160 MPH, about 225 MPH true airspeed. The axis of attack was 300 degrees magnetic, and the bombardiers' bomb release interval setting was 25 feet for these big 1,000 pound bombs. Twenty-five photos of the target were taken by six K-22 cameras. Bombing results were rated as good. Tracks, rolling stock, dock installations, and repair shops were hit by the enormous 1,000 pound bombs. A nearby oil storage depot also received a direct hit. Of the six thousand pound bombs we had aboard the ship we were flying, "Yo Yo," two hung up on the left side of the bomb bay, and quick acting bombardier, Lt. Foss salvoed them on the target. They smashed some of our planes' fuel lines and damaged rudder-cable guides, but no fuel leaked and I could control the rudders satisfactorily.

The Group made a descending left turn after bomb release, to foil any flak gunners, but there were none. The thirty-nine B-24s in the Group formation arrived back over our airfield at 1234 hours. I logged 6 hours and 25 minutes by the time my plane was on the ground.

There were no casualties, and all planes returned safely. This was the Group's 56th accredited mission and its 64 mission flown in Italy. It was my 37th accredited mission.

June 8, 1944   No Mission.

Weather at all possible targets were too bad for a mission. No flying this day.

June 9, 1944 Munich East Marshaling Yards, Austria (An Alternat Target).

My crew was not selected to fly on this mission to the Munich area in Austria. However, S/Sgt Thomas S. Delaney my radio operator, was assigned to fly with Lt. Douglas C. Richards' crew in his plane, "Purple Shaft," in the lead position of the 2nd Box of the 1st Unit. Our nose turret gunner, Bill Halper, flew with Lt. Walter Addis' crew of my 746th Squadron and his plane received heavy flak damage.

Crews were originally briefed to bomb the Bayerische Moterenwerk that was producing aircraft engines, but cloud cover of this primary target required the Group to bomb the Munich East Marshaling Yards instead. The Group finally resorted to using Pathfinder radar because that target also had cloud cover.

Each crew's sleep was interrupted in the tents at an early hour, 0315 hours. Crew members had a quick breakfast, followed by a cold trip in the back of open Army six-by-six trucks to attend a briefing at 0415 hours. Stations time at the aircraft was 0520 hours, start engines time for the first aircraft was 0530, taxi out at 0545 hours, and the first B-24 too off at 0555 hours. Thirty-seven bombers followed the lead, taking off at 45 second intervals after him. Three planes returned before reaching the target because one had a sick pilot, one had inoperative top and tail gun turrets, and one had a loss of oil pressure on #4 engine which occurred at 0914 hours, about an hour before target time. This later B-24 was attacked by one Me-109 enemy fighter at 0921 hours as it was returning home, just seven minutes after it left the formation, but the damaged plane and crew were able to return safely to our airbase.

The 304th Wing had P-38s and P-51s as escort fighters, but this did not prevent enemy fighters from attacking stragglers of our bomber formations. At 0921 hours an Me-109 attacked the plane that left our Group formation and returned early because its #4 engine oil pressure was lost. The Me-109 attacked from the eight o'clock high position.

Seven Me-109s were seen attacking stragglers of one of the Wing's other formations at 0852 hours, twenty minutes before the Group reached the target. Fifteen more Me-109s were seen at 0921, and they were engaged by our escort fighters. Ten more enemy fighters were seen in the target area at 1015 hours, but our Wing's escort kept them away and they didn't attack our Group. Our gunners claimed no enemy planes shot down and enemy fighters did not shoot down any of our bombers.

One reason that escort fighters were late arriving to protect the bombers was that P-51s of the 52nd Fighter Group had met some enemy fighters while flying enroute to their assigned rendezvous point to meet the bomber formations. The Group leader recognized that the intention of the enemy fighters was to engage the escort P-51 so they would all drop their drop tanks early, and thus cause them to have insufficient gas to enable them to reach the bomber rendezvous point and provide sufficient escort time for the bombers. The fighter group leader sent a small force of his P-51s to disperse the enemy fighter, then he took the rest of his group to join the bombers as he was supposed to do. When the P-51s finally reached the bombers, their pilots saw the bomber groups with their hands full fending off repeated attacks by enemy fighters. They engaged the enemy fighters, and as a result none of the bombers were lost, none of our fighter escort were lost, and our escort fighters destroyed 14 enemy planes, probably destroyed 2 more, and damaged another.

Radio operator T/Sgt Delaney noted in his diary, ".... Bill Halper (my nose turret gunner) flew with Lt. Addis' crew, and they really caught the flak! Their tail gunner had a piece of flak with his initials on it! They had several holes in their plane..."   Our Group lost no planes to enemy fighters, and none were lost to flak. However, eight of our Group's bombers were damaged from enemy fire, one of them seriously, and there were three members of crews wounded, one of them seriously. Among the wounded were Capt. Walter F. Mulligan of the 744th Squadron who was wounded in the foot, Lt. Charles P. Hundley who received a knee wound, and a top turret gunner was hit in the thigh. The enemy had 268 heavy guns in the target area firing at the Group's formation. The Group also encountered flak over the Udine, Pola, and Regensburg. Over the target, flak was intense and accurate with ugly, heavy black, red, and white bursts. S/Sgt Thomas S. Delaney, my radio operator flying on the "Purple Shaft" with Lt. Douglas Richards crew, said in his diary, "....The flak was plenty thick and accurate over the target. We came through again without a scratch! Thank God!"

The weather in the target area was too bad for visual bombing. The target was covered by altocumulus clouds with tops at 15,000 feet. The Group's Pathfinder radar plane had to find the target through the clouds. It dropped its bombs on the target and all bombardiers of the formation dropped their bombs as soon as they saw the Pathfinder-directed bombs released. The temperature at 23,300 feet was minus 25 degrees centigrade.

There were two different kinds of bombs loaded on the Group's B-24s. The 1st Unit of the formation had bundles of 100 pound incendiaries (AN-M126A1 types) and 19 bombers in that formation dropped 37.7 tons of these (754 bombs) on the Munich East Marshaling Yards at 1012 hours from an altitude of 23,000 feet on an axis of attack of 180 degrees magnetic. The 2nd Unit of the Group formation was loaded with the giant 1,000 pound general purpose bombs and 15 bombers in that Unit dropped 41.5 tons of them (83 bombs) at the same time from an altitude of 21,000 feet on the same axis of attack. Thus, a total of 34 Liberators dropped on the target. One of the planes in the formation, number 275 flown by Lt. Stan Sagert's crew with Lt. Werner "Judge" Foss the bombardier, had a bomb rack malfunction that caused one of his 1,000 pound bombs to hang up after his other four big bombs were released. After trying to repair the problem at high altitude, using a portable oxygen walk-around bottle in the bomb bay, Foss decided to return his bomb to our airbase. Two planes carrying the 100 pound incendiary bombs had six of them hang up in the bomb bay, and they were brought back to our base. After bombs were away, the Group made a descending left turn to confuse the aim of flak gunners.

Results of the bombing could not be accurately assessed because the target was covered by clouds, but many of the crews were able to see, through breaks in the clouds, bombs falling on the marshaling yards. The majority of crews could not see the target. Seventeen photos were taken by six K-22 cameras, but all they were able to see were parts of the target through occasional breaks in the clouds.

The Group's formation of 34 Liberators returned to our airbase at 1251 hours. Flying time was 7 hours. This was the Group's 57th credited mission and its 65th mission flown in Italy. There were no bombers lost from this mission, only eight damaged, one of them severely. There were three personnel casualties. One pilot was hit seriously by flak, another pilot was slightly injured below the knee by flak, and a top turret gunner was hit slightly by flak.

June 10, 1944 Ferrara Airdrome, Italy .

My crew was selected to fly this short, 4 hour and 5 minute mission to bomb the Ferrara airdrome in Italy, and I had another short flight in the afternoon to pick up a new B-24J at the aircraft replacement depot. Except for the fact that we encountered flak at the target that damaged seven of our Group's planes, and one bombardier was hit by flak, it was a milk run. Flak was moderate and accurate with ugly, heavy black bursts. No enemy aircraft were seen, there were no casualties other than the bombardier, and all of our aircraft returned safely to our airbase. I flew our wonderful "Porky' on the mission, and I had another good bombardier temporarily filling in on our crew with our regular navigator-bombardier Duston, Lt. Werner C. "Judge" Foss. We were able to "sleep in" until 0515 hours this morning, briefing was held at 0620, stations time at our aircraft was at 0730, and start engines time for the first Box was set for 0735 hours, but this was delayed for ten minutes, for some reason. Then the lead plane with Captain Louis M. Abernathy of the 745th Squadron flying it taxied out to the end of the runway and took off ten minutes late at 0755 hours. Thirty-six bombers followed him off the runway at 45 second intervals. My position in the Group formation, flying "Porky," was number 3 in the 2nd Box of the 2nd Unit. As usual, there were six Boxes in the Group formation.

S E C R E T
BATTLE ORDER

10 June 1944

1st Unit: 1st Box

Formation Leader: ABERNATHY, Callan AP 791
No. 3: Brabon   AP 799   Dep Leader: REID, Witkin 279
                            No. 4: Nunimaker AP 338
No. 6: Dysinger   AP 501   No. 5: Hendrickson   AP 947

2nd Box

Leader: Rudd   AP 295
No. 3: Bruce   AP 275   Dep Leader: Lambert   AP 072
                            No. 4: Jones   AP 077
No. 6: Whitaker   AP 319   No. 5: Goza   AP 493

3rd Box

Leader: Newhouse AP 777
No. 3: Ogden   AP 225   Dep Leader: Rawlinson AP 293
                            No. 4: Blackwell AP 364
No. 6: Shetterly   AP 485   No. 5: Hall   AP 912
                            No. 7: Ceretti   AP 284

2nd Unit, 1st Box

Leader: GRUBER, Clark, W.D. AP 768
No. 3: Johnson   AP 8275   Dep Leader: Webster   AP 098
                            No. 4: Williamson AP 810
No. 6: Hill   AP 199   No. 5: Scott   AP 256
                            No. 7:   AP _____

2nd Box

Leader: Ensign   AP 486
No. 3: Capps   AP 306   Dep Leader: Hundly   AP 853
                            No. 4: Smith   AP 489
No. 6: Dean   AP 934   No. 5: Wood   AP 201
                            No. 7: Gullick   AP 442

3rd Box

Leader: Gardner   AP 309
No. 3: Solcher   AP 882   Dep Leader: Nilsson   AP 304
                            No. 4: Wilkinson AP 329
No. 6: Marler   AP 113   No. 5: Reicher   AP 334
                            No. 7: Walker   AP 203

456 BG: SEARCHLIGHT THREE   RECALL: LOOSELIP.
52nd FG: DAYLONG

Stations: 0730. Start Engines: A 0735   B 0740   C 0745
                               D 0750   E 0755   F 0800
Taxi Out: 0745. Take-off: 0755.

S E C R E T

Again, we saw a 459th Bomb Group Liberator crash and burn on takeoff. The flames and large plume of smoke at the end of the runway was clearly visible as we circled to form our Group. We are becoming more convinced that it is sabotage, and the rumors are growing that it was. We have had no crashes on takeoff in the 456th Group, as precarious as our takeoffs were, while the 459th has had many.

After catching up with the Abernathy's lead plane and forming our Group formation, we were joined by other groups of the 304th Wing over Stornara at 4,000 feet. The Wing formation of groups, with the 456th Group leading, departed Stornara climbing on course at 0847 hours. The rate of climb was 250 feet per minute and 160 MPH indicated airspeed, about 210 MPH true airspeed, until we reached 15,000 feet altitude, then the rate of climb was reduced to 150 FPM until 21,000 feet was reached. As a tribute to our hard working ground crew, there were no early returns from this mission, all 37 bombers flew over the target. Once at altitude our cruise speed to the Initial Point, Porto Maggiore, was at 165 MPH indicated airspeed, about 238 MPH true airspeed this day.

Our Wing had long range P-38Js and P-51s for escort, starting at 0944, about 45 minutes before target time, but they were not needed. We only saw 10 Italian Macchi 202s flying at 19,000 feet at 1045, but they didn't attack our formation. Maybe they were some Italian pilots just getting flying time since Italy had already surrendered to the Allies.

The weather enroute had our formation covered with seven to ten-tenths of cirrostratus clouds above us. The cirrus had bases at 22,000 feet for the entire route. Below us, enroute, we had three-tenths cloud cover with bases at 6,000 feet and tops at 8,000 feet.

Weather in the target area, below our bomber formation, was composed of two cloud formations. One cloud formation had one-tenth cloud cover with bases at 3,000 feet and tops

401

at 12,000 feet, and the other cloud coverage below us had three-tenths altocumulus cloud coverage with bases at 8,000 feet and tops at 15,000 feet. The cloud cover above us was the same cirrus coverage that we had enroute. The temperature at 21,000 feet was minus 15 degrees centigrade.

Flak at the target was moderate, accurate, with ugly black bursts. We also encountered some flak enroute at Rimini and Porto Garibaldi. Seven of our bombers had flak damage and one bombardier was hit.

From the Initial Point, Porto Maggiore, on an axis of attack of 305 degrees magnetic, 37 bombers flew over the target. Three bombers had bomb rack malfunctions that prevented them from dropping on the target, and they brought their bombs back home. Thus, 34 of our Group's B-24s dropped 79.98 tons of 20 pound fragmentation bombs (7,998 of them) on the Ferrara Airdrome at 1037 hours from 21,000 feet for the 1st Unit of the formation and 20,000 feet for the 2nd Unit. The indicated airspeed was 160 MPH, a true airspeed of 228 MPH. S/Sgt Delaney's diary recorded that Judge Foss, our replacement bombardier, had trouble with the bombs and he had to salvo some of them. Delaney saw the bombs hit right on some hangers and JU-88 planes. It was a good job of bombing.

After bombs were dropped, the Group formation made a descending left turn to confuse flak gunners, staying north and east of Altedo, Italy, to avoid another flak area. Six K-22 cameras took pictures of the target area and bombing results were rated as fair. Many hits were scored on the main target area, including the aircraft dispersal area, hangars, and crew living quarters.

Our Group formation of 37 bombers returned to our airbase at 1227 hours. There were no planes lost, only 7 damaged from flak, and there were no casualties.

On this day, the Fifteenth Air Force sent the 82nd Fighter Group of P-38 Lightnings, each loaded with a single 1,000 pound bomb, on a low level mission to bomb the Romano Americano Oil Refinery, with the intent of bombing it before people on the ground had sufficient warning to allow them to start their smoke screens. This was the Fifteenth's number one target. They were escorted by other P-38s. Their mission succeeded, and the P-38s were able to pick out the specific targets they had studied before smoke pots were started. They dropped thirty-six 1,000 pound bombs, hit a cracking plant, and a storage tank went up in flames. Three refinery units were partially damaged.

June 11, 1944   Giurgiu Quay Railroad Sidings, Rumania.

My crew was selected to fly "Porky" on this mission, its second day of flying in succession. Our Group's target was seventy miles due south of Ploesti. It was the Giurgiu Quay Railroad Sidings in Rumania, the west half. We had excellent flying weather with ceiling and visibility unlimited (CAVU) the entire route and at the target. Although eight Me-109s were seen, they didn't attack. We lost no bombers, and only one plane was damaged by flak. We had no casualties. Again we were able to fly our Porky but we had some problem with the bomb bay doors after we dropped our bombs.

It was another extremely early wake-up call in our tents, at 0245 hours in the dark, briefing was conducted at 0345, stations time at our planes was 0455, start engines for the first Box was 0505, and the lead plane with Major Robert L. Reid flying it taxied out to the end of the runway at the early hour of 0515. Major Reid took off at 0525 and 40 of us followed him off the runway at 45 second intervals. Lt. Dave E. Tavel was in the lead plane of the 2nd Unit. I was flying "Porky" in the deputy lead, the #2 position, of the 2nd Box of the 2nd Unit. Five B-24s returned before reaching the target; one had a gas leak due to a gas cap being left loose, two had turbo-superchargers out, and two had engines

CONFIDENTIAL

BATTLE ORDER

11 June 1944

1st Unit, 1st Box

Formation Leader: Maj. REID. Thomas AP 817

No. 3: Hall	AP 345	Dep Leader: PARKS, Palis	AP 764
		No. 4: Ward AP 768	
No. 6: Powell	AP 947	No. 5: Strombom	AP 912
		No. 7: Loathers AP 098	

2nd Box

Leader: Bishop   AP 328

No. 3: Rawlinson	AP 293	Dep Leader: Mapa	AP 485
		No. 4: Riddle AP 777	
No. 6: Toselli	AP 364	No. 5: Richscheidt	AP 225
		No. 7: Klinger AP 284	

3rd Box

Leader: Phifer   AP 501

No. 3: Dengler	AP 338	Dep Leader: Nix	AP 233
		No. 4: Lunt AP 799	
No. 6: Whitaker	AP 319	No. 5: Cava	AP 493
		No. 7: Huls AP 285	

2nd Unit, 1st Box

Leader: Taval, Eckor AP 227

No. 3: Scott	AP 256	Dep Leader: Monahan	AP 487
		No. 4: Laszewski AP 309	
No. 6: Gullick	AP 486	No. 5: Hill	AP 199
		No. 7: Hendrickson AP 295	

2nd Box

Leader: Gutting   AP 831

No. 3: Shober	AP 8275	Dep Leader: Capps	AP 306
		No. 4: Addis AP 489	
No. 6: Dean	AP 934	No. 5: Wood	AP 201
		No. 7: Ashley AP 853	

3rd Box

Leader: Douglass   AP 304

No. 3: Marler	AP 203	Dep Leader: Savage	AP 377
		No. 4: Wilkinson AP 329	
No. 6: Solcher	AP 810	No. 5: Phillips	AP 882
		No. 7: Roicher AP 113	

Time at stations: 0455

Engines: A 0505 B 0510 C 0515
         D 0520 E 0525 F 0530

Take-off: 0525   Recall: PAPER

456th RETAIN, ONE THREE
Penetration escort: 1st FG- FLYWHEEL
ONE
Target and withdrawal cover: 14th FG-
FLYWHEEL TWO

404

malfunction and their propellers had to be feathered. After we formed our Group formation, we rendezvoused with the 455th Group over Stornara at 4,000 feet before departing at 0617, climbing on course at 160 MPH indicated airspeed, about 210 MPH true airspeed, and 250 feet per minute rate of climb until we reached 15,000 feet, then the rate of climb was reduced to 150 FPM until the bombing altitude of the 1st Unit, 19,500 feet was reached. Our route to the target took us over Kolaj, Prizen, Rosiorii De Vede, to the I.P., Draganesti (note that many names of these cities were changed by Communists when they took control of them after the war).

We had one group of P-38s escorting us starting at 0734, about an hour and twenty minutes before our target time. Eight Me-109s were seen, but our escort kept them away so that none attacked our Group.

It was beautiful flying weather, CAVU all the way. The temperature at 20,100 feet was a relatively warm minus 15 degrees centigrade. We had scant, inaccurate flak at Batulvce, and at the target, the flak was moderate, fairly accurate, with ugly, heavy black and red bursts. Only one of our bombers had flak damage, and there were no casualties. We were not supposed to take evasive action by maneuvering our planes while in formation on the bomb run. However, on later missions, we had someone in the nose of the aircraft toggle the bombs when they saw the lead aircraft drop its bombs on the target, after it had synchronized its bomb sight on the target. On some occasions, when I saw the tracking flak getting close to our aircraft, I would make a small adjustment to the right or left, so the next stick of radar controlled or visually controlled antiaircraft guns would not hit us. On this day, I watched each successive stick of flak bursts getting closer to our plane dead in front of us, and made a slight adjustment by moving "Porky" a few feet to the right. S/Sgt Thomas S. Delaney reported in his diary, after talking with S/Sgt William E. Halper, our nose gunner who always watched and sweated out flak bursts tracking our flight, because he was riding in the nose turret in front of our Liberator, "...The flak was heavy, intense, and accurate! Lt. Capps turned the plane to the right just in time, six straight flak bursts hit where we were! Thank the Lord!"

Thirty-six B-24s flew over the target, but one had a bomb release malfunction and couldn't release its bombs on the target. Thirty-five bombers released 75.1 tons of 250 pound general purpose bombs (601 bombs) on the Giurgiu Quay Railroad Sidings in Rumania, the west half, at 0900 hours from 20,500 feet altitude for the 1st Unit and 19,500 feet for the 2nd Unit at 160 MPH indicated airspeed, a true airspeed of 224 MPH. The axis of attack was on a heading of 130 degrees magnetic from the Initial Point, Draganesti. The bombardier's bomb release interval setting was 50 feet. The front right bomb bay door on "Porky" would not close after our bombs were released, even after someone walked out on the cold catwalk and tried the hand crank to close them, so we had to fly home and land with the door open. I carefully controlled our plane's fuel consumption so we would have enough fuel to make it home with the extra drag generated on our plane by the open door.

Six K-22 cameras took photos of the target area on this clear day, and the bombing results were rated as fair, because of the number of bombs hitting the briefed aiming point. Crews saw a good coverage of the target area. S/Sgt Thomas S. Delaney on my crew reported seeing the bombs hit right in the target. Photos showed that bombs fell across oil loading sidings and facilities. Rail tracks and rolling stock were hit, and hits on oil tanks caused many large fires. Two large barges received direct hits. A strings of bombs carried across oil loading sidings and the quayside, scoring direct hits on facilities, trackage, and rolling stock. Eighteen percent of bombs seen in the photos were within 1,000 feet of the aiming point and 57 percent were within 2,000 feet.

After bombs away, the formation made a descending right turn at 155 to 160 MPH indicated airspeed, about 210 to 224 MPH true airspeed, to foil flak gunners, and the slow speed was to enable the pilots to keep a tight formation in defense against possible enemy fighter attack.

All 36 planes in the formation returned over our airbase at 1211 hours. The combat flying time was 6 hours and 45 minutes. It was the Group's 59 credited mission and the 67th mission flown in Italy. It was my 39th and 40th credited missions, a "two-fer," and I now had 187 hours and 55 minutes of combat flying time. No planes were lost, only one Liberator had flak damage, and we had no reported casualties.

June 12, 1944   No Mission. (Rest and Recuperation on the Isle of Capri).

There was no mission this day because of bad weather. However, this was a day that my crew was selected to take a week's leave. We had a choice of going to the Isle of Capri or spending the time touring southern Italy. Rome was still occupied by Germans, so my copilot 2nd Lt Sidney H. Brooks, our bombardier 2nd Lt. James J. Duston, and I went to the magical Capri. We spent a few days of rest, relaxation and sight seeing. The ruins where the Roman Emperor Tiberius lived was there. The weather, beaches and water were great. The Fifteenth Air Force had taken over some hotels and their restaurants on the island, to be used by aircrews as a rest camp after they had finished flying a certain number of missions. Our Group provided us with a Jeep to drive to Naples where we caught a ferry that took us to the Island. We met another couple of officers from our Group who were returning from Capri at the ferry dock, and they used the Jeep to drive it back to our airfield.

We had a flat tire in a rural area on the way to Naples. While we were changing the wheel of the Jeep, a grubby, dirty, unshaven Italian farmer came over to our Jeep. He had come out of a very low grade, rustic farm hut that had an animal skin for a door and a dirt floor. He looked like he was not far removed from the standard of living of stone-age man. To our great surprise, he said "hello" in excellent English and he talked with a clear Brooklyn accent. He asked us where we were from. After some conversation, while we continued to change the wheel, he explained that he had gone to Brooklyn as a small boy with his parents, attended American schools, worked most of his life in the United States, saved his money, then came to Italy with a small pension, bought this farm, and farmed it to the present time. He seemed to enjoy talking with us.

The Island of Capri was a wonderful, restful, luxurious experience. We had very good accommodations and there were excellent, first-class restaurants in the hotels run by highly skilled Italians. The famous British entertainer, Gracie Fields, owned a large luxurious villa on the island that had a private beach, and she turned it over to the Allied Forces to use as an officers' club. We could swim on her private beach in the clear blue water of the Tyrrhenian Sea, then go into her beautiful villa in our bathing suits, to eat a well prepared and fabulous buffet lunch. It was something far removed from the canned and dehydrated C-ration meals we ate at our airbase, prepared by Army-trained cooks. I can readily understand why the Roman Emperor, Tiberius, decided to make his castle here and live the last years of his life from 26 to 37 A.D on Capri.

There were about three or four hotels where we could eat splendid dinners, which were a far cry from the standard canned "C" rations we were used to having. We were waited on in high style by waiters wearing tuxedos and in the best Continental style. It was a great change from our rough tent life and eating off metal mess kits at our airbase. More important, we didn't have to worry about flying combat missions for a few days. Many meals were served outside on a beautiful verandah, in beautiful June weather, surrounded by hibiscus and blooms of other fragrant flowers. For the first time, I experienced flaming crepe suzettes for desert, served with a flare, by excellent waiters. It was a luxury that almost all of us, in our early twenties, had never experienced before.

Mt. Vesuvius the volcano on the mainland south of Naples, twenty-five miles away, had erupted a few weeks earlier than our visit to Capri. It spouted volcanic ash all the way to Capri, and a thin film of volcanic dust covered everything. We heard that seventy-five B-25 Mitchell twin-engine bombers that were positioned on an airfield at the base of Vesuvius were destroyed by giant rocks that the volcanic eruption rained on them. It was an airfield that one of our Group's heavy bombers had used to make an emergency landing on earlier.

It was difficult to leave that dreamland on Capri, far removed from the realities of war, when our few wonderful days on the beautiful island came to an end. We had to return to reality, the constant threat to our lives, and the rustic style of living we were accustomed to at our airbase. We had to start sweating out combat missions again.

June 13, 1944 Bayerische Motorern Werke, Munich, Germany.

While Lt. Sidney Brooks and myself were still enjoying the good life on the Isle of Capri, the Group flew a very rough mission to bomb the Bayerische Motorern Werke at Munich, Germany. The Group lost two planes on the mission, and another bomber, "Purple Shaft," was so damaged by flak that it never flew another mission. A total of fifteen bombers were damaged on this mission.

C O N F I D E N T I A L

BATTLE ORDER

13 June 1944

1st Unit, 1st Box

Blythe

Formation Leader: Col. STEED, / AP 809   Griffin

No. 3: Gullick   AP 485   Dep Leader: Lambert, / AP 817

No. 4: Laszewski AP 30:

No. 6: Scott   AP 199   No. 5: Shober   AP 487

2nd Box

Leader: Richards AP 489

No. 3: Ragland   AP 255   Dep Leader: Sagert AP 8275

No. 4: Smith   AP 854

No. 6: Ashley   AP 934   No. 6: Marsh   AP 442

No. 7: Bood   A. 621

3rd Box

Leader: Gardner AP 4487

No. 3: Menchan   AP 113   Dep Leader: Nilsson AP 810

No. 4: Little   AP 744

No. 6: Fulton   AP 203   No. 5: Peak   AP 177

No. 7: Wilkinson AP 847

2nd Unit, 1st Box

Leader: Jackson AP 279

No. 3: Jones   AP 077   Dep Leader: Nunimaker AP 338

No. 4: Ward   AP 345

No. 6: Ogden   AP 225   No. 5: Shetterly AP 768

No. 7: Dysinger AP 283

2nd Box

Leader: Rudd   AP 295

No. 3: Bruce   AP 2275   Dep Leader: Dengler AP 285

No. 4: Hillman, (Graber) AP 319

No. 6: Powell   AP 947   No. 5: Hulв   AP 493

No. 7: Luther   AP 290

3rd Box

Leader: LeuXuma AP 313

No. 3: Klinger   AP 465   Dep Leader: Webster AP 098

No. 4: Riddle   AP 777

No. 6: Blackwell AP 912   No. 5: Richtscheidt AP 328

No. 7: Ceretti AP 364

Spares: 747th Sqdn: 284,
744th Sqdn: 739

Stations: 0550

Engines: A 0555 B 0600 C 0605
D 0610 E 0615 F 0620

Take-off: 0615.

456th: "BOULDER THREE ONE"

1st FG: "PIXIE TWO"

Recall Signal: CLASS

325th FG: "PIXIE FIVE"

410

It was another early wake-up call for the crews, at 0345 hours, briefing at 0445, stations time at the aircraft was 0550, and the first Box started engines at 0555. Colonel Steed, in the lead plane, taxied out to the end of the runway at 0605, then took off at 0615. Thirty-eight B-24s followed him off the runway at 45 second intervals. Five of these planes aborted the mission and returned to our airbase before reaching enemy territory. One plane returned to our airbase because of an oil leak, two returned because they had engines go out, one returned because a generator malfunctioned, and one bomber had to return because a turbo-supercharger malfunctioned.

After the Group formation was assembled around Colonel Steed's plane, he led the formation over Stornara at 3,000 feet to rendevous with other groups of our 304th Wing. The formation of groups departed Stornara, climbing on course at 0707hours, flying at 160 MPH indicated airspeed, about 210 MPH true airspeed. The rate of climb was 250 feet per minute until reaching 15,000 feet, then the formation climbed at the reduced rate of climb, 150 FPM, until the 1st Unit's bombing altitude of 21,000 feet was reached. The navigation route took the formation over Tremiti Island, Caorle, Chiem Lake, Landshut, then to the I.P. of Illumnster, Germany, before bombing the target at Munich.

Many Fifteenth Air Force heavy bombers were dispatched on this day to bomb in the Munich general area in a coordinated attack. Fighter escort was provided by P-51s and P-38Js starting at Chiem lake, but this did not stop 21 enemy fighters from attacking our Group's formation. Enemy fighter attacks started at 0905 hours, before the Wing's fighter escort rendezvous, about 1 hour and 10 minutes before the Group was scheduled to reach its Initial Point. Evidently the Luftwaffe knew when the Group's fighter escort would meet the heavy bombers, either by tracking the fighters by radar or from information provided by spy planes in the air. Ten FW-190s attacked singly over the Udine area from the 6 o'clock position. The FW-190 pilots set up an organized traffic pattern to fire on our Group's Liberators, unhampered by our scheduled fighter escort that wasn't due to meet the formation until the Group had flown another 120 miles. Next, at 0945 hours, 8 Me-109s and 5 JU-88s came in from 5 and 7 o'clock positions in very aggressive attacks near Maniago, Italy, still far from the scheduled fighter escort rendezvous at Chiem lake. Our Group's gunners claimed one destroyed.

Also seen, but they didn't attack our Group formation, were 20 Me-109s, 9 Me-110s, 5 Me-210s, and 15 FW-190s. They probably attacked Groups that weren't flying such tight formations as our Group, or they were looking for stragglers. The 484th Bomb Group of Liberators that was scheduled to bomb the Munich Marshaling Yards, near our target about the same time, was attacked by fifty single and twin-engined enemy fighters. The enemy fighters attacked the 484th Group with air-to-air bomb drops, cannon, rockets, and machine guns, and five of their Liberators were shot down. Gunners of the 484th bombers claimed to have shot down eighteen of the enemy fighters.

Flak was encountered by the 456th Group formation at Maniago, Salzburg, Regensburg, and at the target, Munich. The flak at the target was graded as intense, accurate, with heavy black bursts, and our Group lost the services of three B-24s from flak hits, and fourteen bombers were damaged from all types of enemy fire.

The weather enroute was clear from takeoff until enemy territory was reached in the Udine area, then altocumulus clouds began to appear below the formation. In the target area, cloud formations increased to three-tenths of cirrus cloud coverage above the formation with bases at 22,000 feet. Below the formation there were two-tenths of cumulus cloud coverage with tops at 12,000 feet. Temperature at 22,000 feet was minus 20 degrees centigrade.

Thirty-four B-24s dropped 101 tons of giant 1,000 pound bombs (202 of them) on the Bayerische Motorern Werke at Munich, Germany, at 1018 hours from an altitude of 21,000 feet for the 1st Unit and 20,000 feet for the 2nd Unit, on an axis of attack of 178 degrees magnetic, at 160 MPH indicated airspeed, a true airspeed of 227 MPH. The bombardiers' bomb release interval setting was 100 feet. After bombs away, the Group made a descending right turn at 155-160 MPH, about 210 to 228 true airspeed, to foil flak gunners on the ground. Bombing results were later rated as fair. The target was well covered by a good concentration of the huge 1,000 pound bombs. Many fires were started, and hits were scored on machine shops, unloading bays, stores, workshops, and heat treatment shops of the factory.

Two bombers did not return to our airbase and were lost. The Group formation of 32 bombers returned over the field at 1305 hours and landed, but one B-24 that landed, the "Purple Shaft," was so damaged that it had to be retired. The crews logged 6 hours and 45 minutes by the time they were on the ground. This was the Group's 60th credited mission of 68 missions flown while it was in Italy.

The two bombers lost in flight were both from the 744th Squadron, and as mentioned earlier, a plane from the 746th Squadron, "Purple Shaft," had so much damage that it had to be scrapped. Fourteen other B-24s were damaged by enemy fire.

One of the B-24s lost, #41-28817, flown by 2nd Lt. Ralph O. Griffin in the deputy lead position off Colonel Steed's right wing (the number 2 position in the 1st Box of the 1st Unit), was last seen at 1036 hours, about 20 minutes after bombs had been dropped on the target. Griffin's plane had two engines feathered and was reported, by aircrew at the intelligence interrogation after the Group landed, to have been headed for Switzerland. It was learned after the war that the crew bailed out, probably over the Brenner Pass, and there was only one confirmed survivor, the pilot 2nd Lt. Ralph O. Griffin. He was taken Prisoner of War, and he is currently a member of the 456th Bomb Group Association. Other crew members of the plane were listed as Missing In Action, but they haven't been heard from since.

Another B-24 that was lost, number 285 flown by 2nd Lt. John E. Dengler in the number 2 position of the 2nd Box of the 2nd Unit, had its controls shot out and it was reported to have ditched in the Gulf of Venezia at 1230 hours. Three of the crew members were rescued and returned to duty. Six of the crew were killed in action. Of the survivors, S/Sgt Roderick O. Carlson the tail turret gunner, is currently a member of the 456th Bomb Group Association. Another survivor, the bombardier, 2nd Lt Harold F. Wanamaker, was rescued and returned to duty but he was later listed Missing In Action on a mission he flew on July 17, 1944. The other survivor who was rescued and returned to duty, Sgt Robert W. Seaman, turret gunner, is of unknown location.

For the day, our Group had eleven crew men listed as Missing In Action, six killed, and one seriously wounded. Others had lesser wounds.

One of the bombers seriously hit by flak, but able to return to our airbase, was the "Purple Shaft," aircraft number 489. It was flown by the assistant operations officer of my 746th Squadron, 1st Lt. Douglas C. Richards (later promoted to Lt. Col.) who is currently a member of the 456th Bomb Group Association. Two crew members of the "Purple Shaft" were wounded when flak scored a direct hit on the plane after bombs were dropped on the target. It blew a gaping hole three to four feet in diameter in the back end of the airplane, right behind the ball turret gunner, Sgt Russel W. Brown.

Richards said that the flak hit caused him to lose his flight control trim tab and he had to use extra force on the control wheel to regain and maintain control of the plane. He said the experience shook his crew up. The 88mm explosive shell did not explode on contact as it was designed to do, and as we had seen it do on other occasions. The unexploded flak shell passed clearly through the bomber, otherwise he and his crew would not be alive today if it had detonated. The shell only made a gaping hole through the bomber. Sgt Jerry Krenek, the flight engineer and waist gunner, was seriously hit in the feet and legs by flak, and he almost slipped through the huge hole in the floor near his feet because the plane was bouncing about while Richards tried to regain control of the plane after his trim control had been shot out. The other waist gunner saved Krenek by grabbing him and pulling him away from the hole to safety. The oxygen system had been shot out in the waist and they were still at bombing altitude. Sgt. George E. Rich, radio operator, on seeing how severely Krenek was wounded, secured a portable oxygen bottle for him, sacrificing his own needs, and administered first aid. Soon after, Sgt Rich noticed that he too had been wounded. Lt. Daniel F. Curran, bombardier, went to the back of the plane to give Rich first aid.

Before Lt. Richards' plane was struck by the flak, the ball turret gunner, Sgt Russell W. Brown, was looking out from his ball turret, when he saw flak bursting just ahead of his plane. Because the flak was tracking his plane so closely, he realized that his ship was being zeroed in on by gunners on the ground and that the next burst could be near his position. As a precaution, he unlatched the hatch of his ball turret and threw the door open. Sure enough, the next flak burst hit the "Purple Shaft" just behind his ball turret and the force of the blast threw him up through his hatch, out of the turret. He received a bump on the head and several pieces of flak as momentos of the experience.

Krenek's wounds were so bad that he was sent home to the States after being treated at our large hospital in Foggia. That ended his combat career. He was never able to walk correctly afterward. Rich's wounds were not as severe, and he was treated at our Cerignola hospital. The "Purple Shaft's" wounds were so severe that it was retired after, and it never flew another mission.

June 14 and 15, 1944   No Flying.

The weather was too bad for flying, and there were no Group missions. My copilot and I were still enjoying the good life on the Isle of Capri.

June 16, 1944   Vienna Winter Hafen Oil Storage Area, Austria.

While I was still on the Isle of Capri, the 456th Bomb Group flew another rough mission, this time to bomb the Vienna Winter Hafen Oil Storage Area in Austria. All missions to Vienna were tough ones, and this one was no exception. With 300 antiaircraft guns on the ground firing at our formations and large concentrations of fighters in the area, Vienna was second only to Berlin as the most heavily defended target in Europe. Two of our B-24s failed to return from the mission, one shot down by flak and the other was lost to fighters. Fourteen other Liberators of our Group received damage from enemy fire.

The Fifteenth Air Force heavy bombers were scheduled to attack oil facilities in and around Vienna on this day. The Apollo Oil Refinery thirty-three miles east of Vienna was one of the ten largest refineries outside of Rumania.

The 304th Wing divided its four groups into two separate formations, each consisting of two groups to bomb two different oil targets in the Vienna area this day. One formation consisting of the 449th and 454th Groups bombed the Nova Schwechat Oil Refinery. The other formation, consisting of the 455th and our 456th Group, bombed the Vienna Winter Hafen Oil Storage Area. The returned to our airbase early, one because it had a supercharger malfunction, and the other because it had an engine failure.

Aircrews were given the following escape and survival instructions for this target and all targets above the Alps. "If you are forced down in the primary target area you should endeavor to reach the Yugoslavia border and attempt to cross it near Novi-Sad, as there is a safe area directly south of that point on the Yugoslav side of the Danube. There are also several safe areas south of that vicinity where you can obtain aid from the Partisans who can be identified by the red star on their cap (they never wear a helmet) and by their salute of raising the clenched fist to the right temple. Be sure to have good shoes along, and wear your identification dog tags."

Our Group rendezvous with the 455th Group was over Stornara at 4,000 feet, then the two groups departed Stornara climbing on course at 160 MPH indicated airspeed, about 210 MPH true airspeed, and a rate of climb of 250 feet per minute until 15,000 feet was reached, then the rate of climb was reduced to 150 FPM to climb the rest of the way to bombing altitude. The route took the formation over Sazziol Island, Csallokozaranyos, Trnava, to the Initial Point of Ganserndorf, then to the target at Vienna.

The weather was good enroute, with cirrus above the bomber formations at 23,000 feet. There were no clouds below the formation until the Alps were reached. From there to the target, cloud coverage increased from two-tenths cumulus cloud coverage, tops at 7,000 feet, until it became six-tenths coverage from cumulus clouds over the target, with bases at 5,000 feet and tops at 9,000 feet. Return weather was the same as for the route out. Temperature at 21,000 feet over the base was minus 21 degrees centigrade.

417

C O N F I D E N T I A L
BATTLE ORDER

16 June 1944

1st Unit: 1st Box

Formation Leader:: Abernathy, Callan AP 764
No. 3: Hundly   AP 853   Dep Leader: Parks, Ragland AP 887
                    No. 4: Little   AP 7
No. 6: Dean   AP 934   No. 5: Butcher   AP 810
                    No. 7: Hendrickson AP 072

2nd Box

Leader: Ensign   AP 486
No. 3: Gullick   AP 256   Dep Leader: Johnson   AP 831
                    No. 4: Smith   AP 549
No. 6: Scott   AP 306   No. 5: Addis   AP 199
                    No. 7: Schober   AP 437

3rd Box

Leader: Douglass   AP 749
No. 3: Savage   AP 897   Dep Leader: Nilsson   AP 297
                    No. 4: Palic   AP 487
No. 6: Miller   AP 309   No. 5: Roocher   AP 113
                    No. 7: Ruck   AP 277

2nd Unit: 1st Box

Leader: Jackson, C.Y.   AP 277
No. 3: Strombom   AP 912   Dep Leader: Monohan   AP 334
                    No. 4: Klinger   AP 345
No. 6: Goza   AP 493   No. 5: Richtschaidt AP 364
                    No. 7: Huls   AP 338

2nd Box

Leader: Gruber, Phifer   AP 501
No. 3: Bruce   AP 275   Dep Leader: Powell   AP 947
                    No. 4: Brabon   AP 799
No. 6: Jones   AP 077   No. 5: Luther   AP 233
                    No. 7: Whittaker   AP 319

3rd Box

Leader: Chandler   AP 777
No. 3: Rawlinson AP 293   Dep Leader: Mapa   AP 485
                    No. 4: Toscalli   AP 284
No. 6: Leathers   AP 225   No. 5: Hall   AP 328
                    No. 7: Blakkwoll   AP 768

Stations: 0620   456th SIXHORN THREE FOUR

Engines: A 0625 B 0630 C 0635   Fighters: "A"
          D 0640 E 0645 F 0650

Take-off: 0645   Recall: CRANK

Fifty enemy aircraft, FW-190s, Me-109s, Ju-88s, and Me-210s, were waiting in the target area, but only twenty aggressively attacked our Group formation. Two FW-190s attacked at 1010 hours, forty minutes before target time, attacking from the 3 and 6 o'clock positions level, firing rockets. Two Me-109s attacked at 1040 hours, ten minutes before target time, and they came in from the 6 o'clock level position. Eight FW-190s attacked the Group formation 1055, five minutes after bombs away, attacking from the 12 o'clock level position and from the 8 o'clock low position. Their attacks were very aggressive as they closed to within 50 yards of the Group formation. Some enemy fighters flew right through the formation of bombers.

The fighters in this area were so aggressive that one Luftwaffe fighter rammed into a B-24 of the 376th Bomb Group, knocking its right wing off and both planes crashed in flames. The 376th Bomb Group of Liberators that was attacking a target thirty-three miles to our east was attacked by forty single and twin engine enemy fighters. Two Liberators were shot down. Gunners of the 376th claimed 12 enemy fighters destroyed.

One of our straggling bombers, discussed later, was shot down by fighters before it reached the target. Our gunners did not report shooting down or damaging any enemy fighters. Over the target the flak was intense, very accurate, and heavy. It was the radar tracking type as well as the barrage type. One of our planes was shot down by flak hits. Fourteen other B-24s were damaged from all causes, flak and fighters.

Thirty-nine B-24s flew in our Group formation over the target, but one plane had a bomb rack malfunction that prevented it from dropping its bombs on the target. Thirty-eight aircraft were able to drop 84.63 tons of 250 pound general purpose bombs (677 bombs) on the target at 1050 hours from 22,000 feet for the 1st Unit and 21,000 feet for

419

the 2nd Unit at 160 MPH indicated airspeed, a true airspeed of 232 MPH, on an axis of attack of 238 degrees magnetic. The bombardiers' bomb release interval setting was 40 feet. A cloud immediately over the target caused difficulty in accurately aiming at the target, but a fair concentration of bombs filled the target area. Clouds obscured photographic results of the bombing. Twenty target photos were taken by 7 K-22 cameras and only portions of the target could be seen through the clouds. However, many fires were started and smoke billowed up thousands of feet through the cloud layer. Most crew members reported that they saw a fair concentration of bombs in the target area while peering through breaks in the clouds. Fires in the area could be seen up to seventy miles away.

With two planes shot down, the remaining 38 bombers in the Group formation headed back to friendly territory. Fourteen were shot up with wounded aboard some of the planes. Two of the planes with wounded aboard landed at Foggia where there was a better level of medical attention immediately available. The procedure for planes landing at our airbase with wounded aboard was for the planes to notify the formation leader, then dive down ahead of the formation and enter the landing traffic pattern before the rest of the planes in the formation entered the traffic pattern. On the downwind leg of the traffic pattern the crew had to shoot a red flare to let the ambulance on the ground know that there were wounded aboard.

The formation of 36 remaining bombers arrived over our field at 1315 hours and crews logged 6 hours and 55 minutes by the time they were on the ground. This was the Group's 61st credited mission of 69 missions flown in Italy.

The B-24 that was shot down by enemy fighters during the air battle was "Sky Gazer," flown by 2nd Lt. Paul E. Miller of the 745th Squadron. It was singled out for attack because it had been having engine trouble during most of the flight and it had difficulty keeping up with the Group formation. He was flying in the #6 position of the 3rd Box of the 1st Unit. Two FW-190s, always on the alert for stragglers because fewer bomber guns would be firing at them, attacked "Sky Gazer" from the six o'clock low position. Lt. Miller took good evasive action, violently maneuvering his crippled plane as much as possible, but as he made a left bank, fire from an FW-190 hit the underside of his left wing and lower fuselage. The plane went into a flat spin at about 15,000 feet. Two parachutes were seen to come out of Star Gazer at 1040 hours, ten minutes before target time. Five crew members were killed in action and are buried in the American Military Cemetery at Lorraine, France. These include the pilot, navigator, radio operator, ball turret gunner, and tail turret gunner. Five crew members of "Sky Gazer" are listed as missing in action; the copilot, bombardier, nose turret gunner, engineer, and top turret gunner.

The second plane lost, #44-40493 flown by 2nd Lt. Kirk B. Goza of the 744th Squadron, was hit by flak that knocked out engines #1 and #4. The #4 engine was on fire and the propeller could not be feathered, so it was providing much drag on the aircraft causing it to steadily lose altitude. The crew jettisoned all loose equipment, but that didn't help. The pilot gave the order to bail out. Observers aboard bombers of the Group's formation reported seeing nine parachutes open from the plane, but it was learned much later that all ten crewmen were able to get out before the plane was seen to crash at 1210 hours, 1 hour and 20 minutes after bombs away. Eight members of the crew were taken Prisoners Of War, but two, the copilot 1st Lt. Charles L. Thompson, and navigator 2nd Lt. Raymond C. Miller, were able to evade capture and return to Italy. Miller was killed on a later flight, November 5, 1944. Two members of the crew who were

POWs are currently members of the 456th Bomb Group Association: Sgt Stewart H. McFarland, ball turret gunner, and Sgt Thomas H. Williams, upper turret gunner. The status of the rest of the crew is unknown.

Three crewmen on the mission were seriously wounded by flak. Wounded were two bombardiers, one navigator, and one pilot. Most were flying in the 1st Box of the 1st Unit. One interesting story is that of Lt. Benjamin L. Smalley, squadron bombardier of my 746th Squadron, who had barely missed being killed on the spectacular crash on our airfield March 2, 1944. I had witnessed the wounded Smalley, miraculously running from the flaming plane that had killed his two pilots, his navigator and his engineer. On this mission, June 16, 1944, he was bombardier in the plane flown by Capt. Samuel W. Parks in plane #887, in the deputy lead (#2 position) of the 1st Box of the 1st Unit. He was on the bomb run synchronizing his bomb sight when he was struck in the back by a piece of flak. It perforated his thoracic cavity, causing his left lung to collapse. The force of a flak burst that hit the nose of his plane threw Smalley away from his bombsight to the floor. He waived away the navigator who came to his aid, and despite his intense pain, he quickly pulled himself back to his position over the bombsight. He made final corrections to the bombsight and was able to make a timely release of his bombs on the target. He was an outstanding example of the quality of character we had on our aircrews.

The pilot that was hit by flak was Lt. Charles P. Hundley, also of my 746th Squadron, and also flying in the 1st Box of the 1st Unit, in position #3. Flying aircraft #853, he was struck in the leg by flak, and his copilot, 2nd Lt. Edmund A. Sajeski, took over the ship and flew it safely back to our base.

June 17-21, 1944   No Missions These Five days.

No missions were flown during these five days because of fowl weather all around. Lt. Sidney Brooks and myself returned from our taste of the good life on Capri, and I vowed to return there someday, preferably after the war's end. (Many years later I did succeed in visiting the island two more times, and I enjoyed it as much on each subsequent visit.)

I made a non-mission flight in "Porky" for 2 hours on the 21st, but I don't remember why. It may have been a test flight after some repairs, or it may have been a transition training flight to give my copilot Lt. Brooks some experience flying the plane.

June 22, 1944   Chivasso Motor Transport and Repair Depot, Italy.

This was another milk run mission that my crew was not selected to fly. However, S/Sgt Thomas Delaney my radio operator flew on the mission with Lt. Henry F. Lunardi's crew in "Bottoms Up."

It was a mission to bomb the Chivasso Motor Transport and Repair Depot in Italy, bomb results were graded as superior, and no flak or enemy fighters were seen.

While the Group was on this mission, I flew the Link Trainer on the ground at Group Headquarters for one hour.

Group used a four-Box formation for the first time on this mission.

The new formation consisted of flying four Boxes of ten bombers in each Box, in a diamond configuration. This new formation replaced the previous six-Box formation that the group had been using, which consisted of flying two Units each made up a "V" of three Boxes, each Box consisting of from six to seven bombers.

S E C R E T

(a) Battle Order.   Date: 22 June 1944.

1st Box

Formation Leader: Miller, Sinclair AP 790   Ryde

No.3: Powell   AP 623   Dep Loader: Johnson /   AP 831
                      No.4: Bruce   AP 275
No.6: Huls   AP 295   No.5: Hendrickson   AP 501
                      No.7: Jones   AP 077
No.9: Whitaker   AP 319   No.8: Brabon   AP 799
                      No.10: Luther   AP 233

2nd Box

                      Leader: Snee   AP 8275
No.3: Scott   AP 306   Dep Leader: Smith   AP 549
                      No.4: Addis   AP 853
No.6: Lumardi   AP 0487   No.5: Hill   AP 486
                      No.7: Ashley   AP 442
No.9: Vosbell   AP 201   No.8: Dean   AP 934
                      No.10: Wood   AP 199

3rd Box

                      Leader: Gardner   AP 628
No.3: Nilsson   AP 297   Dep Leader: Lasnewski   AP 304
                      No.4: Monahan   AP 749
No.6: Marler   AP 113   No.5: Savage   AP 807
                      No.7: Roak   AP 177
No.9: Walker   AP 203   No.8: Solcher   AP 487
                      No.10: Dysinger   AP 637

4th Box

                      Leader: Clark   AP 768
No.3: Ball   AP 485   Dep Leader: Strombom   AP 912
                      No.4: Riddle   AP 777
No.6: Ogden   AP 225   No.5: Cerretti   AP 328
                      No.7: Russel, Rawlinson AP 293
No.9: Shotterley   AP 964   No.8: Richtscheidt   AP 470
                      No.10: Klinger   AP 345

SPARES: 744th # 279, 338 :: 748th # 256, 299 :: 747th # 637.

Time at Stations: 06:40   456th: "PUSSCAT TWO TWO".

Start engines: 1st-06:50 ‖   52nd FG: "EXCEED TWO".
06:55 - 3rd 07:00 4th - 07:05
                                Recall: "TAVERN".

Taxi out: 07:00

Take-off: 0710

S E C R E T

From this day on, the diamond formation of four Boxes was to become our standard combat formation. It was an easier formation to assemble, less difficult to organize, it provided a tighter pattern of bombs dropped on the target, and it provided a tighter concentration of our bombers' guns available for firing at attacking enemy fighters. The four box formation was less spread out than the six box formation.

Crews were awakened for this mission at 0430 hours, briefing was held at 0530, and stations time at the aircraft was at 0640 hours. The lead plane, with Major John R. Sinclair flying it, started engines at 0650 hours, it started to taxi to the end of the runway at 0700, and then took off at 0710 hours. Thirty-nine B-24s followed him off the runway at 45 second intervals. After assembling the group's diamond formation, Major Sinclair led the formation to rendezvous with other groups of the 304th Wing over Stornara at 3,000 feet. The Wing formation departed Stornara at 0800 climbing on course at 160 MPH indicated airspeed, about 200 MPH true airspeed, climbing at a 250 feet per minute rate of climb to the bombing altitude. There were no aircraft making early returns this day and all 40 planes went on the mission. The ground crews did a superior job getting the B-24s ready for this mission.

The route took the formation over Lido Di Roma, Pianosa Island, to the Initial Point, which was three miles east of Chieria, Italy, which is about 10 miles southeast of Turin, to the target at Chivasso which is about 20 miles northeast of Turin. Five wings of Fifteenth Air Force bombers went to the target, including our 304th Wing, the 55th, 5th, 47th and 49th Wings. All were B-24s except the 5th Wing which was composed of all B-17s.

The weather was CAVU until Pionosa Island, then five-tenths of cirrus clouds, bases at 20,000 feet (above the formation), and eight-tenths of alto cumulus coverage (below the formation) with bases at 6,000 feet and tops at 8,000 feet. The target could be seen between the clouds.

425

The temperature at 17,000 feet was minus 10 degrees centigrade.

The 40 Liberators flying in our Group formation dropped 88.75 tons of 250 pound bombs (710 bombs) on the target at 1052 hours from 18,500 feet for the 1st Unit and 17,500 feet for the 2nd Unit at 160 MPH indicated airspeed, 218 MPH true airspeed, on an axis of attack of 10 degrees magnetic. The bombardiers' bomb release interval setting was 40 feet. After bomb release, the formation made a descending right turn at 160-165 MPH indicated airspeed, about 218 to 228 MPH true airspeed. Bombing results were graded as superior, and there was an excellent concentration of bombs completely covering our Group's aiming point at the target. Six K-22 cameras in the group photographed the target results.

All 40 Liberators of our Group formation returned to our airbase safely, undamaged, at 1344 hours. There were no casualties. Flight time was 6 hours and 40 minutes by the time planes were on the ground. This was the Group's 62nd credited mission in 70 attempts.

June 23, 1944 Nis Marshaling Yards, Yugoslavia.

Again, my crew was not selected to fly on this day's mission, but my radio operator and bombardier, Delaney and Duston, were selected to fly with Lt. Henry F. Lunardi's crew in "Bottoms Up" on the mission. Delaney celebrated his twenty-first birthday on the mission. The Group was briefed to bomb the Bucharest Chitilla Railroad Station in Rumania, but bad weather forced it to bomb an alternate target, the Nis Marshaling Yards in Yugoslavia. After the superior bombing results that were achieved by using the four Box formation, instead the standard six-Box formation, our Group was again flying its diamond formation of only four boxes, with ten Liberators in each box. No fighters

426

S E C R E T

(a) Battle Order.   Date: 23 June 1944.

1st Box

Formation Leader: Thomas;Reid AP 791

No.3: Rugland	AP 256	Dep Leader: Cutting	AP 279
	No.4: Smith	AP 549	
No.6: Ashley	AP 201	No.5: Doan	AP 934
	No.7: Addis	AP 853	
No.9: Wood	AP 199	No.8: Lunardi	AP 0487
	No.10: Scott	AP 831	

2nd Box

Leader: Lee AP 338

No.3: Luther	AP 275	Dep Leader: Brabon	AP 799
	No.4: Jones	AP 077	
No.6: Hendrickson	AP 501	No.5: Fields	AP 233
	No.7: Huls	AP 295	
No.8: Powell	AP 623	No.8: Whitaker	AP 319
	No.10:	AP	

3rd Box

Leader: Newhouse AP 470

No.3: Rawlinson	AP 293	Dep Leader: Strombom	AP 912
	No.4: Blackwell	AP 777	
No.6: Leathers	AP 637	No.5: Mapa	AP 485
	No.7: Hall	AP 225	
No.9: Richtscheidt	AP 362	No.8: Cerretti	AP 328
	No.10: Shetterly	AP.	

4th Box

Leader: Tavel AP 177

No.3: Nilsson	AP 297	Dep Leader: Monahan	AP 304
	No.4: Douglas	AP 749	
No.6: Roak	AP 628	No.5: Marler	AP 365
	No.7: Lassewski	AP 807	
No.9: Walker	AP 203	No.8: Solcher	AP 810
	No.10: Raicher	AP 119	

SPARES: 744th = 072, 290 :: 745th = 487 :: 746th = 8275, 442, 201 ::
747th = 768 ::

Time at stations: 0555.   456th: "MOSES THREE".

Start engines: A 0605 B 0612   Fighters: "CARTLOAD".
                C 0620 D 0627
                                     Recall: "REALTY".
Taxi out: 0615.

Take-off: 0625.

S E C R E T

were seen and flak was meager, inaccurate, and none of our bombers reported damage. The most dangerous hazard on this mission was the poor weather.

It was another early wake-up call for the crews in their tents, at 0400 hours, briefing at o450, aircraft stations time was 0555, and Major Robert L. Reid of the 744th Squadron, flying in the lead plane started engines at 0605 hours, started to taxi to the end of the runmway at 0615, then he took off at 0625. Thirty-eight Liberators followed him off the runway at 45 second intervals. After our Group's B-24 assembled the diamond formation around Major Reid's plane, our Group rendezvoused with the 455th Group over Stornara at 4,000 feet, then departed climbing on course at 0718 hours, climbing at 160 MPH indicated airspeed, 200 MPH true airspeed, and a rate of climb of 200 feet per minute. The Group's route to the target was scheduled to take it through Yugoslavia to Gaesti, Rumania, to the Initial Point, Cojasca (half way between Ploesti and Bucharest), then to the target at Bucharest. However, weather prevented the Group's formation from coming anywhere near this target.

The weather was atrocious! There were 12 bombers that became separated from the rest of the group formation as the formation dodged around and through some formidable clouds. One entire Box of ten Liberators lost the formation and returned to our airbase without bombing. Two other planes lost the formation and had to return before dropping their bombs. Only one of the 12 bombers that returned early had penetrated enemy territory deeply enough to be given credit for the mission. All of the other eleven bombers that returned early received no mission credit.

The 14th Fighter Group of P-38s were scheduled to provide cover for the 304th Wing of B-24s starting at 0946, over Gaesti, and the 14th was scheduled to provide penetration, target, and withdrawal cover. However, no enemy fighters were seen by aircrews of our Group. Either our fighter escort did an excellent job of protection for the Liberators, or they were not needed. The weather was probably too bad for enemy fighters to risk taking off, flying through the layers of clouds, then being able to find their airbases again through the clouds to return.

However, to the north of our scheduled target, at Ploesti, Fifteenth Air Force bombers from the southern tip of Italy succeeded in bombing that oil center because the weather was much better on the southern route, and at Ploesti, than on our Group's route and at Bucharest. Liberator groups stationed in the heel of the boot of Italy, east and south of Taranto, flying a route more southern than our Group's northern route, found the weather better and were able to fly to Ploesti. The oil production facilities at Ploesti were truck by 139 Liberator bombers that dropped 283 tons of bombs. Six bombers were lost. Fighter escort for the bombers destroyed 24 enemy fighters, twelve of them claimed by the hot P-51 fighters of the 52nd Fighter Group. The hot 52nd Fighter Group holds the record of destroying 102 enemy aircraft in a thirty-day period.

After the twelve Liberators of the 456th Bomb Group had aborted the mission due to weather, the remaining twenty-seven bombers in the Group formation ran into a wall of clouds that prevented it from reaching the primary target, Bucharest. Major Reid the Group leader selected an alternate target that could be reached, the Railroad Marshaling Yards at Nis, Yugoslavia. Weather at the alternate target was not very good either but the target could be seen by the Group bombardiers. There were five-tenths of altocumulus clouds below the formation covering the alternate target, with cloud bases at 10,000 feet and tops at 16,000 feet. The formation was flying under a cloud cover of three-tenths cirrostratus clouds, bases at 20,000 feet and tops at 22,000 feet. Thus the Group could fly to the alternate target between a sandwich of clouds.

Twenty-seven bombers succeeded in dropping 53 tons of 100 pound bombs (1,060 bombs) at 0935 from 20,000 feet on an axis of attack of 215 degrees magnetic, flying at 160 MPH indicated airspeed, 222 MPH true airspeed. The bombardiers' bomb release interval setting was 35 feet. The air temperature at 20,000 feet was minus 20 degrees centigrade. Flak was meager, inaccurate, with

Delaney, flying as radio operator on Lt. Henry F. Lunardi's crew in aircraft number 831, "Bottoms Up," stated in his diary, "....We came over the target and the left bomb bay doors wouldn't open, so I took off my flak suit and went out on the bomb bay catwalk to crank the doors open. I was about a foot away from the hand crank when my chute caught and I couldn't reach It. I got kind of dizzy so I got back and started to take off my chute, and then the bombs went out just barely clearing the bomb bay doors! I should have taken my chute off before I went out on the catwalk. I should have used my head, but we didn't have much time (before bombs away)!...."

The twenty-seven Liberators in the Group formation returned safely over our airbase at 1146 hours. No aircraft had damage, and there were no casualties. By the time the Liberators were on the ground they had logged 5 hours and 30 minutes. It was the Group's 63rd accredited mission in 71 attempts. Most crews were very happy to be on the ground after the chancy weather conditions they encountered. Close formation flying in bad weather conditions was an additional enemy that aircrews had to endure. There was the very real danger of colliding with other bombers while weaving in and out and around the clouds.

June 24, 1944   Craiova Railway Repair Depot, Rumania.

My crew received an unusual early morning wake-up call at 0315 hours to fly our beloved "Porky" on this day's

430

mission. After a brief, abbreviated breakfast of coffee and pancakes (one of the better "C" ration items that I liked, with peanut butter and jam piled on top), dehydrated milk and dehydrated eggs, I joined the rest of the aircrews to ride in the back end of open Army six-by-six trucks up to our headquarters on the hill. We attended the briefing at 0430 hours. As we walked into the briefing room, we saw that the yarn on the wall map at the end of our briefing room wasn't too long, and though our target, the Craiova Railway Repair Depot, was in Rumania, it was only 115 miles west of the heavily defended Ploesti and Bucharest areas. Our Wing was scheduled to have fighter escorts that consisted of P-47s, P-38s, and the hot new P-51s as security blankets. Lt. Judge Foss was flying with his own crew on this mission, so my Navigator-bombardier accomplished both tasks alone this day and he did a very good job! Our bombs went into the center of the target.

We were told at the briefing that our previous bombings of Axis railroad repair facilities had made them critically scarce and overtaxed. The Craiova Repair Depot was servicing the German armies in the southern front that were in a life and death struggle with the invading Russian armies, and that the yards were also servicing the trains that are transporting refined and crude oil out of Rumania.

Aircrews were told at the briefing that if we were to bail out in Rumania we should work our way across the Danube River to the west and southwest of the town of Nis, and find Partisan soldiers to help us. We were told, again, that we could recognize Partisans by the red star on their hats, and by their salute which was a clenched fist to their right temple. We were to ask for the Allied Military Mission representatives. We were also told, again, to wear good strong walking shoes and to wear our Dog Tags (metal military identification tags).

431

S E C R E T

Date: 24 June 1944.

(a) Battle Order.

1st Box

Formation Leader: STEED, Witkin AP 809   Parks
                                Dep Leader: Ragland / AP 768
No.3: Leathers   AP 364
                  No.4: Riddle   AP 777
                                        No.5: Mapa   AP 485
No.6: Ogden   AP 912
                  No.7: Blackwall   AP 964
                                        No.8: Klinger   AP 345
No.9: Hall   AP 328
                  No.10: Dysinger   AP 634

2nd Box

                  Leader: Richards AP 299
                                    Dep Leader: Sagert   AP 8275
No.3: Johnson   AP 831
                  No.4: Capps   AP 306
                                        No.5: Tosselli   AP 364
No.6: Scott   AP 477
                  No.7: Shober   AP 0487
                                        No.8: Hill   AP 853
No.9: Vosbell   AP 201
                  No.10: Wood   AP 199

3rd Box

                  Leader: Douglas   AP 749
                                    Dep Leader: Fleming AP 297
No.3: Wilkinson   AP 807
                  No.4: Williamson   AP 810
                                        No.5: Phillips   AP 628
No.6: Little   AP 304
                  No. 7: Monahan   AP 334
                                        No.8: Marler   AP 365
No.9: Walker   AP 203
                  No.10: Reicher   AP 113

4th Box

                  Leader: Ecker, Grubor AP 470
                                    Dep Loader: Rudd   AP 295
No.3: Whitaker   AP 319
                  No.4: Bruce   AP 947
                                        No.5: Brabon   AP 0799
No.6: Fields   AP 233
                  No.7: Luther   AP 338
                                        No.8: Jones   AP 077
No.9: Hendrickson AP 501
                  No.10: Powell   AP 623

SPARES: 744th - 290, 279 :: 745th - 487 :: 746th - 549 :: 747th - 637th

Time at stations: 05:35   456th: "RADCLIFF-ONE".

Start engines: 1st 05:45 2nd 05:52   Fighters: "TANKSTOP".
               3rd 06:00 4th 06:07
                                      Recall: "PORTRAIT".

Taxi out: 05:55

Take-off: 06:05

S E C R E T

When the briefing was finished we climbed into the back end of open six-by-six army trucks and were driven to our planes, to be at our aircraft for the scheduled stations time of 0535 hours. Start engines time for the lead plane, with Colonel Steed flying in it, was 0545 hours. Each of the rest of the group's three Boxes started their engines at five minute intervals. I was scheduled to fly in the 2nd Box, the number 4 position, so my copilot. Lt. Brooks, and I carefully started our four reliable Pratt and Whitney R-1830-43 engines that each produced 1200 horsepower. After some early problems with these engines during training back in the States, we now had engines that had been modified by the factory so that they were very reliable. We also had maintenance ground crews that had become more experienced and familiar with the engines. We knew that our lives depended, to a great extent, on these engines so we watched them very closely, as did most other crews. If we could not keep up with the Group formation because of a faulty engine we knew that enemy fighters would single us out for their guns. We carefully checked each engine's magnetos, oil pressure, fuel pressure, and cylinder-head temperature before we made the decision to takeoff on the mission.

Colonel Steed's plane started to taxi to the end of the runway at 0555, then took off at 0604 hours. Thirty-nine B-24s followed Colonel Steed's plane off the runway at 45 second intervals, then each flew to catch up with his plane and to take its place in the Group's diamond formation around his lead plane. My plane, "Porky," was number fourteen to takeoff. The number two aircraft of my box, number 8275 flown by Lt. Stanley A. Sagert, could not get his landing gear to retract, so he aborted. I was ordered to fly our "Porky" to take his position as the deputy lead of the 2nd Box (according to notes of my radio operator, S/Sgt Stanley S. Delaney). After we had formed our new diamond formation Colonel Steed led the Group over Stornara at 3,000 feet where we joined the 455th Bomb Group. Both of our groups departed Stornara flying in a trail formation of groups. We climbed on course at a 200 feet per minute rate of climb and 160 MPH indicated airspeed, a true airspeed of about 200 MPH. For this mission, the four groups of the 304th Wing were divided into two separate, smaller "Wings" for this bombing, the 455th and 456th Groups in one formation, and the 459th and 454th Groups in a separate formation. Each two group wing bombed the same target within a ten minute window.

Our Group, flying with the 455th Group, crossed the Yugoslavian coast enroute to Rumania at an altitude of 16,000 feet, headed for our Initial Point, Segarcea, Rumania. Four B-24s returned to our airbase before our formation entered the target area, aborting their mission. Two of the bombers that aborted had faulty landing gears that would not retract, one bomber had its electrical system go out, and one returned early because it had low oil pressure on an engine.

Our Group formation passed over Lake Ohrid and Prilep in Yugoslavia, then flew direct to the Initial Point, Segarcea in Rumania, thence to the target in Craiova.

No enemy fighters were seen. Weather enroute and at the target was not the best, but our Group's bombardiers were able to see the aiming point through breaks between the clouds and get good bombing results. The weather on the way to the I.P. was a messy one with up to six-tenths cloud coverage. There were two different layers of clouds below our formation, cumulus and altocumulus clouds, that extended from 4,000 feet up to 15,000 feet. Above our formation were three to four-tenths of cirrus cloud coverage that had bases at 21,000 feet and tops at 23,000.

At the target area the weather improved a little below our formation. Cloud coverage dropped from six-tenths down to four-tenths of cumulus and altocumulus clouds, bases at 3,000 feet and tops at 15,000. Above the Group formation there were the same cirrus clouds that had been with us enroute. The visibility was 20 miles, and the air temperature at 19,000 feet was minus 12 degrees centigrade. While there was no flak at the target, we encountered meager, inaccurate flak with heavy black bursts on the way to the I.P. None of our Liberators were hit by it.

Our Group formed a column of Boxes prior to the I.P., and the bomb run was made in that formation. The thirty-six B-24s that remained in the formation dropped 88.5 tons of 500 pound general purpose bombs (354 bombs) on the target at 0930 hours from 19,000 feet for the lead Box and 17,500 for the 4th Box in the diamond, on an axis of attack of 14 degrees magnetic. The bombing airspeed was 160 MPH indicated airspeed, 222 MPH true airspeed. The bombardiers' bomb release interval setting was 50 feet. Six K-22 cameras took pictures of the results, and the bombing was graded good. A good pattern of bombs covered the target, hitting many buildings, and a few secondary explosions and fires were seen in the target area as a result of our bomb hits. My radio operator who was manning one of the waist guns, S/SGt Thomas S. Dleaney, had recorded in his diary that he watched the bombs from our plane hit right in the center of the Main Depot.

After bombs away the Group's rally was a descending slight turn to the right, then a left turn around north of the town of Craiova at a reduced indicated airspeed of 155-160 MPH, a true airspeed of about 210 to 222 MPH, to keep our formation tight.

Our Group's Liberators had no damage from enemy action. Only one B-24 of our 304th Wing received damage. That one was a 459th Group plane that was hit by enemy fighter fire while it was straggling from its group formation near the target. A total of 162 B-24s in our 304th Wing bombed the Craiova Railway Repair Depot this day with overall results that were graded as excellent. My radio operator, S/Sgt Thomas S. Delaney, recorded in his diary, ".There were no enemy fighters, and no flak over the target! "Porky" brought us back again! Pilot and copilot flew wonderful formation again! Thanks, God!"

All of the 456th Bomb Group's formation of 36 bombers returned home with no reported damage and no casualties at 1226 hours. Six hours and 20 minutes flying time were logged for the mission. This was the Group's 64th credited mission in 72 attempts. It was my 41st credited mission, a single credit mission, and I now had 194 hours and 15 minutes of combat flying time.

Today a Soldiers Medal was awarded for heroism to my friend and my 746th Squadron Flight Surgeon, Captain Louis A. Tripi. Beside much heroic action that he demonstrated on our airbase while saving lives of wounded airmen from wrecked planes, the energetic Tripi who was a gynecologist by training volunteered to deliver babies free of charge to Italian citizens in the local area. It was his only chance to keep proficient at his preferred profession. Also receiving the medal were Major Sherman Masler of Group Headquarters and Sgt. Alan S. Cameron of my 746th Squadron.

The Group's enlisted men's softball team trounced the 454th Bomb Group team today by a score of 11-0.

June 25, 1944   Avignon Bridge and Marshaling Yards, France.

My crew was awakened for the second day in a row for a mission, at the early hour of 0300, to bomb the Avignon Bridge in France. Our plane "Porky" was being repaired, so we flew another crew's plane, number 839, "Gin Rae." It was a long mission, 7 hours and 55 minutes. Bombing results were excellent. Weather at the target was clear. Three

436

of our planes were damaged from flak, none from enemy fighters, although some Me-109s and FW-190s were seen. A Ju-88 fighter dropped aerial bombs on our formation,

S E C R E T

(a) Battle.

Date: 25 June 1944.

1st Box

Formation Leader: Ladd, Miller AP 809

		Dep Leader: Gardner	AP 628
No.3: Nilsson	AP 297	AP 810	
	No.4: Williamson	No.5: Lassewski	AP 334
No.6: Solcher	AP 113	AP 203	
	No.7: Flemming	No.8: Roak	AP 177
No.9: Savage	AP 807	AP 365	
	No.10: Wilkinson		

2nd Box

Leader: Phifer AP 501

		Dep Leader: Brabon	AP 799
No.3: Hendrickson	AP 077	AP 338	
	No.4: Luther	No.5: Powell	AP 623
No.6: Whitaker	AP 319	AP 275	
	No.7: Bruce	No.8: Fields	AP 233
No.9: Huls	AP 295	AP 345	
	No.10: Klingler		

3rd Box

Leader: Ensign AP 486

		Dep Leader: Johnson	AP 853
No.3: Gullick	AP 442	AP 839	
	No.4: Capps	No.5: Wood	AP 934
No.6: Ashley	AP 275	AP 487	
	No.7: Shober	No.8: Lunardi	AP 549
No.9: Hill	AP 256	AP 201	
	No.10: Voshall		

4th Box

Leader: Clark, W. D. AP 768

		Dep Leader: Strombom	AP 912
No.3: Corn	AP 777	AP 293	
	No.4: Rawlinson	No.5: Ceretti	AP 328
No.6: Ogden	AP 225	AP 485	
	No.7: Ball	No.8: Shetterly	AP 964
No.9: Richtsheidt	AP 637	AP 634	
	No.10: Dysinger		

SPARES: 744th - 290 :: 745th - 304 ::

Time at stations: 04:55.   456th: "SCHOOL-ROOM TWO-FOUR".

Start engines: 05:00 2nd 05:05   52nd FG: "GREEN-HERD".
                05:15 4th 05:25
                                    Recall: "WHISTLE".
Taxi out: 05:10

Take-off: 05:20

S E C R E T

but they didn't hit any of our Liberators. Except for this incident, our fighter escort did a good job of keeping enemy fighters from attacking us. We had trouble with the plane's interphone and with its tail turret guns, but they were fixed by our competent radio operator before we reached enemy territory. Again, our navigator-bombardier, 2nd Lt. James Duston, flew the mission without help and he did an excellent job.

At that early hour, I couldn't eat much breakfast, except some C-ration dehydrated coffee, and some toast and jam. We were supposed to have boxes of K-rations for in flight meals on the long mission. We rode up to the Group briefing room in the back of open Army six-by-six trucks for a briefing that started at 0345 hours. We were all astonished when we saw the length of yarn that depicted our route for the day on the map that covered the wall at the end of the briefing room. The yarn led northwest to southern France. We were told that we would have P-38s and P-51s for fighter escort. They were to provide protection from the time we penetrated enemy territory, over the target area, and during withdrawal from the target.

Our stations time at the aircraft was an early 0455 hours. Major Chester Ladd, a West Pointer, flying in the lead plane started his engines at 0500 hours and the Liberators of the other three Boxes of the diamond formation started engines at 5 minute intervals following his. Ladd started taxiing to the end of the runway at 0510 and he took off at 0519 hours. The rest of us, 38 more Liberators, followed his plane at 45 second intervals. I was the 24th plane to take off because I was flying in the number 4 position of the 3rd Box. After we had assembled our diamond formation around Ladd's plane, our Group joined the 455th Group over Stornara at 5,000 feet before departing at 0612 hours, climbing on course at 160 MPH indicated airspeed, about 200 MPH true airspeed, and a rate of climb of 200 feet per minute. Our

Initial Point for the bomb run was St. Remy, France. Our scheduled bombing altitude was unusually low, 16,500 feet, and the bombing formation was unusual, a column of Boxes at the target, rather than our usual diamond formation. Each Box of the column of Boxes were assigned slightly different aiming points for their targets.

One B-24, number 853 flown by Lt. Johnson of the 746th Squadron and deputy leader of the 3rd Box, returned early because he had to feather two engines that had problems while he was over our field and his bombardier jettisoned their bombs into the Adriatic.

Thirty-eight bombers remained with the formation and continued to the target. Although there were clouds below the formation all the way to the coast of France, the weather over the target area in France was excellent, with ceiling and visibility unlimited (CAVU). The temperature at 16,500 feet was minus 7 degrees centigrade.

Flak was encountered as soon as we reached the French coast, enroute to the target, at Maussanne, Salon, Tarascon, and Marseilles, but most of it was scant, inaccurate, and moderate, with heavy black bursts. Flak over the target was also scant, inaccurate, with heavy black bursts. Only three of our planes were damaged by flak. One Liberator dropped out of the formation between the Initial Point and the target at 0955 hours and was not seen afterward. It did not drop its bombs on the target. We learned later that it had three engines malfunction near the target and its crew had to jettison the bomb load before reaching the target, at 0953 hours, sixteen minutes before the group reached the first bomb release point. That plane, number 256 flown by Lt. Hill, was able to make it to the Island of Corsica where there was an Allied airbase. His plane was originally reported as missing in action from the mission, but we learned much later about the emergency landing on Corsica.

439

Two Boxes of the Group's formation, totaling 16 Liberators dropped 47 tons of giant 1,000 pound general purpose bombs (94 bombs) on the Avignon Highway Bridge at different times: the first Box of this section dropped its bomb load at 1009 hours on an axis of attack of 055 degrees magnetic from an altitude of 18,000 feet; and the second Box of this section dropped its bombs on a second pass at the target, making a right turn to bomb the same Avignon Highway Bridge on an axis of attack of 260 degrees, dropping at 1018 hours, nine minutes after the first Box. All bomb runs were made at the same bombing speed, an indicated airspeed of 160 MPH, and a true airspeed of 212 MPH.

Another 13 Liberators of our 456th Group dropped 39 tons of the giant 1,000 pound bombs (94 bombs) at 1009 hours on the Avignon Railroad Marshaling Yards from 17,000 feet on an axis of attack of 355 degrees magnetic.

Another 8 bombers of our Group dropped 24 tons of the 1,000 pounders (48 bombs) on the Avignon Rairoad Bridge at 1009 hours on an axis of attack of 354 degrees magnetic.

The bombardier's bomb release interval setting for these huge thousand pound bombs was set at the minimum interval. After the last box had made its bomb release at 1019 hours, the Group formation made a descending right turn to Mirabeau, then headed home.

Six K-22 cameras took photos of the target area. Overall bombing results were graded as excellent. Fifty-seven percent of our giant 1,000 pound bombs hit within 1,000 feet of the aiming points of the targets, and 71 percent of them hit within 2,000 feet of the aiming points. The Avignon Highway Bridge was believed to have been cut at both ends. All bombs aimed at the Marshaling Yards hit within its general area, at least one very large explosion was seen, rolling stock and tracks were destroyed. The Railroad

Bridge had very near misses that the 94 powerful 1,000 pound bombs striking near it probably damaged. Bombardiers of the one Box that was aiming at the Railroad Bridge were unable to pick up their target in time to properly aim at it effectively because smoke had drifted over it from previous bombing of the Marshaling Yards, but the near misses of the huge 1,000 pound bombs exploding at close interval probably rendered structural damage to the bridge.

Our Group was congratulated for its excellent bombing on this mission by General Twinning, Commander of Fifteenth Air Force.

One Ju-88 appeared at 1005 hours, above our formation at 30,000 feet. It dropped aerial bombs on us but they were not effective and none of the bombs hit any of our planes. We also saw 3 Me-109s and 2 FW-190s but they didn't attack our Group formation, thanks to our fighter escort.

All four groups of the 304th Wing struck communications targets in the Avignon area on this day, flying in two separate mini-Wings, the 454th and 459th in the first small wing, and the 456th and the 455th making up the second "wing." The 456th had the best bombing record of the 304th Wing on this day. All targets the 304th Wing set out to bomb were well covered. A total of seventeen enemy fighters were encountered by all groups of the Wing, and one of these was probably shot down by gunners of one of the groups. None of our bombers were lost, except that the one crippled plane, noted above, had engine trouble and had to land at Corsica for repairs. It was repaired and my crew was given the interesting assignment to pick it up four days later.

It was a long flight home and three planes had to land at airfields on the way home due to low fuel. Two of our planes landed at Corsica to refuel, joining the Liberator that had to land there due to engine trouble. The third plane that had low fuel landed at an airfield at Naples to refuel.

The remaining 34 Liberators in the Group formation returned to our airfield at 1327 hour. I logged 7 hours and 55 minutes. We were given two-mission credits. I now had 202 hours and 10 minutes of combat flying time.

June 26, 1944 Moosbierbaum Oil Refinery, Vienna, Austria.

My crew was selected for a long, two-credit mission the second day in a row, the roughest up to this time. I was anxious to reach my fifty missions so I didn't mind. I learned later that there was a brief reduction of qualified crews available for flying in our Group during June because no new replacement crews were assigned to our Group from June 10 until late July, to replace those that had been lost. My crew was happy to get to fly its beloved "Porky" again, as it had been put back in commission in time for this mission by our tireless ground maintenance crews. Lt. Werner "Judge" Foss joined our crew again for this mission to assist our navigator-bombardier, Lt. James Duston. This was our roughest mission to date, and our good old "Porky" performed impeccably.

The mission this day was to the tough defense zone of Vienna with its 300 heavy antiaircraft guns and many enemy fighters, to bomb the Moosbierbaum Oil Refinery. It was a tough mission, and we were attacked by 53 enemy fighters, we lost two B-24s, and 12 of our planes, including mine, were damaged by enemy fire. Our formation consisted of what had become our standard since our June 22 mission, a tight four Box diamond formation. This formation not only provided a tighter concentration of bombs on the target, it also provided a tighter concentration of our bombers' machine guns to fire at attacking enemy aircraft, and it proved effective this day. We experienced one of the most massive air battles that the 456th Group was to encounter the entire war and it was a good test of the new formation.

442

S E C R E T

(a) Battle Order.   Date: 26 June 1944.

1st Box

Formation Leader: Thomas, Sinclair   AP:791

No.3: Ruls   AP 501   Dep Leader: Gruber,Lee AP 338
                    No.4: Bruce   AP 623
No.6: Brabon   AP 799   No.5: Whitaker   AP 319.
                    No.7: Luther   AP 295
No.9: Jones   AP 077   No.8: Hendrickson   AP 290
                    No.10: Fields   AP 233

2nd Box

Leader: Bishop   AP 470
No.3: Leathers   AP 293   Dep Leader: Blackwell AP 225
                    No.4: Riddle   AP 777
No.6: Richtschiet   AP 637   No.5: Mapa   AP 485
                    No.7: Webster   AP 912
No.9: Shetterly   AP 964   No.8: Hall   AP 328
                    No.10: Dysinger   AP 634

3rd Box

Leader: Douglass   AP 749
No.3: Savage   AP 807   Dep Leader: Monlhan   AP 628
                    No.4: Little   AP 304
No.6: Walker   AP 203   No.5: Marlar   AP 365
                    No.7: Solcher   AP 810
No.9: Roak   AP 177   No.8: Hutchins   AP 297
                    No.10: Reicher   AP 113

4th Box

Leader: Tavel   AP 279
No.3: Ragland   AP 486   Dep Leader: Snee   AP 549
                    No.4: Capps   AP 306
No.6: Scott   AP 853   No.5: Gullick   AP 831
                    No.7: Shober   AP 477
No.9: Dean   AP 934   No.8: Lunardi   AP 8275
                    No.10: Wood   AP 442

SPARES: 744th - 072, :: 745th - 487 :: 747th - 345, 638.

Time at stations: 05:10.   456th: "BOOKCLUB-ONE-TWO".

Start engines: 1st 05:20 2nd 05:27   Fighters: "PUSSCAT".
                3rd 05:35 4th 05:42.
                                       Recall: "ORANGE".
Taxi out: 05:30.

Take-off: 05:40.

S E C R E T

Our Group was paired with the 455th Group in a mini-Wing formation of two groups to bomb Moosbierbaum, with the 455th in the lead of our mini-Wing. Other heavy bomber groups of the Fifteenth Air Force bombed four other oil refineries in the Vienna area about the same time.

It was another early wake-up call in our tents, at 0300 hours, an early briefing at 0400, and time to be at stations in our aircraft of 0510 hours. Major John R. Sinclair was in the lead aircraft, and he started his engines at 0520 hours. The start engine time for each of the Boxes was increased from the routine five minute lag between start engines for each of the Boxes. The 2nd Box started engines seven minutes later, at 0527 hours, the 3rd Box at 0535, and the 4th Box at 0542 hours. This was designed to save fuel by decreasing the engine idle time on the ground while our planes waited for takeoff.

Major Sinclair taxied his bomber toward the end of the runway at 0530, then coaxed his heavily loaded B-24 off the runway at 0538 hours. Thirty-eight B-24s followed his plane off the runway at 45-second intervals. I was flying in the number 4 position of Box number 4, the last Box, so I bounced my sweet silver "Porky" off the bumpy runway fourteen and a half minutes after the leader. Lt. Dave E. Tavel was flying the lead plane of my Box.

Two bombers returned early: Lt. Dilmar T. Hutchins in B-24 number 297 "The Imp" returned early because two superchargers malfunctioned, and Lt. John W. Little in aircraft number 304 "Barbara Jane" returned early because engines number 3 and 4 were running at high RPM, his rudder was shaking because cowl flaps were stuck too far open, and his nose turret had its right charging handle malfunction.

After our Group formed its diamond of Boxes around Major Sinclair's plane, we rendezvoused over Stornara with the 455th Bomb Group at 3,000 feet to form our mini-Wing formation of groups before departing on course. The mini-Wing formation departed Stornara climbing on course at 200 feet per minute and 160 MPH indicated airspeed, a true airspeed of about 200 MPH, until the lead plane reached its bombing altitude of 21,000 feet. Our route took us over Varansko, Yugoslavia, to the Initial Point, Wetzleinsdorf, Austria.

Weather was great for the entire trip, with ceiling and visibility unlimited (CAVU). It was a beautiful day! There were only a few scattered stratus clouds in the valleys over the mountains of Yugoslavia, but north of the mountains visibility was 20 to 25 miles with a slight haze.

We had fighter cover from P-38s and P-51s, starting at 0840 hours at Keszthely, Hungary. Our fighters were from the 52nd fighter Group. Fighter cover was scheduled to continue with other fighter groups providing cover to and from the target. Fighters flew about 3,000 feet above our bomber formation. However, our Group and our companion group, the 455th, were attacked by such a massive number of enemy fighters that it was more than our fighter escort could handle. Our fighter escort had it hands full in a separate massive dogfight of fighter planes so that they couldn't prevent other enemy fighters from attacking our bombers.

The beginning of what was to become a massive air battle began at 0908 hours when fifty Me-109 enemy fighters began attacking our Group's planes, 34 minutes before our target time. Our fighter cover engaged the enemy fighters, but many were free to attack our Group. I was flying in the number four position of the Tail-End Charlie box, Box four of the Group's diamond formation. The swarm of fighters fired rockets, cannon, and machine guns at us in numerous aggressive attacks. They made attacks from 3 and 6 o'clock high, and from 5 and 7 o'clock level.

445

The first of our B-24s lost had been flying off my right wing, the "Belle of the Brawl," number 41-28638 flown by Flight Officer George J. Gullick of my 746th Squadron. Gullick's plane gradually fell back, and it could not keep up with the Group's formation because it had lost its superchargers. It was being attacked by six Me-109s that inflicted much damage to it because they had singled the crippled plane out for destruction. Finally, the crew had to bail out at 0910 hours.

Our crew members could also see, going on at the same time, a huge fighter attack on the 455th Bomb Group ahead of us, as well as a colossal, separate dogfight between our escorting fighters and a large number of enemy fighters. At 0910 hours, five FW-190s flying at great speed made very aggressive head on passes at our Group formation, flying through our tight diamond formation of bombers. They were trying, unsuccessfully, to break up our Group formation. At 0920 hours three Macchi-202s attacked from 5 and 7 o'clock level. Eight Me-210s and four Ju-88s were below our formation.

The second B-24 shot down from our Group formation was number 42-52233 flown by 2nd Lt. Dudley B. Field of the 744th Squadron. He was flying as "Tail-End Charlie" in the 1st Box, position number 10, and was so severely damaged by enemy fighter fire that its crew also had to bail out at 0920 hours. Both Field's and Gullick's crews were reported as missing in action, but we learned their fate later, as discussed below.

It was estimated that there had been 200 enemy fighters defending the target area that day. The only two Liberators we lost were shot down by fighter attacks before our formation reached the target. Twelve other bombers in our formation received damage by flak and fighters on the mission. Eleven enemy fighters were confirmed destroyed by our Group's gunners, an additional six were claimed as probables, and four enemy fighters were reported to be damaged by our gunners.

Again, referring to the diary of our radio operator, S/Sgt Thomas S. Delaney who was manning a waist gun, he recorded: "The Jerries threw everything they had at us! There were more than 200 enemy fighters around us. About 10 to 15 made attacks on us! Carl Ezuck, our tail gunner, claimed 1 destroyed, and 2 probables. Bill Halper, our nose gunner, claimed 1 destroyed! One fighter came at my waist position head on, and I put a barrage of 50 calibers in front of him and he peeled off. I never did see him again. I think it was an FW-190. It was the greatest sky battle we had ever seen. Four planes in Baker Box (the 2nd Box) had injured men. Planes in Able box (the 1st Box) also had injured men! The top turret gunner was killed by flak in Able 2 (the 1st Box), The P-38s knocked the heck out of the Jerries. I saw one P-38 shoot down 2 Jerries! The Me-109s ran when the P-38s came around!.The fighters came in 4 and 5 at a time at our tail gunner! One came in head on at our nose turret gunner and went under us. He was about 10 feet from us! Our ball turret guns were out which saved the Jerry! Hamlin (S/Sgt Clyde W.), was flying ball turret for us today. He was really sweating it out because it was his 51st mission! He found out after the mission that it was actually his 52nd mission and he didn't have to fly that mission! He had his bible, and my rosary beads over his turret. He really had guts to point his guns and bluff, plus watching Jerries throwing rockets and 20mm cannon shells at us! The crew performed excellently, from the pilot to the tail gunner. Everyone did their job well, and it paid dividends! The pilot and copilot flew a wonderful formation, they kept us right under Dog 1 (number 4 position of the 4th Box), and they gave us plenty of fire power too! It was a fine mission for all of us, everyone was cool and alert. I was proud to be a member of such a good crew. It was the roughest mission for all of us and we were flying in the Tail Box too! I saw two B-24s crash and blow up! Ray Dickson saw three B-24s crash and 20 parachutes open! Thanks God!..............Nine B-24s in the group ahead of us went down over our target! They had a straggling formation (fighters delight)..."

Enemy fighters liked to attack stragglers and loose formations. Our Group flew a tight formation, an intimidating sight for enemy pilots to face, with its tight concentration of guns. This may account in part for the fact that enemy fighters only shot down two of our Liberators on a day when so many groups around us lost many more.

The 455th Bomb Group, our companion group in our mini-Wing formation, was flying ahead of our formation to the same target. Its formation consisted of 36 Liberators, and it was attacked about the same time our 456th Bomb Group was being attacked. It was first attacked by 60 enemy fighters that used similar tactics as those that attacked our Group. Among many other attacks, enemy fighters made vicious head-on attacks on the 455th Group formation trying to break up their formation as they did on our Group formation. The enemy fired rockets and cannon. All the while, our escort fighters were busy engaging 20 Me-210 twin-engined enemy fighters.

Near the target, sixty more enemy fighters aggressively attacked the 455th Group. One of the 455th's Liberators was rammed by a single-engine fighter during a head-on attack, but the B-24 that was rammed stayed in its group formation until after bombs were dropped. It went down in flames after dropping its bombs on the target. Two other Liberators of the 455th Group were set on fire as they approached the target, and they also remained with the 455th's formation until bombs were dropped on the target. It too exploded in the air soon after dropping its bombs. In all, our companion group, the 455th, lost 10 bombers on this mission, but its gunners claimed 34 enemy fighters

448

destroyed. As we approached the target, after they had left it, the sky was filled with parachutes from enemy as well as friendly planes. Parachutes from our 456th Bomb Group planes added to the sight.

Weather at the target was clear and the wind at 19,000 feet was only 20 knots from 290 degrees. The temperature at 21,000 feet was minus 16 degrees centigrade.

The 459th Bomb Group, flying ahead of us, was being hit hard in a huge air battle. A huge swarm of fighters of all types were attacking the Group. It appeared that three of their planes went down in flames, at least ten enemy fighters were shot down, and numerous chutes were blooming in the sky ahead of us.

The remaining 35 Bombers of our 456th Group fought their way to the I.P through a heavy cloud of black flak bursts, then dropped their bombs on the target at 0942 hours. One bomber had its bombs hang up in the bomb racks, and it was not able to release bombs on the target. Thus, 34 of our Liberators were able to drop 75.5 tons of 250 pound general purpose bombs (604 bombs) on the Moosbierbaum Oil Refinery from 21,000 feet for the 1st Box and 20,000 feet for the 4th Box of the formation on an axis of attack of 235 degrees magnetic, at an indicated airspeed of 160 MPH, a true airspeed of 228 MPH. The bombardiers' bomb release interval setting was 35 feet.

Flak at the target was moderate, accurate, with heavy black bursts. Flak had also been encountered at three different points enroute to the I.P. After bombs were released, our Group formation made a descending left turn at an indicated airspeed of 155 to 160 MPH, a true airspeed of 208 to 218 MPH, to deceive flak gunners on the ground. The airspeed was purposely kept low so the B-24s could maintain a tight formation throughout the descending turn for maximum fire power protection against enemy fighter attacks.

449

Six K-22 cameras took pictures of the target. Bomb bursts and explosions of previous group drops obscured the aiming point of most of the plant. Oil storage tanks on the south-eastern side of the plant received several direct hits from our bombs, resulting in at least two violent explosions and fires. A new storage tank area under construction at the eastern corner of the plant suffered many hits, and bombs wrecked personnel buildings to the south of the plant. Results indicated the target was well covered, and that the oil refinery was demolished. Fires and smoke rose thousands of feet into the air.

Our 456th Group's crippled formation of 35 Liberators returned to our airbase at 1224 hours, and it logged 6 hours and 50 minutes by the time it was on the ground. It was the Group's 66th accredited mission of 74 missions flown in Italy. It was my 44th and 45th credited mission, a two-credit mission, and well earned! I now had 209 combat flying hours.

The casualties for the day for the 456th Group were 20 airmen missing in action, one upper turret gunner was killed, and one bombardier seriously wounded. The gunner killed, S/Sgt Elmer J. Stallman, a member of Lt. Taylor's crew from the 744th Squadron, was killed by a piece of flak that hit his head and he died instantly.

Gullicks crew from the 744th Squadron, we learned later, had all bailed out and were taken prisoner of war except Sgt Edward J. Bastian who bailed out but was killed by some undetermined means, death by a faulty parachute or by soldiers on the ground. He is interred in the American Military Cemetery at Ardennes, Belgium. Sgt Adolph J. Stadnicki was wounded in the foot by Me-109 machine gun fire before he bailed out, but he survived. Second Lieutenant James B. Dixon, navigator, and S/Sgt Albert A. Wolz, engineer, are currently members of the 456th Bomb Group Association.

It was also learned later that seven members of Field's crew, also from the 744th Squadron, successfully bailed out and were taken prisoners of war. The pilot, 2nd Lt. Dudley B. Field, the upper turret gunner, S/SGt Henry A. Barrett, the bombardier, 1st Lt. Paul E. Busse, nose turret gunner, S/Sgt Archie G. Hatch, navigator, 2nd Lt. Wilson D. Smith, engineer, Matthew G. Beland, and turret gunner, T/Sgt William J. Harvey. Field, Busse, and Hatch are current members of the 456th Bomb Group Association. Beland, a former member, died March 6, 1993.

June 27, 1944 No mission this day.

Evidently the weather was bad at all targets, or our high level commanders decided we needed time for our hard working maintenance crews to get our shot-up planes back in condition.

*June 28, 1944 Karlova Airdrome, Bulgaria.

Our air crews weren't allowed to rest more than one day. My crew was scheduled for this day's mission to bomb the Karlova Airdrome in Bulgaria. We had excellent results. This was my crew's fourth mission in five days, but I was glad to keep working toward my magic fifty for a ticket home. We flew our reliable "Porky" on the mission. Lt. Judge Foss flew with us again today to help our navigator-bombardier, Lt. James Duston. The Karlova Airdrome was the most active airdrome in Bulgaria and it had 57 planes on it. The weather was clear the entire route, another great day for flying! To top it off, we saw fighters, but none attacked us. Although we encountered scant flak at three different locations enroute to the target, at Sopot, Pirdop, and Krnarc (many of these names were changed after the war by communist rulers), there was no flak at the target.

S E C R E T

(a) Battle Order.   28 June 1944

1st Box

Parks
                Formation Leader: Richards,/ AP 764   Phillips
No. 3: Ball   AP 485   Dep Leader: Tosselli,/ AP 790
                No. 4: Riddle   AP 777
No. 6: Leathers AP 293   No. 5: Stromben   AP 912
                No. 7: Blackwell AP 964
No. 9: Ogden   AP 225   No. 8: Ceretti   AP 328
                No.10: Klingler   AP 345

2nd Box

                Leader: Gutting   AP 442
No. 3: Ragland   AP 486   Dep Leader: Johnson AP 831
                No. 4: Capps   AP 306
No. 6: Wood   AP 487   No. 5: Dean   AP 934
                No. 7: Addis   AP 199
No. 9: Ashley   AP 477   No. 8: Scott   AP 853
                No.10: Lumardi   AP 201

3rd Box

                Leader: Rudd   AP 338
No. 3: Jones   AP 072   Dep Leader: Huls   AP 501
                No. 4: Luther   AP 275
No. 6: Hendrickson AP 799   No. 5: Powell   AP 947
                No. 7: Lunt   AP 279
No. 9: Roak   AP 177   No. 8: Dysinger   AP 364
                No.10:   AP

4th Box

                Leader: Monahan   AP 334
No. 3: Williamson AP 810   Dep Leader: Gardner AP 628
                No. 4: Little   AP 749
No. 6: Floming   AP 807   No. 5: Wilkinson   AP 487
                No. 7: Nilsson   AP 297
No. 9: Marlar   AP 365   No. 8: Hutchins   AP 203
                No.10:   AP

SPARES: 744th - 295,:: 745th - 113,:: 747th - 768, 634, 637, 470.

Stations: 0550.   456th FLAK FAIR THREE

Engines :A 0555 B 0605   Fighters: FIRTREE
         C 0615 D 0625
                                  Penetration: RETAIN
Take-off: 0620.
                                  Recall Signal: DIAMOND

We had a wake-up call in our tents on this mild summer morning at 0400 hours. After I had some C-ration pancakes, one of the best items on this breakfast menu, and some dehydrated coffee, my crew and I climbed aboard the back end of open Army six-by-six trucks for our ride up to the Group briefing room on the hill to attend briefing, a little before 0500 hours. The sight of the long piece of yarn on the wall map at the end of the briefing room gave us some concern at first until the briefing officers told us that it should be a long milk run. It would be a single credit mission. Our Group formation was our new standard four-Box diamond formation.

Our stations time at our aircraft was set for 0550, and the mild spring air was very pleasant at this early hour. Some of my crew members were having a last minute cigarette away from the aircraft, to avoid a fire hazard around the 100 octane gasoline, while I completed my external preflight inspection of my beautiful "Porky." They wanted one last smoke before we took off and they had to start wearing their oxygen masks for a long time.

Lt. Col. Samuel Parks of my 746th Squadron was flying in our lead aircraft this day, and he started his engines at 0555 hours. He started taxiing toward the end of the runway at 0610, then pulled his heavily loaded B-24 off the bumpy runway at 0619 hours. Thirty-six of our Liberators followed his at 45 second intervals. My plane was assigned to the number 4 position of the 2nd Box, so I was the fourteenth plane to takeoff. After we caught up with Parks' plane and assembled our Group's diamond formation, Parks lead our Group formation to a rendezvous with other groups of our 304th Wing over Stornara at 4,000 feet, before departing on course at 160 MPH indicated airspeed, about 200 MPH true airspeed, and climbing at 200 feet per minute toward the Initial Point in Bulgaria. We had P-47s and P38s covering our penetration of enemy territory, the target area, and our withdrawal.

453

Three B-24s returned early this day. One Liberator had number 4 supercharger malfunction, one plane had a bad oil leak, and another Liberator had number 4 propeller governor go out.

It was a beautiful day as we flew over the Adriatic, then crossed the mountains of Yugoslavia to the mountains in Bulgaria. Only three scant, inaccurate flak firings were made at our formation enroute to the target, but none of our planes received damage. No flak was fired at us in the target area. We expected to be attacked by fighters from Sofia as we passed the city, but none came up. Our fighter escort was doing a good job. We saw some Me-109s in the target area, but none attacked our formation.

Thirty-four Liberators in our Group flew over the target, but two planes didn't drop its bombs on the target. One plane had its bombardier's toggle switch for releasing his bombs fail and the other plane accidentally released its bombs before reaching the target. Thus, 32 bombers in our Group successfully dropped 79 tons of 500 pound bombs (316 bombs) on the Karlova Airdrome at 0944 hours from 19,900 feet for the 1st Box and 18,700 feet for the 4th Box. The indicated airspeed was 160 MPH, and true airspeed was 222 MPH. The axis of attack was 360 degrees magnetic, and the air temperature at 19,000 feet was minus 18 degrees centigrade, very warm compared to what we had been used to enduring during the winter months. The bombardiers' bomb release interval setting was 25 feet.

Six K-22 cameras took pictures of the target area, and they revealed excellent results. There was a good pattern of our Group's bombs on the target. Direct hits were made on planes, repair shops, hangars, and nearby buildings were completely destroyed. Many fires were seen as our Group left the area. Thirty-one of the airdromes planes were destroyed by the Wing, of which eleven were destroyed by the 456th Group.

Our Group formation of 34 Liberators arrived back at our field at 1245 hours, no planes or crew members lost or damaged. The Group logged 6 hours and 35 minutes. It was the Group's 67th accredited mission of 75 flown in Italy. It was my 46th credited mission, and as much as I tried not to think about it, I was getting close to the magic fifty! I now had 215 hours and 35 minutes of combat flying time.

Again, our radio operator S/Sgt Tom Delaney's diary recorded, "We plastered the airdrome at Karlova! It was a good run, we saw very little flak, and no enemy fighters! Lt. Capps and Lt. Brooks were sick, but flew a darn good formation anyway! We caught 20 enemy planes on the ground! Lt. Douglas C. Richards (our assistant operations officer) flew lead plane, and did a good job! It was a very successful mission. Thanks, God!"

June 29, 1944   Another Stand Down Day.

The weather appeared good, so there must be another reason why we weren't flying. I was given the pleasant task of flying up to the Island of Corsica to pick up one of our planes that had landed there for repairs after the Avignon mission on June 25, 1944. The crippled plane had two engines inoperative and couldn't make it back to Stornara. It had been repaired, and it was supposed to be ready for me to fly home. To my enjoyment the plane was not ready, so I had to spend the night on Corsica, in the comfortable bachelors' officers quarters, which was a considerable upgrade from the standard of living I was used to in my tent at Stornara. I knew that this was the birthplace of the famous emperor of France, the great Napoleon Bonaparte, and I was curious about it ever since we flew by it on our way to bomb Avignon five days ago.

The Allied Airbase was an interesting one on the east coast of the Island of Corsica, with British and French troops occupying it. That night I enjoyed talking with people in the officers club, where I got to know, over a few drinks, a British assistant operations officer of the airbase. We talked about flying fighters versus flying bombers. When I told him I had flown American P-40 fighters a few hours, he said that he would arrange for me to fly one of his Spitfire fighters early the next morning before I had to leave with my B-24. I was so excited at the prospect of flying a Spitfire, I had a difficult time sleeping that night!

June 30, 1944   Kaposvar Marshaling Yards, Hungary.

While I was on Corsica this day, our Group flew a mission that was an attempt to bomb the Odertal Oil Plant in Czechoslovakia. Weather prevented it, and a target of opportunity, marshaling yards at Kaposvar, Hungary, was bombed instead.

The crews had a wake-up call in their tents at 0415 hours, briefing at 0520, stations time at their planes of 0630 hours. Captain Chester R. Ladd started engines of his lead plane at 0635, started to taxi out to the runway at 0645, then took off at 0655 hours. Thirty-seven B-24s followed him off the runway at 45 second intervals.

Six planes aborted the mission before reaching the target. One of the returning planes had a gas leak on number 2 engine. Another plane returned early because it had an engine that ran too hot. One plane was so late taking off that it could not catch the Group formation because the plane ahead of him on the runway was having engine problems and it delayed its takeoff. One B-24 had low fuel pressure that dropped off when it reached high altitude, and another plane had a hydraulic fluid leak. One bomber had its number 1 and 4 electric generators go out. All but one of these planes returned their bombs to our airbase and landed with them. The plane with a fuel leak jettisoned its bombs in the Adriatic before landing.

S E C R E T

(a) Battle Order.   Date: 30 June 1944.

1st Box

Formation Leader: Miller, Ladd   AP 132   Russel
No.3: Johnson   AP 831   Dep Leader: Ensign / AP 791
                    No.4: Shober   AP 0487
No.6: Scott   AP 853   No.5: Ashley   AP 442
                    No.7: Ragland   AP 839
No.9: Sajeski   AP 275   No.8: Dean   AP 934
                    No.10: Lanardi   AP 201

2nd Box

Leader: Leukuma   AP 470
No.3: Rawlinson   AP 293   Dep Leader: Webster   AP 777
                    No.4: Mapa   AP 485
No.6: Klingler   AP 345   No.5: Reichscheidt   AP 313
                    No.7: Hall   AP 912
No.9: Shotterly   AP 964   No.8: Cerrotti   AP 225
                    No.10: Dysinger   AP 364

3rd Box

Leader: Douglas   AP 749
No.3: Nilsson   AP 297   Dep Leader: Little   AP 304
                    No.4: Wilkinson   AP 810
No.6: Reicher   AP 334   No.5: Roak   AP 177
                    No.7: Palis   AP 365
No.9: Savage   AP 807   No.8: Walkor   AP 203
                    No.10: Hutchins   AP 487

4th Box

Leader: Gruber, Breeding AP 768
No.3: Huls   AP 295   Dep Leader: Phifer   AP 501
                    No.4: Luthor   AP 275
No.6: Powoll   AP 947   No.5: Whitaker   AP 338
                    No.7: Lunt   AP 279
No.9: Jones   AP 077   No.8: Hendrickson   AP 799
                    No.10: Vosholl   AP 306

SPARES: 744th Sqdn: 290, 072.   745th Sqdn: 113, 283.
         746th Sqdn: 199.   747th Sqdn: 634, 637.

Time at stations: 06:30   456th: "DAYLONG FOUR-ONE".

Start engines: 1st 0635. 2nd 0642. Fighters: "IMPISH".
                3rd 0650. 4th 0657.
                                     Recall: "ROBBIN".
Taxi out: 06:45.

Take-off: 06:55.

457

The Group's diamond formation of four Boxes rendezvoused with the 455th Group over Stornara at 3,000 feet, then they departed at 0748 hours climbing on course. The formation's route was scheduled to take it over Cazziol Island, Csallikzaranyos, Sternberg, Neustadt, to the Initial Point, Ober Glogau, then to Odertal. The weather up to Lake Balaton was good, but from that point on there was a solid, ten-tenths cloud coverage with altocumulus clouds with bases at 14,000 feet and tops too high to measure. This prevented bombing at Odertal, or the secondary target, so a target of opportunity was selected in Hungary. Fighter escort was provided by P-38s, P-47s, and P-51s.

Thirty-two B-24s in the Group formation dropped 79 tons of 500 pound general purpose bombs (316 bombs) on the Kaposvar Marshaling Yards, Hungary at 1037 hours, from 12,500 feet for the 1st Box and 10,500 feet for the 4th Box of the diamond formation, on an axis of attack of 255 degrees magnetic. The indicated airspeed was 160 MPH, and the true airspeed was 205 MPH. The temperature at 12,000 feet was a warm minus 3 degrees centigrade. The bombardiers' bomb release interval setting was 30 feet. Six K-22 cameras took pictures of the target area, and results were good. There was a tight pattern of bombs that hit the railroad choke-point and rolling stock. No fighters or flak were seen, there were no planes damaged, and no aircrew casualties.

The Group formation of bombers returned to our airbase at 1245 hours. It was the Group's 68th credited mission in 76 attempts. Flight time was logged as 6 hours and 5 minutes by the time planes were on the ground.

Operations of the 304th Wing during June had been entirely of a strategic nature, none against troop concentrations. All our missions hit transportation facilities, oil production and supply installations, and airdromes.

While my Group was flying this mission, I got up extra early in the morning on the tranquil Island of Corsica this day, so that I could fly the British Spitfire fighter plane as the British assistant operations officer had promised me the night before. I wanted to fly the Spitfire before I had to fly the B-24 back to our base in Stornara. When I went to base operations and met my new British friend, we saw many French Army troops lined up on the only available runway at the airbase. An extremely tall French officer was reviewing what looked like a few thousand troops. It took a long time while we waited patiently. In fact, it took so long that I didn't have time to fly the Spitfire before I had to depart with my B-24 for Stornara.

The French troops marched in review along the runway. I learned later that the tall French general was General Charles De Gaulle, and he was reviewing the French troops in preparation for their invasion of the France Riviera that finally took place in August 15, 1944 in "Operation Dragoon," formerly called "Anvil."

By the time the French parade was over, it was too late for me to fly the Spitfire, much to my disappointment! I knew we had to get the B-24 back to our home base as soon as possible before dark, because it had already taken one more day than we had planned to bring the plane home. We needed the plane and my crew. We were short of aircrews.

The Luftwaffe fighter force was on its last gasp. During June 1944, the Luftwaffe lost 48.3 percent of the operational fighter force, per a study by Williamson Murray in his book "Luftwaffe." (The Nautical and Aviation Publishing Company of America, Baltimore, Maryland, 1985).

July 1, 1944   There was no mission flown this day.

My crew was scheduled to fly the number 4 position of the 3rd Box on a mission with the Group, but it was canceled before we were briefed.

July 2, 1944 - Shell Oil Refinery Budapest, Hungary. (Our 456th Bombardment Group was awarded its second Distinguished Unit Citation for this mission).

My crew was selected to fly our beloved "Porky" with the Group this day, to bomb the Shell Oil Refinery at Budapest, Hungary. This was probably our Group's roughest mission to date. We were attacked by 60 enemy fighters, the flak was intense, accurate, with ugly, heavy black bursts, and six of our B-24s were shot down. We had a substitute navigator-bombardier on our crew for this mission, Lt. John K. Zwiebel, and he was severely wounded by a piece of flak in the shoulder that nearly tore his arm off. "Porky" received many holes from enemy fire. Bombing results were good as we bombed in a column of Boxes. Our 456th Bombardment Group was awarded its second Presidential Distinguished Unit Citation for this mission, for "outstanding performance of duty in armed conflict against the enemy." The citation states, "In preparation for a maximum effort bombing mission to Budapest, Hungary, ground personnel worked feverishly, enthusiastically and with untiring vigor to get all B-24 type aircraft in the best possible mechanical condition to insure success for the operation." I know from personal experience that our competent crew chief on "Porky," M/Sgt. Candelario R. Aguilar Jr., worked very hard, for long hours in the open air to get our plane ready.

We had a 0400 wake-up call in our crew tents on this mild, windless summer morning day. After a hearty breakfast of powdered eggs, powdered milk, toast, dehydrated coffee, toast and jam, we washed our metal mess kits, returned them to our tents, then climbed aboard the back end of open Army six-by-six trucks for our usual ride up to our briefing room on the hill. Briefing was held at 0500 where we were told about our target for the day. We knew it to be a rough one. The Shell Oil Refinery was the largest crude oil distillation plant in Hungary and it had never been bombed. Our

460

S E C R E T

(a) Battle Order: 2 July 1944

1st Box

Formation Leader: Thomas, Reid   AP 279

No. 3: Monahan	AP 334	Dep Leader: Gardner	AP 749
	No.4: Williamson	AP 810	
No. 6: Reicher	AP 628	No.5: Fleming	AP 297
	No.7: Little	AP 304	
No. 9: Walker	AP 177	No.8: Marler	AP 365
	No.10: 'whe'	AP 4 7	

2nd Box

Leader: Leo   AP 338

No.3: Lunt	AP 501	Dep Leader: Powell	AP 947
	No.4: Luther	AP 275	
No. 6: Whitaker	AP 799	No.5: Jones	AP 077
	No.7: Huls	AP 295	
No. 9: Hutchins	AP 487	No.8: Hendrickson	AP 072
	No.10:	AP	

3rd Box

Leader: Ensign   AP 486

No.3: Scott	AP 839	Dep Leader: Sagert	AP 8275
	No.4: Capps	AP 306	
No.6: Doan	AP 934	No.5: Voshall	AP 201
	No.7: Shober	AP 0487	
No.9: Ragland	AP 831	No.8: Sajoski	AP 549
	No.10: Addis	AP 199	

4th Box

Leader: Jackson, C. Y. AP 470

No.3: Rawlinson	AP 293	Dep Leader: Stromben	AP 912
	No.4: Riddle	AP 777	
No.6: Webster	AP 345	No.5: Ball	AP 364
	No.7: Mapa	AP 485	
No.9: Leathers	AP 284	No.8: Ogden	AP 225
	No.10: Shotterly	AP 637	

SPARES: 744th Sqdn: 290. 745th Sqdn: 807. 747th Sqdn: 634, 328.

Time at stations: 0605.   456th BG: "BUTLER ONE-FOUR".

Start engines: A 06:15 B 06:22   Fighters: "CLEARSOUP", with suffix
                C 06:30 D 06:37.   numbers in order of contact.

Taxi out: 06:25.   Recall: "DEER".

Take-off: 06:35.

S E C R E T

previous attacks on Ploesti and German synthetic oil plants had cut the vital Axis production of petroleum products by fifty percent. A successful mission this day would reduce the remaining supply by forty-percent more. Because of the essential nature of this remaining oil plant we expected it to be heavily defended. From 75 to 95 fighters were expected to attack our bomber formation, and flak was expected to be very intense and accurate.

The entire Fifteenth Air Force armada of heavy bombers made coordinated attacks on oil refineries and railroad marshaling yards in Hungary, this day, directly challenging the Luftwaffe and attempting to deliver crippling blows to some strategic targets. All bomb Groups of our 304th Wing were attacking installations near our 456th Group's target, and all other wings of the Fifteenth's heavy bombers were attacking nearby targets.

We were again told that if we were forced to bail out in enemy territory we should make our way south into Yugoslavia and seek help from the Partisans who could be identified by the red stars on their caps and by their distinctive salutes of raising their fists to their heads.

Anticipating a huge air battle, there were a total of six of our fighter groups from the 306th Fighter Wing patrolling in the immediate target area. Two of the fighter groups provided cover during penetration over the target, and during withdrawal for the B-17s of the 5th Bomb Wing which was bombing targets near ours. One of the fighter groups provided "free lance" cover over the entire target area. The other three fighter groups of the 306th Wing provided penetration, target, and withdrawal cover for the other four Liberator wings that were bombing targets in the area, the 49th, 55th, 47th, and our 304th Wings. As it turned out, our fighter cover was spread too thin to protect our Group from such a massive enemy fighter attack, and the

Luftwaffe ground control directed the enemy fighters where our fighter escort was not.

Another problem that our crews foresaw was that we were briefed to go into the target from the I.P., flying in a column of Boxes, instead of our normal Group's diamond formation that provided us more protection from enemy fighters by concentrating our Groups guns together. We were told in the briefing room that this was the most effective procedure for knocking out a small target. Lt Werner C. "Judge" Foss Jr. noted in his diary that during the morning briefing his pilot, Lt. Stanley A. Sagert who he was flying with this day, was among others who objected to this type of bomber formation because it was dangerous. They made the case that it would make us very vulnerable to heavy fighter attack, but our commander Colonel Steed who was not flying on this mission said that while he agreed with the Group's crews that this was not the best procedure, he had to abide with the order passed down by the 15th Air Force Headquarters. As will be seen, we had a difficult battle because of this new procedure. However, this was the most accurate way of hitting the target.

With mixed feelings, we climbed on the back end of the six-by-six trucks for the ride to our planes where we had a stations time of 0605 hours. The weather was beautiful as the sun was coming up. We usually arrived at our planes long before our formally designated stations time so that we could give our B-24s careful preflight checks to ensure that everything was in order and to brief our crews about what was going to happen. Our ground crews, and my flight engineer T/Sgt Edward W. Broom (later killed on a mission aboard "Porky" July 21, 1944 as discussed elsewhere), usually did a very thorough job before we arrived at the plane, but my preflight inspection of the outside of "Porky" was a double check to see that nothing was overlooked, and that the plane was safe to fly. I was getting near to the magic fifty missions and I was concerned that something would prevent my reaching that goal. Some crew members had last minute cigarettes at a safe distance from the 100 octane gasoline of Porky before climbing on our plane. They knew that they'd soon have to wear their oxygen masks for a long time without cigarettes. It was also a means of easing their nervousness. I didn't smoke cigarettes so that wasn't a problem for me.

Major Robert L. Reid and Colonel Thomas of Group were in the lead plane for today's mission and they started their engines at 0615 hours. Thomas began to taxi to the end of the runway at 0625, then took off at 0635. The rest of us, 36 more planes in all, followed him off the runway at 45 second intervals. I was flying in the number 4 position of the 3rd Box of our diamond formation, so I positioned myself in the taxi line to the runway so that I was the 24th plane to takeoff, 18 minutes after Reid's plane. After we all caught up with Reid in the air and formed our Group's diamond formation around Reid's plane, the Group formation flew over Stornara at 4,000 feet to join in trail formation with the 455th Group, then we departed, climbing on course, at 0730 hours. Our climb speed was the standard 160 MPH indicated airspeed, about 205 MPH true airspeed.

One of the 455th Bomb Group's B-24s crashed while taking off for this mission. We saw the fireball and plume of smoke at the end of the San Giovanni airfield, home of the 455th Group, while we were flying to assemble our formation before departing on the mission. I was wondering if this Liberator was another one that was a victim of sabotage.

Seven of our 456th Group bombers returned early before reaching the target. One Liberator had a gas leak, three bombers had oil leaks, two had turbo-superchargers go out, and one B-24 had an engine failure. I was lucky in that I never had to abort a mission for any reason while flying as an aircraft commander. I flew every mission I was scheduled to fly.

The weather was good all the way to the target, with only one-tenth cirrus cloud coverage above our formation, bases at 20,000 feet and tops at 21,000. There were two-tenths cumulus cloud coverage below our formation with bases at 7,000 feet and tops at 10,000 feet, until we reached Belgrade. After Belgrade, the cloud coverage below us increased to three-tenths coverage until we arrived in the target area. Over the target, we had two-tenths of thin cirrus clouds above us with bases 21,000 feet and tops at 24,000. Below our formation at the target, there were four-tenths of cloud coverage with altostratus clouds, bases at 8,000 feet and tops at 13,000 feet. Visibility was 10 miles, and the temperature at 21,500 feet was minus 19 degrees centigrade.

We had little enemy opposition on the way to the target, except for flak. As we passed Brod and Metkodic in Yugoslavia the flak was scant, accurate, with heavy black bursts, but at Sarajevo the flak increased to moderate intensity, accurate, with heavy black bursts. As we approached the Initial Point and formed our column of Boxes, and from there past the target, the flak was very intense, accurate, with heavy black bursts. Flak was of the tracking type as well as the barrage type. Many of our planes received flak hits, but none went down before bombs were dropped.

Thirty-one Liberators flew over the I.P. flying in a column of four Boxes. Two of our Liberators had bomb release malfunctions and couldn't drop on the target. The remaining twenty-nine B-24s that didn't have bomb release malfunctions were able to drop 65.13 tons of 250 pound bombs (521 bombs) on the Shell Oil Storage and Refinery Plant at 1022 hours from 22,200 feet for the 1st Box, and 19,900 feet for the 4th Box of the column of Boxes, on an axis of attack of 275 degrees magnetic. The indicated airspeed was 160 MPH, giving a true airspeed of 227 MPH, and the bombardiers' bomb release interval setting was 30 feet.

The diary of S/Sgt Thomas S. Delaney, radio operator and waist gunner on my crew, described what happened on our plane during the bomb run. It says, "....Our navigator-bombardier (Lt. John K. Zwiebel) got hit by flak, a bad flesh wound in the shoulder. Just before bombs away, I heard the bombardier over the interphone say coolly, 'Nose-gunner I'm hit.' Bill Harper, our nose gunner, volunteered to getting out of his nose turret to help the bombardier! Bill found him lying over the bombsight! The top turret gunner said over the interphone that the lead plane was dropping its bombs, so Bill toggled out the bombs, and by gosh they hit right in the center of the Oil Refinery! Our Sperry ball turret gunner watched the bombs all the way down!"

Lt. Werner "Judge" Foss, who had flown some missions as my bombardier, was flying in Sagert's plane off to my right. I saw his worried eyes looking out a window of his plane all the way home, looking at the gaping hole in the nose of my plane, where he would have been flying if he wasn't with his regular crew this day. He could easily have been in the nose of my plane where my substitute navigator-bombardier was hit.

Nine K-22 cameras took pictures of the target area, and they revealed good results, but smoke and fire over our target area that resulted from bombings by other groups of other nearby targets prevented precise assessment of our bombing results. After bombs were away, the Group formation made a descending left turn after we had cleared the target area.

It was then, at 1025 hours, three minutes after bombs were released, before we had reformed our diamond formation, and after we had emerged from the intense black cloud of flak over the target, that a huge cloud of enemy fighters composed of 50 Me-109s and 10 FW-190s, began

466

their attacks on our formation. We were the most vulnerable right after bombs away because we had dropped our bombs in a column of Boxes. It was a hectic, fierce air battle. All attacks were from the 3 and 9 o'clock positions, mostly from level to low positions, and the attacks were very aggressive, with enemy fighters closing to within 50 to 100 yards of our formation. They fired machine guns, 20mm cannon, and rockets at us. There were no head-on attacks this time, but the enemy fighters made their attacks singly, in pairs, four and eight fighters abreast and some attacks were made with fighters line astern. Some dived away low after making their passes while other fighters zoomed upwards. Many fighters exposed their bellies as they finished their passes, making good targets for our gunners. Much of this was because the pilots had little combat experience because most of the experienced Luftwaffe pilots had already been killed or maimed. The bottoms of FW-190s had armor plate, so they may have felt it was all right to expose their planes' bellies to us. One Ju-88 fired rockets at us from the rear. The fighters were painted blue with large black Maltese crosses on wings and fuselages, and some were painted silver with similar crosses. One Me-109 was painted an unusual olive drab color.

Some of our crews reported seeing our own gunners, in the excitement of the brawl, shooting at our own P-51 escort as they crossed the nose of our 1st Box in hot pursuit of the enemy fighters. Mustangs looked much like Me-109s from a distance, except for the scoop on the P-51's belly. When P-51s were far enough away so that the American flag painted on the P-51's fuselage couldn't be readily seen, or they were banking so their belly scoops couldn't be seen, it was difficult for our gunners to tell them apart. However, the P-51s were silver, not painted, whereas the Me-109s were painted.

467

"Porky" received seven 50mm machine gun holes in its rudder, in addition to enemy inflicted holes that were discovered on the ground after we had landed, and which had evidently come from the fire of our own gunners as they fired aggressively at attacking enemy fighters that passed behind my plane.

Because I was flying "Porky" in tight formation at the time, under our lead aircraft, I could only see glimpses of the action, hear the conversational descriptions of the action over our aircraft interphone, and feel the fierce vibration from the fire of "Porky's" machine guns that made the whole ship vibrate violently. The excitement caused me to fly as close as I could to the plane ahead and above me, Lt. Robert S. Ensign's plane number 486, "Piece Maker" of my 746th Squadron. I flew close to his plane to concentrate the fire power of our guns as much as possible. I was flying so close to his plane that empty shells from Ensign's machine guns hit the leading edge of my wing, punching many holes in it. My ground crew was not happy that I flew so close to the plane ahead because it created much repair work for them. I decided that next time I would fly a few feet lower so the empty shells from the plane ahead will go over our plane. I definitely felt the flak bursts near our plane that caused it to pitch in the air, and I could hear the flak sprinkling over Porky.

S/Sgt Delaneys diary states about the air battle, "…. All this time enemy fighters were making savage attacks! I didn't knock any down, but kept them away from my side! The top turret gunner (T/Sgt Edward W. Broom our flight engineer) got two Me-109s, the waist gunner (Delaney was the other waist gunner) got two Me-109s, the Sperry ball turret gunner got one probable Me-109, and the tail gunner got one probable Me-109. The flak was the heaviest I have ever seen! God was with us all the way!.....One of my best friends, Jack Bonifield, was on one of those plane shot down (number 42-51077, "Emperor Jones" of the 744th Squadron) ...."

As a result of the gigantic air battle, six of our Group's bombers were shot down by enemy fighters, and thirteen of our B-24s, including our "Porky", were damaged from flak and fighters. Our Group's gunners were credited with shooting down 26 fighters, getting 8 more probables, and damaging 4 more. Sixty-one of our Group's airmen were missing in action, one ball turret gunner was killed, my navigator was severely wounded, and three gunners were seriously wounded, including a left waist gunner, a right waist gunner, and a tail turret gunner. The sky was filled with from ten to twenty parachutes much of the time during the air battle.

The 744th Squadron lost the six planes out of a total of eight Liberators that it had sent on the mission. All of their planes were flying in the 2nd Box. Aircrews of our Group reported that enemy fighter fire was deadly accurate on this mission. As a result of these fighter attacks, two of the six 744th Squadron planes were seen to disintegrate in midair from explosions, two more 744th bombers were seen going down with engines on fire, another was seen spinning out of control with a wing shot off, and one 744th Liberator was seen to have its tail shot off, and diving out of control. Only four to five parachutes were seen to come from all six of the planes shot down, and it was difficult to tell which planes they came from. More information about what happened to the aircrew personnel, described below, was obtained after the war by surviving members of the six aircrews who became members of the 456th Bomb Group Association.

On our "Porky", while I was flying close formation, our navigator, Lt. John K. Zwiebel, received the bad wound in his shoulder as described by Delaney's diary. He had received the ugly flak wound that nearly hit the bone and almost ripped his shoulder off. It was bleeding profusely. Our nose

469

gunner, S/Sgt William E. Halper, volunteered to get out of his nose turret to help him, because he was the only other crewman in the nose section of Porky at the time. Halper found Zwiebel lying over the bombsight, incapacitated, as the top turret gunner (our great flight engineer, T/Sgt. Edward W. Broom) called out over the interphone that the lead plane was dropping their bombs. Quick thinking Bill Halper hit the bomb toggle switch to release our bombs. The Sperry ball turret gunner on the belly of our plane watched our bombs fall all the way to the target, and they hit right in the center of the oil refinery. While Halper was away from his guns the sixty enemy fighters resumed their savage attack on us, Halper continued his aid to Zwiebel during the attack, giving him morphine to ease his pain, and he applied a compress to stem the flow of blood from his shoulder. Later on the ground, our commander Colonel Steed said Halper would be recommended for the Distinguished Flying Cross for his quick action. Our Group's poor administrative procedures held up this award so that I never learned whether or not he finally received it.

The air battle with enemy planes did not end our flirting with danger on this mission. After the enemy fighters ran out of fuel and left us, we ran into heavy and accurate flak on the way back from the target area. Through a navigation error by our lead plane, we flew over Sarajevo and more flak put more holes in "Porky." Some of our crew members had relaxed by removing their heavy flak jackets when we were over Yugoslavia, thinking it was safe. S/Sgt Delaney's diary notes, "...Andy Smyth (Andrew R., Jr.) and Ray Dickson (Raymond M) didn't have their flak suits on during the second flak attack, and they were really sweating it out! Andy Smyth was standing up, and then sat down, and pieces of flak struck again right were he had been standing!"

Our crew brought Zwiebel up to the warmer flight deck for landing. Because our wounded navigator-bombardier had an ugly flak wound in his shoulder, I decided to land at Foggia so that an ambulance could meet the airplane and take him directly to the Foggia Hospital nearby for immediate attention. (I visited with Zwiebel later in the hospital and he was expected to recover, but he was listed as missing in action on a mission after I had returned to the United States. Incidentally, while visiting him in his hospital bed, the famous movie actress, Madeleine Carroll, came around to his bed and talked to us.)

After dropping off Zwiebel we gave our bullet ridden "Porky" a thorough inspection. Though Porky had numerous flak and fighter inflicted holes in it we determined that we could takeoff and land it safely. The plane seemed to be flying well, and the hydraulic pressure, engines, electrical, and gasoline systems were still operating normally. As soon as we dropped Zwiebel off we took off and returned to our airbase a little after the rest of the formation.

The remainder of our Group's battered formation arrived at our airbase at 1250 hours, and it logged 6 hours and 25 minutes after it was on the ground. It was the Group's 69th accredited mission in 77 attempts. It was my 47th and 48th credited missions, and I now had 222 hours of combat flying time. I only had two more to go!

Colonel Steed did not fly on this mission, but he talked with our crew after we were on the ground and after we had been interrogated by intelligence people. He said that we did a fine job, and then shook hands with Bill Halper. It was here that he said that he would recommend Bill for the Distinguished Flying Cross.

Our Group was awarded its second Presidential Distinguished Unit Citation for this mission.

This was quite a day for "Porky" and our crew: Four enemy fighters destroyed, two probably destroyed, and an excellent bombing mission. The dark side of the day was Zwiebel's wound.

More information about the fate of the six 744th Squadron aircrews was learned after the war from surviving members and from the historical archives. One of the planes shot down was the "Emperor Jones," aircraft number 42-51077 flying in the number 5 position of the 2nd Box, piloted by 1st Lt. Edward C. Jones. Five of his crew were killed in action and the rest, all six, were taken POW's. The POWs were imprisoned in Stalag Lufts I and IV. Three that had been taken as POWs are current members of the 456th Bomb Group Association: S/Sgt Jack F. Bonifield, radio operator, S/Sgt Joseph F. Miller, engineer, and 2nd Lt. Vittorio O. Russo, copilot. Killed, were the bombardier, tail turret gunner, ball turret gunner, pilot, and nose turret gunner. The pilot, ball turret gunner, and tail turret gunner are buried in the American Military Cemetery at Lorraine France.

Second Lieutenant Frank O. Powell's plane, number 41-28947 flying in the deputy lead of the ill-fated 2nd Box, had three crew members killed: the pilot, Powell, the copilot, and the navigator. They are interred in the same cemetery in Lorraine, France as the other 744th Squadron members. Two of Powell's crew are still listed as missing in action: his nose turret gunner, Sgt Joseph C. turret gunner; and 1st Lt. George J. Frankovich, copilot. The whereabouts of the other three POWs from this crew are unknown.

General H. H."Hap" Arnold, Commander USAAF Visits Stornara!

Left to right, Colonel Steed, General Arnold, Lt. Nelson, Colonel Fay Updegrove (Commander, 304th Bomb Wing), Major General Nathan F. Twining (Commander, 15th Air Force), Major Douglas Richards (Operations Officer, 746th Squadron), and Lt. Col. Samuel W. Parks (Commander 746th Squadron). Photo provided by Richard C. Hood of the 746th Squadron.

Five Star General Arnold Visits Stornara

The third 744th Squadron plane, number 42-64487 flown by 2nd Lt. Delmar T. Hutchins in the number 9 position of the Box, had two members of the crew killed in action: the pilot Hutchins, and the radio operator, Sgt Louis F. Morris. They are also interred at Lorraine, France. Three members of the crew had successfully bailed out and were taken as POWs and put in Stalag Lufts I and IV: Sgt. John T. Miller, upper turret gunner; 1st Lt. George J. Frankovich, copilot; and S/Sgt Fred Meisel, tail turret gunner. Miller and Frankovich are current members of the 456th Bomb Group Association. Meisel is now deceased. The remaining five crew members are missing in action, and their whereabouts are unknown: the nose turret gunner, bombardier, navigator, and engineer.

The fourth 744th Squadron plane lost was number 42-52295, "Hot and Bothered," piloted by 2nd Lt. Roy F. Huls. He and two others of his crew were killed in action, the engineer and the tail turret gunner. They are buried at Lorraine, France with the others. All seven of the rest of the crew are listed as missing in action, their whereabouts unknown.

The fifth 744th plane shot down on this mission was number 42-99799, "Jean," piloted by 2nd Lt. Lawrence D. Whittaker. Only two of the crew survived, and eight were killed. Killed were Whittaker, his copilot, engineer, tail turret gunner, upper turret gunner, bombardier, ball turret gunner, and nose turret gunner. They are all buried at Lorraine, France with their squadron comrades. The two of the crew that were able to successfully bail out, and taken POWs, were: 2nd Lt. John F. Wark, navigator; and S/Sgt James A. Riley, radio operator. They were imprisoned in Stalag Lufts I.

The sixth 744th plane shot down was number 42-78072 piloted by 2nd Lt. Page C. Hendrickson. When it came time to bail out of the crippled B-24, Lt. Hendrickson's parachute was found to be unusable, so he tried to survive by holding on to his copilot, 2nd Lt. Robert C. Alexander, who bailed out, but Hendrickson was unable to hold on and he fell to his death. Three others on the crew were killed in addition to Hendrickson: his bombardier, upper turret gunner, and tail turret gunner. They are also buried at Lorraine, France. Five crew members were able to bail out of the plane, although four of them were wounded and hospitalized. Taken as POWs and wounded were: 2nd Lt. Edward B. Wagner, navigator; S/Sgt Carl E. Richardson, radio operator; Sgt. John L. Weidrich, nose turret gunner; and T/Sgt Louis C. Plath. Also taken POW, and currently a member of the 456th Bomb Group Association, was Lt. Alexander, the copilot who had tried to save the life of his pilot.

July 3, 1994 Malaxa Locomotive Works, Bucharest, Rumania

My crew was not selected to fly on this mission to bomb what we were told was the largest steel works in Europe. However, S/Sgt Thomas S. Delaney, my radio operator, was selected to fly as the lead radio operator with Captain Douglas Richards and Major Sinclair on this mission in a 747th Squadron plane that was not named. It turned out that the rest of my crew missed a milk run, although there were a potential 100 enemy fighters and 126 antiaircraft guns in the area. No planes were lost or damaged, there were no casualties, bombing results were good, and enemy fighters were seen but they didn't attack.

Crews were awakened in their tents at 0530 hours, attended briefing at 0630, arrived at their planes for a stations time of 0745 hours, and Major John R. Sinclair in the lead

SECRET

3 July 1944

BATTLE ORDER

1st Box

Formation Leader: Sinclair, Richards AP 470

No. 3: Hill AP 290   Dep Leader: Lee   AP 279
                No. 4: Little   AP 304
No. 6: Riddle AP 364   No. 5: Dysinger AP 912
                No. 7:
No. 9:   AP   No. 8:   AP
                No. 10:   AP

2nd Box

Leader: Douglas   AP 749

No. 3: Wilkinson AP 329   Dep Leader: Nilsson AP 297
                No. 4: Palis   AP 334
No. 6: Savage AP 807   No. 5: Marlor AP 113
                No. 7: Williamson AP 810
No. 9: Soloher AP 283   No. 8: Walker AP 628
                No. 10:   AP

3rd Box

Leader: Bishop   AP

No. 3: Ogden AP 225   Dep Leader: Huls AP 345
                No. 4: Webster   AP 313
No. 6: Ball AP 595   No. 5: Klingler AP 328
                No. 7: Blackwell AP 964
No. 9: Richtscheidt AP 293   No. 8: Coretti AP 485
                No. 10:   AP

4th Box

Leader: Ecker, Gruber AP 768

No. 3: Johnson AP 831   Dep Leader: Snee AP 839
                No. 4: Addis   AP 477
No. 6: Dean AP 934   No. 5: Voshell AP 201
                No. 7: Shober   AP 0487
No. 9: Lunardi AP 8275   No. 8: Sajeski AP 853
                No. 10:   AP

SPARES: 744th Sqdn: 501. 746th Sqdn: 306. 747th Sqdn: 284,637.

Stations: 0745   456th, "RECKLESS ONE TWO"

Engines: A 0755 B 080   Fighters, "SURETHING"
          C 0810 D 0817
                                      Recall Signal: "LOCKJAW"
Take-off: 0815

SECRET

bomber started his engines at 0755 hours. Sinclair started to taxi to the end of the runway at 0805, then took off at 0815. Thirty-two B-24s followed his plane off the runway at 45 second intervals.

After forming their four-Box diamond formation around Sinclair's plane, the Group rendezvoused with the 455th Group over Stornara at 3,000 feet, then departed at 0909 hours climbing on course at 160 MPH indicated airspeed and 250 feet per minute rate of climb to bombing altitude. The formation's cruising speed to the I.P. after it reached bombing altitude was 165 MPH indicated airspeed which was 234 MPH true airspeed. The planned route took the formation over Ragusa, Kragujevac, Hinava, Cojasca, then to the Initial Point which was between the towns of Caculati and Moara Saraea (as stated previously, many of these names were changed when Communist Russia took control of them after the war). There was no fighter escort for this mission and it turned out that none were needed. Two planes returned early with their bombs, both of them because they had oxygen leaks.

Weather was not the best. Enroute, below the Group formation, there was seven-tenths of cumulus cloud coverage with bases at 6,000 feet and tops at 14,000 feet. Above the Group enroute to the target was seven-tenths of cirrus cloud coverage with bases at 18,000 feet and tops at 20,000. Over the target the cumulus cloud coverage increased to eight-tenths, bases at 6,000 feet and tops at 12,000. The cirrus clouds above the formation over the target decreased to one-tenth coverage, bases at 20,000 and tops at 24,000 feet. The temperature at 21,500 feet was minus 18 degrees centigrade.

Flak at the target was of moderate intensity, accurate, with heavy black bursts. One bomber had a bomb release malfunction that prevented it from dropping its bombs on the target. The remaining thirty Liberators dropped 76.25

tons of 500 pound bombs (305 bombs) at 1210 hours from 22,000 feet for the 1st Box of the diamond formation and from 20,500 feet for the 4th Box. The axis of attack was 180 degrees magnetic, the indicated airspeed was 160 MPH and the true airspeed was 227 MPH. The bombardiers' bomb release interval setting was a close 25 feet. Seven K-22 cameras took pictures of the target, and their analysis by technicians indicated that bomb results were good. After bombs were released, the T/Sgt Thomas S. Delaney, flying on Captain Douglas Richards' crew as radio operator for this mission, sent a Target Strike Report by radio message back to our 304th Wing Headquarters that said the mission was successful, and he received a message back acknowledging receipt of his message.

The Group's 31 Liberators reached home at 1540 hours. The formation logged 7 hours and 30 minutes by the time they were on the ground. It was the Group's 70th accredited mission in 78 missions.

July 4, 1944   No mission this day, Independence Day!

The weather was too bad at all targets. We had a special dinner meal today, better than normal (I believe it was steak) because it was Independence Day!

July 5, 1944   No mission for the second day in succession.

Weather was still too bad for bombing. We had time to take care of chores around camp. I spent some time at our new club with some of our crew. I only had two missions to complete the magic fifty, and I was anxious to finish. No one in our Group had flown fifty missions at this time, so we weren't sure that the fifty mission policy would still be honored. Our Group was short of crews because we hadn't received our normal quota of replacement crews since June

10. I was the only one of my crew that would be getting fifty missions because the rest of my crew only had about 23 credited missions. I had flown many missions before they joined me. I could be replaced easily by upgrading my copilot, Sydney Brooks, to take over the crew.

July 6, 1944 North Oil Refinery, Trieste, Italy.

My crew was selected to fly this one in our trusty "Porky". It was another milk run as no flak or enemy fighters were seen, no planes damaged, and no casualties. eather was good and bombing results were good. Lt. Werner "Judge" Foss joined ourcrew for this mission to help out Lt. James Duston, our navigtor-bombadier. We bombed in a column of Boxes again, but since no enemy fighters were expected, we weren't afraid of it.

Wake-up calls came to our tents at about 0515 hours, we had breakfast, then attended briefing on the hill at 0600 hours. We had a stations time to be at our planes of 0720 hours, and Major Louis Abernathy started engines of his lead plane at 0730 hours. He started to taxi out to the end of the runway at 0730, then took off at 0740 hours.Twenty-nine Liberators followed him off the runway at 45 second intervals. I was flying in the number 6 position of the 2nd Box. There were only three Boxes in the formation this day, flying in a "V" of Boxes.

S E C R E T

6 July 1944

BATTLE ORDER

1st Box

Abernathy

Formation Leader: Witkin,/ ~~BLACKLER~~ AP 477 Clark,W.D.

No. 3: ~~Ghantler~~ AP ~~299~~ 464 Dep Leader: Toselli/ AP 470

No. 4: Mapa AP 485

No. 6: Leathers AP ~~328~~ No. 5: Shotterly AP 313

No. 7: Strombom AP 912

No. 9: Ball AP ~~595~~ No. 8: Klinger AP 345

No. 10: Richschoidt AP 225

2nd Box

Leader: Gutting AP 8275

No. 3: Ragland AP 549 Dep Leader: Johnson AP 199

No. 4: Addis AP 899

No. 6: Capps AP 306 No. 5: Voshell AP 201

No. 7: Shober AP 0487

No. 9: Scott AP 480 No. 8: ~~Mitsanesky~~ AP ~~301~~ 853

No. 10: Lunt AP 925

3rd Box

Leader: Gardner AP 283

No. 3: Floming AP 807 Dep Leader: Monahan AP 334

No. 4: Palis AP 365

No. 6: Roak AP 177 No. 5: Saleher AP 810

No. 7: Lassowski AP 304

No. 9: Wilkinson AP 329 No. 8: Walker AP 203

No. 10: Hill AP 561

SPARES: 744th Sq. 279,338,290. 745th Sq. 297. 746th Sq. 486,890. 747th Sq. 284,944,

Time at stations: 0720 456th BG: RUBBISH THREE

Start engines: A 0730 B 0740 Fighters: SAXHORN
            C 0750

Recall: ROBBIN

Taxi out: 0730.

Take-off: 0740.

S E C R E T

480

I was the 16th plane to take off, so my wheels left the runway about 12 minutes after Abernathy's lead plane took off.

After forming our "V" formation of three Boxes, we rendezvoused with the 455th Group over Stornara at 4,000 feet beforedeparting at 0825 hours, climbing on course at 160 MPH indicated airspeed, or 210 MPH true airspeed. Only one bomber aborted before reaching the target. He had a runaway propeller.

The weather was clear for the gathering of our formations, but we had four-tenths of alto cumulus clouds below us as soon as we flew over the Adriatic Sea, bases at 7,000 and tops at 8,000 feet. This cloud cover gradually decreased until it was only two-tenths of cumulus cloud coverage below us at the target area, tops at 14,000 feet. No clouds above us. The temperature at 19,700 feet was minus 9 degrees centigrade. There was no fighter opposition and no flak on this bright sunny summer day.

We formed our column of Boxes at the I.P. then twenty-nine B-24s dropped 72.5 tons of 500 pound general purpose bombs (290 bombs) at 1029 hours from 20,000 feet for the 1st Box and 18,500 feet for Boxes 2 and 3, at an indicated airspeed of 160 MPH and 223 MPH true airspeed on an axis of attack of 60 degrees magnetic. The bombardiers' bomb release interval setting was the minimum. Six K-22 cameras took pictures of the target area and the bombing results were good. Practically all crews reported our bombs falling in the target area. We left the target with many fires and smoke at the oil refinery, from our bombs and from bombs of previous groups that bombed the target earlier. Flames at the target were reported to be rising 900 feet into the air and smoke rising to 8,000 feet. After bombs were released, our Group made a descending right turn at 155 to 160 MPH indicated airspeed.

All twenty-nine in our Group formation returned to our airbase at 1205, and we recorded 4 hours and 30 minutes for this short mission after we were on the ground. This was the Group's 71st credited mission of the 80 missions that it had flown in Italy.

This was my 49th credited mission, and I only needed one more for a ticket to return home to family, friends, safety, good food, and particularly to where daily showers and baths were available. Until I came to Italy, I always took the normal amenities of living in the United States, such as safety from harm, flushing toilets, running hot and cold water, good food, and daily showers for granted. My experience in Italy taught me to appreciate them in a way that I never had before, a grateful recognition of their importance that stayed with me the rest of my life!

July 7, 1944 Odertal Synthetic Oil and Coke Plant, on the border between Poland and Czechoslovakia

I was happy to be selected to fly on this, my last mission, but I was also nervous about the possibility that something could go wrong to prevent my being able to return to the States after I had safely flown 49 missions. I only needed one more mission to finish! So did S/Sgt Thomas S. Delaney, our radio operator on "Porky!"

When we walked into the briefing room that morning and saw the length of yarn on the wall map of our briefing room that announced the route for the day's mission, one of the longest missions we ever flew, I was almost certain that we would be shot down on my last mission. The route took us through two different enemy fighter belts. It appeared inevitable that I would not make it home after being so close to the magic fifty missions. This was an eight-hour mission through some of the most heavily defended parts of Nazi Europe. Not only that, but it was a two-credit mission and I only needed one more mission to finish.

482

S E C R E T

Plan: "ABLE"   DATE: 7 July 1944.

Time at stations: 06:10. Start engines: 1st Box: 0620. 2nd Box: 0630.
                                          3rd Box: 0640. 4th Box: 0650.

Taxi out: 06:30. Take-off: 06:40. Take-off interval: S.O. P.

Assembly: S. O. P.

Bomber rendezvous: STORNARA.

Time: 07:38. Altitude: 3,000 feet.

Fighter rendezvous:

Time: Altitude:

Climbing speed: 160. Rate: S. O. P.

Cruising formation: Diamond of nine ship Boxes.

Speed: 165. Route out: Base to KP (42°45'N, 16°43'E) to TP (47°46'N,
                         17°58'E) to TP (49°44'N, 17°18'E) to TP
                         (50°19'N, 17°34'E) to IP to Target. Key-
                         point time 08:14 at 10,000 feet.

Initial point: OBER GLOGAU (50°21'N, 17°51'E). Axis of attack: 71°Mag.

Target: ODERTAL Synthetic Oil Plant.   Target time: 11:00B.

Aiming point:

Bombing formation: 9 ship front of 9 ship Boxes.

Speed: 160. Altitude: 19,000 feet.

Bomb release interval: 30 Foot.

Rally: Slight left then Right. Speed: 160 - 165.

Route home: To Rally Point (49°53'N, 18°37'E) to TP ESLLOKOZARANYOS then
            Reciprocal to Base.

Landing procedure: S. O. P.

Secondary target: BOHUMIN Oil Refinery. IP: KRAFARN (49°56'N, 18°01'E).
                  Axis: 99°M. Rally: Right.

Second Alternate: VIENNA LOBAU Oil Refinery. IP: STRASZHOF (48°19'N,
                  16°38'E). Axis: 220°M. Rally: Left to (47°55'N,
                  16°38'E), staying East of SOPRON on route back.

Call signs: 456th BG: "FLYWHEEL FOUR-ONE". Fighters: "FREIZOL" with suf-
                                            numbers in order of contact.

Recall: "PORTRAIT"   Copy of the Original Briefing
                        454th Bomb Group Battle Order
                        Source:NationalArchives,Wash. D.C.

Copy of Original Briefing

S E C R E T

Battle Order   Date: 7 July 1944.

1st Box

		Formation Loader:	Callan, Sinclair AP 790 Hyde	
No. 3: Ashley	AP 279		Dep Loader: Johnson /	AP 477
		No. 4: Capps	AP 306	
No. 6: Sagort	AP 8275		No. 5: Doan	AP 934
		No. 7: Ragland	AP 0487	
No. 9: Smith	AP 549		No. 8: Scott	AP 480
		No. 10:	AP	

2nd Box

		Loader: Loukuma	AP 470	
No. 3: Ogden	AP 225		Dep Loader: Strombom	AP 912
		No. 4: Riddle	AP 777	
No. 6: Mapa	AP 485		No. 5: Klinglor	AP 345
		No. 7: Hall	AP 293	
No. 9: Shotterly	AP 964		No. 8: Corrotti	AP 328
		No. 10:	AP	

3rd Box

		Loader: Douglass	AP 334	
No. 3: Little	AP 304		Dep Loader: Lassowaki	AP 807
		No. 4: Nilsson	AP 297	
No. 6: Fleming	AP 329		No. 5: Williamson	AP 810
		No. 7: Selchor	AP 628	
No. 9: Roak	AP 177		No. 8: Phillips	AP 393
		No. 10:	AP	

4th Box

		Loader: Tossolli, Clark AP 768		
No. 3: Hill	AP 421		Dep Loader: Loathore	AP 284
		No. 4: Rudd	AP 403	
No. 6: Addis	AP 839		No. 5: Marlor	AP 365
		No. 7: Lunt	AP 925	
No. 9: Richtschoidt	AP 364		No. 8: Dysingor	AP 313
		No. 10:	AP	

SPARES: 744th Sqdn: 279.   745th Sqdn: 113 and 283.

746th Sqdn: 199 and 853.   747th Sqdn: 364.

Time at stations: 06:10.   456th BG: "FLYWHEEL FOUR-ONE".

Start engines: A 06:20 B 06:30   Fighters: "FREEZOL" with suffix
                C 06:40 D 06:50.   numbers in order of
                                                       contact with bombers.
Taxi out: 06:30.
                                             Recall: "PORTRAIT".
Take-off: 06:40.

S E C R E T

Our Vision Of What Would Happen On Our Last Mission. A 15th Air Force Liberator (465th B G.) overturned over Germany after being hit by enemy fire. Photo Provided by the San Diego Aerospace Museum.

15th A.F. Liberator On Fire Over Germany

I bit the bullet and concentrated on the job to be done. I learned, after the war, that we were short of crews at the time because we hadn't received replacements since the 10th of June, a time that we would normally have received between four and eight flight crews. S/Sgt Thomas D. Delaney was flying on his last mission also, and this would give him a total of 51. This was our last mission, one way or another!

The target was only 90 miles from the dreaded target that was always hanging over our heads since we were first briefed to bomb it on March 4, the target of Breslau, Germany where Hitler had his military headquarters, and where he lived. We had aborted the bombing of Breslau earlier because of weather, but we were told that as soon as the weather cleared enough, we would be scheduled to bomb it. Every morning, as we walked into the briefing room after we had originally been briefed to bomb Breslau, we worried that the yarn on the map would be going up to Breslau. It was aspecter that hung over our heads since. It had become the subject of some nervous humor among many of us since that time. It was always nagging us, in the back of the minds of those who attended that briefing.

We had to pass through two fighter belts on the way to the target, and after enemy fighters attacked us for the first time from each the two fighter belts, they would have enough time to land, refuel, then attack us again as we returned on our way home. That was the vision that worried us as we left the briefing room to go out to our planes and fly the mission.

We had an early 0400 wake-up call in our tents in the darkness of a mild summer morning. We had the usual C-ration dehydrated breakfast before we routinely cleaned our metal mess kits, returned them to our tents, then climbed into the back of open army six-by-six trucks for the ride up to our briefing room on the hill. Briefing commenced at 0500 hours and we were all shocked out of our sleepiness by the sight of the long yarn up to the edge of Poland, near the dreaded target, Breslau, where Hitler had located his command bunkers. The gasps of disbelief were clearly audible as the crew members first saw the yarn when they entered the briefing room.

At the briefing, we were told that we would have long-range P-38 Lightnings and P-51 Mustangs for escort, but we all knew that didn't provide us with much security in the past, when as many as 60 enemy fighters attacked us under their "cover." Major John R. Sinclair was to be in our lead plane, and we were briefed to fly our standard diamond formation of four Boxes. I was flying in the number 4 position of the 1st Box, under and behind Sinclair's lead plane. Luftwaffe aircraft had been attacking the 1st Box of our formations with head-on assaults in attempts to break up our formations before we reached our targets. I was worried about it, particularly since this was my last mission, one way or another!

Stations time for being at our planes was 0610 hours. We arrived at "Porky" early and some of our aircrew had their last-minute nervous smokes of cigarettes a safe distance from Porky before we climbed aboard. I told them that we would be wearing our oxygen masks for a long time on this eight hour flight. I gave the plane an unusually tough external check, hoping that I would find something wrong that would give me an excuse to abort. Lt. Brooks and myself were hoping that we could find something wrong with the plane that would be an excuse for aborting the mission so we could return to our safe tents and warm secure beds. No such luck! As usual, the ground crew had done a great job so that everything checked out in excellent condition.

We started our engines at 0620 hours with the rest of the planes of our lead Box. Again, Brooks and I were more than usually critical and careful on our checking each of our four engines, still hoping to find something wrong. We gave each engine a critical, careful check during our standard pre-takeoff run-up of one engine at a time. We checked the two magnetos of each engine, the cylinder head temperatures, oil and gas pressures, oil temperature gauges, propellers, and engine superchargers. Unfortunately, we couldn't find anything that would give us an excuse to abort the mission because the ground crews had done such a good job of preparing the plane. Reluctantly, we had to continue with the mission.

Major Sinclair began his taxi to the end of the runway at 0630 and he coaxed his heavily loaded Liberator off the runway at 0650, ten minutes later than scheduled. Each of the 34 Liberators that were on this mission followed him off the runway at 45 second intervals. My plane was number 4 to takeoff, so I took off 3 minutes after the lead plane. The air was much warmer, and thinner, and we had no head wind, so we used almost all of the bumpy runway before the heavily loaded 'Porky's" wheels left the ground. I had to carefully conserve the fuel of our plane because of the long mission, by avoiding abrupt movements of the throttles and by keeping the propeller revolutions per minute (RPMs) at a minimum for a given setting of the throttles. After we caught up with Sinclair's bomber and the rest of the B-24s assembled into our diamond formation of Boxes, Major Sinclair led us over to Stornara to rendezvous with the rest of the groups of the 304th Wing at 3,000 feet. We departed Stornara, climbing on course at 0738 hours at 160 MPH indicated airspeed. Once we reached our bombing altitude of 19,000 feet, the formation flew at 165 MPH indicated airspeed, which was 224 MPH true airspeed, so we could pass through the enemy fighter belts, that started at Lake Balaton, Hungary, at a fast pace, and because this was the best airspeed for maximum fuel economy on the long mission. Our route of travel took us over Lake Balaton, our usual rendezvous point with enemy fighters, then up to our Initial Point, Ober Glogau, then to the target on the Oder river, on the Polish and Czechoslovakian border, the Odertal Synthetic Oil and Coke Plant. There were no planes returning early, as much as they would like to, again a credit to our hard working ground maintenance crews!

The weather enroute to the target was clear except for some altocumulus clouds below us over the mountains of Yugoslavia as we passed. In the target area, we had three-tenths of alto cumulus cloud coverage, with their tops reaching up to 18,000 feet. There were no clouds above us. The temperature at 19,500 feet was a warm, summery minus 11 degrees centigrade.

We passed through a scant, inaccurate firing of heavy flak as we flew through the Lake Balaton area. As we entered the target area, the flak became very intense and accurate with heavy black bursts. Nine of our planes had flak damage, two of them with severe damage, but they were able to fly home with the formation. "Porky" didn't get a hole in it!

All 35 of our Liberators passed over the target. However, one Liberator had received severe flak damage that required it to drop its bomb load early to enable it to keep up with the Group formation. Thirty-four bombers of our Group's bombers dropped 85.5 tons of 500 pound general purpose bombs (342 bombs) at 1128 hours from 19,500 feet for the 1st Box of the diamond formation, and 19,000 feet for the 4th Box, at an indicated airspeed of 160 MPH, and a true airspeed of 224 MPH, on an axis of attack of 55 degrees magnetic. The bombardiers' bomb release interval setting was 30 feet. After we had released our bombs, the Group made a descending left turn flying at an indicated airspeed that was faster than normal, 160 to 165 MPH, which was a true airspeed of 224 to 230 MPH.

The only fighters our Group saw occurred about one hour after we had already dropped our bombs on our target and we were headed home. We saw some Me-109s at 1220 hours, then we saw fighters at 1240 hours, a few miles south of Lake Balaton. There were only 15 Me-109s and 4 Me-110s, and they didn't attack us, either because we had a tighter formation than other groups in our Wing formation of groups, or because our escort menaced them too much. The Luftwaffe was obviously on last legs, because on previous missions to this area there would be 60 or 80 enemy fighters coming up to intercept us. Post-war studies indicated that the Luftwaffe had lost most of its power by now. It had a shortage of pilots, fuel, and ammunition. We had won the air battle over Europe! The Luftwaffe would collect groups of planes for an occasional, selective, massive attack after today, but it didn't have the experienced pilots or fuel for such attacks on a continuing basis as it had in the past.

S/Sgt Thomas S. Delaney, radio operator on my crew, noted in his diary, "The Jerries sure threw up plenty of flak, but Major Sinclair did and excellent job of leading our formation right down "flak-alley." We didn't get any flak holes in "Porky." Our plane sure brought us through with flying colors! The target was hit and hit hard by our group! All groups of the groups in the 15th Air Force hit the target! Three groups got shot up by fighters. We were lucky, we saw four enemy fighters! Two Me-109s went down and crashed behind us!.I sure prayed plenty on that raid, more than ever! I have plenty to thank God for! Lt. Capps and Lt. Brooks flew excellent formation. Fires were seen all over the target area, and black smoke was seen rising plenty high! Thanks, God!"

On the way home, after we were out of the fighter belt of Hungary, I was beginning to feel elated at the prospect of finishing my missions. Over Yugoslavia, Major Sinclair dropped our formation down to 15,000 feet, so that crew members that smoked cigarettes could take off their oxygen masks for a little while and have a smoke. We had been wearing the masks that pressed hard against our faces for more than six hours. Unfortunately, the altitude of 15,000 feet was only a couple of thousand feet above the Yugoslavian mountains. Here Germans had mounted antiaircraft guns on railroad cars to fire at us as we passed over this well traveled corridor, knowing that it was the route we took while flying to and from the soft underbelly targets of Nazi Europe. Sure enough, some heavy black burst began to explode menacingly through our formation. Ground gunners were so close to us that they were firing at an almost point-blank range! I could visualize my plane being shot down by this last effort by the Germans after we had safely flown over he most dangerous areas. I was so close to completing my mission requirement that I hated to have it end by a flak burst here, merely because some wanted to have a smoke. Luckily, we flew by the flak, out of its range, and no planes were shot down.

Our formation of 35 Liberators reached our airfield at 1445 hours and we logged 7 hours and 50 minutes by the time we were on the ground. It was the Group's 72nd accredited mission of the 80 it had flown in Italy. But more important to me and to S/Sgt Delaney, was the fact that we had completed our missions! We both had 51 missions! I had 234 hours and 20 minutes combat flying time, and Delaney had 227 hours and 5 minutes. No one had finished 50 missions in our Group before so we weren't sure about the policy since we had never seen it in writing. We were among the first to test the policy, and I was worried that the goal would be extended now that I had finally reached it. Looking back on it, I don't believe many, if any, realized that I or S/Sgt Delaney had finished 51 missions until they got around to filling out the flight records.

On the ground, with unusual gusto, I drank my 2 ounces of the medicinal whiskey that the flight surgeon gave us before we entered the interrogation room. The coffee and doughnuts that the Red Cross provided us never tasted better!

The friendly Red Cross attendants were a much welcomed sight! I felt like bending down and kissing terra firma. As tired as I was from the flight, I felt like I was walking on air. I felt so good! I had this type of a wonderful, buoyant, thank-God feeling only a few times during the rest of my life.

I was in a tie for being the first pilot of our Group to finish flying fifty missions (I had fifty-one missions). The orders sending me back to the states dated July 8, 1944 had four other pilots listed on it, sending them home with me, Lieutenants Robert S. Ensign, George H. Gutting, Thomas W. Monahan, and Carl R. Strombom. I believe we were the first pilots to complete fifty missions. Other crew members on those same orders included the following who are currently members of the 456th Bomb Group Association: Lieutenants Robert H.Vanderlaan, Howard B. Liechty, William F. Roberts, Joseph Bungo, Charles W. Ward, and T/Sgt Ralph Dykstra. For some reason, S/Sgt Delaney's orders were issued a few days later then mine.

I was one of the last pilots to come into the Group before the Group had flown any missions and I was tied for first to finish with fifty.

July 8 and 9 1944   My flight to Benghazi, Libya, North Africa.

As I mentioned, I'm not sure that administrators of our Group Headquarters knew how to deal with crewmen finishing their fifty mission tour. They were notoriously poor administrators, due in part to the fact that we had only been operating in Italy for six months. I don't think they had planned ahead for such a situation. There was an uneasy period when we thought that the fifty mission policy would be revoked now that we had reached it.

The day after I finished my missions, on July 8, I still had no official recognition that I had completed my tour with

51 missions. The orders from Headquarters Fifteenth Air Force that sent us home were dated July 8, 1944, but I knew nothing about it and I don't think my squadron operations officers knew about it either because I was ordered to fly a Liberator down to Benghazi, Libya to ferry a passenger that had business there.

After the 3 hour and 30 minute flight down to Africa, when I entered the traffic pattern of the Benghazi airport, I was amazed by the number of wrecked planes that surrounded the airport. Wreckage of United States, British, Nazi, and Italian planes of all descriptions were densely massed around the airport in a manner I had never seen before or since. The wrecks must have numbered five hundred or more in the small area that surrounded the airport. I was curious to learn what had happened there.

My passenger had business there that required me and my skeleton crew of copilot, navigator, engineer, and radio operator to spent the night in Benghazi. In the officers club that evening I learned that Benghazi had changed hands between British and German forces many times in a short period of time. Many planes had been shot down during the great air battles for the base. The town had changed hands so many times in such a short period of time that German and British doctors worked side by side on German and British patients, treating them equally, in the only local hospital. When the Allies finally took Africa for the last and decisive time, driving the German forces out of Africa, causing most of the Axis troops to surrender and enter prisoner of war camps for the duration of the war, the British put the remaining German doctors and patients on a protected ship and allowed it to return to Axis-controlled land. Of course, other captured Germans and Italians were put in prison camps.

My copilot, navigator, and I spent the night in visiting officers quarters living in civilized conditions under a roof and eating reasonably good food. I felt more relaxed than I had been for more than a year, having finished my missions. My crew and I returned to our airfield at Stornarella the next day. My flying time, again, was 3 hours and 30 minutes from Benghazi.

When I returned to our airfield at Stornarella on July 9, 1944, I parked my plane and went to my tent. I wasn't in my tent more than fifteen minutes before I heard an army six-by-six truck pull up outside it, and someone, I believe it was our operations officer Captain Hyde, came into my tent. He hurriedly gave me some orders, handed me a handful of medals, then told me to get on the truck for immediate transport to Naples to catch a boat home! I didn't have time to say good-bye to anyone, and I threw all of my belongings, helter skelter, into my B-4 suitcase, threw it on the back end of the truck, and we were off to Naples. No one had to tell me twice! Evidently, the orders came through while I was in Africa, and I was supposed to leave for Naples the day before. It must have been an administrative "goof." Since I was one of the first to finish my missions they didn't know how to handle it administratively.

The orders dated July 8, 1944 from 15th Air Force Headquarters stated, "... each individual accepts this privilege (of returning to the states) with the understanding that he will be returned to this Theater upon expiration of temporary duty (in the States)." In other words, we were expected to return to Italy, indicating that they hadn't developed a final policy. Afterward, we received orders from 15th Air Force dated July 14, 1944 that rescinded the July 8 orders, relieving us from the requirement to return to Italy.

The truck took me to an abandoned racetrack outside of Naples where many tents had been pitched for use as a staging area for airmen who had completed their missions. We had to wait there until a sailing time was arranged to take us home. Sailing times were kept secret because German submarines still threatened our ships on the high seas. Among the officers from the 456th Bomb Group who were at the Naples race track with me waiting to go home were Lt. Robert S. Ensign, Lt. George H. Gutting, Lt. Howard B. Liechty*, Lt. Robert H. Vanderlaan*, Lt. Carl R. Strombom, Lt. Thomas W. Monahan*, Lt.Robert R. Corn*, Lt. Joseph Bungo*, Lt. William F. Roberts*, Lt. Charles W. Ward*, and T/Sgt Ralph Dykstra* (* Indicates that they are current members of the 456th Bomb Group Association. Ensign is deceased.)

The next day, after my arrival at the racetrack, there were about thirty of us officers who had finished our fifty missions, almost all second lieutenants, who were waiting in line to go into the mess building to eat lunch. We had arrived about five minutes before the door opened because we had nothing else to do. While we were waiting in line, Major General Nathan F. Twining, Commanding Officer of the Fifteenth Air Force came up to us, accompanied by some of his staff officers. They were on an inspection tour of this new facility when General Twining saw us standing in line. He came over to us, talking to each of us in the line, asking if we had completed fifty missions. We all told him yes. He was surprised that we had not been promoted from the grade of second lieutenant during the time that we had all flown fifty missions. The Eighth Air Force in England, we learned later, gave its aircrew officers automatic promotions when they completed half of their required missions, and many received second promotions when they finished their required number of missions.

We went into lunch, and when we came out of the mess hall one of the officers in our group excitedly drew our attention to a military order on the bulletin board that had been put there while we were eating. It was signed by General Twining and it promoted all of us who had been Second

495

Lieutenants to First lieutenants! General Twining must have been so concerned about our delinquent promotions that he required someone to rapidly type the military order with each of our names on it during the short time that it took for us to eat lunch!

The administration and management of the Fifteenth Air Force, in matters that didn't pertain to operations and flying, was notoriously poor. It became more apparent to me after the war, during my research for this book. As I researched the National Archives and the Air Force history libraries, it became apparent that records of the Eighth Air Force were far superior to those of the Fifteenth. The administrative clerks of the National Archives, as well as those of the Air Force libraries, pointed out the difference in quality between the two. Part of the blame for this could be attributed to the fact that the Fifteenth Air Force was less than nine months old, having been activated in Africa November 1, 1943, and it had only been in Italy for eight months, since December 1, 1943. The Eighth Air Force, on the other hand, had its beginnings with its first mission on August 17, 1942. The Eighth was almost a year and a half older than the Fifteenth Air Force. The Eighth had much more time to establish its administrative policies and procedures.

During its early months, the Fifteenth Air Force had to give priority to the organization and management of its operations, and combat missions, and to its routine housekeeping functions at the expense of other administrative details and record keeping.

However, it did not escape the attention of aircrew members that many non-flying officers on the 456th Group Headquarters staff were able to be promoted during this period. It wasn't that they were not deserving, because they were. Without exception, they were all competent, hard working officers. The rub was that we who were being shot at and flying missions, and doing a good job of it, the sole reason for existence of the Group, were being ignored by our headquarters administrators.

Chapter 5
EPILOGUE

The war against the Luftwaffe, the great Air Battle for Europe, was won in time to allow the invasion of Europe, known as Operation Overlord, on June 6, 1944. In only five months we had witnessed and contributed to a complete reversal of the precarious situation where the Luftwaffe dominated the skies over central Europe, to one where the Luftwaffe had been almost completely destroyed and the Allies dominated the skies. The Luftwaffe was only able to launch two Me-109 fighters in opposition to the massive Allied invasion armada on June 6, 1944, and only token Luftwaffe aircraft opposition was seen afterward.

The Luftwaffe still had many planes, but few pilots, scarce fuel supplies, parts, and ammunition with which to fly them. The few defensive fighters able to be launched were quickly shot down by our superior escort fighter force.

One Luftwaffe fighter pilot was heard to say, during the last days of our great battle for air superiority, "every time I closed the canopy of my fighter to take off, I felt like I was closing the lid on my coffin."

The last Liberator of the 456th Bomb Group lost to enemy fighter attack was lost during August 1944, one month after I completed my missions. All of our Group's losses afterward were to stiff antiaircraft fire. The Nazi pulled their 88mm multipurpose guns and 105mm guns back from the east and west fronts as they retreated from rapid allied advances on the ground, and they concentrated the guns around targets near their homeland targets. These guns were the only defenses the Nazis had left to protect their cities and factories after the Luftwaffe was destroyed.

The first six months of 1944 were violently sobering experiences for most of us young aircrew members. By July 7, 1944, when I completed flying my 51st mission, the 456th Bomb Group had lost 45 Liberators, for all reasons, from its normal inventory of 62 bombers. The Group had lost 18 Liberators to enemy aircraft fire, 17 were lost to flak, and 10 were lost for all other reasons. Our gunners claimed a total of 179 enemy aircraft destroyed or probably destroyed (126 confirmed destroyed and 53 probably destroyed).

During those first few months of 1944 most of my comrades and I matured very fast. Like me, many didn't have enough whiskers growing on our faces, only a little fuzz, to require shaving on a regular basis. It was the first time away from home for many of us. Experiences at that rural Italian farm indoctrinated us, rapidly, to the harsh reality of life, death, blood, sweat, tears, and war. It not only made us appreciate the fact that we were allowed to continue living, but it made us appreciate the amenities of living in the United States that we had always taken for granted up to then. We learned to appreciate such luxuries as freedom, security, showers, running water, indoor plumbing that works, good food, and many others, amenities. The average citizen in the United States, particularly the younger generation of today, does not realize what a great advantage he enjoys. That advantage is a reason that so many foreigners want to come to the United States.

The 456th Bomb Group's Experience Afterward.

It was only a period of fifteen months, from the time that our first aircraft began arriving on the Stornara airstrip, February 1, 1994, to the time that the last mission returned from enemy territory on April 26, 1945. The last unlucky crew to be shot down on a 456th Bomb Group mission was hit by a burst of flak on 25 April, 1945 over Linz, Austria, the day before the last mission was flown. The plane was piloted by Lt. Harry Messimer of my old 746th squadron, and all crew members were listed as missing in action except two, who were later reported as prisoners of war, T/Sgt Dale Shebilsky, radio operator, and S/Sgt John S. Mac Pherson, upper turret gunner. (Shebilsky is currently a member of the 456th Bomb Group Association.)

In those few months 7,272 bombing sorties were flown from the rustic airfield. Then, as swiftly as it had arrived, the group returned to the United States. This incredible adventure came to a victorious end with the defeat of Nazi Germany on May 7, 1945, when Germans finally signed peace papers. Victory in Europe was officially declared on May 8.

The 456th's Casualty Rate.

During the fifteen months of air operations there had been 3,267 different officers and airmen assigned at some time or another to the 456th's B-24 bomber crews. With 910 crew members lost or missing in action during that time, it amounted to a 28% loss. Such a high loss rate was typical of the twenty-one other heavy bomber groups of the 15th Air Force in Italy. The 8th Air Force (Heavy Bombers) and 9th Air Force (Tactical Bombers) in England and the 15th

Air Force (Heavy Bombers) and 12th Air Force (Tactical Bombers) in Italy suffered some of the highest casualty rates of all major armed forces during World War II.

If the story were told as a tale of fiction, few could bring themselves to believe it. This was not fiction, although it must have seemed like a nightmare to many of the men who experienced it, and to wives, relatives, and sweethearts of the 910 valiant airmen of the 456th who were lost or missing in action during that time. Although the Group started with 62 B-24H planes, it lost 105 planes in that fifteen month period. The Group flew a total of 249 bombing missions. Most of the 910 lost were victims of air battles fought four miles above fiercely defended enemy territory in Germany, Austria, France, Italy, Rumania, Bulgaria, Hungary, Czechoslovakia, and Yugoslavia.

The 456th's Bombing Accuracy.

The 456th's bombing accuracy was the best of the other three groups in the 304th Bomb Wing. Bombing accuracy, although not very impressive in light of modern technology that employs laser-guided "smart bombs" that can be sent down chimneys, was very good by standards of World War II state-of-the-art technology. Strategic bombing was in its infancy, and we were just beginning to experiment with air to ground radar (the H2X Pathfinder equipment) to enable us to see through clouds, smoke, and darkness.

Though our bombing accuracy wasn't great by modern standards, the massive numbers of bombers we employed and the persistent and redundant bombing of the important targets allowed us to completely destroy them. All strategic bombing objectives were attained, the Luftwaffe was completely destroyed, and the ability of Germany and its allies to wage war was almost completely destroyed. The British, Canadian, and Russian Air Forces, in addition to the USAAF, made major contributions to the success of the battle for the air. They must share the credit for the air victory.

As the 456th Group gained experience and training, and as the weather improved from the winter months of February 1944 to the spring months, allowing better visual bombing conditions, our bombing accuracy gradually improved. While only 20.1 percent of our bombs hit within 1,000 feet of aiming points for the month of March, 1944 and 36.3 percent for the month of June, 1944, by March of 1945 accuracy had reached 71.9 percent of the Group's bombs hitting within the 1,000 foot circle. The 456th's monthly bombing record consistently led the other groups of the 304th Wing and its average bombing record for the entire fifteen months of operations in Italy led the nearest average of other groups in the 304th Wing by 1.4 percent.

For the fifteen months of its combat operations in Italy the 456th dropped its bombs on targets in the following order of importance, as measured by tonnage of bombs dropped: Communication Lines, 6,328 tons (about 45%); Oil Refineries and Storage, 2,543 tons (18%); Airdromes, 1,893 tons (14%); Factories, 1,603 tons (12%); Troop Concentrations, 896 tons (6%); and Miscellaneous Towns and Harbors, Etc., 675 tons (5%). These and many other figures quoted herein were taken from the 456th Bomb Group's final official report prepared by Captain Paul A. Doorley, Statistical Officer; Lt. Col. Dave E. Tavel, Operations Officer; and signed by Colonel Thomas W. Steed, Commander.

The 456th Group's Maintenance Record.

The 456th Bombardment Group's maintenance personnel consistently out performed all other groups of the 304th Wing with their ability to keep our Liberators repaired and ready to fly combat missions. During its entire time in Italy, maintenance crews of the 456th Bomb Group were able to keep an average of 83 percent of its 62 assigned aircraft ready for combat. The next highest group record in the 304th Wing was 5 percent less than our Group record for the entire period of the Italian combat tour.

The Fate of "Porky" and My Crew After I Left.

When I completed my 51 missions on July 7, 1944, only S/Sgt Thomas S. Delaney, radio operator and gunner on my crew, had sufficient missions to earn his ticket home. The rest of my crew had a little more than half that many because I flew many missions before they joined me. Delaney flew extra missions with other crews because his talent as a radio operator was in great demand. Thus, the rest of my crew was not eligible to return to the states and they were required to fly more missions after I returned home.

My copilot, 2nd Lt. Sydney H. Brooks, was checked out as first pilot and given command of our ship ""Porky"." Two weeks after he took command of my crew, on a mission July 21, 1944, ""Porky"" had a wing knocked off by enemy fire and it collided violently with another plane in his formation. "Porky" spun violently to the ground out of control, and the other plane exploded. Nine parachutes were seen coming from the two planes that carried twenty crewmen. That happened three minutes after "Porky" had dropped its bombs on the Brux oil refinery in Czechoslovakia.

Brooks and his (our) bombardier, 2nd Lt. James J. Duston, miraculously survived the violent crash. Duston had been officially reported as missing in action, but Brooks who is a member of our 456th Bomb Group Association reported that Duston was with him in the Prisoner Of War Camp at Stalag Luft I, Barth, Germany. Four of the crew were reported killed, including T/Sgt Edward W. Broom, engineer; S/Sgt Robert M. Gafner, his new radio operator; S/Sgt Arthur P. Arseneaux, his new nose turret gunner; and 2nd Lt. Roy S. Dubs, his new copilot. Two other members

503

of the crew are still listed as missing in action, S/Sgt Carl Ezuck, tail turret gunner, and S/Sgt George Youngquist, ball turret gunner. Those killed are buried in the American Military Cemetery at Lorraine, France.

Of course I had a close personal feeling for all crew members of "Porky", but I owe a special debt of gratitude to T/Sgt Edward W. Broom, flight engineer on "Porky," who saved our lives many times with his brilliant, ingenious, emergency stopgap procedures. He helped keep our battle-damaged plane flying on many occasions. He had a sincere, devoted, unselfish love of the airplane and he had a detailed knowledge of it. He was a true professional, and in all my experience since that time (thirty years in the USAF) I have seldom met a better, more competent, dedicated or talented man. He was a true gentleman and an exemplary engineer whom I admired and respected very much. I never heard him utter a curse word or saw him become emotionally out of control, although there were many occasions where it was amply warranted. He was killed as a result of "Porky's" demise and is interred in the American Military Cemetery in Lorraine, France.

Memorial to the 456th Bomb Group.

Survivors of the Group have formed the 456th Bomb Group Association, 428 Natchez St., Pittsburgh, PA 15211, and they meet annually. This Association has placed a memorial plaque and planted a tree in the Memorial Park of the oldest and largest military aviation museum in the world, the U.S. Air Force Museum at Dayton, Ohio.

The Association has also published a pictorial and biographical history, *"456th Bomb Group, 1943- Steed's Flying Colts-1945,"* Turner Publishing Company, 412 Broadway, P.O. Box 3101, Paducah, KY 42002-3101, phone (502) 443-0121. Our Association's historian and current president, Fred Riley, formerly a lead bombardier in the 746th Squadron, wrote the excellent book after much research and help from many survivors of the Group.

The 456th Bomb Group Association also placed a memorial in Cerignola, Italy.

My Return to the United States.

After living on the edge of existence for seven months, I had much time to think during my July 10 truck trip in balmy weather from Stornara, in the fertile Foggia valley of Italy, over the Apennine mountains to the race track outside of Naples (the 19th Replacement Battalion). The race track was being used as a staging area for aircrews waiting for transportation home to the United States. Until coming to Italy, learning to fly and flying airplanes, wearing the handsome U.S. Army "pinks and green" uniform with its silver pilot wings, and flying high performance, state-of-the-art aircraft had me mesmerized by the adventure and glamour of it all. It had been a great adventure, mostly fun and games for me, a twenty year old former hard working engineering student who had a routine, quiet future outlook ahead of him. The war, pilot training, and the experiences in Italy had radically changed that!

I was returning to the United States a much different, more adult person than when I arrived in Italy. During those first few months of 1944 most of my comrades and I matured very fast.

I was promoted, along with other second lieutenants, by the personal action of General Nathan F. Twining, Commander Officer of the Fifteenth Air Force who was on an inspection trip while we were in the camp waiting our shipment home. We spent about a week in that camp. We couldn't leave camp because we were on standby to board a transport and could be ordered to board at any time.

Finally, at 1530 hours on July 17, 1944 we were taken from the camp and put on board the *MV Henry Gibbons*, a Victory Ship at 1700 hours. Lt. Robert H. Vanderlaan, a navigator from the 745th Squadron who finished his missions the same day as I, was put on the ship at the same time, but I didn't know it until recently because he was billeted in another cabin on the ship and we never met on the ship. Vanderlaan kept a detailed diary and he provided valuable details of our trip, and I remembered much of it after he read me his notes. He is a member of the 456th Bomb Group Association.

While we were waiting on board the ship in the Naples Harbor, we watched a fast twin engine plane, a British Hurricane, that was maneuvering around the harbor area to give gunners on board the ships in the harbor practice tracking their antiaircraft guns. As a pilot, I was interested in the plane because it was one of the fastest planes of the war, made of wood instead of metal. The Hurricane suddenly went into a 90 degree bank, had a high speed stall, and it crashed into the water before our eyes. The pilot must have been killed instantly. This was the last violence we were to see in Italy.

We finally departed Naples Harbor headed for New York on the evening of July 17 and we were put in cabins that held 8 men. Food and accommodations were very good compared to what we were used to at Stornara, no C-rations or tent living to which we were accustomed. The cabins were designed for field grade officers and were very good. Vanderlaan noted that the *MV Henry Gibbons* was a converted Army Transport carrying 120 hospital litter cases, and numerous Jewish refugees in the lower decks. Because it had a fast cruising speed of 18 knots, faster than U-boats, our ship was able to travel solo, not in a convoy.

After a beautiful, relaxing seventeen day voyage during which we sun-bathed and became very tan on calm seas, we passed the beautiful Statue of Liberty in the evening of August 3, 1944. It was one of the greatest days of my life as our ship sailed past the beautiful Lady. There wasn't a dry eye in my small group of companions. It was a very dramatic moment for us, not only because of what the grand old lady meant symbolically, but also because we felt we finally reached secure territory after living under the ordeal of rough and violent wartime conditions.

We arrived in New York Harbor, Pier 84 at 1730 hours on August 3, 1944, then we were transported to Fort Hamilton, New Jersey, by bus arriving there at 2200 hours. I was told that the train to California, my destination, wouldn't be leaving for two days, so we were allowed to go into New York the next day for some sight- seeing. One of the officers billeted in the same cabin as mine on the *MV Henry Gibbons*, Lt. Robert E. Locke a navigator from the 459th Bomb Group, was also headed for my home, San Francisco. He told me during the sea voyage that he knew the manager of the famous *Billy Rose's Diamond Horseshoe,* a famous dinner theater in New York. He said that he would take me to the show if we had time to visit New York before taking the train. I passed his comments off as bragging, but he and I went to New York together and we were greeted as heroes by the Diamond Horseshoe staff. We were given front row tables for the dinner and show that evening, the emcee of the show introduced us as war heroes to the crowd in the theater, and our table was flooded with free drinks and food. The entire evening didn't cost us anything except for the underground rail transportation fare.

Those of us headed for California departed Fort Hamilton by train on August 5, 1944. We were headed for "the Redistribution Center nearest our homes." Mine was Santa Monica, with a 2 week delay (leave) enroute to spend at my home. I spent the wonderful two weeks with my wife at home in Daly City, a suburb of San Francisco, before we traveled down to Santa Monica.

507

At the Redistribution Center in Santa Monica we spent a week being processed, during which we were treated to a tour of a movie studio and were introduced to some movie stars. We were given a choice of assignments, anywhere in the United States. I remembered what the Ferry pilot had told me in Italy, that he was making seven dollars a day more than pilots flying in combat who were being shot at, and he was joy-riding around the world. I was able to get assigned to the 3rd Ferry Group, flying out of the Wayne County Airport in Romulus, Michigan. We ferried new B-24 aircraft from the nearby Ford Motor Company's Liberator production line at Willow Run, Michigan.

It was some of the most enjoyable flying I ever had! At the Ford Willow Run plant, all planes coming off the assembly line at the rate of one an hour had the same priority. There were about 12 to 14 planes on the operations board at all times, ready to be ferried out to such places as China, Italy, Britain, Canada, New Guinea, and various airfields in the United States. I went to all of those destinations, a different one each time. Once I signed for a Liberator at Willow Run, I was on my own, and I could take any route to get to the plane's destination. For example, when I signed for a plane to ferry a Chinese crew (that couldn't speak English) to China, I had the option of taking the east or the west route from the United States to get to China. I had a copilot, navigator, an engineer, and sometimes a radio operator. We usually worked out the most interesting route to take to our destination. Going to China, I took a route from Bermuda to the Azores, then across the Libyan Desert battlefields, and sightseeing in North Africa, with a three day stop in Cairo, Egypt, for periodic maintenance on the new plane. From there we mapped our flight so that we toured at low level over historic Israel and Jerusalem, before stopping at Abadan, Iraq; a stop at Karachi which was then part of India; and the Assam Valley in India before, going over the Hump to China.

Ferry pilots flew on commercial aircraft or on military transport aircraft, on a priority basis, to return to Willow Run after their planes were delivered. During the war, the government had a four-level priority system for determining who would fly on the scarce airline seats. First priority went to top level government officials, such as departmental secretaries, presidential aides, and such. Ferry pilots had number two priority, and I never met anyone who had a number one priority. Whenever my crew entered a commercial airport within one hour of takeoff time, the airline was required by law to give us seats on the airliner. This meant that more than one passenger had to be bumped off the airliner to make room for each of us because we traveled with parachutes and other flight gear that weighed many pounds. Except on over water flights, almost all airliners were the two engine DC-3 that had strict weight restrictions.

On one occasion, when we entered the San Francisco airport an hour before the plane's scheduled takeoff, seven passengers had already boarded the plane by the time that the slow airline clerks finished our paper work. They had to get off the airliner to make room for four of my crew. We were getting on the plane as the passengers we had to bump were getting off of it. One of the bumped passengers was a brigadier general, who saw my flight engineer, a corporal, getting on the plane. Generals were very uncommon during the war. He gruffly challenged my corporal, demanding to see his orders. I quickly pulled out a copy of them to show that the corporal had the required number two priority. The general, who was traveling on military orders only had a number three priority, thus, he had to get off the plane and my corporal got on.

509

I didn't intend to make the military service a career after the war. Instead, I wanted to return to school and become a aeronautical engineer. However, as I was being discharged from the service after the war ended, a sergeant in the processing line asked me if I wanted to become a U.S. Air Force Reserve Officer and fly military aircraft on weekends when I returned to civilian life. I enjoyed flying, especially the high performance military aircraft, and I decided that this would complement my engineering training, so I signed up. Besides, everyone believed that World War II was the war to end all wars, and the United Nations was being formed to ensure it.

If there hadn't been a Korean War, my military career probably would have been ended, except that I continued to fly Air Force planes out of Hamilton Field while I was studying at the University of California in Berkeley. I intended to continue flying after graduation. The Korean War required President Harry Truman to call the reserve forces to active duty. I was recalled to active duty on April Fool's Day 1951, and sent to the Strategic Air Command base at Spokane, Washington, where I flew B-29's for a short period before being transferred to Travis Air Force Base to fly the giant ten-engine Consolidated reconnaissance RB-36. It had six huge 3,600 horsepower pusher-type propeller engines and four 5,200 pounds of thrust jet engines. It was the first aircraft that I ever flew up to that time that had enough engine power to continue takeoff, fully loaded, at maximum emergency takeoff weight with two engines inoperative. That was a great advance in aircrew security, because every plane up to that time usually meant that the plane would crash to the ground if it lost only one engine during takeoff while fully loaded. We had many flights in the RB-36 that lasted 24 hours, because the plane had such a great endurance and it flew at such a high altitude. It flew so high at the time that no fighter interceptor planes could reach it.

When I saw the hot new B-47, with six-jet engines that each had 7,200 pounds of thrust, during a refueling stop it made at Travis Air Base one Sunday while it was on an experimental test flight, I became determined to fly that sleek beauty. I succeeded. It was love at first sight! I flew the Boeing B-47 for seven years in the Strategic Air Command at March Air Force Base, California. I flew it over much of the northern hemisphere of the world and the Arctic. It was about that time that I decided to become a Regular Air Force Officer, instead of remaining in the Reserve. I applied for a regular commission and was accepted.

The B-47 was the sweetest, most reliable multi-engine plane I ever flew. The sweetest single-engine plane I ever flew was the Lockheed T-33 that we learned to fly as part of our checkout in the B-47, and which I flew for many years after.

All pilots of B-47s at that time were sent through navigation, radar, and bombardier training for a year before checking out in the B-47. After my tour in the B-47, the Air Force sent me to obtain a Masters Degree from the University of Southern California, before being assigned to the Flight Test Center at Edwards Air Force Base in the Mohave Desert, where the old Muroc Airbase was located. At Edwards, I was assigned as a flight test project officer on the supersonic North American B-70 bomber, but budget problems and other delays postponed building the bomber until after my tour at Edwards was finished. While waiting for the B-70, I kept busy flying many more USAF planes, including the B-52, B-47, T-39, U3A, T-33, among others.

I had two tours in the Pentagon and in the U.S. Air Force Headquarters in Wiesbaden, Germany, before retiring. In Germany I belonged to a tennis club that had many ex-Luftwaffe pilots as members. We used to talk war stories, and I met many that were shooting at me on raids over European cities which we determined we were flying on at the same time. I met one ex-Luftwaffe fighter pilot who had three fingers missing, and he told me that it may have been gunners on my plane that shot off his fingers. I visited many of our World War II targets in Germany and Austria during that tour of duty.

After retiring from the Pentagon in Washington D.C., I obtained a Doctorate from the George Washington University and entered the University teaching profession. I taught at the George Washington University in Washington D.C., the George Mason University in Fairfax, Virginia, where I was an Assistant Professor. I also did consulting work in the Washington D.C. area until final retirement in 1987.

In my retirement I wrote a book, a biography of Hannibal the ancient Carthaginian, *"Hannibal's Lieutenant: A Unique Biography of the Brilliant Hannibal* (1994)*,"* by Robert S. Capps, published by Manor House Publications of Alexandria, P.O. Box 19427, Virginia 22320. My interest in Hannibal started when I learned that Hannibal's greatest battle was fought only twenty miles from our old base at Stornara.

I have been happily married for the past thirty-five years to the former Eve Margaret Chapen of Sacramento, California. We live in Alexandria, Virginia which is across the Potomac River from Washington D.C.

I have three children by my first wife, the former Barbara M. Foreman, who is deceased. My children, all at or nearing fifty years of age at the time of this printing, are Wendy (NMI) Winton of Milpitas, California; Robert Randall Capps, of Dallas, Texas; and Dennis Daniel Capps of Agoura, California. Through them, I have five grandchildren and two great grandchildren

THE END.

About the Author

Dr. Robert S. Capps served in the USAF thirty years and retired in 1972 as a Colonel and Command Pilot. He also received a doctors' degree from George Washington University (1978), a masters' degree from the University of Southern California (1959), and a bachelor of science degree from the University of California (Berkeley-1948).

After retiring from the USAF, Dr. Capps taught at George Washington University, George Mason University. Prior to that, he also taught for UCLA and Southeastern University. He also did management consulting work in government and industry.

In 1994 he wrote *"Hannibal's Lieutenant,"* about the life of the Carthaginian, Hannibal, who was famous for taking his elephants and army over the Alps into Roman Italy in 218 BC.